RETROACTIVE JUSTICE

RETROACTIVE JUSTICE

Prehistory of Post-Communism

István Rév

STANFORD UNIVERSITY PRESS

STANFORD, CALIFORNIA

2005

Stanford University Press
Stanford, California

Printed in the United States of America
on acid-free, archival-quality paper.

Library of Congress Cataloging-in-Publication Data
Rév, István.
    Retroactive justice : prehistory of post-communism / István Rév.
        p. cm.—(Cultural memory in the present)
    Includes index.
    ISBN 0-8047-3642-1 (cloth : alk. paper)—ISBN 0-8047-3644-8 (pbk. : alk. paper)
    1. Hungary—History—Revolution, 1956. 2. Public history—Hungary. I. Title.
II. Series.
DB957.R475 2005
943.905—dc22   2004021121

Original Printing 2005

Last figure below indicates year of this printing:
14   13   12   11   10   09   08   07   06   05

Typeset by Classic Typography in 11/13.5 Adobe Garamond.

To my grandfather, known through my mother's memories,
Dr. István Földes (1890–1944)

Let's talk of graves, of worms and epitaphs . . .
—SHAKESPEARE, *The Tragedy of King Richard the Second* (III.ii.145)

Contents

RETROACTIVE JUSTICE

Introduction

Nullius in verba! Trust not in words! At the beginning of a book of history, built on words found in the depths of archives, the motto of the Royal Society, itself a misappropriated fragment of a line from Horace, is a self-defeating warning. The documents in the archives of repression are, however, largely fabrications: misinformation, blatant lies, overdramatizations, or their opposite: trivializations of dramatic events. The witnesses, the sources of forced confessions, the scribes who took the forged notes, are no longer here to testify; the historian is in the business of death. Still, *"quoniam valde labilis est humana memoria"*—"because human memory is very weak," as typical medieval charters begin—the historian has no choice but to make use of what has been left behind by bad times. Oftentimes the documents preserve nothing but the record of loss, the unrecoverable traces of that which can no longer be found. As the inscription by the irresponsible clergyman in the *Book of Memory*, the *Liber Memorialis* from Reichenau puts it: "The names that were to have been inscribed in this book but which I have through my negligence forgotten, I commend to you, Christ, and to your mother, and to all the celestial powers, in order that their memory be celebrated here below and in the beatitude of eternal life."[1]

The modern historian tries relentlessly to share responsibility with others: he (in my case) or she is in need of others to verify the words. The

---

1. Quoted by Jacques Le Goff, *History and Memory* (New York: Columbia University Press, 1992), p. 73.

voice of the sources is evoked in order to support words with facts, to guarantee the reliability of historical assertions. But facts, in the field of history, come wrapped in words. The historian working in archives of misinformation, where the documents have been consciously deformed, had better take the hermeneutic suspicions of the Royal Society seriously. Still, after due consideration, the student of the past should override the forewarning from on high. The historian is not always denied good luck: sometimes, relying on the involuntary help of interrogators, secret agents, or the *mouton des prisons*, I am able to learn even what the accused, the tortured, the executed thought or did before the sentence was carried out; I find intercepted messages, acquired by wire-tapping—although, under Communism, in the midst of grave shortages, where it was mostly the privileged who had telephones in their homes, it was usually unguarded voices in sublet apartments that were tapped.

The interrogation reports or the court documents sometimes reveal connections of which the accused themselves were unaware. The highly centralized regimes did everything to atomize their subjects, who, in most cases, had to act, read, or think alone. The interrogator, however, always suspects conspiracy, organized sabotage, concentrated illegal action, and secret societies behind the hopelessly individuated acts. The policeman is like the typical historian, looking for regularity. And he is right: almost always the cases show more regularity; they are more revealing than what each individual act might otherwise suggest in its singularity.

After the end of "classical" State Socialism, from the beginning of the 1960s, in most of the Central European countries repression became somewhat shy. Open terror was used less and less for pedagogical or mobilization reasons. Reports about the activities of the enemy, about arrests, trials, and sentences were rarely published in the press. ("The Politburo has decided that the report should not be made public [*sic*] in the black-and-white digest [the classified daily information bulletin for the highest echelon of the party]; only department heads of the Central Committee, and the first secretaries of the Budapest and county party committees should have access to the report"—was the top leadership's decision about the fate of the report on the anti-Communist demonstrations on March 15, 1973, in Budapest.)[2] Information traveled in a haphazard, unreliable, informal

2. Magyar Országos Levéltár (Hungarian State Archive) (MOL) 288. Fond. 1973, 5/609 ő.e. Published in János Kenedi, *Kis Állambiztonsági Olvasókönyv*, Október 23–

way, even between prison cells. The participants in real acts, not only the imagined enemy, did not know much about the others, who used the same available repertoire of social, cultural, and political action. The very first report to be published about crucially important events of the post–World War II period of Central Europe is, in most cases, the work of the historian, who after very long decades, and after the Fall, discovers unknown documents about unknown events in formerly classified archives.

Had the interrogators not tried hard to prove subterranean connections—sometimes, of course, without the slightest trace of any real relationship at all or by reinterpreting the confessions—posterity would not have been able to learn that the isolated acts shared a common logic, the participants had similar ambitions, and the events show naive uniformity. The historian must rely on the documents the secret services fabricated, for these are sometimes not just the only available sources, but the ones that present a detailed picture from a wider perspective. The subterranean perspective sheds light on the surface. The secret agents were the reliable, although untrustworthy, partners of the future historian; we are collaborators.[3]

Writing the recent history of the Central and Eastern part of Europe is unlike the work of the Western historian, who can turn to published sources, contemporary reports, memoirs by participants and eyewitnesses, whose work is embedded in solid, mostly normalized and consolidated public memory. Usually it is not the historian who is the messenger there, unlike in the less fortunate part of the world, where the message is, more often than not, bad news. The recent history of Central and Eastern Europe is the history of bad times.

*

The primary—one might almost say, the primal—scene of this book is Hungary, and this was, in part, a methodological decision. Hungary is a very small country and it was even smaller during the decades of State Socialism. As a consequence of central planning, centrally imagined uniformity, the ambition of central regulation, and the limited range of available choices, everything and everybody was nearer to each other in the countries

március 15–június 16 a Kádár korszakban [Small State-Security Reader, 23 October–15 March–16 June in the Kádár Era] (Budapest: Magvető, 1966), vol. 2, p. 158.

3. On this fundamental epistemological and methodological issue, in relation to a different historical period, see Carlo Ginzburg, "The Inquisitor as Anthropologist," in his *Clues, Myths, and the Historical Method*, trans. John Tedeschi and Anne Tedeschi (Baltimore, MD: Johns Hopkins University Press, 1989), pp. 156–64.

under Communist rule than is usual or customary under normal circumstances. Most people were forced to live near others: in labor or internment camps, in prison cells, in communal apartments, where several families had to share the former bourgeois apartment of a single family, or in unbelievably tiny flats on huge housing estates, where the neighbors could hear every sound from the adjacent unit.

Communism is the regime of compression: long lines, constant waiting, a limited number of extremely crowded places, people jammed in and pressed close to each other, everybody constantly at the same place. The overwhelming majority, especially the urban dwellers, work for the same employer: the state. Planning was meant to eradicate superfluous parallelism, and this led to a finite, very small number of institutions: universities, research and art institutes, journals, newspapers, restaurants, coffeehouses, all owned or controlled by the very same state. It was difficult to travel internally—in the Soviet Union there were closed cities even in the 1980s, and citizens were required to carry a passport for domestic travel; in Hungary, until the second half of the 1970s, special permission was required to visit a city near the western, Austrian border—and for the majority, it was impossible to travel abroad.

Members of the party elite spent their holidays together in the party's holiday resorts and visited the same special shops and medical institutions, while opposition intellectuals read the same books, frequented the same espresso bars, went to the same movies, worked at and were fired from the same workplaces. Everybody knew everybody else, and even if somebody seemed to be unknown, it was quite easy to guess where the unknown person came from. It was far from atypical for the members of the opposition to be the children of the party elite. I am one of them.

The Communist countries were much smaller than their sheer physical size would have implied. Even the Soviet Union, the largest country on earth, one of the two superpowers—where it took at least nine days for the Trans-Siberian express to traverse the nine-thousand-kilometer width of the country, where during the Brezhnev era the Lake Baikal-Amur railway line (the BAM) was allegedly built (it was not built)—was a great deal smaller than what it was—and what the misinformed outside world thought.

Besides all this, Hungary is a hopelessly monocentric country, where Budapest is the only real urban center on a European scale, where everything happens in that single city. Either you lived in Budapest during the Communist times, or you did not live anywhere. There was no chance of internal migration; it was impossible to buy an apartment (if you divorced, and Hungary had the highest divorce rate in Europe, you could not move out of your flat, which you had to share with your divorced spouse); changing your workplace or occupation was administratively regulated; emigration was a complicated alternative. Besides the highest divorce rate, as the only real option, Hungary had the highest suicide rate in the whole world. It was a small place with few choices.

The leaders of the small left-wing and later on the Communist movement, who spent their time together first in deep illegality, then, after World War II in power and in the same prisons, gave up, betrayed, imprisoned, then stabbed in the back, executed, and buried each other over and over again; they married each other's wives, slept with each other's husbands and with the widows of their victims. People, murderers and their victims, especially Communist murderers and their Communist victims, lived in incestuous vicinity.

Retribution, the political repression, classified and imprisoned the members of the opposition within the same social and physical space, irrespective of their motives, aims, and political or ideological convictions. It made no difference where they had come from, or where they intended to move. The authorities and their secret services restricted the living space of the imagined or real protesters, resisters, and dissidents, partly to make surveillance easier. In the absence of any alternative, members of the opposition had to live their lives dangerously near one another. The cramped world of the dissidents further increased the paranoia of the state security services, which suspected signs of highly organized conspiracy in every congested public or private space. Gossip, as informal information, spread extremely fast in this jam-packed world, sometimes fulfilling the wildest fantasies of the secret agents. The obsessions, delusions, and blatant lies of the services, in the end, bring the historian nearer to an understanding of the workings of the Communist system than contemporaries would have suspected.

I know or knew the majority of the protagonists of this book. I know them and I knew or might have known their parents and grandparents, and they know or knew or might have known each other well, too well. I know the victims and their executioners too.

*

Compression under State Socialism was not only spatial but temporal as well. Revolutions, regime changes in general, and Communist takeovers in particular invite historical revision, past actions under new descriptions. New histories are made by category change. After revolutions—and revolutionary changes—as Thomas Kuhn has famously claimed, we live in a different world: "What characterizes revolutions is, thus, change in several of the taxonomic categories prerequisite to scientific description and generalization. That change, furthermore, is an adjustment not only of criteria relevant to categorization, but also of the way in which objects and situations are distributed among pre-existing categories."[4] A new distribution of historic objects—the events, the ideas, and the dead of the past—requires not only a certain number of possible new choices but—as Michel Foucault remarked—new excluded possibilities as well.[5]

In 1918 the Austro-Hungarian monarchy ceased to exist; in November, as a result of a bourgeois revolution, the republic was proclaimed that in March 1919 gave way to a Communist takeover—after the Soviet Union the second soviet regime in the world—which after 133 days was defeated by a right-wing, Christian, anti-Semitic, and chauvinist counterrevolution; as a consequence of the Trianon Peace Treaty, Hungary lost two-thirds of its territory and half of its population; the country became an ally of Fascist Italy and Nazi Germany; Hitler gave back some of the lost territories while two hundred thousand people died at the Don River and more than five hundred thousand Jews and Roma were deported to and annihilated in the concentration camps; the country found itself once more on the losing side after the end of World War II; the Paris peace treaty ordered once again the amputation of the territory of the country; the Hungarian Germans and Slovaks were forced to migrate after the war; the Soviets deported hundreds of thousands to the gulags; in 1948 the Communists seized power and the enemies of the Communist state were hunted down, imprisoned, and executed; in 1956 the revolution broke out and was defeated, and was followed by severe reprisals and mass emigration; in 1968, after Hungary took part in the invasion of Czechoslovakia and the defeat of the Prague Spring, the last hope in the reformability of existing Socialism, with the utopia of "Socialism with a human face," was lost (for the time being, forever). In 1989, without due forewarning, the

---

4. Thomas Kuhn, "What Is a Scientific Revolution?" in *The Probabilistic Revolution*, ed. Lorenz Krüger and Lorraine Daston, vol. 1 (Cambridge, MA: MIT Press, 1987), p. 20.

5. Michel Foucault, *The Order of Things: An Archaeology of Human Sciences* (London: Tavistock, 1970), p. 380.

State Socialist regime, the party-state, together with the protecting iron curtain and the Berlin Wall, fell, and the country found itself once again in an unknown world.

After each turn Hungarians found themselves in a new world, living with a new past. Past actions under new descriptions required not only new taxonomic categories but also the inclusion (and naturally, the exclusion) of certain possibilities, that is, reactivated, until then excluded, left out, censored, forgotten events of the past. At any given moment history became foreshortened, retrospectively foreseen in a different way. The changed perspective created new continuities, new chronologies by exclusion, which in turn compressed the elapsed historical time. The new situations warranted newfangled historical contentions—Hungary's historical or political mission in the Carpathian Basin, traditional cultural superiority over the neighboring ethnic groups, the centuries-long tradition of liberation movements, the historic role of the exploited underclasses, the iron laws of historical progress, historical necessity—and in the face of competing claims, coming from neighboring countries or from rival, defeated political groups, in Hungary, as in the rest of Central Europe, historical arguments have always been used in actual political wars. In fact, historical arguments have always been the ultima ratio in political battles. Historical figures, the dead, the favored dead, have always been our contemporaries. In this part of the world the dead, any dead, might resurface unannounced any moment. I know the dead from close up too; they are my contemporaries.

*

If graves can (and sometimes should) be opened, if the solitude of the dead cannot be honored, if the past is not envisioned as being over yet, then the objects, the events, the ideas, and the dead of the past could be revisited and remade: not as doubles but as if each of them were the original, the real one. The object of my study is the *remake*: the remake of the dead, the martyr turned unknown soldier and back again, the criminal who is redeemed as innocent, holy days banalized, cemeteries restructured, and unremarkable figures presented as historical monstrosities, ordinary places rebuilt as sites of horror.[6] My book is not devoted to traces of times gone by

6. "To give ourselves a past a posteriori, as if it were, a past from which we prefer to be descended, as opposed to the past from which we did descend" (Friedrich Nietzsche, *Unmodern Observations*, trans. Gary Brown, William Arrowsmith, and Herbert Golder [New Haven, CT: Yale University Press, 1990], p. 103).

or representations of past events, but to *phantoms*.[7] It deals with bodies and objects that are presented as visibly, even tangibly, incarnate.

Instead of the notion of substitution, I study manipulation by hand: undoing by remaking. (Note: the Latin prefix *re* = back or again, in some cases has the same force as *un* in English; implying undoing of some previous action, like *recludere* = unclose, open, or as in the case of *revelare*, meaning to unveil.) Each chapter of this book is offered to the story—in almost all cases to the stories—of a particular remake: the dead body, the name of the dead, the cemetery, the holy day, the criminal, the underworld, the funeral, the political transition.

Each part arcs over the Great Divide: 1989, the year of the Fall, of the interval (*promzhutok*), in the formulation of the Russian formalist theoretician, Yury Tynianov. In that year the past fell to pieces and became extinct.[8] Millions, hundreds of millions of people in the former Communist world became lost; they lost their future because they lost their past. One morning—in Hungary it was exactly on June 16, 1989, the day of the reburial of the executed prime minister of the 1956 revolution—they woke up unsuspecting and found themselves in a brand new world, with all their certainties disappearing. History left no time for preparation, as it was not the people who undid the regime; History did it itself. ("This silent collapse—which is sometimes called 'The Velvet Revolution'—has in all probability ruined something in the people, although it is difficult to know exactly what. What was gone was perhaps the ethos of resistance, which

7. "The phantom, created by a god in the semblance of a living person such as the one Apollo fabricates 'like to Aeneas himself and in his armor. . . . It is a simulacrum now that the Greeks and the Trojans confront in battle, a figure that both sides are convinced is the hero in person'" (Jean-Pierre Vernant, "Psuche: Simulacrum of the Body or Image of the Divine?" in *Mortals and Immortals*, ed. and trans. Froma I. Zeitlin [Princeton, NJ: Princeton University Press, 1991], p. 186; see also chap. "Birth of Images," pp. 164–85).

8. In 1988/1989, among other things, I was preoccupied, together with my students, members of a several-year-long seminar, with writing and editing a collection of texts related to the economic and social history of Socialism. By the time the book (*Gazdaság—és Társadalomtörténeti Szöveggyűjtmény a Szocializmus Magyarországi Történetének Tanulmányozásához* [Economic and Social History Sources for the Study of the History of Socialism in Hungary], vols. 1–2 [Budapest: Aula, 1990]) was published in the spring of 1990 the cover of the book was printed with a diagonal black ribbon. By early 1990, the object of the book seemed to be dead. (Despite its untimeliness, I think it is still a good, although not a very useful, book.)

had given cohesion to a form of life, or it was an instance of hope that, although it had never been real hope, had nevertheless provided form and coherence to existence.")[9]

Gone were the certainties, the pillars of one's life: the recurrent familiar events, the rhythm of life, the everydays and the holidays, the well-known street names, the social significance of neighborhoods, the meaning of the photographs in the family album, the social capital, the knowledge of Russian as a usable foreign language, the value of the sociometrical network of one's private and professional world, the stability of memories, the comprehension of private and public history. What remained was unknown. At that point between the lost and the not-yet comprehended, historians, politicians, and professional and amateur self-proclaimed experts offered support: to remake the world. My book is a chronicle of the endeavor.

I am a fieldworker in Hungary, whose object of study is not the history of my country, which I know too well. Dealing with history is not a scholarly task for me; it is an existential undertaking. Hungary is just a particular and particularly suitable case that reveals not the deep structures of history but the possible available relations to the (perpetually remade) past. "Is not the narrow space, where we spend our everyday life, the symbol of all places, of the world, of life itself?"—once asked Imre Kertész, the Nobel laureate survivor of Fascism and Communism, who, in his own words, is a stranger everywhere, as being a stranger everywhere is unavoidable.[10] I am not a stranger; I am at home here, in spite of everything.

*

This book, in a sense, is a string of stories: dozens and dozens of loosely but deeply connected stories. The same protagonists, martyrs and villains, victims and executioners surface in the subsequent stages from different perspectives and under new descriptions. Each chapter is centered on deeply buried traces of the 1956 Revolution, although the subject of the book is certainly not the history of the revolution. My license to write history is my telling of stories. Weaving stories—by using finite structural elements—around the dead is a way to make them familiar. As they are my

---

9. Imre Kertész, "A Boldogtalan 20. Század" [The Unhappy 20th Century], in Imre Kertész, *A Száműzött Nyelv* [Exiled Language] (Budapest: Magvető, 2001), p. 35.

10. Imre Kertész, *Haza, Otthon, Ország* [Fatherland, Home, Country], in Imre Kertész, *A Száműzött Nyelv* [Exiled Language] (Budapest: Magvető, 2001), pp. 111 and 107, respectively.

contemporaries, I want to see them from up close. I cannot do this with the technique of defamiliarization, estranging, displacement (*sdvig*), a modus operandi that the Russian literary formalists, Viktor Shklovskii and Yury Tynianov among them, had learned, probably from Husserl.[11]

The stories cover vast territories and thousands of years but not in quest of deep arch-structures. "The *Necronym*," the second chapter of the book, is indebted to Wittgenstein's notes in his "Remarks on Frazer's *Golden Bough*," although I am definitively not looking for his "family resemblances," or distant relatives.[12] As is so intimately familiar in the practice of writing history, I am dealing with death, with the dead. Death is the ultimate subject of the historian. I know: the dead are produced by differentiated practices; death is not a timeless universal category. ("We do not play chess with eternal figures in the world . . . ; the figures are but what the successive configurations on the playing board make of them"—as Paul Veyne remarked.)[13] Each of the dead is mourned over in a slightly or grossly different way. Death, as we know from the Gospels, is not (just) a biological but a social and cultural fact and idea. Faced with the drama of death, we have no choice but to turn to the repertoire of available practices in order to turn the biological into an artificially slowed-down social process. As imperfectly related members of both temporarily and spatially large groups, we turn to a sort of common pool—the content of which is more or less preserved, although constantly altered, and transmitted by (often misperceived) sacred books, tales, myths, rudimentary practices—the existence of which is, for the most part, unknown to us. I tell these stories, coming from afar both in time and space, in the hope that they might shed light on those features of our contemporary practices that otherwise would have seemed strange or obvious, difficult to comprehend or trivial, complicated or just too simple to accept.[14]

11. On Skhlovskii, and *ostranienie* ("defamiliarizing," "estranging") in his case, as a prehistory of a useful literary device, see Carlo Ginzburg, *Wooden Eyes* (New York: Columbia University Press, 2001), esp. pp. 1–4.

12. Cf. Ludwig Wittgenstein, *Philosophical Occasions, 1912–1951*, ed. J. Klagge and A. Nordham (Indianapolis, IN: Hackett, 1993), pp. 119–55.

13. Paul Veyne, *Foucault révolutionne l'histoire. In: his Comment on écrit l'histoire suivi de Foucault révolutionne l'histoire* (Paris: Editions du Seuil, 1978), p. 236.

14. "Historians and anthropologists most truly love their practice when they alternate constantly between the past and the present, the distant and the near, the immutable and the changing" (Alain Boureau, *Kantorowicz: Stories of a Historian*, trans. Stephen G.

The book starts with an autopsy and after several chapters, after a journey that leads to faraway places in time and locality, ends with a funeral. The book enacts the artificially slowed-down process between death and the final burial. It is a survey of the political technologies—taxonomies, categorization, and distribution: the making—of the dead. I often visit burial places, especially the oldest cemetery in Budapest with the graves and mausolea of the prominent dead. The place, in an attempt at retroactive justice, has changed considerably in the past decade. The visible efforts, the structures elevated above the earth, try desperately to find life in death, immortality in the corpse, justification in sacrifice. It is not only addition, new, mushrooming heroic structures one can encounter in the place of death but also exclusion, the empty sites left behind when bodies are removed. As if following the commandment of the Bible—"the land cannot be cleansed of the blood that is shed therein, but by the blood of him that shed it" (Num. 35:33)—the newly found martyrs cannot rest in the vicinity of those who are chosen for being responsible for past catastrophes.

The process I have followed while working on this book was like the slow cleansing of a found object. The activity has not only revealed hitherto hidden qualities of the object but also gradually changed its nature as well. The object of my study—the dead as contemporary—exhibits, paradoxically, characteristics that make it analogous to what Ian Hacking termed "interactive kind." While repeating the experiments, revisiting the cemeteries and the archives, scrutinizing the sources in the subsequent chapters, I have discovered hitherto-unknown features, which either had lain there buried before and came into light as a consequence of my manipulation, or became visible because I myself had become slightly different, more attentive, more sensitive as a result of my own activities. My work had a looping effect: recognizable both on the object and on myself.[15]

Nichols and Gabrielle M. Spiegel (Baltimore, MD: Johns Hopkins University Press, 2001), p. 108.

15. Hacking distinguished "interactive kinds" from "indifferent kinds": "I do suggest that a cardinal difference between the traditional natural and social sciences is that the classification employed in the natural sciences are indifferent kinds, while those employed in the social sciences are mostly interactive kinds. The targets of the natural sciences are stationary. Because of the looping effect, the targets of the social sciences are on the move" (Ian Hacking, *The Social Construction of What?* [Cambridge, MA: Harvard University Press, 2001], p. 108, esp. pp. 103–24). Hacking, however, does not mention the feedback, the impact of the classification on the scholar who is devising and employing the classification scheme.

The volume is a collection of concomitant fragments. Still, in the course of working on it, I had high ambitions: I wanted to make the world of State Socialism perceptible and to provide tangible experience about the life beyond the party-state. State Socialism is presented from the perspective of the Fall, while life beyond the party-state is shown as a prisoner of its prehistory. The book is both a prehistory of post-Communism and a post-*histoire* of Communism. It is an assemblage of fragments. Providing fragments, however, might be an appropriate way of presenting my history: "The human body could be no exception to the commandment which ordered the destruction of the organic so that the true meaning, as it was written and ordained, might be picked up from its fragments."[16]

Each chapter recounts a multitude of events; quite a few of them seem to be but coincidences. The *Oxford English Dictionary* defines coincidence as "a notable concurrence of events or circumstances having no apparent causal connection." For the contemporaries of unfolding events, however, the lack of causal connection is not apparent either. Causal connection, or the lack of it, becomes visible usually only from the perspective of the end-point of a particular chain of events. What the historian knows after the end was, in most cases, still unclear and uncertain for the contemporaries in the course of the emerging affair. By recording concurrent events, which, either for the contemporary actors or, later on, for the chronicler, sometimes lack apparent connections, the historian might be able to restore the uncertain, open quality of history as experienced *in eventu*.

Inference based on the close study of a set of events, of apparent historical coincidence, opens the way for what Charles Sanders Peirce called "abduction." Abductive or retroductive reasoning could be modestly, in a minimalist way, perceived as connecting observed surprising facts with other, supposedly relevant facts from different, even distant historical periods. In certain cases, however, for the latecomer, the historian, it might be promising to try to infer possible explanations from effects. Historical abduction thus may be imagined as—*posteventum*—inference from concurrent events to supposedly related—temporarily or spatially distant—incidents or sometimes, in the hope of constructive suggestion, even to probable cause(s).[17]

16. Walter Benjamin, *The Origin of the German Tragic Drama*, trans. John Osborne (London: Verso, 1998), pp. 216–17.
17. "The very notion of a meaningful coincidence contains from the beginning a contradiction. It requires both chance and intention. Two things that happen at once

As the book is a record of historical remake, pasts in the making, as a secondary goal, I wanted to organize my work into a "register," a "catalog," a "list" of phenomena, useful, perhaps essential, for the work of a historian: the corpse; the relic; the name; the pantheon; the holy day; the courtroom; the underworld; the transition. Description and interpretation permeate each other.

*

The book started to emerge, unnoticed, in the course of "Memory, Forgetting, and the Archive," a graduate seminar cotaught with friends Stephen Greenblatt and Randy Starn in Berkeley. The course was then repeated in an altered format, as a road show, in the deep South, at the University of Alabama in Tuscaloosa. At a memorable, and I can perhaps add, dramatic, conference, organized by the Getty Research Institute at the Warburg Library in Hamburg, the program of the book was presented in a condensed form.[18] At the time of the conference Reinhart Koselleck was the Warburg Professor in residence of the library, and he attended all the seminars. He sat silently in a corner and after each session he made long, perceptive comments. Probably he too was not able to resist the truly dramatic impact of the symposium. In his comments he persistently used *wir*, we, when referring to Germans living under the Third Reich. On the third day, however, as if almost without prior intention, he changed to the third-person plural: *sie*, they.

The first part of the manuscript was written at Stanford, at the Center for Advanced Studies in the Behavioral Sciences, where I had the good fortune to have regular conversations with the biochemist Paul Berg, who

---

become such a coincidence only when two criteria are met; logic must dictate the event as purely accidental, but the simultaneity must nevertheless tempt one to assume some more remote, mysterious connection between them. Pure chance does not make for a portent; rather, chance must be combined with an uncanny sense of meaningfulness that underwrites the happening" (Peter T. Struck, *Birth of the Symbol: Ancient Readers at the Limits of their Text* [Princeton, NJ: Princeton University Press, 2004], pp. 94–95).

When historians try to follow Epimenides' example, "who made revelations not on future things, but on things past, things invisible," then they experience the sense of meaningfulness in what otherwise might seem to be pure contingency (Aristotle, *On Rhetoric*, trans. George A. Kennedy [Oxford: Oxford University Press, 1991], 3.17.1418A.24).

18. Published as "Covering History," in *Disturbing Remains: Memory, History and Crisis in the Twentieth Century*, ed. Michael S. Roth and Charles G. Salas (Los Angeles: The Getty Research Institute, 2001).

widened my horizon by patiently explaining the biochemical, neurological, and genetic mechanisms behind the working of memory.

I am indebted to my graduate students at Berkeley and at the Central European University in Budapest, most of them from former Communist countries; to close friends, Carlo Ginzburg and Thomas Laqueur among them, who accompanied me on long walks in the cemeteries in Budapest; to Sorin Antohi, Imre Barna, Paul Berg, Carla Hesse, Peter Kenéz, János Kis, Gábor Klaniczay, András Mink, Al Rieber. On different occasions I benefited from comments made by Saul Friedlander, Tony Judt, Marilyn Young, and Hayden White. Ildikó Csikos and Katalin Dobó provided valuable assistance. Without Judit Szira's insistence, the book would not have been finished.

I am especially grateful to my institution and to my colleagues at the Open Society Archives. While I was working on this book we built an archive together, which by today has become one of the most important cold-war archives in the world: it has the richest source collection on the history of Communism and probably the most interesting collection of human-rights documents. Writing the book and building the archives, the primary source for my book, were parallel activities.

There is a figure whose shadow is behind each chapter of this book: Imre Nagy, the executed prime minister of the 1956 Revolution, the martyr of his Communist utopia with a human face. Only after having finished the book and almost the introduction as well, did I realize that I had not referred to his political biography, arguably one of the most important Hungarian historical works of the past decade, the decade after the transition.[19] It is not the life but the death of the martyred prime minister that hovers behind my study; not so much the body as the corpse. The dead are not fictitious characters in this book.

[As a prisoner of war, Nagy became a Communist in the Soviet Union (although formally he became a member of the Bolshevik Party only in 1920). He fought in the Red Army, and later on, he was accused of having taken an active part in the execution of Czar Nicolas II and his fam-

19. János M. Rainer, *Nagy Imre, Politikai Életrajz* [Nagy Imre, A Political Biography], vol. 1, 1896–1953; vol. 2, 1953–1958 (Budapest: Institute of the 1956 Revolution, 1996 and 1999).

ily.[20] He came back to Hungary, worked in and for the party, and from 1930 to 1944 he lived in the Soviet Union, where he received Soviet citizenship. He was expelled from and readmitted to the party, lost his job, and for a short time was imprisoned. Probably in the early 1930s he found himself entangled in the web of the Stalinist secret services and, having no choice, presumably cooperated with them. He most likely played a role in the imprisonment and tragic fate of some Hungarian Communist émigrés in Stalin's Soviet Union, among them Lajos Magyar, the noted Sinologist, who first made use of the term "Asiatic way of production."[21]

At the September 1, 1989, meeting of the Central Committee of the Hungarian Socialist Workers' Party, the last secretary general informed the members of the Central Committee about the content of a dossier that General Kriuchkov, the head of the KGB, had sent a few days before.[22] (There are good reasons to conclude that it was the Hungarian party leadership that had asked for the dossier to be prepared, around the time of Nagy's reburial in June 1989.) On the basis of the documents received, the last secretary general of the party accused Nagy of having worked as an agent of the Soviet secret services and of having been personally responsible for the imprisonment and eventual execution of dozens of innocent Communists. The dossier, together with original and forged documents, contained a list that Nagy had prepared in April 1939 in Moscow with 150 names. At least every fifth person on the list had a family member in prison, in the Gulag, on his or her way to the gallows. This was a list of Nagy's personal acquaintances, not a willful denunciation report prepared

20. See Elisabeth Heersch, *Nicolaus II. Feigkeit, Lüge und Verrat. Leben und Ende des letzten russischen Zaren* (München: Langen Müller, 1992). The accusation has been repeated several times since, among other publications, in *Krasnaia Kabbala* (Red Kabala), an anti-Semite pamphlet published in Moscow in 1992. Rainer denies the reliability of the accusations, although its seems plausible that prisoners of war, former soldiers of the Austro-Hungarian army, took part in the execution (Cf. Rainer, *Nagy Imre*, vol. 1, p. 54).

21. I still eat with a silver spoon that as a small child I received from Magyar's former wife, the famous actress, Max Reinhardt's one-time beautiful lover Blanka Péchy. She was a good friend of my mother's, and after my birth, she gave the spoon to me. It once belonged to her son, who had been shot down as a fighter pilot in the Red Army during World War II. His name was István too; it is engraved on the silver spoon.

22. Cf. Károly Grósz's speech at the September 1, 1989, meeting of the Central Committee, in *A Magyar Szocialista Munkáspárt Központi Bizottságának 1989. évi jegyzőkönyvei* [Protocols of the 1989 Meetings of the Central Committee of the Hungarian

by an agent. Still, at one of the last meetings of the Central Committee, before the eventual collapse of the regime, Nagy was charged with direct collaboration in the perdition of dozens of innocent victims. The charges were echoed in the international press and also in scholarly publications.[23]

Imre Nagy came back from the Soviet Union at the end of 1944 and became a member of the first government as minister of agriculture; he was the minister who signed the land decree that parceled out the large estates among the Hungarian peasantry; he became the speaker of the parliament and held different governmental positions; he was expelled from the party for "right-wing deviation," then readmitted; after Stalin's death, the Soviets chose him as the prime minister in June 1953; he was ousted at the beginning of 1955; he was fired from the party once more; he taught agricultural economics at the University of Economics in Budapest; on the evening of October 23, 1956, on the demand of the tens of thousands of demonstrators in front of parliament, he appeared on the balcony of the parliament and became the prime minister of the revolution. In the early morning hours of November 4 he took refuge in the building of the Yugoslav embassy in Budapest. He was deviously kidnapped—despite written guarantees—and held under house arrest in complete isolation in Romania, where he wrote a diary. He was brought back to Budapest in April 1957 and, after long interrogations, was put secretly on trial on February 5, 1958. Then the trial was postponed until June 9. On June 15, 1958, he was sentenced to death. Early the next morning Imre Nagy, together with two of his fellow prisoners, was hanged. He was buried in the courtyard of the prison.][24]

I also know Imre Nagy, in a way. During the closed and secret trial a film was shot—altogether about forty thousand meters—in the hope that an edited version could be used as propaganda material after the execution. Two edited versions were made, a longer one-hundred-minute one, and

Socialist Workers' Party], ed. Anna S. Koszticz and János Lakos, vol. 2 (Budapest: Hungarian National Archives, 1993), pp. 1514–18.

23. See Johanna Granville, "Imre Nagy, aka 'Volodya'—a Dent in the Martyr's Halo?" *Cold War International Project Bulletin* 5 (spring 1995): 28–37.

Rainer, after careful and persuasive analysis, and weighing all the circumstances, provides a balanced assessment. See Rainer, *Nagy Imre*, vol. 1, pp. 199–212.

24. The secret documents of the trial were kept in a strongbox in the office of János Kádár, Nagy's executioner, ruler of Hungary between the defeat of the revolution and 1988. Only after his death in July 1989 and the collapse of his party in the same year was the safe opened.

FIGURE I.I. Imre Nagy in front of his judges, June 1958. From the never-released film made by the secret police. Open Society Archives, Budapest.

later on, an eighty-minute version. In 1961, on the secret orders of the Ministry of Interior, the films, except for a few copies of the eighty-minute version, were destroyed. My archives somehow acquired a copy of the film, which to this day—with one exception—has never been publicly shown.[25] I saw the film more than once and showed it to the writer Árpád Göncz, president of Hungary between 1990–2000 and a former convict of the 1956 Revolution, whose death sentence was later commuted to life imprisonment. Göncz translated Faulkner in prison. The sight of the emaciated, bespectacled defendant, looking significantly older than his age, with a squared exercise book in his hand, constantly making notes, writing in pencil, listening attentively as if he were participating in an academic debate, lecturing in a quiet, professorial voice, using simple, logical arguments to the court, behaving as if he were really standing before an institution of justice, who, during the whole show, did not implicate any of his fellow defendants, deeply shook the president of the republic too. (See Figure I.I.)

25. In the "House of Terror" (see related discussion in Chapter 6, below), the house of horrors devoted to the crimes of Communism, there is a room dedicated solely to the

My only consolation in this situation is that, sooner or later, the Hungarian people and the international working class will acquit me of those heavy accusations, the weight of which I have to carry now, in the consequence of which I have to give my life but the responsibility for which I have to take. I feel that the time will come when, in a calmer atmosphere, with clearer vision, with a better knowledge of the facts, justice could be administered in my case too. I feel I am the victim of a grave mistake, the mistake of the court. I do not ask for pardon.

These were his last words.

---

viewing of the film, in order to implicate Imre Nagy's fellow defendants, most of them former Communists as well, who admitted the fabricated charges.

1

Parallel Autopsies

"Shadows are nearing me,/Disguised as bygone years,/I watch them with sorrow, and see/that they are empty picture frames. . . . But why? The cross, which I lifted/in the moment of my pride, was just too heavy/But what did I accomplish? Only a grave/in the cold bitter wasteland."[1] This is the voice of an (alleged) exile, the Hungarian martyr-poet of the Revolution of 1848, Sándor Petőfi. I have retranslated into English verse this so-called poem, which was originally written in Russian and then translated into Hungarian prose by an electrical-engineering student who was studying at Lenin University in Moscow. The lines were discovered in a Siberian archive in 1988, around the time of the collapse of Communism. The poem was recited on July 19, 1989, in the cemetery of Barguzin, Siberia, near Lake Baikal, at the supposed grave of the poet. By that time the alleged skeleton of Petőfi was already in a camcorder box in a hotel room, under the bed of Ferenc Morvai, the Hungarian furnace king, who feared the possibility of a burglary. Members of the archaeological expedition that had found the skeleton were afraid that the bed might collapse under the corpulent king of furnaces.[2] The bones had suffered a fate similar to those

---

Chapter 1 is a revised version of "Parallel Autopsies," originally published in *Representations* no. 49 (winter 1995): 15–39.

1. Poem quoted in Edit Kéri, *Petőfi Szibériában?!* [Petőfi in Siberia?!] (Budapest: Eötvös, 1990), p. 200. Unless otherwise noted, translations are my own.

2. Ibid., pp. 196–98.

of Saint Mark, stolen by Venetian merchants from Alexandria. According to the *Translatio Sancti Marci,* "The Venetians put the body under pieces of pork and returned to their ship. On the way they were stopped by Saracens who, on examining their cargo, saw the pork arid and left in disgust."[3]

*

On July 16, 1989, one month after the reburial of Imre Nagy, the prime minister of Hungary executed in 1958, an amateur anthropologist of the archaeological expedition to Siberia found a skeleton with what were identified as the characteristics of a mixed "Dinaric-Pamiric" type. The body, face down, had been covered with a shroud and buried without a coffin. The bones were lying in a newly opened grave in a remote corner of a cemetery that might have belonged either to the Eastern Church or to the Orthodox Jewish community (a fence separating the two sections had long been demolished).

The skull was thin with a high forehead, and from the upper jaw an unusually large cuspid stood out (see Figure 1.1). (According to contemporary descriptions, Petőfi had a "vampire tooth" in his upper jaw.) After quick measurements, the anthropologist—who was to run as a parliamentary candidate of the Small Holders' Party the following year—established that the dimensions of the shoulder corresponded exactly to the size of Petőfi's uniform, preserved at the National Museum in Budapest. Later on, philologists, anthropologists, and military historians raised the question that if the size of the bones corresponded exactly to the uniform, then how could there have been room for the poet's flesh? But the question was quickly dismissed as nonscientific. (In fact, the uniform itself later turned out not to have belonged to Petőfi.)[4]

The skeleton had unusually broad, feminine hips, but the amateur historians of the expedition produced a description of Petőfi, from the 1840s, by an allegedly homosexual contemporary who might have been very sensitive to such details. They determined from it that Petőfi had "elastic, that is, feminine hips . . . which evidently means that he had broader than

3. Patrick J. Geary, *Furta Sacra: Thefts of Relics in the Central Middle Ages* (Princeton, NJ: Princeton University Press, 1990), p. 93.

4. See Gyula Farkas, Gyula Dezső, and Sándor Oláh, "Miért nem azonosítható a Barguzini lelet Petőfi Sándor csontvázával?" [Why Is it not Possible to Identify the Barguzin Remains as Sándor Petőfi's Skeleton?], in *Nem Petőfi!* [Not Petőfi!], ed. László Kovács (Budapest: Akadémiai, 1992), p. 131.

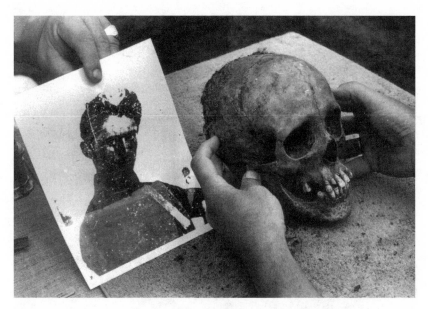

FIGURE 1.1.   Sándor Petőfi's only surviving photograph and his alleged skull.
Photo: Tibor Borzák.

average hips."[5] (In the painting by Miklós Barabás, the fashionable portrait painter of the age, Petőfi is also depicted with rather broad hips [see Figure 1.2].) However, the anthropologists evidently misunderstood the description, which was written in German, of Petőfi's "springy [*elastisch*] steps."[6] On July 31, 1989, the 140th anniversary of the disappearance of the poet, the expedition held a press conference at which Dr. Kiszely, the anthropologist, announced that "on the basis of computer analysis of all the relevant data of the body found, the probability is six trillion to one that the identified remains are those of Petőfi. Consequently, of all the skeletons one can find on this earth, there is no other that could be identified as Petőfi's."[7]

5. Kéri, *Petőfi Szibériában?!* p. 84.

6. Imre Straub, "Petőfi a kortársak vallomásainak tükrében. Emlékezések egy kis sovány emberről. Vajon kit temettek el Barguzinban?" [Petőfi in the Mirror of his Contemporaries. Memories of a Small Thin Man. Who Was Buried in Barguzin?], *Magyar Hírlap* (Hungarian Herald, Budapest), September 8, 1989, pp. 54–55.

7. Quoted in József Kiss, "Petőfi csatatéria halála és szibériai sirjának legendája" [Petőfi's Death on the Battlefield and the Legend of his Tomb in Siberia], in Kovács, *Nem Petőfi!* pp. 54–55.

FIGURE 1.2. Miklós Barabás: Sándor Petőfi's portrait.
Hungarian National Museum.

The feminine body rested near a skeleton, later attributed by the
expedition to a certain Mihail Karlich Küchelbecher, a sailor of German
origin and an exiled Decembrist, who died somewhere in Siberia. On the
other side of the body, nearer to the presumed boundary of the old cemetery of the Eastern Church, was found the skeleton of a Mongolian shaman
two meters tall.

In his biography of Petőfi, Gyula Illyés, the most respected populist
poet in post–World War II Hungary, describes the earlier poet's last hours:

At the beginning of the battle the poet was seen sitting on an oven near the edge
of the burned-down village, taking notes in his pocket notebook. For half an hour
he leaned on his elbow on the banister of the small bridge. Some minutes later, he

went over to the cannoneers; at that moment a cannonball hit the firing position, and the poet was covered with dust. . . . When the attacking Russian army burst into a wild hurrah from three sides at the same time, Petőfi was standing near the medical field station. "The first battalion was less than a thousand steps away. I shouted at him," wrote a doctor from the medical station later on, "and pointed at what was happening. But he remained undisturbed, and only said: 'Bagatelle.' But then I pointed at the left wing, where our general was running. Petőfi turned towards him, looked, and then started to run, too. After he began running, two battalions of ulans followed suit." . . . A mad bloodbath started. The Russians did not want to take any prisoners of war. . . . When the horse almost trampled him, the poet turned his face to his pursuer. He received his mortal wound from the front.[8]

Illyés also mentions the legend—widespread after the death of the poet—that Petőfi was buried alive. A certain V. V. Pahirja, a Ukrainian who rediscovered the story of the Siberian exile in 1985 and had read Illyés's biography in Russian, tried to reconcile the story of the death on the battlefield with the story of the Siberian death: the poet, who had been buried alive on the battlefield, climbed out of his grave during the night but was unfortunately caught by the Russians, who then deported him to Siberia.[9]

It was, however, the poet who died at the age of twenty-six on the battlefield in Transylvania—according to the description, "face to face" with the enemy who personified 1848 in the historical consciousness of the Hungarians. Petőfi translated Pierre-Jean de Béranger, Heinrich Heine, and Shakespeare's *Coriolanus*; he read the works of the French Enlightenment in the original; he was the most prolific poet of his age and an ardent antiroyalist who wrote the most beautiful love poems in the whole of Hungarian literature. (He had a Slovak mother and a father—a village butcher—with a Slavic name, Petrovich, which he later changed to the more Hungarian-sounding Petőfi.) In the memory of the nation, it was he who, by reciting his poem against tyranny, foreign (Habsburg) oppression, and censorship on the steps of the National Museum, ignited the fires of the 1848 Revolution. The day the revolution broke out, March 15, 1848, has always been remembered as the day of freedom of speech, when Hungarian society rose up against foreign and native oppression. After World War II, March 15 became the day the authorities feared most: the day when the defeated revolutionaries of 1956 wanted to start the uprising all over again, the day every year when the democratic opposition, together with university students, took to

8. Gyula Illyés, *Petőfi Sándor* (Budapest: Szépirodalmi, 1963), pp. 650–80.
9. V. V. Pahirja, interview on Hungarian Radio, September 7, 1985.

the streets to demonstrate against censorship and the Soviet military presence, and for freedom of thought and the liberation of the country.

According to witnesses, Petőfi was unarmed when he died. Although he was a major in the revolutionary army, he wore civilian dress. In 1846 he wrote a prophetic poem, in which he foresaw his death on the battlefield, with steeds riding full tilt over his body toward the ultimate victory of world revolution. He even envisioned his grave as the common grave of heroes who died for universal freedom. Still, he did not quite want to die so soon. Shortly after a romantic love affair, he married and had a son he did not want to orphan. But the numerical superiority of the Cossack forces at Segesvár, which came to Hungary at the call of the Habsburgs and in the spirit of the Holy Alliance, overwhelmed the Hungarians. Petőfi was killed, robbed, and buried in a common grave at Segesvár. The grave and his body have never been found.

*

A few months before the small Hungarian expedition (joined by the local Communist Party chief and the chairman of the local soviet) began to dig in the remote Siberian cemetery, excavations started in plot 301 of the biggest cemetery in Budapest in the presence of family members and representatives of the Ministry of Justice and the Citizens' Committee for Historical Justice. Archaeologists, anthropologists, experts in forensic medicine, and police investigators uncovered the graves of five of the most prominent victims of the 1956 Revolution in a remote corner of the cemetery. Four of them—Imre Nagy, the prime minister of the revolution, his minister of defense, who was kidnapped while officially negotiating with the commanders of the Soviet army, and two other high officials—had been hanged thirty-one years earlier on June 16, 1958, following a closed trial. The fifth victim had died in prison before the end of the trial as a consequence of interrogations. Finding these bodies was not part of a routine police investigation. According to a 1953 decree of the Council of Ministers—signed by then prime minister, Imre Nagy—those who had been executed for treason had to be buried in unmarked graves. After the introduction of reforms at the end of the 1960s, family members could be notified and allowed to be present at reburials of these victims. After 1988, as a token of the regime's retreat, family members of the executed could even apply for and receive permission to remove the corpse and bury it wherever they wished to. But Imre Nagy and his fellow victims had been hanged and then secretly buried in the courtyard of the prison. It was only three years later, under pseudonyms, that their bodies were secretly moved. Rumors spread from some drunken grave diggers that plot 301 hid the bodies of the martyrs. From the beginning of the 1980s, on the anniversary of the execution, family members and surviving victims of the revolution began placing flowers on the ground in the darkest corner of the cemetery, at the supposed resting place of the dead. This supposition was strengthened when, after 1982, the police closed down that part of the cemetery on both June 16 and on October 23, the anniversary of the day when the 1956 Revolution broke out.

In July 1988, at the Foreign Affairs Council in San Francisco, Károly Grósz, the last secretary general of the Hungarian Communist Party, answering a question, announced that the family of Imre Nagy would be granted permission to bury the hanged politician in private. By that time, however, Nagy had already been buried in public, if only symbolically. On June 16, 1988, the thirtieth anniversary of the execution, a commemorative monument was erected in the Pére Lachaise Cemetery in Paris. The grave was donated by Jacques Chirac, the conservative mayor of Paris. The monument, an abstract shipwrecked boat, was designed by László Rajk, the son of the executed minister of foreign affairs, the most famous victim of the Hungarian show trials at the end of the 1940s. The monument not only symbolized the shipwrecks of a utopian Communism and of the revolution, but also re-created a familiar image of resurrection from early Christian iconography: the vomiting, that is the reassembling of the pieces of the shipwrecked bodies by the whale that had swallowed them.[10]

At the time of the symbolic burial of Imre Nagy in Paris, a demonstration was held in Budapest at the Eternal Sacred Flame, honoring Count Lajos Batthyány, the executed (and then reburied) prime minister of the 1848 Revolution. At the suggestion of one of the organizers of the demonstration—a man who was to become a member of the Hungarian Parliament in 1990 and who had been sentenced to death after 1956 and spent one year

---

10. In the sermons of the Syrian Saint Ephraim "Death will be overcome by trembling, and will vomit up all it has eaten, so that no dead will be left who is not brought to that place of judgment" (*Das Heiligen Ehpraem des Syrers Sermones III*, ed. Edmund Beck [Lovain: Corpus SCO, 1972], vol. 321.139, p. 13). Quoted by Caroline Walker Bynum, *The Resurrection of the Body in Western Christianity 200–1336* (New York: Columbia University Press, 1995), p. 75.

on death row—the demonstrators renamed the Eternal Sacred Flame the Batthyány-Imre Nagy Flame.

Count Batthyány was shot on October 6, 1849, on the day when the thirteen leading generals of the 1848 Revolution were hanged or shot in Transylvania. He was executed in a prison in Pest, on the site of the present American embassy. He was shot, as he was unfit for hanging. The prison authorities had barely saved his life the previous day when his wife managed to smuggle into the cell a small dagger with which Batthyány cut his own throat in order to avoid a public hanging. Because of his neck wound, the authorities, who had saved his life so they could kill him, had to order his execution by firing squad. His body lay in public at the scene of the execution for three hours.[11]

The Habsburg authorities ordered Batthyány buried in an unmarked grave, but Franciscan monks stole the body from the cemetery and buried it in a crypt in one of the chapels of the order. His initials were inscribed on the inside of the marble slab covering the crypt. (He was officially reburied on June 9, 1870, under the reign of Emperor Franz Joseph, who had ordered his execution twenty-one years earlier.)

Thanks to the Franciscan monks, identifying the corpse of Count Batthyány was an easier task than finding the bodies of some of the executed generals in Transylvania. The brother of one of them had been able to smuggle the body out of the courtyard of the fortress of Arad, where the general had been killed and put in the ground, only by sawing it in two and hiding the two parts in boxes. The body was then reburied twice. The remains of five hanged generals were found only by chance in 1932 during some flood-prevention work. The bodies were then hurriedly laid to rest in the crypt of the Cultural Palace in Arad, Transylvania—at the time Transylvania had already become, as it still is, part of Romania—but in 1974 they were removed and reburied at the site where the hangings supposedly took place. (In fact, they were hanged quite far from the place where they now rest.)

According to one of the undersecretaries of the Ministry of Justice, when the authorities finally agreed to let the families bury the victims of

11. Miklós Peternák, "Catafalque Outside the Palace of Exhibitions," in *Catafalque*, ed. Gábor Bachman, László Rajk, and Miklós Peternák (Budapest: META-R Kft. NA-NE Galery, n.d.), pp. 11–13.

the 1956 Revolution, they first went through hundreds of official documents, then tried to find the hangman, prison officers, grave diggers, and the officials of the cemetery in order to locate the exact burial place of the victims. A special police commissioner from the secret service was appointed to lead the search. When the first corpse was found, to the surprise of the excavators the human remains were mixed with bones that had been taken from the Budapest Zoo. Mingled with the remains of Imre Nagy were the bones of a giraffe. The bodies of the executed were lying face down, wrapped in shrouds and tar paper. On the legs were small metal plates certifying that the prison authorities had paid the sixty-forint fee for the burial.[12]

The Committee of Historical Justice asked the minister of justice to excavate the bodies of five lesser-known revolutionaries who had been executed after the defeat of the uprising. The committee thus wanted to avoid the impression that only the most prominent leaders had been rehabilitated. After long negotiations, a compromise was reached whereby a sixth, empty coffin was buried, to acknowledge the other executed victims.

At first, the government consented to private, family burials and later on, with the weakening of the regime, to nonofficial state funerals. In the end (it was already almost the end of the regime as well), the reburials became quasi official, with the prime minister and important members of the

12. The dog tag fastened to the leg of the corpses certified that the authorities had paid the dues to the ferryman to have the dead carried for certain to the other shore.

Aristophanes was probably the first Greek authority who mentioned the ancient custom of placing two obolos in the mouth of the dead as the duty to Charon, the ferryman of the underworld. According to other traditions the coins placed on the eyes of the dead covered the bridge toll. In Tracie, the coins placed in the mouth of the dead were for the angels, who carried the dead bodies over the famous bridge that is braided of hair and rises above the Danube. The custom still has several variants in Romania, especially in Transylvania. At the beginning of the twentieth century, in Szeged, in southern Hungary, the sum of the toll was four fillers, the exact price of the toll paid by pedestrians on the bridge over the Thais River.

In Russia, the coin placed in the coffin was to pay for the boat, which carried the body over the fire-river that divided this world from Paradise, or the money served as the bribe for the judges of the netherworld. See Géza Róheim, "Kharón és obulus," trans. Éva Hegedűs, in Róheim, *A Bűvös Tükör* (Budapest: Magvető, 1984), pp. 356–423. Originally published as "Charon and the Obolos," in *Psychiatric Quarterly* (supplement) XX (1946): 314–35. Not surprisingly, van Gennep interpreted similar French customs as examples of *rites de passage*. Cf. A. van Gennep, *Manuel de folklore français contemporain*, Tome Premier II (Paris: A Picard, 1946), pp. 720–24.

government present. The Committee of Historical Justice, which organized the ceremonies, asked László Rajk, the well-known opposition activist, architect, and stage designer—and after 1990, a member of parliament—to work out the plans for the architectural installations and the catafalques.

*

Rajk's father, a veteran of the Spanish Civil War, was the most popular Communist leader after World War II. In his capacity as the minister of the interior he played a crucial role at the first show trials, but he was tried and then hanged as a Titoist spy during the most famous of the Hungarian purges in 1949. Together with other Communist leaders, he was secretly buried in the woods not far from Budapest, in the village where Count Pál Teleki, the prime minister of Hungary during the Hungarian and German occupation of Yugoslavia, was put to rest after his suicide. Rajk was then rehabilitated after Stalin's death, and on the demand of large groups both inside and outside of the party, Rajk and three other hanged Communist leaders were reburied on October 6, 1956—the anniversary of the day Count Batthyány was killed. The reburial turned out to be the prelude of the 1956 Revolution. Imre Nagy was present at the ceremony: a photo shows him offering his condolences to the widow and the seven-year-old László Rajk (later to become the stage designer of the Imre Nagy reburial).

The coffins of the elder László Rajk and the other executed Communists were laid out in 1956 in front of Lajos Kossuth's Mausoleum, which was completely covered by black drapery. Kossuth, the governor of Hungary during the 1848 Revolution, died in exile in Turin on March 20, 1894. His body was carried to Hungary, and buried on March 31, 1894 in Budapest. The mausoleum was almost completed by the summer of 1906, when lightning demolished the building. So Kossuth was not reburied in the mausoleum—the non plus ultra of neohistorical architecture—until November 25, 1909 (see Figure 1.3). Kossuth's Mausoleum—featuring above the entrance Hunnia, the allegorical female figure representing Hungary, draped in mourning, immersed in memories of the past and meditating on the woes of the homeland—was an appropriate background for the ceremony in 1956. Rajk and his fellow Communists were buried in the future Pantheon of the Heroes of the Labor Movement. Rajk rested there until 1989, when his son removed the body and re-reburied it near the mausoleum of Count Mihály Károlyi, the first president of Hungary after the dissolution of the Austro-Hungarian monarchy in 1918. (Károlyi died during his second exile

FIGURE 1.3. Lajos Kossuth's remains in front of the mausoleum. Photo Archives of the Budapest History Museum.

in France in the 1950s; he had moved to France as a demonstration against the Rajk trial. His reburial took place in the middle of the 1960s.)

János Kádár's death and burial in 1989 provided the background for László Rajk's decision to remove his father from his grave. In 1949, as minister of the interior—a position inherited from Rajk—Kádár, the leader of Hungary for thirty-three years, played a not-yet-quite-known role in persuading Rajk to confess at the trial. Kádár remained minister until he in turn was tried and imprisoned. The son of the show-trial victim did not want to leave his father in the vicinity of his executioner and so moved him near the exiled and reburied president Count Károlyi in a *depositio ad sanctos*, a well-known practice from late antiquity, when Christian noblemen buried their relatives in close proximity to the martyrs of the church. The latest, simple grave of Rajk is marked by a plaque of a street name on which Rajk's name is crossed out diagonally with red paint.

It is worth mentioning, even in this dry chronicle on recent Central European *danses macabres*, that János Kádár died at exactly the hour Imre Nagy was legally rehabilitated by the Supreme Court of Hungary. On television one could see a small sheet of paper with the news of Kádár's death being passed down the benches of the courtroom. Nagy was legally rehabilitated a month after his reburial; Kádár survived the reburial of his victim, whom he hanged, and did not allow to be buried, by only a few weeks.

*

In Hungary there was no revolution in 1989, not even a velvet one, as in Prague. There were no strikes, no large-scale demonstrations, no signs of massive popular unrest. Hungarians skeptically watched the not-so-dramatic suicide of the system. The dictatorship of the proletariat, in its own version of history, had started with the seizure of power. Perhaps this was why, in 1989, nobody wanted to begin again with "all power to the Soviets," or something similar. The regime melted like butter in late summer sunshine. Even in its demise, Communism succeeded in not denying itself. Its strange death fooled the people one more time by denying them the experience of their sovereignty. Communism killed itself instead of letting the people do it themselves. There were no special dates that could be remembered as decisive in the course of political transformation. The only event that was, and still is, considered in a strange way as crucial was the reburial of the revolutionary prime minister Imre Nagy on June 16, 1989.

The ceremony took place on Heroes' Square, in front of the Millenary Monument, which had been erected as part of the thousand-year anniversary of the Hungarians' arrival in the Carpathian Basin. The monument links a Magyar past with the Hungarian Holy Crown that represents the country's Christian and European civilizing mission in the Carpathian Basin. In a semicircle there originally stood the statues of fourteen kings, among them six Habsburg monarchs.

After World War I and the dissolution of the Austro-Hungarian monarchy, and during the short reign of the First Hungarian Soviet Republic, the statues of the Habsburg emperors were moved away and the statue of Franz Joseph was demolished. On May 1, 1919, the entire monument was covered in red. In place of the conquering pagan chiefs, in front of the obelisk in the middle of the square, was placed a statue of Marx, his arms around two worker figures. The two arcs of the semicircle were transformed into red blocks with the inscription: "Proletarians of the World Unite!" After the defeat of the Soviet Republic, the neobaroque counterrevolutionary regime brought the Habsburgs back, and in 1929 a Memorial to the National Heroes was erected over the Tomb of the Unknown Warrior, the soldier who fought during World War I for the integrity of the thousand years of Hungary. The inscription on the monument read: "For the thousand-year borders!" (This monument served as the background for the altar during the Eucharistic Congress held in Budapest in 1938. During the visit of John Paul II in 1990, the monument was also the background for the mass held on the steps of the Fine Arts Museum on the left side of the square.)

After World War II, the new Communist government removed the statues of the Habsburg kings once more, and replaced them with the figures of national heroes who fought for the independence of the country. Maria Theresa was replaced by Imre Thököly, the leader of the anti-Habsburg uprising in the 1670s and 1680s, who died in exile and was reburied in October 1906; Leopold II was replaced by Ferenc Rákoczi, the leader of the 1703–11 uprising, who died in exile in Turkey in 1735 and was reburied in 1906; the statue of Franz Joseph by Lajos Kossuth, who was exiled by Franz Joseph himself. The Memorial to the National Heroes was also removed, to be replaced in 1956 by a plaque commemorating those who sacrificed their lives for the independence and freedom of the Hungarian nation. The square was the stage for May Day demonstrations and military parades every year on April 4, the day the Red Army—according to the Communist historiography—forced the last German soldier to leave Hungarian soil.

This square, with the coming and going of mostly exiled and reburied figures from its semicircles, was the backdrop for the 1989 reburial of the hanged prime minister.

The figures who disappeared from the semicircles, who were removed from the national pantheon, who were even taken away from the cemeteries, were not only removed from public display but from public discourse as well. (In the 1950s, the composition of one of the oldest Budapest cemeteries was changed. The corpses of the old noble families and members of the bourgeoisie were removed from their proximity to the Pantheon of the Heroes of the Labor Movement. To purify the space—the ground for the newcomer heroes of the new order—the historical setting of the burial place was recomposed.) Nontalk was an important tool of retelling history. In the official Communist chronology certain dates, events, and persons lost intelligibility; they ceased to make sense. Once a topic had become appropriated by official history writing, it lost its historicity. Consequently it became extremely difficult to reconstruct a context in which the person or the event could meaningfully be remembered. From being taboo, historical events and actors sank into the realm of nonexistence, transformed into nonevents, nonproblems, nonpersons. In light of the subsequent developments, it is clear that they were only put aside (*aussparen* is the word Thomas Mann would use here) and were then *reactivated* in a different guise, in a different *persona*, in the context of a different, inorganically recreated narrative.

The post–World War II regime presided not only over the present, the actual subjects of the state, but over the past, over dead souls, as well. Unlike the power of the bishops of late antiquity that derived partly from the tombs of the saints, the strength of the Communist Party stemmed not only from its dead martyrs, the Communist heroes, but also from the unmarked graves of unburied, nameless victims, the persons not talked about. So long as the graves remained unmarked, the victims unnamed, the prosecutors could suppose that they ruled the company of the hanged. However, as Robert Hertz, Emile Durkheim's most promising student, pointed out in his *Contribution á une étude sur la représentation collective de la mort*:

As long as the temporary burial of the corpse lasts, the deceased continues to belong more or less exclusively to the world he has just left. . . . During the whole of this period the deceased is looked upon as having not yet completely ended his earthly existence. . . . In its present distress it remembers all the wrongs it has suffered during its life and seeks revenge. . . . It may "return" of its own initiative through necessity or through malice, and its untimely appearance spreads terror.[13]

Under Communism, unmarked graves—and Hertz's insights are illuminating here, even if not taken literally—testified to the ill-conceived strength of not only those who had the right to take away names, leave graves unmarked, and write history by policing silence. The nameless victims in the graves were also the objects of the executioners' constant horror. They feared the ghosts, the *semianimus*, the half-alive who might return and haunt them, who could not rest peacefully, who might reappear, resurface in memory in a different context. "The dead still muter as shades" (Isa. 29:4) and "feel the worms gnawing at them" (Job 14:22; Isa. 66:24).[14] (Ac-

---

13. I quote from Robert Hertz, "A Contribution to the Study of the Collective Representation of Death," in *Death and the Right Hand*, trans. Rodney Needham and Claudia Needham (Aberdeen: Cohen and West, 1960), pp. 36–37; originally published as "Contribution á une étude sur la représentation collective de la mort," *Année sociologique* 10 (1907): 48–137.

14. Eric E. Meyers, *Jewish Ossuaries: Reburial and Rebirth. Secondary Burials in Their Near Eastern Setting* (Rome: Biblical Institute Press, 1971), p. 13.

cording to testimonies, after 1958 Kádár never mentioned Imre Nagy by name, even in closed sessions of the Central Committee, but referred to him only as "the dead man.")

The silence that surrounded certain events shows that the so-called post–1956 compromise, between the regime and Hungarian society, rested on complicit nontalk. The majority did not, could not, hope for any substantial political change in the foreseeable future. They were unable to make any use of remembering, and many had more or less disturbingly guilty consciences for passive or not-so-passive collaboration before, during, or after World War II and during most of the Communist period. Such people complied with the nontalk that made the historical context even thinner around the fading historical figures, echoing the chorus from Sophocles' *Antigone*: "After the fights, there is the time for long forgetting."

Unlike a Greek chorus, the families of the victims were not able not to remember. Like Polynices in Sophocles' *Antigone*, who died for a lost cause, the victims of the 1956 Revolution lay, in effect, unburied. For the relatives, the families of the victims, the unknown burial was not a real funeral. So long as the executed could not rest peacefully, as proper dead persons, the living were under the obligation not to rest either. In spite—and exactly because of—the horror of the execution, the deceased was not truly dead until the corpse had its final burial.

"As it has no resting place it is doomed to wander incessantly, waiting anxiously for the feast which will put an end to its restlessness," wrote Hertz.[15] The victims had been killed, but their passing away had not been completed, since "Death is not a matter of a moment . . . death is not completed in one instantaneous act."[16] It is not a mere destruction but a transition, a transformation, as well.

Contemporary medical science and legal scholarship tend to see death as a process of transition from life to nonlife, rather than some particular moment of crossing into another realm.[17] But the transformation goes beyond the physiological. Death means the disintegration not just of the physical self but of the social self as well—of the persona with which society invests the individual. It is the duty of the living to help to complete

15. Ibid., p. 36.
16. Ibid., p. 46.
17. See, for example, the Swedish Ministry of Health and Social Affairs, *The Report of the Swedish Committee on Defining Death: The Concept of Death* (Stockholm: Swedish Ministry of Health and Social Affairs, 1984).

the transition, to bury, to mark the grave, to reclaim the victim as a properly dead person, giving him or her social integrity as a dead member of the society of the living: "By giving the deceased a new attire, the living mark the end of one period and the beginning of another; they abolish a sinister past and give the deceased a new and glorified body."[18]

*

There is no need for the testimony of the noble knight Owein from Northumberland, the first eyewitness of the Purgatory, for us to imagine what awaits us after death.[19] For it is not so much the dead, but rather the survivors who find themselves in a liminal position after the departure of an important mortal being. Those who remain among the living undergo a "period of waiting," especially if death strikes suddenly and unexpectedly, by trying to find their new place in the emptied and dangerous world under the heavy weight of irreparable loss. This is probably why the survivors are in need of a period of transition, while death could be tamed, the world reordered, interregnum dealt with. Purgatory, this middle state (not between heaven and hell but between life and death) is not so much for the dead, for the *non valde mali*, the not very bad, than for the living, in order to accommodate themselves to the void left behind by the departed.[20] Purgatory, which "enabled the dead to be not completely dead," served and consoled the living; it is not a stage of afterlife but of afterdeath.[21]

Practices of secondary burial, reinterment, symbolic double burials, bone collecting, erecting charnel houses, all serve the artificial, ritualized lengthening of time between biological and social death. Archaeological evidence from Iron Age Palestine suggests that the practice of secondary burial there might derive from Aegean prototypes, and so Jewish secondary burials, bone collecting, and charnel houses of the Second Temple Period did not represent a major break with the past. "[According to the Israelite conception] death in the strictest sense of the term is the weakest

18. Hertz, "Collective Representation of Death," p. 55.

19. Owein is the hero in "Saint Patrick's Purgatory," composed in Latin by a Cistertian monk at the end of the twelfth century. Cf. Jacques Le Goff, *The Birth of the Purgatory* (Chicago: Chicago University Press, 1981), p. 193.

20. Cf. Peter Brown, "The Decline of the Empire of God. Amnesty, Penance, and the Afterlife from the Late Antiquity to the Middle Ages," in *Last Things: Death and The Apocalypse in the Middle Ages*, ed. Caroline Walker Bynum and Paul Freedman (Philadelphia: University of Pennsylvania Press, 2000), pp. 42–45.

21. Stephen Greenblatt, *Hamlet in Purgatory* (Princeton, NJ: Princeton University Press, 2001), p. 17.

form of life."[22] Elias Bickerman's paper on the double cremation of the Roman emperors and studies of the sixteenth-century French royal funerals, starting with Ralph Giesey's and Ernst Kantorowicz's works, emphasize a "certain distinct vitality" of the dead body that was "not suddenly severed from life, but rather losing contact slowly and deliberately."[23] Funeral images and funerary statues—some of them either buried or cremated later— served to substitute the missing, the departed person on earth. Not only Purgatory but even effigies, wooden or wax images of the dead, sophisticated and complex courtly protocol of dealing with the double of the dead, provided the occasion for an afterdeath "plot" and provided formalized solution for the crises of the postmortem situation.[24]

But according to an old Jewish dictum "[a] corpse does not acquire his place of burial if it be a temporary one."[25] Bickerman, in his *Römische Kaiserapotheose* argued that as death does not mean the end of life on earth, "it is the proper funeral ceremony that ends the life of the body."[26] The temporary funeral is thus just a preparation, a waiting until death (and not the dead) is pacified, until the living gradually transform themselves and are ready for the acceptance of death and the final funeral. But without a proper funeral peace cannot arrive either for the dead or for the living; until then the dead cannot be integrated as a dead member to the society.

22. A. R. Johnson, "A Study in Cultic Phantasy," in *Studies in Old Testament Prophecy*, ed. H. H. Rowley (Edinburgh: T. and T. Clark, 1950), p. 90. Quoted by Meyers, *Jewish Ossuaries*, p. 12.

23. Elizabeth A. R. Brown, "Royal Bodies, Effigies, Funeral Meals, and Office in Sixteenth-Century France," in *Micrologus*, vol. 7 (*Il Cadavere*) (Sismel: Edizioni Del Galluzzo, 1999), pp. 454 and 439, respectively.

24. Cf. Le Goff, *Birth of the Purgatory*, p. 292. "Most important of all, the plot continued after death" (ibid., p. 292). "Burial is also a ritual *against* the dead," wrote Carlo Ginzburg in *Ecstasies, Deciphering the Witches' Sabbath* (London: Penguin, 1992), p. 301; emphasis in original. The other side of this observation is that burial is *for* the living, in order to protect themselves from the danger, the impurity that emanates from death. So definitive (oftentimes, secondary) burial and erecting a gravestone after a time of waiting (in large parts of Europe, usually, after a year, following death, when the widow is eventually liberated from her liminal state and is free to remarry) is the final stage of a difficult and long journey, in the course of which, the biological fact is dealt with and transformed in the process of ritualized acts.

25. Cf. Meyers, *Jewish Ossuaries*, p. 75, n. 10. "Whosoever find a corpse in a tomb should not move it from its place, unless he knows that this s a temporary grave" (ibid., p. 74).

26. In *Archive für Religionswissenschaft* 27, 1929, p. 4.

Without a final and proper funeral, the corpses of those who had been murdered, as folk wisdom holds, "would bleed to accuse their murders."[27]

The first pressure to bury the victims of 1956 came from the families and the survivors of the post–1956 purges. Only later on, with the weakening of the regime, were they joined by those who were searching for historical predecessors in their opposition to the Communist system. When Imre Nagy was placed on the catafalque in Heroes' Square, he was brought back to life from anonymity. Like the prisoners of the Bastille in Jules Michelet's vision, who were not only killed but even forgotten, Nagy was the unknown hero for those hundreds of thousands who came to bury him.[28] The funeral not only provided him with a proper burial place but restored his personality by giving him back his name: "What once has been, cannot thus be annihilated."[29] But as Hertz insisted, "Even forgetting is not a simple and purely negative process: it entails a whole reconstruction."[30] What had been forgotten or pushed back in memory was Nagy's historicity, his place in the context of post–1945 Hungarian history. He could not be remembered because the context—hope in the feasibility of another revolution that might change the post–World War II world order—in which he could have occupied a meaningful place was lost. In order to produce an official Communist interpretation of modern Hungary—State Socialism as the inevitable and unchangeable outcome of the logic of twentieth-century history—it had been necessary to leave him out.

Those who wanted to use him, the victim of Communism as the anti-Communist hero, had to solve some serious problems. The problem with the martyr-prime minister was that he died as a Communist, as a naive believer in the reformability of the State-Socialist system. He had to be purified; it had to be shown that by fighting against Stalinism, he actually fought against Communism in general. He had to be cleansed of his impurity, and only then could he be fit for the final funeral. Death recasts the role of the mortal who has died: it gives his or her life a new interpre-

27. Walker Bynum, *Resurrection of the Body*, p. 326.

28. See Jules Michelet, *History of the French Revolution* (Chicago: University of Chicago Press, 1967), esp. p. 73.

29. Ibid., p. 73. On forgetting in Michelet's text, see Hayden White, *Metahistory: The Historical Imagination in Nineteenth-Century Europe* (Baltimore, MD: Johns Hopkins University Press, 1973), pp. 156–57.

30. Hertz, "Collective Representation of Death," p. 150, n. 320.

tation. Those who wanted to make political use of him had to change his social body before the final ceremony. As Hertz writes, "This transformation does not differ essentially from a true resurrection."[31]

At the same time, those last Communists in power, who had no other choice but to consent to this clear political demonstration against themselves in the summer of 1989, gave permission in the hope that the body of the reform-Communist prime minister could help them find a new historical and political legitimation. They tried to portray themselves as the heirs of that very reform Communism for which the prime minister gave his life. The history of the State-Socialist period had been hastily revised and presented as the history of a permanent fight between reformers and hard-liners. The late, too-late, Communist leaders hoped to stand at the catafalque as close relatives of their own victim.

The leaders of the ancien régime hoped to repeat the effect that a contemporary had reported about the Batthyány reburial in 1870: "The sight of the catafalque does not arouse any thought of revenge."[32] As Peter Brown remarks, the discovery, translation, and burial of a relic "announced moments of amnesty. They brought a sense of deliverance and pardon into the present."[33]

Imre Nagy's fellow revolutionaries, who formed the hard core of the Committee of Historical Justice, were once reform Communists themselves. They wanted rehabilitation but were ready to forgive. By contrast, those who wanted to use the event as a demonstration against the Communists, without differentiating between killers and simple party members, between the high officials of the classical period and the quick converts of the last days of the regime, turned the dead prime minister into an uncompromising, ardent anti-Communist.

Most of those hundreds of thousands (me, among them) who went on a pilgrimage to the burial probably felt free to seek forgiveness for their silence, forgetting, and amnesia, for their willing or unwilling collaboration. The regime of the executioners, from the perspective of its inevitably nearing collapse, seemed to be—even retrospectively—surprisingly weak. The pilgrims were seeking signs of solidarity, the companionship of those

31. Ibid., p. 74.
32. Quoted in Peternák, "Catafalque Outside the Palace of Exhibitions," p. 13.
33. Peter Brown, *The Cult of the Saints: Its Rise and Function in Latin Christianity* (Chicago: University of Chicago Press, 1982), p. 92.

other thousands who were as silent as they themselves had been. Being present at the mourning could be a kind of therapy; not "un thérapie par l'espace," as Alphonse Dupront saw pilgrimage, but a therapy of closeness, of taking part, being present at the historical occasion. Those who attended the funeral, who were seeking the closeness of the tortured bodies, tried to cure, to purify, themselves in the presence of the other mourners, the other sinners.

"Pilgrimage is an individual good work," observed Victor and Edith Turner.[34] It is a "good work" partly because it is voluntary, an internal decision of the individual; it is penitence, it is self-sacrifice. But it is extroverted spiritual work that brings the pilgrim "into the fellowship of like-minded souls," so that the process of internal cleansing—the individual, unselfish penitence—becomes visible to others.[35] Seeing one's self-sacrifice mirrored in the eyes of others is a self-affirmation for the individual pilgrim. Thus even if an internal, individual impulse brought the people to Heroes' Square, it was undoubtedly a comforting feeling for people to see the other thousands there who were also trying hard to be seen in the crowd. But the pilgrimage to Heroes' Square could have a further meaning. While peregrination usually marks "the transition of an individual or group from one state or status to another within the mundane sphere," in Hungary, in June 1989, it was evident that the transition would affect not only those present on the square but each and every person, that the whole nation faced a long and probably painful pilgrimage.[36] Nobody had any doubts whatsoever that "transition" in the coming years would denote a different process from what Arnold Van Gennep had in mind in 1908 when he published *The Rites of Passage*. The country was to undergo an initiation into something unknown to anybody.

The sight of the catafalque could not have been very comforting to those who wanted to purify the martyr's Communist past. It was a neo-constructivist structure evoking, quoting, and—from a distance—referring to the style of Russian and Soviet revolutionary constructivism; it was designed in the spirit of Vladimir Tatlin and Aleksandr Rodchenko although the candelabra were rented out from the opera house, where they were be-

34. Victor Turner and Edith Turner, *Image and Pilgrimage in Christian Culture* (New York: Columbia University Press, 1978), p. 31.
35. Ibid.
36. Ibid., p. 35.

ing used for Verdi's *Aida*.[37] It was not just an abstract scaffold of the revolution; rather, it referred to a particular historical moment, an important historical event: the revolution of the East. In this way the ghost of the Bolshevik Revolution hovered above the steps of the Palace of Exhibitions, where the coffins were laid on display. The scene evoked the revolution, and thus it served as a historical statement: 1956 was a revolution. In fact, it was a left-wing revolution, the uprising of the workers and the university students, led by reform Communists, who wanted not to restore the pre–World War II political structure, but to get rid of the Stalinist version of Socialism.

The director of the institute of the 1956 Revolution, reflecting on the situation of 1989, wrote in 1992: "At that time we thought that our task would be just to deepen and complete with local events the cleansed, well-known and accepted picture of 1956. . . . We were prepared for some minor professional debates and disagreements, but did not expect that the very nature of the Revolution would be questioned."[38] So long as it was impossible to have any public discussion of the revolution, those who were still able to remember thought that the revolution had one single, closed reading. This was the narrative, advanced and kept alive by the former reform-Communist intellectuals and Western left-wing thinkers like Hannah Arendt, Jean-Paul Sartre, and Albert Camus, for whom the supposed reform-Socialist alternative, hidden in the depths of the turbulent events, meant one last hope to save the Socialist utopia. There was, or seemed to be, one single story so long as it was impossible to speak. At the very moment the mourners arrived at Heroes' Square, however, they discovered that although the physical remains of the leaders of the revolution had been found, the silent story of the revolution—that is, the revolution itself—had been lost.

The national symbolism of the ceremony was also peculiar, with references to the flag of the revolution, the tricolor from which the Stalinist coat of arms was cut. This hiatus, the empty middle of the flag, duplicated the emptiness of the sixth coffin in the middle of the stage. In that empty

37. László Rajk, "Nagy Imre temetése és az 56–os emlékmű születése" [Imre Nagy's Burial and the Birth of the '56 Memorial], interview by Zsófia Mihancsik, *Budapesti negyed* (Budapest Quarter) 2 (spring 1994): 199.

38. György Litván, "Az 1956–os magyar forradalom hagyománya és irodalma" [The Tradition and Literature of the 1956 Hungarian Revolution), in *'56–os évkönyv* ['56 yearbook], ed. György Litván (Budapest: 1956-os Intézet, 1992), p. 7.

coffin lay symbolically the hundreds of until-then anonymous and im-
properly buried revolutionaries. In the course of the reburial, the anonymous martyrs got their names back too: the names of 277 victims of the
postrevolutionary trials were read repeatedly during the ceremony, like the
names of the early Christian martyrs in the catacombs.[39] In the absence of
any considerable popular movement, the ceremonial interment served to
reconstruct, if only for a single historical moment, a virtual community.

The care of the dead has always been one of the most important instruments in establishing and reestablishing the bonds of a community.
Dead bodies laid out on public display can create a feeling of belonging-
ness for the definable community of the mourners. The reburial also served
as an occasion for public mourning, in which every person, in the presence
of a large group, could act out in a visible way his or her personal catharsis.

The sight of the catafalque was a sure sign that June 16, 1989, was the
dies illa, the last day of the past. Standing near the coffins, among the
mourners, one could hope to be reintegrated into a concrete community:
the communion of people who had lost those who had been killed, a sort
of *consensus omnium* in the presence of the named martyrs. "The final ceremony," as Hertz has remarked, "always has a pronounced collective character and entails a concentration of the society. . . . Here it is not the family or the village but the nation that intervenes directly to reintegrate the
dead into social communion."[40]

The final funeral not only liberated the executed from their uncertain, liminal, not-quite-dead existence but offered liberation to the relatives as well. Until the final ceremony, the relatives of the victims were
treated—and not only by the representatives of the regime—as impure
persons, as they had once been too close to those who had disappeared,
nameless in unknown graves. At the final rite, the visible and invisible cordon that separated the families from the rest of the community was lifted.
The relatives were reintegrated, together with the deceased, into society.

39. Early Christianity of the catacombs, as the movement of the oppressed, the forerunner of the illegal, underground Communist movement, received positive treatment in
Communist history books. The progressive role of the underground Christians was set
against the institutionalized church on the surface, the arch-protagonist of retrograde social
forces.

40. Hertz, "Collective Representation of Death," p. 71.

The corpses in the coffins—or, in the case of the empty coffins, the completely invisible dead

carried the dark shadows of their origin. [They] not only once died an evil death: but this evil death has been inflicted by an evil power. The martyrs had been executed by the persecutors. . . . Their death, therefore, involved more than a triumph over physical pain; they were vibrant also with the memory of a dialogue with and a triumph over unjust power. . . . The feast of the martyrs, and the reading of their passions, on that occasion, did more than allow individuals to live through a drama of the resolution of pain and illness; the local community as a whole could live through, at the martyrs' feast, a tense moment when potent images of clean and unclean power came together.[41]

Peter Brown's image of the funerals of the martyrs in late antiquity applies as well to the scene at Heroes' Square. The dialogue between just and unjust powers was literally evoked. Radio stations broadcast Imre Nagy's last words in front of his judges. The mourners heard the voice that did not ask for pardon. On the right side of the square, the Yugoslav embassy guarded the background. (When the Soviet troops reentered the city on November 4, 1956, Imre Nagy was granted asylum in this building, from which—in spite of the written promise of János Kádár—he was later kidnapped.)

The majority of the crowd was looking to heal the evils of power and found themselves confronted with the evils that had been inflicted on the bodies lying in front of them. Most of them wanted to end a story, to dig the final graves in a country where the relatives of hundreds of thousands had no grave, where people, as a survivor of the Holocaust once wrote, "dig graves in the air." Contrary to their expectations, "the passion brought the past back into the present."[42]

While most of those present at Heroes' Square wanted concord and consensus, the reburial turned out to be the *adventus* of the new regime. This new regime was inaugurated by showing wounds and pointing to the executioners. The martyrs were elevated, but it was the executioners who were revealed. The *elevatio* and *translatio* of the martyrs were quickly translated into a direct political discourse.

Hungarian history is a history of battles lost, and consequently a continual history of executions, exiles, and political suicides. The normal

41. Brown, *Cult of the Saints*, pp. 101–2.
42. Ibid., p. 82.

public rituals of Hungarian history are, accordingly, not victory parades but funerals and reburials. As the reburial was the only mass action in the story of post-Communist political transformation, it served as the foundation myth for the new political regime. Those who came to power after the funeral, like the vast majority of the population, could not disclose a past of resistance. But by being there, by appropriating those bodies on which the rites of death were acted out, by purifying them, the new leaders could present themselves as those who stood at the side of the executed, who were near them both physically and spiritually. This foundation myth at the grave immediately turned into a "continuation myth," with the present being the direct descendant, the continuation of the anti-Communist fight of 1956. The stress in this myth is naturally on anti-Communism in general, not on the particular form of anti-Communism, for which the victims died.

*

As the new regime was conceived at the grave, mourning over the bodies that served to legitimize it, the reburial could not stop at the edge of the grave. Historical justice had to be done! Not only did the heroes have to be named but the executioners did too. This was not the world of Victricius's *De laude sanctorum*, where "We see no executioners on this spot, no bared sword . . . no bloodthirsty enemy is present . . . no torturer hovers in the background."[43] Instead, the torturer is forced to appear in the foreground, together with the scapegoats, so that the naming and sentencing gives dispensation to the silent majority. Trying and sentencing them is a retroactive act, not just of justice but of resistance. Those daring to name the sins could not be sinners themselves. The hand that points to the executioner shows that mark of the elect few. This is why and how the new judges can promise new forgiveness to society.

This is how the postburial funeral of the select could be used to cleanse those who were elected into office immediately after the funeral. What Philippe Ariès called "promiscuity between the living and the dead" can turn past collaborators into ex post facto resisters.[44] Retroactive political justice brings the past closer to the present. The embarrassing times can thus be erased by turning past time into *Jetztzeit*. By changing the length

43. Victricius, quoted in ibid., p. 101.
44. Phillippe Ariés, *Western Attitudes Toward Death* (Baltimore, MD: Johns Hopkins University Press, 1974), p. 25.

of eclipsed time, history is shortened. The *elevatio* of the victims, with the accompanying *passio*, the replay of the past execution, makes the moment of the killing vivid and intense. The intensity of the dramatic recital produces temporal proximity. The replay of the sins brings certain episodes of the past nearer and can help in compressing time.

Time compression is a tool of historical healing. By bringing back and reburying the repressed, whose quasi-earthly existence has spread horror, the time between the temporary burial and the final funeral is put into brackets. History is remade, rewritten. A new chronology is created by the immediatization of the remote. This immediatization plays a key role in the new political legitimation by forming the basis of a continuity myth: we are the immediate heirs of those whom we bury, whose persecutors we are going to punish immediately after the funeral. The now flows naturally from the then; there is no time between the two historical points.

It was only a short step from the generalized anti-Communist interpretation of 1956 to the tradition of archconservative, nationalist, neo-baroque anti-Communism of the 1920s and 1930s. Immediately after the reburial, the postfuneral government of post-Communist Hungary began trying to (re)construct a fictional historical continuity in order to erase the whole period of Communism from national consciousness.

In December 1993, József Antall, the first prime minister of the post-Communist period, died. The choreographers of his funeral designed an emphatically anachronistic show. The State Folk Ensemble, dressed in the costumes of the various ethnic groups of the Magyar tribal confederation, for instance, were meant to symbolize *all* Magyars, both inside and outside the country, as they filed past the catafalque of the man who had declared himself prime minister of all Magyars everywhere. This was calculated to emphasize the restoration of historical continuity. In the last of the series of tableaux set around the catafalque, a man, a woman, and a child, clothed in traditional Hungarian dress, walked up to the coffin with measured steps: it was "The Family" that stood, heads bowed, at the bier of the *pater patriae*, the father of the nation. The premodern iconography—the traditional display, the gun carriage drawn by six horses, the honor guard of hussars in seventeenth-century uniform—was meant to demonstrate the unbroken continuity of Hungarian history. All this served to proclaim that the national tradition was as robust as ever in the post-Communist era; it was stronger than Communism, stronger even than death. In death, József

Antall became the incarnation of the vision that had been his beacon as prime minister: the continuity of Hungarian history after, and in spite of, the Communist detour forced on the country by a foreign power.

One of the last acts of the deceased prime minister (a former history teacher) was a ceremonial visit to the grave of Hungary's recently reburied interwar regent, Admiral Miklós Horthy. It was a symbolic gesture, coming from a man who had subordinated his own political role to his ambition to rewrite history; for him politics was writing history by other means. He had aspired to transform post-Communist Hungary so as to make it seem as if the forty-odd years after the Second World War had never been.

According to post-Communist revisionism, Communism in Hungary was the tragic result of a conspiracy organized from abroad; it was the work of outsiders in the service of foreign powers and, as such, was no part of Hungarian history. The continuity with the nation's past was broken on March 19, 1944, the day the German occupation began. From then on, Hungary was merely the plaything of external forces and not responsible for its history (including the deportation of the Hungarian Jews), for that was not really *Hungarian* history. In this narrative of historical caesura, Fascism and Communism, the Holocaust and the Gulag, became congeneric, thus interchangeable and indistinguishable.

Horthy's reburial was not a rite of commemoration but a unique kind of *damnatio memoriae*: the obliteration of Communism from the nation's memory. Those weeping over Horthy's new grave mourned the hundreds of thousands of soldiers who fell along the Don River in the Second World War against the Soviet Union just as they mourned the man who sent them to their death, and they sought to camouflage their own recent past with the corpse of the regent. They wanted to believe—they wanted to make the whole country, the whole world, believe—that they and the Hungarian people had already fought Bolshevism in the Second World War, had resisted in advance, and thus had paid their dues for all the years when they had suffered Communist rule without demur. Those who were present at the funeral hoped that their physical proximity to the regent's remains would prove that they had always been implacable anti-Communists, the secret opponents of his enemies. (By implication, it follows that those who refuse to see the sacrifice of Hungarian soldiers on the altar of Fascism as an anti-Bolshevik crusade are what they have always been, Communist collaborators, and their repudiation of Horthy simply bears this out.)

The fact that Miklós Horthy was reburied in the autumn of 1993 just one month before Prime Minister Antall was laid to rest was crucial to the rather idiosyncratic interpretation of Hungary's historical "continuity." It was necessary to reinterpret Horthy as a historical person in order to locate the post-Communist prime minister within the regent's historical proximity. The reburial of the admiral and regent was thus seen as the immediate predecessor of the burial of the conservative prime minister, and the two events together allowed a revision of history. Horthy passed from the Hungarian political scene in 1944, nearly fifty years before Prime Minister Antall's death. However, the reburial and the funeral followed one after the other, as the post-Communist era follows the pre-Communist era in the new, revised framework of Hungarian history. Everything in between has been consigned to oblivion.

*

Aleksandr Solzhenitsyn's *Gulag Archipelago* was first officially published in Hungary in 1988, when, after long decades, it became possible for the first time to talk about the Hungarian victims of the Gulag system. Ferenc Morvai, the Hungarian furnace king, and his archaeological expedition hoped to find the body of Petőfi, the archetype of the Hungarian Gulag victim. They were led by, as Johan Huizinga called it, "an ultra-realistic conception" of the saint, on the one hand, and by a historicized, abstract anti-Communism, on the other.[45] Morvai entertained the vision of wounded revolutionaries as the secret labor reserve of the czar in the sparsely populated Siberia: the prisoners of the war, Petőfi among them, working as invalid miners in the future camps of the Gulag. This nightmare, according to a noted Petőfi scholar, served as "the prefiguration of the *malenkaja rabota*—in its folk version, the *malenkii robot*—of the post–Second World War period, placed back in the time of Nicholas I."[46] (Immediately after the Second World War, the Soviet army collected, literally kidnapped, hundreds of thousands of East and Central European people, mostly men, from the liberated countries and held them as slave laborers for years in the Soviet Union. This slave labor was called *malenkii robot*, "small work" or "cage" in the slang of the period.)

45. Johan Huizinga, *The Waning of the Middle Ages*, trans. F. Hopman (Garden City, NY: Doubleday, 1956), p. 166.
46. Sándor Fekete, "Egy történeti vita tényei" [Facts of a Historical Debate], in Kovács, *Nem Petőfi!* p. 24.

The Siberian legend had already been used for direct political purposes in a different political situation. The *Magyarság*, the daily of the Fascist Arrow-Cross Party, published a forged picture of Petőfi's Siberian grave in its August 4, 1940, issue. "One can conclude with good reason," mused a respected literary scholar, "that the publication of the picture and a version of the legend of Hungarian prisoners of war in Siberia, in a Fascist newspaper in 1940 and 1941, served as a kind of sentimental preparation for Hungary's joining the war against the Soviet Union."[47]

The self-styled archaeologists wanted to dig up the arch sin of the Russians, this time if not as a sufficient cause for war, at least as an added historical element of the proof of Soviet criminality.[48] At the time of the mass production of historical revisions, they thought that they could present Petőfi as another taboo of the last regime that did not wish to remind the Soviets of the crimes of their Russian predecessors. Instead of the twenty-six-year-old hero who died on the battlefield and was buried in a common grave, they proposed a thirty-three-year-old, gray-haired Siberian prisoner, who, after having forgotten his beautiful young wife, married the daughter of the local postmaster at Lake Baikal. Instead of the romantic young prophet, they found a man with bad teeth, with a pocked jaw, with a lost kneecap. ("Perhaps a badger took it from the grave," the amateur anthropologist gave as the scientific explanation.)[49]

In the interpretation of the expedition, even the lack of any official document about Petőfi's years in the mines strengthened their case. "As Petőfi was too important a figure, and his case politically too sensitive, it was the order of the czar to destroy all the documents on Petőfi after his death. The lack of documents proves that Petőfi had to stay in Siberia," wrote a dilettante historian after careful investigation.[50] "Where are Wal-

---

47. Kiss, "Petőfi csatatéri halála és Szibéria sírjának legendája," p. 48.

48. One of the furnace king's co-diggers made the accusation that "the Communist government had signed a secret agreement with the government of the Soviet Union, in order to hide further from the public the fact that the Russians had deported the freedom fighters to Siberia" (Ferenc Morvai, quoted in Róbert Hermann, "Jelentés a Tudományos Akadémia Petőfi Bizottságának munkájáról. A Bizottság állásfoglalása a Morvai Ferenc által benyújtott 'újabb Bizonyitékokról'" [Report on the Work of the Petőfi Committee of the Hungarian Academy of Sciences, Statement of the Committee Concerning the "New Proofs" Supplied by Ferenc Morvai], in Kovács, *Nem Petőfi!* p. 252).

49. Dr. Kiszely, quoted in *Petőfi Szibériában?!* p. 73.

50. Miklós Mikolás, "Segesvártól Barguzinig" [From Segesvár to Barguzin], *Pesti Hírlap* (Pest Herald), February 4, 1991, p. 8.

lenberg's letters? How is it possible that such a courageous and intensely practical man was incapable of sending any message, of informing the outside world?" asks the former actress who wrote the history of the expedition. "If somebody is an important prisoner . . . he is never able to send messages."[51] Petőfi's fate, in the story of the resurrectionists, was similar to that of Raoul Wallenberg, the Swedish diplomat who saved the lives of thousands of Jews in Hungary during the Second World War. After the war Wallenberg was taken to the Soviet Union, where he probably died in a Moscow prison. International organizations, together with his family, hoped for decades that he was alive. From time to time witnesses allegedly saw him alive in different prisons, wandering silently from camp to camp in the Gulag.

"The elect could be identified . . . only posthumously," writes Peter Brown.[52] There is no life after death—at least not for the martyrs on this earth. Death makes the martyr, and his death rewrites, reinterprets, his whole life. A martyr is a martyr from the heights of his death. He can be reburied (he is almost always reburied), but he cannot have a new death, a new version of death; he cannot live after the death that made him a martyr. His life freezes at the moment of his death, and one cannot warm up his body and give a new worldly life and then a new death to him.[53] A martyr who survives the death that made a martyr of him is an antimartyr, a poor mortal figure.

Petőfi or his martyrdom almost fell victim to a fatal misunderstanding. Morvai, the furnace king, the prototype and caricature of the new post-Communist capitalist, wanted to act not only as a real Maecenas but as the impresario of a new version of a saint cult, too. The self-styled impresario mixed up the unmarked common grave on the battlefield—the authentic resting place of a revolutionary poet—with a ditch in the most

51. Kéri, *Petőfi Szibériában?!* p. 18.
52. Brown, *Cult of the Saints*, p. 71.
53. "'A man who dies at the age of thirty-five,' said Moritz Heiman once, 'is at every point of his life a man who dies at the age of thirty-five.' Nothing is more dubious than this sentence—but for the sole reason the tense is wrong. A man—so says the truth that was meant here—who died at thirty-five will appear to *remembrance* at every point of his life as a man who dies at the age of thirty-five. In other words, the statement that makes no sense for real life becomes indisputable for remembered life" (Walter Benjamin, "The Storyteller," in *Illuminations*, trans. Harry Zohn [New York: Schocken Books, 1969], p. 100; emphasis in original).

remote corner of a public cemetery, where the hanged were thrown after 1956. The excavator wanted to give a present to his transforming country. He wanted to show that the *translatio* was a sign to the nation of God's capacity to forgive. He wanted to offer a prisoner from the Gulag, instead of the soldier from the battlefield. In doing so, however, he was substituting for the martyr the body of a mere mortal. By trying to find Petőfi the man, he threatened to kill Petőfi the martyr.

The business-minded impresario also used the occasion to promote his furnaces. He organized exhibitions and promotional shows in several cold Siberian cities and had a furnace exhibition in Ulan-Ude while the expedition was busy digging in the cemetery.[54] And like the Roman noblemen of late antiquity, he tried to "privatize the holy." When the reluctant Hungarian government refused to grant an official burial of the body of such dubious origins, he decided to rebury it in the garden of his own house.

Except for the possessed members of the expedition, most people prayed for a negative result of the process of identification. The overwhelming majority of the Hungarians were not like Pausanias, who in his *Description of Greece* had the ambition to claim, "the inexactitudes of the tradition have been corrected."[55]

Instead of the body, they wanted to have the martyr, who died a proper death and was properly buried in the unmarked grave in the battlefield. This called for not the forensic but the martyrological truth. Hungary did not want to find a skeleton but to keep Petőfi.

In the case of the secular martyr, a miracle, like the one described in the *Vita Sancti Abbani,* could not have offered a comforting compromise. After the death of Saint Abbanus, when two monasteries claimed the body of the sixth-century Irish saint, "a miracle provided each community with an identical body of the saint."[56] But who knows? The former president of the Hungarian Academy of Sciences, a famous anatomist himself, wrote:

Who can force me to believe that a young genius, who speaks Slovak, German, French, and even English, a person of high culture, a hero, suddenly makes a cow-

54. Kéri, *Petőfi Szibériában?!* p. 76.
55. Pausanias, "Description of Greece 1.28.7," quoted in Paul Veyne, *Did the Greeks Believe in Their Myths? An Essay on the Constitutive Imagination,* trans. Paula Wissing (Chicago: University of Chicago Press, 1988), p. 74.
56. *Acta Sanctorum* Oct. XI I, pp. 276–93, quoted in Geary, *Furta Sacra,* p. 116.

ardly compromise with his fate, keeps his mouth shut just to escape execution? I apologize to my compatriots, but to believe all this would be tantamount to disgracing one of the greatest heroes of the Hungarian nation and to our common history as well. Such an idea would in itself be a high crime and "sacrilege" in our old religious language.[57]

Morvai did not understand that an unknown grave is a historical fact, that it has a definite historical place, in spite of, in fact as a consequence of, the fact that its exact location is not known. Had Morvai been able to find credible scientific authorities to support his fragile case (and skeleton), perhaps the country would have invented, or discovered, another Petőfi, still lying in an unmarked grave. The nation would then have had to live with two programs of truth, contradicting each other but residing in the same minds.[58]

But finally Hungary got what it hoped for. An international group of experts—anthropologists, forensic experts, archaeologists, and literary scholars from the United States, the Soviet Union, and the German Democratic Republic—together with some worried members of the Hungarian Academy of Sciences, reexamined the corpse found in Barguzin between the cemeteries of the Eastern Church and the local Jewish community. (The furnace king accused the scholarly team of "communist academic sabotage against the interest of the nation.")[59] With due scientific authority it was finally determined that the skeleton, instead of being the remains of a young but mature Christian male, belonged to a sexually immature, Orthodox Jewish female, the perfect antithesis of a real hero.[60] The lack of a coffin and the shroud in which the body was wrapped were not the signs

57. János Szentágothai, introduction to Kovács, *Nem Petőfi!* p. 7.

58. "Since interests and truths do not arise from 'reality' or a powerful infrastructure but are jointly limited by the programs of chance, it would be giving them too much credit to think that the eventual contradiction between them is disturbing. Contradictory truths do not reside in the same mind-only different programs, each of which encloses different truths and interests, even if these truths have the same name" (Veyne, *Did the Greeks Believe in Their Myths?* pp. 85–86).

59. Morvai, quoted in Hermann, "Jelentés a Tudományos Akadémia Petőfi Bizottságának munkájáról," p. 246.

60. On the basis of both metric data and morphological characteristics of the skull and the bones, a so-called sexualized index was determined. Out of the eighty-two observed characteristics, forty-five referred to a female and fifteen to a male, while twenty-two were indifferent. "The final result, gained from the 82 characteristics, was a gender index of -0.71,

of blasphemy, as in the case of the burial of Imre Nagy; they reflected Orthodox Jewish mortuary ritual.[61]

Alexandr Petrovich Gromov and Victor Nikolaievich Zvaiagin, two experts from the Legal Forensic Research Institute of the Soviet Ministry of Health, dissented from the "sexually immature" thesis. According to the learned forensic scholars, the skeleton showed the signs of either undernourishment or "what seemed to be more probable—a certain physiological state, like pregnancy. . . . However, as a result of the fractional state of the pubic bones, we were not able to determine whether a delivery had actually occurred."[62] Alexandr Petrovich, the name of one of the forensic experts,

---

which unequivocally qualifies the remains as a female skeleton" (Farkas, Dezső, and Oláh, "Miért nem azonosítható a Barguzini lelet Petőfi Sándor csontvázával?" pp. 112–18).

61. At a conference on "DNA and Human Rights" in April 2001, organized jointly by the Human Rights Center at Berkeley and the Open Society Archives, I met a young DNA expert who had taken part at the DNA analysis of the Barguzin bones. She worked at the Armed Forces Institute of Pathology at the Office of the Armed Forces Medical Examiner, Washington DC. The Institute of Pathology had been asked by Morvai and his team to carry out supplementary DNA analysis of "Petőfi's remains." The institute undertook two analyses, one in April 1991, the other in October 1996. According to the first report sent out on May 6, 1994, "Skeletal remains were received by the Armed Forces DNA Identification Laboratory (AFDIL) for DNA analysis. The laboratory was asked to determine the sex of the submitted skeletal remains. . . . Conclusion: The results show that the individual from which this specimen was obtained was a female." Signed by Deborah L. Fisher, Chief Nuclear DNA Analyst, Armed Forces DNA Identification Laboratory. The second report, dated October 18, 1996, states, "This is the second report of DNA analysis performed by the Armed Forces DNA Identification Laboratory to determine the sex of skeletal remains purported to be Sandor Petofi, a Hungarian Patriot. . . . An amelogenin profile was generated on the submitted right humerus fragment. The results indicate that the individual from whom the right humerus fragment was obtained is a female." Signed by Jeanne W. Willard, MFS, DNA Analyst, Armed Forces DNA Identification Laboratory; Mitchel H. Holland, PhD, Branch Chief, Armed Forces DNA Identification Laboratory; Jacqueline S. Raskin, MS; Victor W. Weedn, M. D. J. D. LTC, MC, USA Program Director, DoD DNA Registry.

The laboratory conducted a mitochondrial DNA test as well and compared the Barguzin remains with specimen of a database of unrelated individuals. According to a table, attached to the cited document, comparisons were made in the following databases: "U.S. Caucasian, English Caucasian, African American, Afro-Caribbean, African and Hispanic." The bones resembled most closely U.S. Caucasian database. It seems that the woman, who had lived and then been buried in Siberia, and whose bones were sent to the U.S. laboratory, resembled most closely a U.S. Caucasian individual.

62. Alexandr Petrovics Gromov and Viktor Nyikolaievich Zvaiagin, "Petőfi Sándor Barguzini 'azonosítása'" [Sándor Petőfi's "identification" in Barguzin], in Kovács, *Nem Petőfi!* pp. 142–43.

was also, according to the hypothesis of the expedition, Petőfi's Russian name. They were looking for the grave of a certain Alexandr Petrovich. This was the name on the forged picture of the grave published in 1940 in the Fascist newspaper. Alexandr is Sándor's Russian equivalent, while Petrovich is the Slavic form of Petőfi, and the original name of Petőfi's father. Perhaps the forensic expert is the grandson of the Siberian prisoner, the pregnant Jewish poet.

"If the skeleton found in the seventh grave of the Barguzin cemetery really did belong to Sándor Petőfi, then this would prove that the poet was in fact a woman."[63] This would surely be too much for the Magyars. Petőfi was not a Joan of Arc: he was killed, it is still believed, by a Russian Cossack, not by a Hungarian furnace king. Temporarily, the country can rest, at least for the time being, in peace.

*

Under the title "Author's Plot, Not," the *San Francisco Examiner* issued a short report on April 5, 1995:

Poland has paid the ultimate tribute to its playwright of absurd, mistakenly burying the wrong corpse, that of a woman, in his place.

A special commission confirmed that the purported body of writer and painter Stanisław Ignacy Witkiewicz, solemnly brought home from the Soviet Union in 1988, had turned out to be that of a woman.

Witkiewicz, whose plays are recognized as masterpieces of the absurd, killed himself after learning that Moscow's troops had entered Poland in 1939, and was buried in what later became part of the Soviet Union. His reburial in his beloved Polish mountains was accompanied by an outpouring of patriotic sentiment, but doubts emerged as to the identity of the body.

The commission head said blame for the mistake appeared to lie with certain Polish officials and a Soviet doctor who failed to spot the difference in age and sex.

63. Farkas, Dezső, and Oláh, "Miért nem azonosítható a Barguzini lelet Petőfi Sándor csontvázával?" p. 133.

2

The *Necronym*

The Dead

Perhaps you have not heard me for quite some time; so you will bear with me. . . . You will have something strange from me: . . . What is my responsibility? . . . It is not me, I haven't put it this way myself; it was a man from the West, in the presence of the Soviet tanks, who said "The Danube's flow is too quick." . . .

My illness, the reason for my forgetfulness, is that I often know what I want; this is why I am losing weight. . . . My problem is that my mind is constantly whirling round and round and this requires energy. . . . I do not mind whatever you say afterward, and whatever you say, as anybody can shoot me dead. I was aware of the responsibility not to name anybody. (And now I want a lot of water because I am nervous.) . . .

The doctor says that my real problem is that I keep thinking about my responsibility . . . and they say, "You are the chairman of the party, and you still do not speak. If you are the chairman, why are you not able to speak?"

Now I am not the same, not who I was a long time ago . . . but I will not name anybody. . . . I don't know why my presence is important for anybody, as I am a scapegoat in the biblical sense. Because I am older than anybody else. . . .

If I remember correctly—the man who died since then, had refused to sign. . . . Now, in retrospect, I see everything differently too. . . . I had to sign it too, somewhere, God knows where. . . . For how long have I been talking now? I will come to the end. . . . I just cannot stand, cannot bear remaining passive, unable to respond. I cannot stand this. . . . And this what makes me ill. I have a different illness than what my wife has.

Chapter 2 is a revised version, of "Necronym," *Representations* no. 64 (fall 1998): 76–108.

And what is memory? . . . And what is leaking words? . . . I am a very old man, and I have so many kinds of illnesses that I do not even mind if somebody shoots me to death. . . . I apologize. . . .

And please remember that whenever I remember, since this is already what I have to do, I will always tell the truth. . . . I cannot refuse that, for everybody says that I am the living one; I must speak. . . . Now I remember, it started on the twenty-eighth when by pointing at the dress or the color of the skin or pointing at I know not what, unarmed people were killed in a pogrom. And they were killed before, before Imre Nagy and those belonging to him were . . . killed. And if I look at it historically then I too would quietly say, and if I look at it from a distance of thirty years, then I feel sorry, yes, for everybody.[1]

On April 12, 1989, at the opening session of the meeting of the Central Committee of the Hungarian Socialist Workers' Party the chairperson announced, "Because of health problems two of our comrades. István Horváth [the minister of the interior] and comrade János Kádár are not able to take part in our meeting." At around 3:20 PM, Károly Grósz, the secretary general of the party, took the floor because he had something unexpected to report:

Dear comrades! I have a very difficult, even humanly very difficult task now. I would like to inform you that comrade János Kádár is in very poor health. He has been preparing for this session for many days; he has very much wanted to take part, and he has formulated a lot of thoughts. Until yesterday, or at least yesterday, it seemed that he understood my—our—request to keep himself away from our meeting today. But now he is here, he has arrived. Yesterday we parted under dramatic circumstances. But now he is here, and he wants to come into the meeting. We have neither the option nor the right to prevent him, but I would like to warn you that he is in very bad condition both psychologically and biologically. I am not a medical doctor, but I have concrete information about his medical condition. If he takes the floor—I sincerely ask you—please make an effort to understand [him or this whole issue].[2]

At 3:30 PM the Central Committee withdrew for a lunch break, during the course of which the members of the Central Committee elected a new Politburo. At 4:30 PM the session was reconvened. The chair of the

---

1. *A Magyar Szocialista Munkáspárt Központi Bizottságának 1989. Évi Jegyzőkönyvei* [The Proceedings of the 1989 Meetings of the Central Committee of the Hungarian Socialist Workers' Party] (Budapest: Magyar Országos Levéltár, Hungarian State Archive, MOL, 1993), vol. 1, p. 756. Unless otherwise noted, all translations are my own.
2. Ibid.

election committee announced the result of the vote, read the names of the new members of the Politburo, and gave the floor to János Kádár, who wanted to speak.

Kádár was seventy-seven years old, and until May of the previous year he had been the secretary general of the party since October 31, 1956. In May 1988 an extraordinary party conference took place in which Kádár was ousted as general party secretary and was given instead a titular position as chairman of the party. At about the same time he underwent hand surgery that he considered to be more serious than it really was; he thought that this incapacitated him and led to the loss of his faculties.

It is now April 1989. Kádár's best-known victim is about to be reburied in June. He knows that the party, which has no choice, has already given its consent to the reburial; he knows that there is no longer any way to stop it. Imre Nagy, the hanged prime minister of the 1956 Revolution, whose body was thrown into a ditch in the most distant corner of a cemetery on the outskirts of Budapest, is coming back. Kádár will survive the reburial by three weeks and will die on the morning of July 6, 1989, on the very same day, in fact during the course of Imre Nagy's retrial at the Supreme Court, when the executed leader of the 1956 Revolution is rehabilitated.[3] (See Figure 2.1.)

Kádár kept talking for one-and-a-half hours in disjointed words and associations; the Central Committee sat in complete silence.[4] When he finished, the meeting was suspended; some members of the Central Committee, mostly women, were crying.

From the mosaic of his thoughts it is more or less obvious that his mind was occupied by the coming reburial, his role and responsibility in ending the revolution, in bringing the Soviet troops back in, in executing the "dead man," "the man who died since," as he kept referring to Imre Nagy in the speech. At the very end of his monologue, on the very last

---

3. In the film made about Imre Nagy's retrial, one can see that suddenly a small sheet of paper was circulating in the benches of the courtroom. It turned out later that on that sheet of paper was written the news of János Kádár's death.

4. Emil Kimmel, who was deputy press secretary of the party at that time, gives a detailed description of the scene in his memoirs: *Végjáték a Fehér Házban. A helyettes szóvivő titkai* [The Last Scene in the White House: The Secrets of the Deputy Press Secretary] (Budapest: Téka-Szikra Kiadó, 1990), esp. pp. 122–31.

FIGURE 2.1. János Kádár at the time of his last speech. Photo: András Bánkuti.

page of the published minutes he pronounces the name: ". . . before Imre Nagy and those belonging to him were killed."[5]

According to published documents and testimonies, Kádár almost never referred to Imre Nagy by name after 1958, after the prime minister was hanged—as if there had been a self-imposed prohibition on pronouncing the name of the dead. As if by referring to Nagy by name, a relation, *a relational* term would have been produced. In fact, this is exactly what happened in 1989 when it became possible for the first time to pronounce the name of the dead publicly: Kádár lost his proper name and acquired *a necronym* instead: "Imre Nagy's executioner."[6]

5. Immediately after the speech, rumors started to circulate in the city about a "dramatic, monomaniacal, mad speech" by Kádár. The full text was published in 1993 in *A Magyar Szocialista Munkáspárt Központi Bizottságának 1989*, vol. 1, pp. 758–67. The deputy press secretary of the party secretly taped the speech. In order to prevent any future manipulation of the text, he simultaneously recorded, on the same tape, the radio announcement of the exact time. On a copy of the original that I have in my possession, the exact time is announced in the background every ten seconds.

6. About the term necronym, see Claude Lévi-Strauss, *The Savage Mind* (Chicago: University of Chicago Press, 1966), esp. chap. 7, "The Individual as a Species," pp. 191–216. I

"What does the logical identity of sign and thing signified really consist in?"—asks Ludwig Wittgenstein in his *Notebooks*. He has an answer to his question: "Die logische Identität von Zeichen und Bezeichnetem besteht darin, dass man im Zeichen nicht mehr und nicht weniger wiedererkennen darf als im Bezeichneten."[7]

But contrary to logic, or at least to Wittgenstein's somewhat cryptic reasoning here, it seems that sometimes there is more in the sign than in what it stands for.[8] Even the early Wittgenstein contemplates this possibility; when playing with the problems caused by proper names, he writes: "Composer names. Sometimes we treat the method of projection as given. When we ask for instance: what name would fit this man's character? But sometimes we project the character into the name and treat this as given. In that case we get the impression that the great masters we know so well have just the names which suit their work."[9] In this case, what one supposedly recognizes in the name is not only the nominatum—as Gottlob Frege would call the composer—but even the work of the great master, the direct referent of the name. When commenting on J. G. Frazer's *Golden Bough*, Wittgenstein asks: "Why should it not be possible that a man's own name be sacred to him? Surely it is both the most important instrument given to him and also something like a piece of jewelry hung round his neck at birth."[10]

---

use the term differently. Lévi-Strauss understands it in the following way: "The necronym contains no proper name at all and consists in the statement of a kinship relation, which is that of an unnamed 'other' relation. And finally, this relation is negative since the necronym mentions it only to declare it extinct" (p. 192). Lévi-Strauss's reading of the necronym, as a category of classification, did not enter into wider circulation. The lack of reference to it encourages me to resurrect it by attaching a different meaning to it. See, for example, "Since his fall he [Kádár] is called a 'tyrant' or an 'executioner'" (Gáspár Miklós Tamás, "Veszélyben a demokrácia" [Democracy Is in Danger], *Világ* 28 [September 1989]: 34).

7. "The logical identity between sign and thing signified consists in its not being permissible to recognise more or less in the sign than in what it signifies" (translation is from Ludwig Wittgenstein, *Notebooks, 1914–1916*, ed. G. H. von Wright and G. E. M. Anscombe [New York: Harpers, 1961], pp. 3e and 3–4, respectively).

8. As we know, the Wittgenstein of the *Philosophical Investigations* changed his mind and no longer thought that the sign had as its meaning only the object it signified.

9. Ludwig Wittgenstein, *Culture and Value*, ed. G. H. von Wright (Chicago: University of Chicago Press, 1980), pp. 24e–25e.

10. "Warum sollte dem Menschen sein Name nicht heilig sein können? Ist es doch einerseits das wichtigste Instrument, das ihm gegeben wird, anderseits wie ein Schmuckstück, das ihm bei der Geburt umgehangen wird" (*Remarks on Frazer's* Golden Bough [Be-

"Unable to discriminate clearly between words and things, the savage commonly fancies that the link between a name and the person or thing denominated by it is not a mere arbitrary and ideal association, but a real and substantial bond which unites the two. . . . In fact, primitive man regards his name as a vital portion of himself and takes care of it accordingly." This is how Frazer summarizes his conclusions about his long list of examples that follow these introductory sentences in his chapter on taboo words.[11]

These are almost the same words that Sigmund Freud would use more than once in *Totem and Taboo*, where he relies heavily on Frazer's work. The taboo upon names—writes Freud—"will seem less puzzling if we bear in mind the fact that savages regard a name as an essential part of a man's personality and as an important possession: they treat words in every sense as things."[12] Of course, Frazer and Freud are not alone in their convictions. In a book published much later, in 1957, on the intricate problem of the tetragrammaton, or the origin of the prohibition on pronouncing the name of God, Max Reisel writes, "A substantial difference exists between the importance attributed to certain names by primitive man and that attached to names in general by people of a more rational frame of mind."[13] Among the tribes of central Australia, wrote Frazer,

every man, woman and child has, besides a personal name, . . . a secret or sacred name, . . . which is known to none but the fully initiated members of the group. This secret name is never mentioned except upon the most solemn occasions; to utter it in the hearing of women or of men of another group would be a most serious breach of tribal custom, as serious as the most flagrant case of sacrilege among ourselves. When mentioned at all, the name is spoken only in a whisper, and not until the most elaborate precautions have been taken that it shall be heard by no one but members of the group.[14]

---

merkungen über Frazers *Golden Bough*], ed. Rush Rhees [Atlantic Highlands, NJ: Humanities Press, 1979], pp. 5e and 5, respectively).

11. J. G. Frazer, *The Golden Bough: A Study in Magic and Religion*, 12 vols., *Part II: Taboo and the Perils of the Soul* (London: Macmillan, 1911), vol. 3, p. 318.

12. Sigmund Freud, *Totem and Taboo* (New York: W. W. Norton, 1952), p. 56, and see pp. 81, 112.

13. Max Reisel, *The Mysterious Name of Y.H.W.H.: The Tetragrammaton in Connection with the Names of Ehyeh-Huha-and Sem Hammephoras* (Assen, Netherlands: Van Gorcum, 1957), p. 1.

14. Frazer, *Golden Bough*, vol. 3, pp. 321–22.

This alleged rule of whispering, of pronouncing the name in an indistinguishable way, closely resembles the prohibition of pronouncing the Name. The Hellenistic writer Artapan relates a midrash according to which

Moses released by supernatural power from prison went to the royal palace, found the gates open, the guards fast asleep, awoke the king, who was at first terrified at the sight of Moses, then told him mockingly to *name the God who sent him*. Moses *whispered* the name in the king's ear, whereupon the king dropped down; *caught* by Moses he revived. Later on Moses wrote the Name on a tablet and sealed it. A priest who blasphemed the writing died in great agony.[15]

Moses, we are told, did not pronounce, only whispered, the Name; even in this form of reduced sonority the Name was allegedly strong enough to do its work.

According to scholarly sources, "since the death of the High Priest Simon the Just, the other priests no longer considered themselves worthy to pronounce the Tetragrammaton distinctly and completely in the daily priestly blessing."[16] There is even an allegedly reliable eyewitness, "R. Tarphon, who was of priestly descent and himself a priest who testifies to the effect that '[o]nce I followed my uncle to say the priestly blessing, and I inclined my ear near the High Priest, and I have heard that he mixed the Name with the tune of his brethren, the priests.'"[17]

One can see, as Reisel admits, that "the Old Testament though certainly not 'primitive,' sometimes attributes a great significance to names and thus also to the giving of names. . . . This 'taboo' applies of course in

15. Quoted in A. Marmorstein, *The Old Rabbinic Doctrine of God: I. The Names and Attributes of God*, Jewish College Publications, no. 10 (London: Oxford University Press, 1927), p. 30; emphasis in original.

16. Reisel, *Mysterious Name*, p. 64. In Reisel's view this offers the *terminus ad quem* for the blessing in which the tetragrammaton occupied a central place. Now in this case the question remains: When exactly did Simon the Just live? According to learned sources, a date around 198 BCE would be a defensible date for his death. See S. Dubnow, *Weltgeschichte des Judischen Volkes* (Berlin: Judischer Verlag, 1937), p. 102. Although it is unrelated to our topic, perhaps 70 CE, the date of the destruction of the second Temple, offers an alternative terminus ad quem, when the High Priest started to refrain from pronouncing the tetragrammaton. See J. Neubauer, *Bibelwissenschaftliche Irrungen* (Berlin: L. Lamm, 1917), p. 23. Reisel quotes Neubauer, thus contradicting himself; see Reisel, *Mysterious Name*, pp. 65–66, and p. 116, n. 352.

17. See Marmorstein, *Old Rabbinic Doctrine*, pp. 21 and 25–26. "We must assume that after Simon the Just the name of God was not pronounced. Later on, when the opposition to the rule of the priests grew stronger, a compromise was effected; the name of God should be

particular to the name of God."[18] It seems that we are dealing with a more general problem than Frazer's text and Kádár's struggle with words might otherwise suggest.

As to the origin of this taboo, some scholars have emphasized the "motives of reverence and the desire to avoid profanation. Philo, and later Maimonides, saw clearly that to attach a name at all to God is to delimit him and to set boundaries, for God is more than his attributes."[19] A. Marmorstein is inclined to give a historical answer. "Hellenistic opposition to the religion of the Jews, the apostasy of the priests and nobles, introduced and established the rule not to pronounce the Tetragrammaton in the Sanctuary."[20] Reisel's reasoning is somewhat different; the slight change in emphasis, however, leads to a different conclusion:

In my view the most decisive reason [for the prohibition] was the growing expansion of Hellenism (inter alia in Alexandria) and the ensuing gradual contact of the Jews with Egyptian circles exercising magical practices by means of divine names. This contact, and the fact that what had so far been considered a sacred possession of the Jewish people now left the confines of Judaism, called for precautionary measures. . . . The attempt to avoid the Tetragrammaton and to reserve its normal use for the distant future has here been explained as the result of a reaction to Hellenism and to magical practices: This, in my view, is the explanation of this remarkable interruption of a tradition which had been followed for centuries, rather than referring to a number of passages in the Pentateuch which were apparently used retrospectively in support of the restriction of the pronunciation of the Tetragrammaton.[21]

---

pronounced in the priestly blessing but . . . not distinctly" (pp. 21–22). "It has often been pointed out, and found very strange that the author of the Scroll of Esther never mentions the Name of God. Yet the matter seems so simple. The author lived in an age and in a country where and when the pronunciation of the Name was strictly forbidden. It is exactly the time after the death of Simon the Just. . . . We assume that at some later period the innovation of the priests became antiquated and was removed by a reform, which made it a duty to pronounce the name in greetings" (pp. 30–31). See also Samuel S. Cohon, "The Name of God: A Study in Rabbinic Theology," *Hebrew Union College Annual* 23 (1951): 591–92.

18. Reisel, *Mysterious Name*, pp. 2–3.

19. In G. H. Parke-Taylor, Yahweh: *The Divine Name in the Bible* (Waterloo, Ont.: Wilfrid Laurier University Press, 1975), p. 95.

20. Marmorstein, *Old Rabbinic Doctrine*, p. 35.

21. Reisel, *Mysterious Name*, pp. 66–68. See, for example, the prohibitions of the Decalogue: "You shall not take the name of [YHWH] your god in vain" (Exod. 20:7).

Michel de Certeau has also dealt with the enigma of the tetragrammaton: "The tetragrammaton YHWH, 'Yahweh,' inscribes what is *being* withdrawn. It is not the sacrament of a being who is there, nor does it signify something else which might be hidden behind it,

"Undoubtedly, one of the factors operative in forbidding the use of the divine name was the avoidance of magical practices," concurs G. H. Parke-Taylor.[22] This conclusion would be familiar and acceptable even to Frazer, who, on the basis of his long list of examples, thinks that the taboo on proper names serves primarily to prevent the infliction of harm on a person with the help of the knowledge of his or her real name. ("The native thinks that a stranger knowing his secret name would have a special power to work him ill by means of magic.")[23]

Frazer's subchapter on the names of the dead starts with Strabo's *Geographica*, with the custom of abstaining from all mention of the names of the dead in antiquity by the Albanians of the Caucasus. The reason for "drawing the veil of oblivion [this is not John Rawls's 'veil of ignorance'] over the names of the dead" is foremost a reluctance "based on a fear of the ghosts, whose attention might be attracted by the mention of their names."[24] "Although the natural unwillingness to revive past sorrows undoubtedly also plays a role," the most important root of the taboo, as Frazer interprets it, is the belief that "to call a dead man by his name is deemed most unlucky, and is never done except with the intention of doing harm to his surviving family, who make great lamentations on such occasions."[25] Freud states that all such obsessive acts are connected to the complex notion of the "demonic"; to the dread of contact with what is either/or, or both unclean and sacred; to charms or countercharms "designed to ward off the expectations of disaster . . . whenever I have succeeded in penetrating the mystery, I have found that the expected disaster was death."[26]

Relying on the insights of Frazer, Freud, and Wilhelm Wundt, whom Freud uses extensively, that taboos "have their origin in the source of the

---

but it is a trace of evanescence. It is *not pronounced*. It is the *written figure* of a loss, the very operation of being erased" (*The Writing of History*, trans. Tom Conley [New York: Columbia University Press, 1988], p. 341; emphases in original). This is what Jan Assmann identifies as "the *revalation of anonymity*" (cf. Assmann, *Moses the Egyptian* [Cambridge, MA: Harvard University Press, 1997], p. 120). Assmann devotes a short part of his book to the problem of the tetragrammaton on pp. 118–21, but his beautiful and learned analysis leads to direction beyond my actual concern at this point.

22. Parke-Taylor, Yahweh: *The Divine Name in the Bible*, p. 87.

23. Frazer, *Golden Bough*, vol. 3, p. 322; see esp. chap. 6, sec. I, "Personal Names Tabooed," pp. 318–34, and sec. 3, "Names of the Dead Tabooed," pp. 349–74.

24. Frazer, *Golden Bough*, vol. 3, pp. 350 and 353, respectively.

25. Ibid., pp. 350, 355.

26. Freud, *Totem and Taboo*, p. 87.

most primitive and at the same time most lasting of human instincts—in fear of 'demonic' powers," would not help me reach a tangible, satisfactory answer to my original problem.[27] The path that leads from the tetragrammaton via Frazer and Freud to the fear of death is a dead-end street for me. According to Wundt, "The distinction between 'sacred' and 'unclean' did not exist in the primitive beginnings of taboo. . . . It is precisely this neutral and intermediate meaning—'demonic' or 'what may not be touched'—that is appropriately expressed by the word 'taboo,' since it stresses a characteristic which remains common for all time both to what is sacred and to what is unclean: the dread of contact with it."[28]

Freud, as one might expect, did not stop at this point. He went further, into the unconscious ambivalence of the living, the killing of the father, and even much further than that, where I do not want to follow him.[29] Instead, I would like to call attention to a reference in the chapter on "The Taboo upon the Dead," in which Freud makes use of a volume by Rudolf Kleinpaul, who

reaches the final conclusion that the dead, filled with a lust for murder, sought to drag the living in their train. The dead slew; and the skeleton which we use today to picture the dead stands for the fact that they themselves were slayers. The living did not feel safe from the attacks of the dead till there was a sheet of water between them. That is why the men liked to bury the dead on islands or on the farther side of rivers; and that, in turn, is the origin of such phrases as "Here and in the Beyond." Later the malignity of the dead diminished and was restricted to special categories which had a particular right to feel resentment—such as murdered men, for instances, who in the form of evil spirits went in pursuit of their murderers.[30]

It might seem that Kleinpaul's use of the remnants found "among civilized races of the ancient belief in spirits, to throw light on the relation between the living and the dead," could be relevant to my story and could provide a sort of answer to my initial problem of the taboo on certain

27. Wilhelm Wundt, *Mythus und Religion* (Leipzig: Engelmann, 1905–06), vol. 2, p. 307.

28. Wundt quoted by Freud, *Totem and Taboo*, p. 25.

29. For a critical, though sympathetic, reading of *Totem and Taboo* that is willing to follow closely the path Freud proposed, see René Girard, *Violence and the Sacred*, especially the chapter "*Totem and Taboo* and the Incest Prohibition" (Baltimore, MD: Johns Hopkins University Press, 1977), pp. 193–222.

30. Freud, *Totem and Taboo*, pp. 58–59. The work to which Freud refers is Rudolf Kleinpaul, *Die Lebendingen und die Toten in Volksglauben* (Leipzig: G. J. Göschen, 1898).

names, especially on the names of those whom one should dread with good reason.[31] This is definitely not what I am after; I am not interested in the revenge of the dead.

I have a friend, László Rajk, whose father, László Rajk senior, then minister of foreign affairs, previously minister of the interior, was hanged as a victim of the Stalinist show trials in 1949. At the time of the execution of his father, the younger Rajk was six months old. János Kádár, who was the minister of the interior when Rajk was executed, was the godfather of the son. (See Figure 2.2.) (Kádár admits, as we know from a handwritten document composed one or two days before he was to be released from prison on July 20, 1954, that as interior minister, "I was present at the execution of Rajk."[32] A few days later, perhaps because the experience shocked him so much, he asked for permission to resign from that post and transfer to another high-ranking position in the top leadership of the party that he held until his imprisonment in 1951.) The mother was sent to prison, and the six-month-old infant was taken to an orphanage, where his name was changed to István Kovács. (Kovács is a very common name in Hungary, something like Smith in the United States; there are thousands of

---

31. Freud, *Totem and Taboo*, pp. 58–59. Frazer writes:

Rules of the same sort are often imposed even more stringently on warriors after the victory has been won and when all fear of the living corporeal foe is at an end. In such cases one motive for the inconvenient restrictions laid on the victors in their hour of triumph is probably a dread of the angry ghosts of the slain; and that the fear of the vengeful ghosts does influence the behaviour of the slayers is often expressly affirmed. . . . The Apaches, the enemies of the Pimas, purify themselves for the slaughter of their foes. . . . These ceremonies they perform for all the dead simultaneously after their return home; but the Pimas, more punctilious on this point resort to their elaborate ceremonies of purification the moment a single one of their own band or of the enemy has been laid low. . . . "This long period of retirement immediately after a battle," says an American writer, "greatly diminished the value of the Pimas as scouts and allies for the United States troops operating against the Apaches. The bravery of the Pimas was praised by all army officers having any experience with them, but Captain Bourke and others have complained of their unreliability due solely to their rigid observance of this religious law."

The source of Frazer's quote is F. Russel, The Pima Indians: Twenty-Sixth Annual Report of the Bureau of American Ethnology (Washington DC: Smithsonian Institution Bureau of American Ethnology, 1908), p. 204. Frazer devotes a whole subchapter to the rites performed on manslayers: "Manslayers Tabooed," in *Golden Bough*, vol. 3, pp. 165–90.

32. Kádár quoted by Tibor Hajdú, "Kádár és Farkas Rajknál" [Kádár and Farkas Visiting Rajk], *Társadalmi Szemle* 10 (1992): 73.

FIGURE 2.2. László Rajk (left) gives over his office as minister of the interior to János Kádár. Photo Archives of the Hungarian News Agency (MTI).

Kovács in the Budapest telephone directory, dozens of them in the telephone directories of every major American city.)[33]

After Stalin's death, when the younger Rajk was five years old, his grandparents received an anonymous phone call—after years of unsuccessful attempts to recover the boy. They were told they could get their grandson at the corner of Pannonia and Katona József streets, where they lived. (In 1969, Pannonia Street was named after László Rajk; in 1990, after the Fall of Communism, the street was once more renamed and returned to its previous name: Pannonia.) When the grandparents arrived at the corner, a car stopped, a boy was discharged, and the car drove off in a hurry. Although the grandparents immediately recognized him, as he resembled and even today resembles his father so much, the small boy did not respond to

33. "There are some impressive similarities in naming practices across different languages, such as the use of names based on professions. Smith, and its foreign-language equivalents, is the best-known case, being the most common surname in many parts of Europe: Arabic Haddad, Hungarian Kovács, Russian Kuznetsov, Portuguese Ferreiro, German Schmidt, Spanish Hernandez/Fernandez, French Le Fevre/La Forge, and so on" (*The Cambridge Encyclopedia of Language*, vol. 112 [Cambridge and New York: Cambridge University Press, 1997], pp. 1–12).

his name. A few hours later at home, when playing with a teddy bear, the boy—according to the recollection of the grandparents—said to himself, "Pisti has a bear." (Pisti is one of the nicknames for István.) In the 1970s the same László Rajk, then an architecture student, founded an experimental theater workshop and named it the "István Kovács Studio."

What I want to understand is not the working of the psyche of the executioner, the mechanism of remorse, or the repression of the feeling of guilt (we know that the executioners in 1949 did not feel guilty; they knew very well that the interests of the party had priority over personal fate). My question is, rather, why is it not enough to execute; why must the name be extinguished as well? Or as Tatyana Tolstaya has phrased it, "Why pretend that those destroyed never existed if everyone remembers that they did? Why instead of simply settling accounts with vanquished enemies and collecting their skulls, was it necessary to make believe that the enemies had never really existed?" Although I agree with this line of questioning, I cannot, I do not agree with Tolstaya's solution; I would like to find an answer that could make sense to a historian.[34] And despite my hesitation and aversion, I have to go back to Freud to find the clue I am looking for.

34. Tatyana Tolstaya, "'Missing Persons': Review of David King's *The Commissar Vanishes: The Falsification of Photographs and Art in Stalin's Russia*," *New York Review of Books* 45, (January 15, 1998): 12. Tolstaya gives the following answer:

> It seems to me that besides the obvious reason (the desire to attribute all good to oneself, elevate oneself to the status of God, and so on), the tyrant's dark soul was troubled by mystical irrational notions as well. There is an old rule of magic: evocation calls forth epiphanies, that is, speaking a name brings forth the spirit, the demon, the divinity; thus, God's name must not be spoken in vain; thus, religious people speak of the devil indirectly, using nicknames; thus, in many languages the names of frightening creatures (bears, wolves, snakes) are constantly replaced with euphemisms, and they in turn, with new euphemisms. This is the source of the ban on depicting God, and the source of blasphemy when God's image is destroyed or distorted; this explains the jealous destruction of icons after the 1917 revolution, and their equally jealous conservation. Hence the hatred with which early Christians hammered away at the marble faces of pagan sculptures. The motivation here is not that "this never was," but that "this will never again be," a purge not so much of the past as of the future. Which makes it even more frightening. (p. 12)

King's book *The Commissar Vanishes* is a portrait gallery of disappeared and nameless Communist functionaries, of high-ranking—mostly Soviet—officials and officers whose pictures and names were erased. Almost without exception, all the faceless and nameless shadows in *The Commissar Vanishes* were comrades in arms at the founding of the Bolshevik state. All Communist victims of the Stalinist show trials in the other Socialist countries,

In *Totem and Taboo* Freud tells a story: "The dread of uttering a dead person's name extends, indeed, to an avoidance of the mention of anything in which the dead man played a part; and an important consequence of this process of suppression is that these peoples possess no tradition and no historical memory, so that any research into their early history is faced by the greatest difficulties."[35] Freud refers here to a certain page in the *Golden Bough*. I happened to consult the same edition of Frazer's work that Freud used to work from, and on the page referred to (362) I read the following: "[Among the natives of the Nicobar Islands] a most singular custom"— says Mr. De Roepstorff—"prevails . . . which one would suppose must most effectually hinder the 'making of history,' or, at any rate, the transmission of historical narrative. By a strict rule, which has all the sanction of Nicobar superstition, no man's name may be mentioned after his death! . . . This extraordinary custom not only adds an element of instability to the language, but destroys the continuity of political life, and renders the record of past events precarious and vague, if not impossible."[36] This is already closer to what an historian might hope for, but we still have, not an explanation, but the historical consequence of a strange prohibition.

I remembered, however, that I had come across yet another version of the same story, this time without references to Roepstorff, Frazer, or Freud:

Imagine a primitive hunter-gatherer community with a language containing proper names. (And it is not at all implausible to imagine a language used by a primitive community, as far as we know it was in such communities that human languages evolved in the first place.) Imagine that everybody in the tribe knows everybody else and that newborn members of the tribe are baptized at ceremonies attended by the entire tribe. Imagine, furthermore, that as the children grow up they learn the names of people . . . by ostension. Suppose also that there is a strict taboo in this tribe against speaking of the dead, so that no one's name is ever mentioned after his death.

---

together with their would-be executioners, played an important role in the foundation of the Socialist state. Without obliterating the names of these victims, who were accused of treason, sabotage, terror, and so on, it would have been difficult to explain the historical inevitability of the victory of Communism and the superiority of the regime over any previous and contemporary system.

35. Freud, *Totem and Taboo*, pp. 55–56.

36. Frazer, *Golden Bough*, vol. 3, pp. 362–63. Frazer here quotes F. A. de Roepstorff's "Tiomberombi: A Nicobar Tale," *Journal of the Asiatic Society of Bengal* 53 (1884).

The example comes from *Intentionality: An Essay in the Philosophy of Mind* by John R. Searle.[37] The anonymous story is used here in the service of a broader attempt to refute a rival theory of proper names that is usually referred to as the "causal" theory or the "external causal chain of communication" theory, most prominently connected to Saul Kripke's work *Naming and Necessity*.[38]

In Kripke's own words

a rough statement of [the causal-chain] theory might be the following: An initial "baptism" takes place. Here the object may be named by ostension, or the reference of the name may be fixed by a description. When the name is "passed from link to link," the receiver of the name must, I think, intend when he learns it to use it with the same reference as the man from whom he heard it. If I hear the name "Napoleon" and decide it would be a nice name for my pet aardvark, I do not satisfy this condition.[39]

Searle's retelling (a version) of the story about the tribe without history was meant to challenge Kripke's picture of the "causal-chain" approach to proper names.

What is the nature of the problem with proper names? What is the object of disagreement in the debate? "The problem of proper names ought to be easy," says Searle:

We need to make repeated references to the same object, even when the object is not present, and so we give the object a name. Henceforward this name is used to refer to that object. However, . . . objects are not given to us prior to our system of representation; what counts as one object or the same object is a function of how we divide up the world. . . . And how we divide it is up to our system of representation, and in that sense that is up to us, even though the system is biologically, culturally, and linguistically shaped. . . . The problem of proper names used to be put in the form, "Do proper names have a sense?" and in contemporary philosophy there are supposed to be two competing answers to that question: an affirmative

---

37. John R. Searle, *Intentionality: An Essay in the Philosophy of Mind* (Cambridge and New York: Cambridge University Press, 1983), p. 240.

38. In connection with the "causal chain theory," besides Saul Kripke, see Keith Donellan, "Speaking of Nothing," *Philosophical Review* 83 (January 1974): 3–32; Gareth Evans, "The Causal Theory of Names," in *Readings in the Philosophy of Language*, ed. Peter Ludlow (Cambridge, MA: Harvard University Press, 1997), pp. 635–55.

39. Saul A. Kripke, *Naming and Necessity* (Cambridge, MA: Harvard University Press, 1980), p. 96. The title of the book is a direct reference to Rudolph Carnap's *Meaning and Necessity*.

answer, given by the "descriptivist" theory, according to which a name refers by being associated with a description or perhaps a cluster of descriptions, and a negative answer given by the "causal" theory according to which a name refers because of a "causal chain" connecting the utterance of the name to the bearer of the name or at least to the naming ceremony in which the bearer of the name got the name.[40]

To put it bluntly, with the help of one of Kripke's own examples, "Although someone other than the U.S. President in 1970 might have been the U.S. President in 1970 (e.g., Humphrey might have), no one other than Nixon might have been Nixon. . . . Proper names are rigid designators [that is, in every possible world they designate the same object], for although the man (Nixon) might not have been the President, it is not the case that he might not have been Nixon (though he might not have been *called* 'Nixon')."[41]

What makes the causal theory attractive is its counterintuitive nature: it does not take the consequences of associative learning into consideration; it claims that the speaker, even if he or she has no individuating information—or does not associate any individuating characteristics to the name—will be able to denote a concrete individual.[42] It is simply enough to introduce the name; this is what Kripke calls "baptism"—and that is not intended to be taken literally—and with the help of the historical chain, the denotation will be unambiguously tied to the object it denotes. Misreading, misunderstanding, is ruled out.

40. Searle, *Intentionality*, pp. 231–32.

41. Kripke, *Naming and Necessity*, pp. 48–49. Kripke is very straightforward on this point:

> It . . . is not, in any intuitive sense a necessity, a necessary truth that Aristotle had the properties commonly attributed to him. There is a certain theory perhaps popular in some views of the philosophy of history, which might both be deterministic and yet at the same time assign a great role to the individual in history. Perhaps Carlyle would associate with the meaning of the name of a great man his achievements. According to such a view it will be necessary, once a certain individual is born, that he is destined to perform various great tasks and so it will be part of the very nature of Aristotle that he should have produced ideas, which had a great influence on the western world. Whatever the merits of such a view may be as view of history or the nature of great men, it does not seem that it should be trivially true on the basis of a theory of proper names. It would seem that it's a contingent fact that Aristotle did *any* of the things commonly attributed to him today, any of these great achievements that we so much admire. (pp. 74–75)

42. On this point, see Evans, "Causal Theory of Names," pp. 635–55.

According to another example provided by Kripke, it is a contingent fact that Hitler committed all the horrors that he is held responsible for, that are attributed to him.

Hitler might have spent all his days in quiet in Linz. In that case we would not say that then this man would not have been Hitler, for we use the name "Hitler" just as the name of that man, even in describing other possible worlds. . . . Suppose we do decide to pick out the reference of "Hitler," as the man who succeeded in having more Jews killed than anyone else managed to do in history. That is the way we pick out the reference of the name; but in another counterfactual situation where some one else would have gained this discredit, we wouldn't say that in that case that other man would have been Hitler.[43]

There is no question that Kripke is undoubtedly sympathetic with Bishop Butler's maxim that "everything is what it is and not another thing."

According to Frege's original reasoning, "It is plausible to connect with a sign . . . not only the designated object, which may be called the nominatum of the sign, but also the sense (connotation, meaning) of the sign. . . . A proper name . . . expresses its sense, and designates or signifies its nominatum. We let a sign *express* its sense and *designate* its nominatum."[44] Frege's text is not absolutely clear on whether what is meant here is

43. Kripke, *Naming and Necessity*, p. 75. I think this is a rather unfortunate example, one that I will not have great difficulty challenging (especially if I take Kripke's *baptism* in a strict literal sense). Hitler wouldn't be Hitler in that case, not least because Hitler was not Hitler originally; this is not how he was "baptized" in the first place. According to my great-aunt Mimi, her brother, Marcel Breuer, who happened to be my great-uncle, shared an apartment with a certain Adolf Schickengruber in Vienna. When Breuer tired of the academicism of the Vienna Academy and decided to move to Berlin before joining the Bauhaus, he found another student from the academy, a Jewish student of painting, to share the apartment with Schickengruber who was not able to pay the rent on his own. This student later dropped out of the academy and supported himself by selling the painting he had stolen from his roommate. When Schickengruber found out, he turned anti-Semite, and later on, when he was already called Hitler, he decided to pay the Jewish student back for the humiliation. "This is the true story of the Holocaust," according to Aunt Mimi, who felt it her duty to remind the family of its role in the tragedy of the Jews. (Despite the excellence of her story, her memories played a trick with Aunt Mimi. Breuer attended the Vienna Academy much later, so he could not share his apartment with Schickengruber.)

44. Gottlob Frege, "Über Sinn und Bedeutung," *Zeitschrift für Philosophie und Philos. Kritik* 100 (1892). Originally published in English as "On Sense and Nominatum," in *Readings in Philosophical Analysis*, ed. H. Feigl and W. Sellars (New York: Appleton-Century-Crofts, 1949), pp. 85–102. Reprinted in A. P. Martinich, ed., *The Philosophy of Language* (New York: Oxford University Press, 1996), pp. 186–98, quotes from pp. 187 and 189, respectively.

one and only one definite meaning, sense, connotation, or description connected to the object. He says, for example, that "the regular connection between a sign, its sense, and its nominatum is such that there corresponds a definite sense to the sign and to this sense there corresponds again a definite nominatum; whereas not one sign only belongs to one nominatum (object). In different languages, and even in one language, the same sense is represented by different expressions."[45]

In a note attached to the main text Frege plays with an example that will have a long career: in the case of genuinely proper names like "Aristotle" opinions as regards their sense may diverge. As such may, for example, be suggested: Plato's disciple and the teacher of Alexander the Great. Whoever accepts this sense will interpret the meaning of the statement "Aristotle was born in Stagira" differently from the one who interpreted the sense of "Aristotle" as the Stagirite teacher of Alexander the Great. So long as the nominatum remains the same, these fluctuations in sense are tolerable. But they should be avoided in the system of a demonstrative science and should not appear in a perfect language.[46]

Kripke refers to this particular example, concluding that, "according to Frege, there is some sort of looseness or weakness in our language. Some people may give one sense to the name 'Aristotle,' others may give another."[47] Wittgenstein, in his *Philosophical Investigations*, was struggling with the same problem when he analyzed the possible meanings of the name "Moses." What Wittgenstein intended to demonstrate with the example of Moses was that we associate a name with a family of descriptions or, as Searle would put it, a cluster of properties, rather than with a particular description. And at this point we are almost back to Searle, and with him to the hunter-gatherers, the tribe without history, the people who do not speak the name of the dead. In his original essay on proper names, published in 1958, Searle makes extensive use of the "Aristotle" example:

Suppose, for example, that we teach the name "Aristotle" by explaining that it refers to a Greek philosopher born in Stagira. . . . Let us suppose it is discovered later on that Aristotle was not born in Stagira at all, but in Thebes. We will not now say that the meaning of the name has changed, or that Aristotle did not really exist at all. . . . Though proper names do not normally assert or specify any

45. Frege, in Martinich, *Philosophy of Language*, p. 187.
46. Ibid., pp. 197–98.
47. Kripke, *Naming and Necessity*, p. 30.

characteristics, their referring uses nonetheless presuppose that the object to which they purport to refer has certain characteristics. . . . Referring uses of "Aristotle" presuppose the existence of an object of whom a sufficient but so far unspecified number of . . . statements are true. To use a proper name referringly is to presuppose the truth of certain uniquely referring descriptive statements, but it is not ordinarily to assert these statements or even to indicate which exactly are presupposed. Unlike definite descriptions, [proper names] do not in general *specify* any characteristics at all of the objects to which they refer.[48]

If there were general agreement in advance on the precise characteristics that constitute Aristotle's identity, then it would be possible to use his name to refer to him in a precise way. There would be no disagreement or misunderstanding, or certainly less. "But this precision would be achieved only at the cost of entailing some specific predicates by any referring use of the name. Indeed, the name itself would become superfluous for it would become logically equivalent to this set of descriptions. . . . If the criteria for proper names were in all cases quite rigid and specific then a proper name . . . would function exactly like an elaborate definite description."[49]

In his *Speech Acts: An Essay in the Philosophy of Language*, Searle refines his original stand on proper names.[50] Here Searle concurs with Frege to the extent that there is a sort of looseness in our use of language: indeed, "Proper names are logically connected with characteristics of the object to which they refer . . . in a loose sort of way."[51] (This is an answer to Wittgenstein's original question: "What does logical identity of sign and thing signified really consist in?") And here Searle's answer diverges from the early Wittgenstein's: "The logical identity between sign and thing signified consists in its not being permissible to recognize *more or less* in the sign than what it signifies" [emphasis added]. But Searle argues in a commonsensical way that "if both the speaker and the hearer associate some identifying description with the name, then the utterance of the name is sufficient to satisfy the principle of identification, for both the speaker and

---

48. John R. Searle, "Proper Names," *Mind* 67 (1958): 166–73. Reprinted in Ludlow, *Readings in the Philosophy of Language*, pp. 585–92, esp. pp. 587, 590, 589.

49. Ludlow, *Readings in the Philosophy of Language*, pp. 590–91.

50. John R. Searle, *Speech Acts: An Essay in the Philosophy of Language* (London: Cambridge University Press, 1969), chap. 7, "On Proper Names," pp. 162–74.

51. Ibid., p. 170.

the hearer are able to substitute an identifying description. The utterance of the name communicates a proposition to the hearer."[52]

If we associate "some identifying description with the name," if names were not, are not, used just as "rigid denominators," referring directly, without any associated characteristics to the object, then we cannot deny the (somewhat) vague and ambiguous nature of names. Vagueness and ambiguity in turn make communication riskier and misunderstanding more likely. Despite vagueness and ambiguity, however (as we all experience every day when referring to persons), communication takes place with the help of the self-disambiguating mechanisms of the use of language and partly as a consequence of our conscious efforts to make sense of a reference.[53]

Despite the risk involved, there is no need to give detailed instructions for every name, to employ a traffic officer for each utterance of a name. Despite the possibility of misunderstanding, which could be corrected, real and meaningful communication takes place without using the name as a "rigid denominator" in Kripke's sense, especially if the speaker and hearer have similar background information; they know that a connection between the name and the object has already been established, and they do not intend to use the name in a way that is "wildly inconsistent with the [vaguely established] fact about the object."[54] They use the same language (in a loose sort of way); they come from the same world (whatever that might mean, in a broad sense), and so on.

Even if, as Kripke thinks, the primary function of the proper name is just to denote an object (and, contrary to Searle's conviction, we have some reason to believe this to be the case), still in everyday *use* we usually aim at something besides simply referring to a person when uttering a name.[55] As Gareth Evans remarked in a somewhat different context, "With

52. Ibid., p. 171.
53. We try to minimize the attribution of inexplicable. This might be a very weak variant of the principle of charity. See Evans, "Causal Theory of Names," p. 638. On the principle of charity, see Donald Davidson, "Truth and Meaning" *Synthese* 17 (1967): 304–23.
54. Searle, *Intentionality*, p. 259.
55. It is a well-observed fact that elderly people who develop problems with memory start to have difficulty remembering proper names first. They are able to recall important characteristics of the person in question, they are able to give vivid and identifiable descriptions, and still they are not able to recall the name. One possible explanation is that while individual characteristics could be described in alternative ways (a geneticist could be

names as with other expressions in the language, what they signify depends upon what we *use* them to signify."[56]

This evidence suggests that one uses proper names not only to refer but also to make (in fact we do make) "factually informative *identity* statements using proper names."[57]

"Proper names are not connotative," argued John Stuart Mill, however, countering, in his *System of Logic*, the views of the descriptivists; proper names "denote the individuals who are called by them; but they do not indicate or imply any attributes as belonging to those individuals. When we name a child by the name of Paul, or a dog by the name Caesar, these names are simply marks used to enable those individuals to be made subjects of discourse."[58] But we have at hand, a real-life example, Saul Friedländer's experience with the very same name:

"Paul-Henri." I couldn't get used to my new name. At home I had been called Pavel, or rather Pavlíček, the usual Czech diminutive. . . . Then from Paris to Néris I had become Paul, which for a child was something quite different. As Paul I didn't feel like Pavlíček anymore, but Paul-Henri was worse still: I had crossed a line and was now on the other side. Paul could have been Czech and Jewish; Paul-Henri could be nothing but French and resolutely Catholic, and I was not yet naturally so.[59]

---

referred to as a microbiologist or as a biologist, a natural scientist from this university or from the university in that city), an individual name cannot be referred to alternatively (one cannot say "Peter" instead of "Paul"; "Paul Berg" cannot be substituted for "Alban Berg." But anybody who has read Frazer knows that in certain parts of the world people have not one but two or more names. This certainly complicates the case, especially the case of the "chain theorists"; however, the problem seems to be solvable, even inside the framework of the "causal chain theory."

See the distinction between "what the speaker denotes" and "what the name denotes," in Evans, "Causal Theory of Names," p. 635; emphasis in original.

56. Ibid., p. 644; emphasis added.

57. Searle, *Intentionality*, p. 171; emphasis added.

58. John Stuart Mill, *A System of Logic* (New York and London: Longmans, 1965), book 1, chap. 2, sec. 5.

59. Saul Friedländer, *When Memory Comes* (New York: Farrar, Straus, Giroux, 1991), p. 94. Friedländer, one of the most renowned scholars of the Holocaust, fled from the Nazis as a small child during World War II and found shelter in a French Catholic boarding school, while his parents were deported to a concentration camp where they perished. The continuation of the passage quoted goes like this: "What was more, that was not the last of the name changes: I subsequently became Shaul on disembarking in Israel, and then Saul, a compromise between the Saül that French requires and the Paul that I had been. In short,

Contrary to Mill, Searle thinks that Frege's original instinct was sound (and this is what Friedländer's experience points at): "Sentences containing proper names can be used to make identity statements which convey *factual* and not merely linguistic information."[60]

What was a weakness for Frege, what "should be avoided in the system of a demonstrative science and should not appear in a perfect language," becomes a natural property of the institution of proper names for Searle, even a virtue of language. In his original paper, Searle draws out the significance of this imperfection: "But the uniqueness and immense pragmatic convenience of proper names in our language lie precisely in the fact that they enable us to refer publicly to objects without being forced to raise issues and come to an agreement on what descriptive characteristics exactly constitute the identity of the object."[61] (With this statement in mind, we are in fact back at the "paronomastic" aspect of the Name—at the formula: "I am who I am"—"a stylistic method of expressing either something undetermined, *idem per idem*, i.e., that which cannot be fully defined, or the idea of totality or intensity.")[62]

But something else still follows from this insight that could be directly relevant to my original problem: "The question of what constitutes the criteria for 'Aristotle' is generally left open, indeed it seldom in fact arises, and when it does arise *it is we, the users of the name, who decide more or less arbitrarily what these criteria shall be.*"[63]

If we are able to make factually informative identity statements with the help of proper names, without the need to offer detailed, exhaustive descriptions, then the institution of proper names is inherently unstable. Then the proper name is by definition un(der)determined; no fixed cluster of description could be secured to it once and for all. Then it is we who, when using the name, (re)define the actual (loose) "sense" of the name in a more or less arbitrary way. Nobody can guarantee *in advance* the precise

---

it is impossible to know which name I am, and that in the final analysis seems to me sufficient expression of a real and profound confusion" (p. 94).

60. Searle, *Speech Acts*, p. 165; emphasis added.

61. Searle, "Proper Names," p. 591. (Searle repeats almost the same statement in *Speech Acts*, p. 172.)

62. Theodorus Christian Vriezen, Ehje *aser ehje*, in *Festschrift Alfred Bertholet zum 80*, ed. W. Baumgartner, O. Eissfeldt, K. Ellinger, et al. (Tübingen: Mohr, 1950), pp. 498–512. Quoted by G. H. Parke-Taylor, Yahweh: *The Divine Name in the Bible*, p. 52.

63. Searle, "Proper Names," p. 590; emphasis added.

meaning and scope attached to the name of an individual in public. Nobody is able to rule out the possibility of redefining a name by establishing or remembering a relation between names.

This is at once both frightening and liberating. The indeterminacy and polysemic nature of proper names are fundamentally unsettling. We know how folk etymology tries to dig up and grasp the supposedly original and singular true meaning of proper names. We have ample documentation of the paranoia of Soviet censorship from the 1930s testifying to the drive toward *odnoznachnost*, "onemeaningness," whereby the censors tried to reduce possible multiple meanings, the association of names with unwanted predicates or adjectives. And we know from none other than Roman Jakobson that "the refusal to utter one's own name may become a social custom." He refers to Guy de Maupassant, who "confessed that his name sounded quite strange to him when pronounced by himself." In fact, Jakobson theorizes, "*I* is so rigorously substituted by the child for his proper name that he readily names any person of his surroundings but stubbornly refuses to utter his own name. . . . This attitude may persevere as an infantile survival."[64]

It is not only the name that is unstable (the instability of a name in itself does not mean anything), and it is not just the relation between the name and the object it refers to that is ambiguous, but if we are able to express identity statements with the help of proper names, then it is identity that is affected by the lack of a precise (implicitly), attached predicate agreed upon in advance of the name's utterance.[65]

There are all sorts of techniques used to overcome this (linguistically grounded or expressed) instability of identity: taboos, strict rules, and alleged prohibitions enumerated by Frazer describe some such practices.[66]

64. Roman Jakobson, "Shifters and Verbal Categories," in Roman Jakobson, *On Language*, ed. Linda R. Waugh and Monique Monville-Burston (Cambridge, MA: Harvard University Press, 1990), p. 389.

65. Naturally, the events of history are open to reinterpretation. But historical events are almost always intimately connected to certain proper names. Thus the linguistic instability of proper names has an impact on reinterpreting the events of history, and vice versa; when rewriting events of the past, the unstable identity connected to the ambiguity of the meaning of the name helps in finding the space necessary for reinterpretation.

66. Besides Frazer, there are several other known cases, reports, and descriptions of a direct relationship between name and identity.

> Yet even here names and identity are involved too, in the interaction of the living and the dead, for names are often more than *a* label *for* the person, they are rather part

The tradition of giving the name of a deceased father, grandfather, grandmother, or ancestor to a newborn child—or the opposite, the rule of not naming an infant after a certain relative—could point at other versions of the same impulse to overcome instability.[67] The change of name as a reflection of a changed situation might also be related to efforts toward securing unambiguous identity. "In a new situation, according to the Biblical account, new names are sometimes given which are meant to influence the future and the character of the bearer of the name. . . . Even a further step is taken: *the name given to a certain person may also influence others. . . .* Similar views are held in the Talmud: 'the giving of names cannot remain without effect.'"[68] (According to the Babylonian Talmud, "four matters annul the verdict pronounced by God against a person: charity; fervent prayer; *change of name*; change of conduct.")[69]

These naming strategies, in the end, may not be in vain for the individual or his or her close relatives. But the historian is in a different position. In a specific and limited sense, there is not much difference between the natural sciences and the historical profession: both require experiments

---

of it. The chief motive for headhunting among the Marind-Anim of New Guinea was the shortage of names. Each child should receive the name of a headhunter's victim. Should such a boy meet with relatives of the deceased, these would accept him as their kinsman's replacement so that instead of exacting vengeance they would dance and sing for him and even give him presents. (Nigel Barley, *Grave Matters* [New York: H. Holt, 1997], p. 96)

See also G. Zegwaard, "Head-Hunting Practices of the Asmat of Netherlands New Guinea," in *Peoples and Cultures of the Pacific*, ed. Andrew P. Vayda (Garden City, NY: Natural History Press, 1968).

67. "It was common practice [in 1640] to name a newborn child after a living older brother or sister on the assumption that only one of them would reach adulthood; as late as the mid-eighteenth century, the father of the historian Edward Gibbon was still naming his children in this way" (Clare Gittings, *Death, Burial, and the Individual in Early Modern England* [London: Routledge, 1988], pp. 7–8).

68. Cf. "nomen est omen"; see Reisel, *Mysterious Name*, p. 2; emphasis in original. The quoted text continues as follows: "Thus the parents of Noah hope that the choice of this name for their son may have a favourable effect on the achievements of the community in which he lives" (p. 2). See also "A change in name means a change of character: . . . In a narrative containing a number of aetiological elements, Jacob's name is changed to Israel (Gen. 32:28). . . . The meaning of the new name Israel, 'He who strives with God' or 'God strives,' represents a popular etymology. Nevertheless, there is a significant change in the character of the crafty Jacob from this time forward" (G. H. Parke-Taylor, Yahweh: *The Divine Name in the Bible*, p. 3).

69. Reisel, *Mysterious Name*, p. 89, n. 12; emphasis added.

that can be repeated and then checked, verified, confirmed, or falsified using the same data. For a historian, one of the most important sets of data is the set of names, names of individuals connected to certain events. Historians go back to the archives, sources, and documents to find, to check, the names in order to analyze them one more time in a new or different context. In consequence of the linguistically grounded instability of names, the repetition of these experiments understandably leads to slightly or grossly different results, to names under new descriptions. Depending—at least in part—on the surrounding context, the attributes attached to the names will differ from text to text, from one experiment to the next one. The inherent ambiguity that characterizes the use of names in itself could lead to historical revisionism; the instability of names invites revision, the inherent lack of precision—in use—is, in turn, one of the preconditions for historical revisionism.

If the criteria for what constitutes the named is generally left open, if one cannot secure in advance of public circulation the precise "meaning" of the name, then it is rational not to pronounce it, to remain silent about it, not to recall it (as each recall might lead to different connotations), to reach back to the practice of the hunter-gatherers from the Nicobar Islands. ("The name, is in the framework of the doctrinal logic of the Pentateuch, always *godesh* [q-d-sh, holy] because it establishes a relationship; *it has*, so we primitives think, *to be pronounced in order to exist*.")[70] If *one* cannot force a definite description on a name, as "it is *we*, the users of the name who decide" what the criteria shall be, then it is wiser to remain cautious with the use of a name. Then it is in the nature of proper names that one *cannot force* an agreement on the potential users as to what the generally agreed upon fixed criteria should be. There is simply no agreement; there could not be an agreement, as there is no need to come to an agreement when uttering a name. But in the absence of that agreement, the name can still refer.

"When the living Penan enters the system," writes Claude Lévi-Strauss, referring to a particular hunter-gatherer tribe, "he assumes a necronym, that is to say, he becomes one of the terms in a relationship, of which the

---

70. Franz Baermann Steiner, "Taboo," in *Franz Baermann Steiner: Taboo, Truth, and Religion*, vol. 1: *Selected Writings*, ed. J. Adler and R. Fardon (New York: Berghahn Books, 1999), p. 163; emphases added. Steiner originally presented "Taboo" in 1950–52, as a twelve-lecture series in Oxford. The lectures were first published as *Taboo*, with an introduction by E. E. Evans-Pritchard (London: Cohen and West, 1956).

other—since he is dead—no longer exists save in that relation which defines a living person with reference to him."[71] Had Imre Nagy, the executed prime minister, existed as a dead person, had he been referred to (by his proper name), a relation could have been created between him, the dead, and János Kádár, the one who was very much alive. Instead of having *a fixed* cluster of meanings attached to his name, instead of existing in a system of positions (instead of being the chairman of his party, instead of being "János Kádár, the chairman," or the "Old Man," as his closest aides affectionately used to refer to him), there would have been a chance for Kádár to be defined by or locked in a system of unwanted and dangerous relation. (As a consequence of the inherent instability of proper names and thus the uncertainty of identity, no authoritative word, voice, or deed of force could have come to the rescue.)[72] In consequence of the undeterminable nature of proper names in *use*, even the censors of the party would not have been able to guarantee the dissociation between Kádár and the unburied, thus improper, unnatural, dead. The relational sign was not only born; it was displayed, literally, in public when demonstrators carried the name on a banner.

When March 15, the date when the 1848 Revolution broke out, and traditionally a day of anti-Communist demonstrations (or attempted demonstrations after 1956), was last commemorated under the Communist rule, in 1989, demonstrators carried banners with the sign: "Kádár-Haynau, Imre Nagy-Batthyány." (See Figure 2.3.) Julius von Haynau, known as the "hyena of Brescia" was Emperor Franz Joseph's henchman. He was sent to Brescia to suppress the uprising there and execute the revolutionaries, and, as military governor of Hungary after the defeat of the 1848 Revolution, he was in charge of the retribution, the execution of the military and civilian leaders of the revolution. He ordered the execution of the thirteen leading generals of the Hungarian army on October 6, 1849, in Arad, in Transylvania,

71. Lévi-Strauss, *Savage Mind*, p. 198. I use the necronym in this sense: "Brutus, the murderer of Ceasar" ("Et tu Brute, fili mi!"—this is what is remembered when uttering Brutus's name).

72. The birth of the propaganda state and the nationalization of the mass production of history books evidently played a role in the centralized attempt to obliterate certain names. Despite the state's control over the writing of history, the unexpected reappearance or resurrection of certain names could threaten even the proper name of the executioner, which might then itself have been substituted with a relational term. On the propaganda state, see Peter Kenez, *The Birth of the Propaganda State: Soviet Methods of Mass Mobilization* (Cambridge and New York: Cambridge University Press, 1985).

FIGURE 2.3.   Haynau-Kádár; Batthyány-Imre Nagy. Banners at a demonstration in 1989. Photo: András Bánkuti.

and the hanging of the first moderate prime minister of the revolution, Lajos Batthyány, on the same day in Pest. Haynau appears in elementary school history textbooks; his name is a synonym for *henchman*. (On one of the central squares of Budapest there is a memorial, an eternal flame, commemorating the death of Batthyány. On June 16, 1988, on the anniversary of the date Imre Nagy was hanged in 1958, a small group of political demonstrators unofficially renamed the eternal flame the "Batthyány-Nagy Memorial.")

Let me make a remark: I have an illness. And my illness is similar to my wife's: she is losing weight; and I am losing too. The medical opinion is the following. My wife has been walking with a stick for five years; she has to use a stick, and she is losing weight because she had to undergo a radical stomach operation while I was in prison. And she was called to repudiate me, but she did not do that, and then she was forced to renounce my name, she was forbidden to use her husband's name.[73] [See Figure 2.4.]

What happened to the younger László Rajk, happened also to the wife of his godfather, the wife of the person who was the minister of the

73. János Kádár quoted in *A Magyar Szocialista Munkáspárt Központi Bizottságának 1989*, p. 758.

interior when his father was executed: the same authorities that took away
László Rajk's name, because it so clearly referred to (the nonexistence of)
his father, forced Mrs. János Kádár to change her name too, as it would in
the same way clearly point to her husband's absence.

"And please remember," says Kádár in front of the Central Committee, "that whenever I remember, since this is already what I have to do, I
will always tell the truth. . . . I cannot refuse that, for everybody says that
I am the living one; I must speak." What he clearly says is not "I am alive"

FIGURE 2.4. János Kádár leaving the party congress
with his wife, after having been ousted as secretary
general of the party. Photo: MTI Photo Archives.

but "I am the living one" [*én vagyok az élő*], and without a doubt, this refers to the one whose death is connected to the living, who is dead, who
cannot testify (On February 3, 1989, a two-page article was published in
the most important, most widely read Hungarian literary weekly with the
title "What Has János Kádár to Say?" The journalist urged Kádár to speak,
to recall: "Now it is high time for János Kádár to say something. Not about
the future, for visions are seldom fulfilled, but about the past. . . . János
Kádár is a chief witness on any account in the Rajk case and in the Imre
Nagy case. . . . He cannot disappear silently.")[74]

74. István Tanács quoted in *Élet és Irodalom*, February 3, 1989. According to tapes
recorded secretly in László Rajk's prison cell, it was Kádár, Rajk's successor as minister of
the interior, who convinced Rajk that he had no choice but to confess and cooperate in his
own destruction. Kádár, together with one of the chief designers of the show trials who was
minister of defense at that time, visited Rajk in his cell on June 7, 1949. "We came here to
give you an opportunity to talk with the party for the last time in your life," Kádár began,
his logic resembling Rubashov's interrogation in Arthur Koestler's *Darkness at Noon*. "Tell
me Rajk, why do you think that we are so stupid?" asked Kádár. "Why isn't Farkas [the
minister of defense] or me sitting here in your place?" After Rajk's execution it was then
Kádár's turn: he was imprisoned and tortured in 1951 and was released in 1954, after Stalin's
death. After 1956 the secret tapes, along with the documents of the interrogation and Rajk's
trial, disappeared (most probably in either 1959 or 1961), but one transcript survived. Still,
in 1955 at Rajk's retrial a technical officer of the secret police was questioned about the authenticity of the then-existing tapes. He testified that "the transcripts were made on the basis of the tapes that I had personally recorded. The pages between 353 and 376 contain the
transcripts of the conversation between János Kádár, Mihály Farkas, and László Rajk during the night of 7 June 1949, that were made on the basis of the recordings I myself had
made." The two secretaries who transcribed the tapes also verified their authenticity and
stated, "when transcribing the tapes we were able to recognize the voices of some of the defendants, as we had previously taken part in taping the telephone conversations of some of
the accused, Rajk among them." Either at the end of 1958 or the beginning of 1959, an
archivist at the Central Party Archive secretly made a copy of the transcript and hid it
among other papers of the archive. Only in December 1991 did it become possible for the
first time to find and consult the hidden transcript. The text was published by T. Hajdú;
see Hajdú, "Kádár és Farkas Rajknál," pp. 70–89, quotes from pp. 76 and 88, respectively.
The document is to my knowledge by far the most valuable and chilling source for understanding the mechanism of self-incrimination. In the only long interview Kádár gave, a few
months before his death, the reporter asked him about the role he played in the Rajk case:
"According to some Western analysts you have played an important role in Rajk's trial. Others, even in Hungary, state that it was you who eventually persuaded Rajk to incriminate
himself." "I do not know who they are who state such things, but they are not true," answered Kádár, who at that time did not know about the existence of the transcripts of the
secret tapes (*János Kádár: Last Will* [Budapest: Hírlapkiadó Vállalat, 1989], p. 277). The interviewer was András Kanyó and the interview was made in March–April 1989. It is not

The "death-names," as Rodney Needham—the first anthropologist to analyze this classificatory category seriously—refers to necronyms, "are not vehicles or evokers of sorrow, but merely classes of persons with reference to the deaths of true kin."[75] According to Needham, "The principle [involved in the] application of death-names is that on the death of a true kinsman or kinswoman a Penan assumes a name *according to his relationship to the deceased.*"[76]

On October 31, 1956, János Kádár and Imre Nagy re-form the Hungarian Communist Party and create the Hungarian Socialist Workers' Party, which would exist until the collapse in 1989. Kádár is a member of the Imre Nagy government when the government decides to withdraw from the Warsaw Pact and announces the neutrality of Hungary (on November 1, 1956); he gives a significant speech on the revolutionary radio in which he says that "the glorious uprising of our people achieved the freedom of the people and the independence of the country. . . . We are proud that you held strong in the armed struggle," and so on. Then he vanishes, goes over to the Soviets, rematerializing "in public," that is, on the air, when he announces on the radio that he has asked the Soviet troops to invade Hungary and that he has formed a new government to defeat the counterrevolutionary government of Imre Nagy. On the morning of November 4, 1956, the day the Soviet invasion starts, Nagy flees to the Yugoslav embassy. There, along with some other members of his government—including Georg Lukács and such close associates as the widow of László Rajk—Nagy is granted refuge.

Nagy later refuses to sign the letter in which the Soviets were asked retroactively to invade the country, the one Kádár referred to in his last speech: "The letter . . . the man who died since then refused to sign. I had to sign it too, somewhere, God knows where." Kádár said:

I have guaranteed the safety of him who stayed—yes, I have really guaranteed it—in that embassy. But I am such a naive man, I gave a guarantee, because I thought

---

clear whether it was made before or after Kádár's last speech at the meeting of the Central Committee. On the Rubashov case, see Louis Michael Seidman, "Rubashov's question: Self Incrimination and the Problem of Coerced Preferences," *Yale Journal of Law and the Humanities* (winter 1990): 160.

75. Rodney Needham, "The System of Teknonyms and Death-Names of the Penan," *Southwest Journal of Anthropology* 10 (1954): 428.

76. Ibid., p. 418; emphasis added.

that on my request the man would make a statement in order not to create the basis on which one could find support later. Well now, I too see every thing as historically different. But if I gave a guarantee according to his wish . . . but it was his wish to leave home freely. I could not carry this through effectively, as I never read my old writings when I speak, not even those in which that statement was, for they might influence me, believe it or not. Unfortunately, there was a simple sentence in that statement. And since then there have been all sorts of consequences rooted in that simple sentence.

On November 19, 1956, D. Vidic, the Yugoslav deputy minister of foreign affairs, arrives in Budapest and hands over to János Kádár the letter in which the Yugoslav leadership urges the Hungarian party to solve the Imre Nagy conflict. On November 21, an agreement is reached between the Yugoslavs and the Hungarians according to which the Hungarian politicians who found refuge in the embassy might leave the building freely, with Kádár personally guaranteeing their safety. Vidic informs Nagy of the agreement in person, and the next day the Hungarians leave the embassy. Then, with prior consent from the Hungarian party leaders, the asylum seekers are kidnapped by the Soviets and transported to Romania—this with the consent of Gheorgiu Dej, the general secretary of the Romanian Communist Party, who has arrived in Budapest earlier that day.[77] Nagy stays in Romania until the beginning of his trial, at the end of which he is hanged. Kádár struggles in the speech (not) to refer to that guarantee, "the simple sentence" and "all sorts of consequences of the simple sentence." He never mentions Nagy by name, using "he" and vague personal references (there is no personal pronoun in the Hungarian text) like "the man" (who is clearly Nagy) instead. "I never read my old writings when I speak, not even those in which that statement was, for it might influence me, believe it or not," fights the old man of broken promises in the shadow of the dead man.

77. In his last interview, the journalist asked Kádár about this "letter of guarantee." Kádár responded:

> The Yugoslav comrades claimed that they were not interested at all in the personal fate of the refugees, for—according to them—it was an internal Hungarian affair. However, they wanted to save face; this is why they asked us to state that those in the embassy would not be harmed for mistakes committed in the past. Vidic wanted a sentence to the effect that the refugees could leave the embassy freely and return to their homes. We told him that there was no way for them to stay here, in Hungary but after three hours of discussion, we wrote that [what the Yugoslavs wanted] into the text. . . . If I were able to write down, or even to show in a film, how discussions were conducted in those days; then one could see more clearly what happened in those weeks. (János Kádár, *Last Will*, p. 129)

Imre Nagy never signed either an antedated letter of resignation or the letter requesting the Soviet intervention. From a legal point of view, Kádár's government was and remained illegitimate. The government, the new regime, was conceived in that simple sentence, the break of the promise. Nagy had to perish for Kádár to be reborn.

Had Imre Nagy been alive as a dead person, had his name been referred to, mentioned in public, then the original sin would have constantly threatened Kádár's name, thus his identity, and it would have undermined the claim of the regime—connected to his name—to legality and thus to legitimacy. (The post–1956 period is referred to in Hungary as "the Kádár era" or "the Kádár regime.") "Systems of relations," says Lévi-Strauss, taking Rodney Needham's original observations further, "unlike systems of positions whose discontinuous nature is evident, tend rather to be *continuous*."[78] It was not enough to kill Imre Nagy; his personal name had to be taken away, otherwise there would have been no way of erasing any continuity between the treason, which finished the revolution, and the Communist restoration. An unforgettable and unerasable relationship between the hanged prime minister and his successor and executioner would have remained.[79]

On June 16, 1989, the day of Imre Nagy's reburial, the deputy press secretary of the party visited Kádár and stayed at his house for several hours. He was sent by the Central Committee to console the sick man. Hungarian television aired live coverage of the reburial. The event lasted

78. Lévi-Strauss, *Savage Mind*, p. 198; emphasis added.

79. Rodney Needham ("System of Teknonyms," p. 431)—in an exemplarily modest way—does not provide an airy solution to the problem of death names. At the end of his paper he summarizes:

> The point to which we have come in our examination of the death names is this: We cannot invoke sociological laws to explain them, for one can maintain either that there are none, or that what some anthropologists consider such are of no use in this matter. Similarly, we cannot invoke psychological laws. We cannot use expressed purpose to explain them, for this is just what the Penan cannot state, and we cannot properly indulge in sociological teleology. We cannot speak of the symbolic function of the death-names, because the lack of consistent usage of all the names precludes a single type of symbolic relationship that would satisfy, and because they do not symbolize either to the Penan . . . or to the anthropologist . . . either replacement (1), mourning (2), commemoration (3), economic obligation (4), or the perpetual struggle between life and death (5).

> I do not pretend that I have presented and examined all possible hypotheses, but I think the five I have examined are by their immediate plausibility the major ones that might be offered, and by their congruence with certain facts possibly true. I cannot see that any of them should be accepted.

for more than six hours. Kádár was physically sick and emotionally shaken. He did not watch television but rather sat in almost complete silence, asking from time to time "Is *it* today? . . . Is *that* happening? . . . Does *that* take place now? Is this *the day*?"[80]

The Name

The freely elected new parliament considers it as its urgent task—one that cannot be postponed—to enshrine the historical significance of the revolution and freedom fight of the Fall of 1956 in a bill. This glorious event of modern Hungarian history can only be compared to the revolution and freedom fight of 1848. The Hungarian revolution of the Fall of 1956 created a foundation for the hope that democratic social order can be created, that no sacrifice is in vain for the independence of the fatherland.

These are the introductory words of the first bill passed by the first post-Communist parliament, minutes after the last Communist government officially stepped down.[81] On the previous day, May 1, the draft of the proposed bill still contained Imre Nagy's name. The name was there, even during the night when representatives of the different new parties of the parliament were adding the final touches to the text. By the time the youngest member of the parliament read the text of the bill in front of the plenary session of the House, in the name of the new, conservative, anti-Communist prime minister, who had played a minor role in the events of 1956, Imre Nagy's name had been erased. According to the festive protocol of the opening day of the parliament, no room was left for debate. The new conservative speaker of the House, himself a historian, an authority on the 1848 Revolution, remarked, "1956 is the supreme link between us and our historical past."[82] With 366 supporting votes and 2 abstaining, the parliament passed the bill.

On April 30, 1996, not long before the centenary of Imre Nagy's birthday (June 6 or 7, 1896), six parliamentarians introduced a bill in the House. Among the six signatories of the draft were the leader of the Social-

80. Emil Kimmel, "Az utolsó beszéd" [The last speech], *Magyarország*, May 18, 1990, p. 25; emphasis added.
    81. Law XXVIII of the year 1990 (available online at *http://wwwmkogyhu/naplo34/001/0010029.htm*).
    82. *The Diary of the Hungarian Parliament* (*http://wwwmkogy.hu/naplo34/001/0010028.htm*).

ist parliamentary majority; a Socialist Lutheran clergyman, himself the son of a deceased member of the Nagy government (the father was in prison between the World Wars, then imprisoned by the Stalinists at the beginning of the 1950s, and after 1956, naturally, once more imprisoned by Kádár); László Rajk, the son of the show-trial victim, who was the stage designer of the Imre Nagy reburial in 1989 and became a liberal member of the parliament in 1990; the chairman of the Defense Committee of the parliament, who was sentenced to death after 1956 and spent a whole year on death row before his sentence was commuted to life in prison; and another post–1956 prisoner, who later joined the Socialist Party. The proposal was clearly initiated by the Socialists—one of the successor parties to Kádár's Hungarian Socialist Workers' Party—who succeeded in persuading a few symbolic figures to support the bill that would "enact the memory of Imre Nagy, prime minister of Hungary, who suffered martyrdom."

After a very long, politically and emotionally charged debate, the parliament passed the law on June 25, 1996 (missing the deadline of Imre Nagy's birthday), with 167 votes supporting the law, 77 against, and 64 abstaining. (Out of the 167 votes in support, 163 came from the Socialists.)[83]

The lead speaker of the Hungarian Socialist Party, the head of the parliamentary majority, reminded the House that Imre Nagy first became known in the country as the Communist minister of agriculture in 1945, who signed the decree on the parceling of the landed estates and their partition among the millions of landless peasants.

From 1955 onward the name of Imre Nagy became the symbol of the possibility of humanistic, *National and Democratic Socialism*. In light of this, it was no accident that the reform Communists gathered around him in order to prepare for the revolution. . . . His was a human life, exactly because it was not a uniform life history. Had Saul remained a Christian-bashing agent of Rome, nobody would remember his name today, but he turned Paul on his way to Damascus. Although this road has been truly crowded in the past six or seven years, nobody can deny the possibility of true awakening. . . . There are people who might question his idea of a Socialism that could be achieved by rational and democratic means. . . . And he is the symbol of the political transition of 1989–1990 too. It was at his coffin that the Hungarian society made a decision by judging the past and promising the future. We propose to commemorate the name of a person who approached the impossible.[84]

83. Ibid. (*http://wwwmkogy.hu/szavaz/szavlist/66pi2510.htm*).
84. Ibid. (*http://www.mkogyhu/naplo/183/1830042.htm*).

The Socialists not only attempted to tie the name to an imagined democratic and humanistic version of Socialism, but by reading the revolution as an attempt to introduce "Socialism with a human face" and a fight for national sovereignty at the same time, they also connected Socialism with the attribute "national." "He who approached the impossible" refers to the forerunners of the post-Communists, who are presently engaged in the heroic struggle of building a free-market economy in order to create, finally—on the ruins of Communism—a just society, fulfilling Karl Marx's dream and filling their pockets at the same time.

"Imre Nagy's execution prevented him from becoming a true Social Democrat, so he had to die as a National Democratic Communist. But he was, nevertheless, a forerunner of Alexander Dubcek [the leader of the Czechoslovak Communist Party during the 'Prague Spring' and the speaker of the Czechoslovak Parliament after the 'Velvet Revolution']."[85] By using the Czech parallel, the speaker clearly tried to implicate even Vaclav Havel, the quintessential dissident who became the Czechoslovak president after Dubcek had withdrawn his own nomination at the end of 1989 and, on the basis of an agreement with Havel, became the speaker of the parliament instead. In this salvational narrative there is a direct connection between Communists, reform Communists, Social Democrats, and dissidents; there is a road leading from Stalinism to an alliance between former Communists and anti-Communists. Without the former Communists, there would be no place for the former anti-Communist on the political stage. The seeds of the post-Communist transformation had already been sown in 1956 and even before, in 1953, when Imre Nagy became prime minister for the first time.

One of the conservative speakers in the debate, a representative of the right-wing Small Holders' Party, in a modifying proposal suggested that not only the name of the martyred prime minister but also the names of all those victims who were executed in the course of the postrevolutionary terror should be preserved and inscribed in law: "Imre Nagy, who fought against the Stalinist cult of personality, would no doubt agree with the inclusion of all these names; he has never wanted to isolate himself from his fellow revolutionaries." After this rhetorical turn, the speaker read more than 270 names; the members of the House stood in silence.[86]

---

85. Ibid. (*http://www.ywwmkogy.hu/naplo/184/1840307.htm*).
86. Ibid. (*http://www.mkogy.hu/naplo/183/1830046.htm*).

When the representatives recovered their voices, a historiographical and philological debate erupted. One of the original signatories of the bill, the liberal chair of the Defense Committee of the parliament, remembered that he had spent a few months on death row after 1956 together with one of the victims whose name was included in the list. As the Defense Committee chair recalled—on the basis of his personal, firsthand knowledge—this alleged victim of the revolution had, in fact, killed his wife and cut her into pieces, exploiting the favorably chaotic situation created by the revolution. The Communists had included him in one of the postrevolutionary political trials in order to prove that those responsible for the revolution were criminals, the most dangerous elements of the society.[87]

The inclusion of the names of common—and former war criminals—some of them retried and sentenced to death after 1956, including Mihály Francia Kiss, who had been sentenced to death in absentia after World War II on sixty-six counts of murder, in order to implicate the revolutionaries—served to challenge again the reform-Communist reading of the revolution.[88] What the right-wing in the parliament proposed instead in 1996 resembled, in fact repeated, the picture the Communists had painted of 1956 that they called the counterrevolution before 1989: the struggle of déclassé elements, former landowners and the right-wing losers of the Communist regime who tried to go back in time, back before March 19, 1944, when the Gestapo and the German army came to occupy Hungary. The conservatives redrew the earlier accusations of the Communists that had confirmed the counterrevolutionary nature of events: that the real aim of the uprising was to resume the authentic history of the nation from the moment when it had been stopped in 1944.

The conservative parties represented in parliament unequivocally opposed the bill. While to the Socialists, Imre Nagy's name stood for the man "who approached the impossible," to the conservatives, his fate taught instead that "democracy and Communism are incommensurable. . . . Only his death could solve this otherwise insoluble dilemma."[89] "In order to have democracy—this is what we had to learn—it is not enough to take the power back from those who usurp it, but we have to take the past, our

---

87. Ibid. (*http://www.mkogy.hu/naplo/188/1880313.htm*).

88. These other names, besides common criminals, included a general of the interwar regime and the first conservative speaker of the post–World War II parliament.

89. *Diary of the Hungarian Parliament* (*http://www.mkogyhu/naplo/184/1840028 .htm* and *1840044.htm*, respectively).

history, back too," argued the representative of the Young Democrats (a party that started as a liberal, new-age organization of the young in 1989 but, after having sensed real political opportunity in the center-right, reinvented itself as a right-wing, populist conservative party).

The real aim of the bill is to smuggle Communism one more time into the mainstream of Hungarian progression. . . . We have to ask the question: what is the real aim behind this bill? The bill is plainly an initiative to build a historical foundation for the Socialists. This is why it is unavoidable for them to repaint 1956 as a democratic and Socialist revolution. . . . If it were true as the Socialists claim, that Imre Nagy remained a Communist even beneath the gallows and identified himself with his ideas, with democracy, and with his Hungarianness, then his name might be suitable for commemoration. But in this case, the Hungarian Socialist Party would be clearly inappropriate in taking part in the formulation of a bill commemorating him. The forebears of present-day Socialists first repudiated the nation and disavowed democracy, then—in order to be able to privatize what they had previously nationalized in the name of Communism—renounced their ideology.[90]

"16 June, the day of Imre Nagy's execution, was baptized as the 'day of Hungarian freedom.' But this day cannot become the day of rejoicing; this should rather be the day of mourning: One cannot celebrate Good Friday and Easter Sunday on the very same day," a Christian Democrat well versed in the Bible reminded the House.[91]

Perhaps this remark was the impetus for a conversation in the corridors of the House between a liberal parliamentarian, who had spent some time in prison as a young student after the revolution, and the Lutheran clergyman, one of the signatories of the proposal who, as a child with his parents, had also been a refugee in the Yugoslav embassy. "During the intermission, I had a conversation with my fellow parliamentarian, the learned theologian," the liberal told the House, "who reminded me of the fact that Pilate's name is in the credo. . . . The name of evil is also part of the story of salvation."[92] The theologian, a member of the parliamentary group of Socialists, reaffirmed the words of his liberal colleague:

There is a need at every mass and at every worship for mentioning the name of Pilate. And there are several reasons for this: . . . Traditionally two-thousand-year-

90. Ibid. (*http://www.mkogy.hu/napto/184/1840044.htm* and *http://www.mkogy.hu/ naplo/194/1940214.htm*, respectively).
91. Ibid. (*http://www.mkogy.hu/naplo/184/1840289.htm*).
92. Ibid. (*http://www.mkogy.hu/naplo/188/1880331.htm*).

old Christianity lives together with anti-Judaism, but in opposition to it; the confession of the first Christian clearly states who is responsible for the death of Jesus. Instead of accusing randomly, instead of seeing a criminal in everybody each Christian in all times, in historical fairness, should know who has political responsibility; I think of Pilate. Salvation is a historical difference that means that redemption on this earth has no meaning unless somebody is victorious over evil. We too are unable to deny that there was somebody who thought it his historical mission to become the executioner. One cannot pronounce the name of Imre Nagy without thinking of the name of the executioner.[93]

What the two speakers had on their minds was most probably a version of what Mikhail Bulgakov had written in *The Master and Margarita*, when he described the dream of Pontius Pilate, Procurator of Judea: "'You and I will always be together,' said the ragged tram-philosopher who had so mysteriously become the traveling companion of the Knight of the Golden Lance. 'Where one of us goes, the other shall go too. Whenever people think of me, they will think of you—me an orphan child of unknown parents, and you the son of an astrologer-king and a miller's daughter, the beautiful Pila!'"[94]

It was the speakers' clear intention to use Pontius Pilate's name as a necronym, "he who is responsible for the death of Jesus," despite the probable intention of the text of the synoptic Gospels. The Gospels, in fact, portray Pilate in a relatively neutral tone. (See for example Luke 23:13: "Pilate then called together the chief priests and the rulers and the people and said to them, 'You brought me this man as one who was perverting the people; and after examining him, before you, behold, I did not find this man guilty of any of your charges against him; neither did Herod, for he sent him back to us. Behold, nothing deserving death has been done by him; I will therefore chastise him and release him.'" Or, Matthew 27:24: "So when Pilate saw that he was gaining nothing, but rather that a riot was beginning, he took water and washed his hands before the crowd, saying, 'I am innocent of this man's blood; see to it yourselves.' And all the people answered, 'His blood be on us and on our children!'"[95]) As one could have expected, the leader of the Christian Democrats was not able to let these words go unanswered: "I

93. Ibid. (*http://www.mkogy.hu/naplo/188/L880333.htm*).

94. Mikhail Bulgakov, *The Master and Margarita*, trans. Michael Glenny (New York: Meridan, 1993), p. 311.

95. Luke 23:13; Matt. 27:24, in *The Holy Bible: Revised Standard Edition*: Philo of Alexandria, who was most probably a contemporary of Pontius Pilate and far from an

think that in Jesus' case, it would not be worthwhile to present Pilate as the scapegoat, for it is not he who is the main character here. Likewise, in this case too, it is not those who signed the sentence that are the chief actors. According to theology, we, all of us sinners, are responsible for Christ's death," the Christian Democrat concluded his sinister speech. For him saving Pontius Pilate or the interpretations of the synoptic Gospels carried more weight than the pardoning of János Kádár.[96]

The main speaker for the liberals—the party of the former anti-Communist dissidents who, after 1994, as a strange and risky compromise, entered into the coalition government with the Socialists—was the widow of one of the codefendants of the Imre Nagy trial. She recalled and re-minded her audience of the fact that it was a strange Hungarian parlia-mentary practice to enshrine the name of certain individuals in the law. The last "name bill" passed as the First Law of the Year 1953, when the Hungarian Parliament enshrined in law the memory of Generalissimus Stalin. "If we seriously think that Hungary lives under the rule of law to-day, if the country takes the law seriously but refuses Stalinism, then what are the consequences of that valid law now? If the country decides not to venerate Stalin, does it act in an unlawful way?"[97] But Stalin is not alone in his commemoration in the Diary of the Hungarian Parliament. Saint Stephen, the first Hungarian king; Lajos Kossuth, the leader of the 1848 Revolution; even the person who defeated that revolution, ordered the ex-ecution of its leaders, and forced Kossuth into emigration, Franz Joseph I, who ruled Hungary for sixty-nine years, all got their names enshrined in law.[98] Mihály Károlyi, the first president of Hungary, who as the leader of the short-lived 1918 democratic revolution dethroned the Habsburgs, got not one but two entries in the books of the parliament.[99]

---

impartial observer, however, describes Pilate in a letter Herod Agrippa I sent to Caligula as "'inflexible by nature because of his stubbornness,' accusing him of graft, insults, robberies, assaults, wanton abuse, constant executions without trial, unending grievous cruelty" (Philo, *Embassy* 38, pp. 301–2).

96. *Diary of the Hungarian Parliament* (*http://www.mkogy.hu/naplo/188/1880335.htm*).

97. Ibid. (*http://www.mkogyhu/naplo/183/1830044.htm*).

98. The "Franz Joseph bill" was passed in February 1917, in the middle of World War I, at the time of the death of the emperor.

99. A few months after the proclamation of the Hungarian Republic and the victory of the democratic revolution that ended World War I for Hungary, on March 21, the Com-munist Party placarded Budapest announcing the resignation of Mihály Károlyi, who, ac-cording to the text, gave over power to the Communists. Károlyi had not, in fact, handed

"At twelve noon on Sunday, the parliament at an extraordinary mourning session of the House remembered the Liberator of our country, the Great Dead of Humankind, I. V. Stalin." The members of the House were standing while listening to the opening address of the speaker of the House: "The Hungarian working people are staggered to the depth of their hearts by the death of our Great Friend, our Liberator, our Wise Teacher

---

over the power to anyone, but he did not protest; he thought that the Communists might be able to resist some of the harsh conditions the Entente tried to force on defeated Hungary. A few months later he went into exile. After the defeat of the First Hungarian Soviet Republic, when Admiral Horthy's right-wing counterrevolutionary forces took over, Károlyi became the scapegoat not only for allegedly having given power to the Communists but also for the heavy losses of territory the country had to suffer for its participation in World War I.

In 1927, while in exile in London, Károlyi wrote a play, which would be published in Hungary only in 1971. Ravelszki, the hero of the drama, whose name is the title of the play, is the chairman of a party that bears his name. ("The Károlyi Party"—this is how Károlyi's party was known in Hungary.) The imagined country lives under tyranny, and when rumors spread that Ravelszki has been killed by an agent of the government, the revolution breaks out. Despite the attempted murder, Ravelszki in fact stays alive, but the leaders of his party convince him that it is in the interest of the country and the revolution to confirm the rumors, so Ravelszki agrees to go secretly into exile. The revolution is victorious, Ravelszki becomes the martyr of the country, and time goes on. The new leaders naturally betray the revolution and Ravelszki's ideas, and he decides to return secretly: on the occasion of the inauguration of his mausoleum, in order to reveal his existence, the abuse of his name, and the grand camouflage.

His former comrades in arms also prepare for his return, and when in the National Cemetery Ravelszki discloses his identity, he is taken to a mental asylum as a schizophrenic pretending that he is the great revolutionary, who—as everybody well knows—died years ago. Having no other choice left, Ravelszki tries to escape in order to get killed, and so to awaken his country. The country, however, remains indifferent; nobody cares anymore (Mihály Károlyi, *Ravelszki*, ed. and with an intro. by Miklós Hubay [Budapest: Magvető Könyvkiadó, 1971]).

"For every emigrant it is comforting to know that in the twentieth century historical processes are much quicker, and man lives much longer than before. This is why we have the opportunity to live through the opposite of everything, even several times" (Károlyi, *Ravelszki*). On February 14, 1946, the Hungarian Parliament passed a law commemorating Károlyi's name and his invaluable service to the country. When he returned from his emigration, it was László Rajk who greeted him in the name of the Hungarian Communist Party. Károlyi became the Hungarian ambassador to Paris, but when he was barred from testifying at Rajk's trial—he had been witness to an incident that the prosecutor falsely and purposely attributed to Rajk—he resigned and went into exile for the second time. He died in 1955. His remains were brought back to Hungary where he was reburied on March 18, 1963. The day of the burial was a Sunday (Ravelszki's Mausoleum was inaugurated on a Sunday too); his mausoleum is not far from Lajos Kossuth's, in the vicinity of the Pantheon of the Heroes of the Workers' Movement, near László Rajk's third burial place.

and Leader, Iosif Vissarionovich Stalin. The Greatest Friend of our Nation, the One whom we thank for our dearest treasure, our Liberty, parted the company of the living." After his opening remarks, the speaker of the House announced that "the deputy prime minister introduced a bill to the effect of preserving the immortal memory of the Dearly Loved Generalissimus Iosif Vissarionovich Stalin, the Leader of Progressive Humankind, the True Friend of the Hungarian Nation."

The deputy prime minister, who in his words was "hit by the grievous disaster," stepped up to the podium "in front of a whole nation plunged into mourning, to introduce a bill that would preserve forever the immortal memory of Stalin." The bill stated:

the name, the work, and the teaching of Iosif Vissarionovich Stalin have been united inextricably with the history of our country. Sovereignty of the Hungarian nation, the liberty of the Hungarian people, the rise of the Hungarian workers have forever been connected with what Comrade Stalin created and represented for both the peoples of the Soviet Union and for progressive mankind. . . . In view of these, the parliament inscribes in law the memory of Iosif Vissarionovich Stalin for all that He achieved in the liberation of Hungary; in establishing and guaranteeing the freedom of the Hungarian nation; in the political, economic, and cultural betterment and rise of the Hungarian working classes.

The deputy prime minister was struggling with words as he commented on the bill: "With my heart constricted I am searching in vain for the appropriate words to find a way to express who Stalin was for mankind." But he found the words and spoke for more than one and a half hours. "Stalin is dead," announced the deputy prime minister at the end of his shocking oration,

but his name will live until the end of time in his work. The faithful and thankful Hungarian people have decided to preserve His glorious memory in law. By passing the law that I have introduced in the name of the Council of Ministers of the Hungarian People's Republic we are binding an imperishable wreath out of the love and gratitude of our people around the deathless memory of our dear and great Comrade Stalin.[100]

According to the testimony of the Proceedings of the Hungarian Parliament, with these words ended the memorial address of March 8, 1953, by the deputy prime minister of the Hungarian People's Republic, Imre Nagy. (See Figure 2.5.)

100. The description of the event is from *Szabad Ifjúság*, March 10, 1953, p. 5.

FIGURE 2.5. Imre Nagy at the extraordinary mourning session of the Hungarian Parliament, March 8, 1953. Photo Archives of the Hungarian National Museum.

3

A Pantheon

Two copies were made of the minutes of the October 7, 1957, meeting of the secretariat of the Budapest Party Committee. The only surviving carbon copy shows clearly that in 1957, unlike in 1989, "the other side," that is, the counterrevolutionary one of the 1956 dividing line, was still very much—although not literally—alive. In his briefing, the chief of the Budapest Police reassured the comrades present that

the police will be especially alert on October 31, as well as on November 1 and 2, as November 1 is All Saints Day, while November 2 is the Christian day of the dead. On these days we should be prepared for the appearance of black flags on the houses, lighting of the windows, candles, and memorial services in the cemeteries. . . . The comrades know the situation in the Kerepesi Cemetery. There, *opposite* to the graves granted at public expense to the Communist martyrs, the dead of the counterrevolution are buried.[1]

One of the functionaries immediately reacted: "In public life, we have succeeded in pushing back the counterrevolutionary elements of the society.

---

1. This is the so-called 21st parcel of the cemetery. Between November 1, 1956, and January 9, 1957, 457 people were buried here. From the cohort between age ten and nineteen there are 62 boys and 7 girls among the dead. From the age group between twenty and twenty-four, 68 men and 6 women; between twenty-five and twenty-nine, 51 men and 6 women; and between thirty and thirty-four, the ratio is 29 to 6. This "abnormal statistical average" clearly shows that most of those buried here should have died during the armed fighting. See Kenedi, *Kis Állambiztonsági Olvasókönyv*, vol. 1, p. 24, n. 10.

Why should we tolerate the heroic adjectives on the gravestones of the counter-revolutionaries? Why is the cemetery another world? [*sic!*]"

The secretary explained the difficulties of the issue:

The first suggestion presented to us was to remove the counterrevolutionaries from the graves granted at public expense. A special committee of the secretariat of the Central Committee, however, after due consideration of the issue, decided that this would be somewhat unfortunate to do and could lead to rather upsetting consequences. According to the law still in force, exhumation of bodies can take place only in the presence of the relatives. Imagine, comrades, what would happen if we deliberately gathered the relatives of the counterrevolutionaries and started to dig out their dead one after the other from the graves? You see, comrades!

After very careful consideration, the Central secretariat of our party, in turn, reached the following sound decision: we do not have to exhume the counterrevolutionaries, but to enclose with hedgerow, with some carefully planted bushes, that parcel of the cemetery where the counterrevolutionaries are interned.

(According to the minutes, at this point one of the participants intervened and shouted, "In this way we, ourselves, would emphasize the presence and the graves of the counterrevolutionaries.") "But," continued the secretary, "we should, at the same time, dig out our comrades from their present graves and erect a suitable heroic monument at another point of the cemetery and move, in proper way, their bodies there."[2]

The session of the secretariat of the party, which was referred to at the Budapest party meeting, took place a few weeks earlier. The planned memorial and the mausoleum of the heroes of the workers' movement were on that session's agenda. The secretariat considered two plans; a rather intense—although, from an aesthetic point of view, sadly unprofessional—discussion developed about the best possible sculptural and architectural approach for honoring the veterans of the Communist movement. In the course of the discussion, the problem of mixing up the bodies and the politically embarrassing layout of the cemetery emerged. A deputy prime minister member of the Politburo reported that "the bodies of the revolutionaries are somewhat mixed with the bodies of the counterrevolutionaries around Kossuth's Mausoleum. The comrades suggest here that the bodies of those comrades who died while defending the People's Democracy should be moved. But wouldn't it be better to do this, the other way round?"

2. (Hungarian State Archive) (MOL) BB. 1. Fond. 1957/13. ő.e. Quoted in Kenedi, *Kis Állambiztonsági Olvasókönyv*, vol. 1, pp. 21–26. I have used the original typewritten version.

One of the oldest members of the Politburo, who was a member of that body even before 1956, addressed the deputy's concerns:

We went there and consulted with leading comrades from the cemetery, the director of the cemetery included. The wounds are still fresh, comrades. There are all sorts of dead bodies here: children killed in the street, passers-by, even people who had nothing to do with the events; they make up the majority, and then, yes, our dead. To move ours is much easier; there is no point in assembling and upsetting quite a few hundred working families now. This would be superfluous. According to the design of the memorial of the heroes, bushes would be planted around, and this would clearly separate our great dead from the other bodies that will not remain so visible.[3]

The secretariat ultimately suggested the "use [of] horticultural methods" to separate and cover those who were "not our dead."

*

Using "horticultural methods" to cover embarrassing sites was not a unique Hungarian countercommemorative technique. On June 25, 1976, the workers of the Polish industrial city Radom took the streets to demonstrate against sudden, drastic increases in the price of basic foodstuffs. Workers of the largest plants of the city built barricades, and during the demonstration, the headquarters of the local party committee was set ablaze. The Communist authorities, with the help of the militia and units of the military, quickly regained control of the streets, killing two demonstrators, wounding several workers, and arresting hundreds of those who were involved. Radom became stigmatized as a city of hooligans, alcoholics, and antisocial and marginal elements. In 1981, after the official establishment of the "Solidarity" trade union and the temporary withdrawal of the Communists, the people of the city, together with trade-union activists decided to erect a memorial to commemorate the anti-Communist demonstration and the victims of the uprising. On the fifth anniversary of the event, Lech Walesa unveiled a temporary stone memorial to mark the site of the future monument. Inside the stone were placed three urns containing earth from three important cities that played a role in the chain of Polish anti-Communist movement: Poznan (1956); Gdansk (1970 and 1980); and Radom (1976).

On December 13, 1981, six months after the unveiling of the temporary monument, martial law was declared in Poland. The Radom rehabil-

3. MOL 288. Fond. 7/11. ő.e. (August 9, 1957).

itation committee disbanded, and the prosecutor of Radom ordered the seizure of a bulletin, "*Radom, Czerwiec '76*" [Radom, June '76], which had been published by the rehabilitation committee and narrated the events of the uprising.[4] When the city government published a book about the city in 1985, it covered the history of Radom only up to 1975; the June protest had become a nonevent again.[5] The authorities decided to turn the intersection in the center of the city, where the temporal memorial sat, into a no-man's land and planted bushes around the stone to make it invisible.[6]

When in 1991 (after the Fall of Communism) the city, now controlled by a group closely allied with the Catholic Church and the Solidarity trade union, began to make preparations to receive the visit of the (Polish) pope, John Paul II, in June, arrangements included making several alterations to the memorial site.[7] The memorial space thus transformed from a memorial to the workers' protest against price rises into a Catholic event. The first of these alterations involved relocating a cross-topped obelisk that commemorated the Kosciuszko uprising of 1794 against the Russians to the site where it had been moved sideways by the Communist government sometime during the 1960s. In turn, the monument to the events in 1976 had to be pushed to one side, off center, in order to position the obelisk in its original place. Several months later the city ordered another granite stone, similar to the memorial to 1976, engraved with a quotation from one of the sermons of the sixteenth-century Jesuit priest, Piotr Skarga, a famous personality of the Counter-Reformation from the sixteenth–seventeenth century. Skarga's sermons had been a source of patriotic rhetoric during the struggle for independence in the eighteenth and nineteenth centuries. The new stone with the quotation, to commemorate the pope's visit, was placed on the other side of the cross-topped obelisk, making the obelisk the symbolic center of the site. As a result of these changes, the monument seemed now to commemorate not the postwar tradition of working-class revolt against Communist dictatorship, as intended in 1981, but as the historic alliance of the Polish people and the church in their struggle for an independent and Catholic Poland.

4. Cf. David Morgan, "We Don't Make Heroes from the Lumpenproletariat: Remembering the 1976 Protest in Radom," *Polish Sociological Review* 2, no. 118 (1997): 133–47.
5. Stefan Witkowski, ed., *Radom* (Warsaw: PWN, 1985).
6. David Morgan, "The 1976 Radom Protest," unpublished manuscript, 1995.
7. The following description is based largely on David Morgan's manuscript.

There is a cross at the top of the Kosciuszko obelisk, and just below that is a small reproduction of the "Black Madonna," Poland's most venerated icon. On the front of the monument is an inscription: "The peasants under the protection of the National Government will be granted freedom and the right to private ownership of land, so that no one may deprive them of it. Tadeusz Kosciuszko. From the manifesto of Polaniec, May 7, 1794."[8]

Although the obelisk is marked with the date 1794, it is actually of much more recent vintage and was originally erected by the villages named on the back of the memorial for a completely different reason: not to commemorate Kosciuszko, but to commemorate the emancipation of the peasants by the imperial edict of Alexander II, the Russian "Czar Liberator," in 1864, a time when Russia—partly as a result of the defeat of the Kosciuszko revolt—ruled this part of Poland. It was only in 1917, after the Romanov dynasty had been swept away by the revolution, that the face of the monument was changed on the 100th anniversary of Kosciuszko's birth. Now, the Germans occupied this part of Poland; only a year later—in 1918— would come the rebirth of the Polish state. What had originally been a memorial from a peasantry grateful for their liberation from serfdom to a Russian czar, had become a monument to an earlier failed struggle against Russian occupation.[9]

(After the Fall of the Communist regime, the newly reconstituted rehabilitation committee decided not to go forward with the original plan to erect a permanent monument in memory of the 1976 anti-Communist uprising in place of the temporary stone memorial. The surfacing of the fact

8. The uprising led by Kosciuszko attempted to reverse the effects of the earlier two partitions of Polish territory by the Prussian, Austrian, and Russian empires. Kosciuszko was able to mobilize the peasants to support the uprising by promising them an end to their feudal obligations in the manifesto of Polaniec, May 7, 1794. After the failed uprising, on the Polish territory ruled by the Russians, the czar finally liberated the serfs seventy years later, in 1864. Kosciuszko lived twice in America. First he arrived there a month after the Declaration of Independence. As a military engineer he was assigned the task of designing and supervising the fortification at the heights of West Point, which Washington called the "key to America." West Point is the site of the U.S. Military Academy. The first monument erected on the land of the academy by the cadets was to Kosciuszko. He befriended Jefferson, and, after he left the United States for the second time, he appointed Jefferson the executor of his will. After having sold his estate and all his possessions in the United States, the money, according to his will, was to be used to buy slaves in order to free them.

9. David Morgan, "We Don't Make Heroes from the Lumpenproletariat," pp. 144–45.

that the sculptor, the designer of the original plan in 1981, Bronislaw Kubica, had sculpted a memorial to Boleslaw Bierut, the first Communist president and party secretary of Poland who was Stalin's close ally, served as a plausible argument for revising the original plan. The Bierut monument was commissioned in 1979 for Lublin, where Karol Wojtyla had taught at the Catholic University and served as a bishop. When Wojtyla was elected pope in 1978, the authorities decided to erect a monument to the Stalinist president and party secretary, who went to school and started his political career in Lublin. Bierut and his memorial were presented as a clumsy counterpoint to John Paul II, and the ridiculous sculpture, the figure in a short and female-style buttoned coat, disqualified the sculptor from building a memorial after 1989. So the stone remained . . . jut a bit off-center. In 1996 at the time of the twentieth anniversary of the Radom events, the local Catholic weekly pointed out "the almost miraculous symbolic resemblance of the three stones to the Holy Trinity.")[10] Instead of bushes, now the Holy Trinity.

*

In March 1957, in a memorandum, the Temporary Executive Secretariat of the Budapest Party Committee called the attention of the highest leadership of the party to "the undignified state of the graves of some of the martyrs of the 1956 counterrevolution, especially that of Imre Mező, Sándor Sziklai, and Lajos Kiss."[11]

We find it essential for the Central Leadership to decide about erecting a proper gravestone and later on a fitting memorial for the martyrs of the labor movement and the party. We suggest setting up a committee that . . . would recommend the names of those martyrs of the counterrevolutionary events, who could be buried in the Kerepesi Cemetery, *adjacent to* Kossuth's Mausoleum. . . . The same committee should also recommend a proper memorial, commemorating the 1919 martyr Communists and those who died during the time of Horthy's Fascism between the two World Wars.[12]

Already in May 1956—before the revolution—the Budapest City Council declared that the Kerepesi Cemetery should function as "The

10. Ave: Pismo Diecezji Radomskiej, Nr. 26 (105), August 24, 1996. Quoted by David Morgan, "We Don't Make Heroes from the Lumpenproletariat," p. 145.

11. Imre Mező was one of the secretaries of the Budapest Party Committee, one of those truce-bearers, who was killed on October 30, 1956, in front of the headquarters of the Budapest Party Committee on Republic Square.

12. MOL M-Ks-288-7/3. ő.e.; emphasis added.

National Pantheon," where only the greatest figures of the political, cultural, scientific, and social life could be buried in the future and only the important graves could stay in place.[13] From the documents of the party it is obvious that the real impulse for creating the "National Pantheon" and setting up the "Pantheon of the Working-Class Movement" was the urge to put the cemetery in order, to clear and homogenize the mixed graveyards, and to place, after 1956, the recent dead of the party in proper context. The proximity of Kossuth's Mausoleum—the largest, most decorative, and most famous funerary architecture of the country—would establish and reaffirm the martyr status of the dead, who finished their life on the good side. The other noteworthy element of the suggestion was to embed the victims of the counterrevolution in the epic of the long struggle between whites and reds, Communists and Fascists, hence the recommendation to bury the victims of the post–1919 white terror together with the Communist martyrs of 1956, "the second coming of the white terror."

The martyr cult—that, without exception, included only Hungarian Communists but no foreign, not even Soviet soldier victims of the events—provided the base and served as an integral part of the Communist understanding of 1956. While the summary courts tried still-alive perpetrators of the 1919 white terror and suddenly discovered Hungarian Fascists, who were involved in the 1944 events, together with the participants of the 1956 Revolution—in order to implicate the latter "by association"—in the Kerepesi Cemetery, a similar logic forced a new arrangement on the dead bodies. The name of the main road leading to the cemetery was changed in 1957 to Imre Mező Avenue (after the Budapest party secretary killed in front of party headquarters in 1956—the old name was restored after the Fall in 1990). In 1957 the Budapest City Council ruled that no ecclesiastical ritual—that is, no burial with the involvement of any of the churches—could take place in the cemetery. In the same year, the city council ordered a new and thorough arrangement plan for the burial ground. The clearing of a large area continued; already in the early 1950s a large number of bodies had been exhumed and transported to other cemeteries, in order to diminish the density of aristocrats and other former enemies of the people buried there. All the bodies from three large plots were exhumed to make room for the planned "Pantheon of the Workers' Movement" and for the "Mausoleum."[14]

13. Cf. Vilmos Tóth, "A Kerepesi Temető—1 (The Kerepesi Cemetery—1)," *Budapesti Negyed* VII, no. 2 (summer 1999): 93.

14. Ibid., pp. 94–99.

In the meantime, the secretariat of the party discussed a list presented by a special committee. The committee—along the lines of the "ideology of filiation"—was given the task of martyr naming. The list contained those who were considered worthy of being buried either in the "Pantheon" or under the planned monument: Socialist activists of the nineteenth century; Social Democrats from the beginning of the twentieth century; veterans of the 1919 First Hungarian Soviet Republic; internationalists of the Spanish Civil War; members of the interwar trade-union movements, anti-Fascists; Communists killed during the Stalinist purges in the Soviet Union; Communists and Social Democrats who died as a consequence of the show trials of the 1950s; Communist functionaries who passed away in old age or because of illness; and at the end of the list, military officers who were members of the secret police and who fought against or were killed by the "counterrevolutionaries" in 1956. The five most representative Communist victims who were killed during the 1956 fights (three of them while defending the party headquarters on Republic Square) were last on the roll call. There was a suggestion to include one of the heroes of the 1848 Revolution among the Communist martyrs. At this point the official historian of the party, a member of the Politburo himself, remarked that although the old nineteenth-century veteran was "the editor of the 'Workers' Journal,' he was in fact a peasant and for this reason was disqualified and disclosed from the Workers' Association."[15]

According to the original plan, the Pantheon was to be unveiled on November 20, 1958, on the fortieth anniversary of the foundation of the Hungarian Communist Party, but as a result of the difficult task of sorting out the right bodies and proper names, finding the most fitting design, locating some of missing bodies, and completing the necessary secondary burials, the Pantheon was finally opened—and not accidentally so—on the occasion of the fortieth anniversary of the 1919 First Hungarian Soviet Republic.

Some bodies intended for the new Pantheon were moved from other, less representative parts of the Kerepesi Cemetery. Others were transferred from various cemeteries around the city. Dead Hungarian veterans like Leo Frankel, commissioner of labor in the Paris Commune and member of the General Council of the First International, whose corpse was brought back from the Pére Lachaise Cemetery in Paris, arrived from abroad. Special

15. MOL 288. Fond. 5/83. ő.e. (June 17, 1958).

consideration was given to bodies and symbolic burial of personalities who could, in any way, be related to the year 1919. The names of all the important leaders of the 1919 Soviet Republic, whether they died in the course of the post–1919 white terror, or—as was the case with the overwhelming majority of them—as victims of the Stalinist show trials in Moscow, as emigrants in the Soviet Union, or as a result of natural causes, became inscribed on the gravestones. The name of the head of the First Hungarian Soviet Republic, Béla Kun, was also inscribed on the pylon of the Pantheon, although his body is still hiding in an unknown grave, perhaps in the courtyard of one of the Moscow prisons, where he was executed. His widow was granted a grave in the Pantheon.

The Politburo of the party ordered the minister of the interior to find the body of the commissar of the interior of the 1919 Soviet Republic, the head of the infamous "Lenin boys" who was killed by fleeing from the white terror following the defeat of the short-lived Bolshevik experiment in Hungary. In a secret memorandum, written to the Politburo, the minister of the interior explained all the extraordinary efforts, which the Hungarian secret services undertook in order to find the body in Eastern part of Austria, not far from the Hungarian border. The Hungarian ministry identified the three witnesses of the execution, smuggled one of them from Czechoslovakia into Austrian territory, searched for another witness in Transylvania, and questioned an Austrian police inspector who took part in the execution. But they could not find the body.[16] At the end of the 1950s, in the midst of the cold war and political tensions between Hungary and its Western neighbor, it was extremely difficult to search for the body of the infamous commissar, one of the initiators of the red terror during the 133 days of the First Hungarian Soviet Republic; he had been, after all, on the Western side of the iron curtain. Still, to include some of the best-known victims of the 1919 white terror besides the Communist martyrs of 1956 was of special importance for the planners of the new arrangement in the cemetery.

During and after the 1956 Revolution, altogether 574 bodies were interred in the Kerepesi Cemetery. When the Communist bodies were exhumed in 1958, the less-important officers, in most cases, officers of the hated secret police, were interred in a special parcel, where the uniform gravestones were arranged in a circular form. In the middle of the circle there is a not-so-spectacular sarcophagus with the laconic inscription: "Eter-

16. MOL 288. Fond. 5/238. ő.e. (July 20, 1961).

nal gratitude and glory to the heroes, who fell while fighting the counter-revolution" (the inscription is invisible now, because the sarcophagus is surrounded by densely planted evergreen bushes). The memorial does not specifically refer to 1956 and remains silent about the presence of the officers of the secret police; it is a rather shy construct. The inscription on the gravestones simply mentions the military rank of the deceased, as if they had been officers of the military and not of the secret police. Opposite to the entrance to the circle, the central gravestone of the memorial is dedicated to Colonel László Lukács. His life, his deeds, even the circumstances of his death do not seem to be exceptional, compared to the others buried under the uniform, gray stones. The dates, however, that frame Colonel Lukács's biography are the focal points of the Communist interpretation of the counterrevolution: László Lukács—as a fateful coincidence—was born in 1919 and died in 1956. He was born in the year of the counterrevolutionary white terror and died in 1956, as the victim of another "white terror," during the time of "the second counterrevolution."

*

The Pantheonization of the Kerepesi Cemetery started most probably with the reburial of Count Lajos Batthyány, the prime minister of the 1848 Revolution who was executed on October 6, 1849, and reburied in 1870. Until that time the cemetery was named on maps as Allgemeiner Kerepesser Friedhof, the Kerepesi Common Cemetery. On March 15, 1860, students organized an unofficial celebration in front of and in the cemetery, to commemorate the outbreak of the revolution twelve years before. The police shot into the crowd, killing a law student, Géza Forinyák. Besides the funeral of the great poet, Mihály Vörösmarty, in 1855, Forinyák's funeral on April 4, 1860, in the Kerepesi Cemetery turned into the largest anti-Habsburg demonstration in the city. His grave is in the wall of the cemetery, together with that of his brother, who died in 1906 as a general of the cavalry, a genuine secret counselor to the court (who ordered the shooting that killed his brother), and a deputy chief of the military academy. In the last third of the nineteenth century, the cemetery was turned more and more into the privileged resting place of the rich and famous. In 1874 a special segregated plot was opened for those who took their own life or were executed, who could not receive an ecclesiastical burial.

In January 1945 the Soviet offensive reached the Kerepesi Cemetery, where German troops were stationed. Engineering corps blew open the fence, and the Soviet army entered the cemetery, which became a battlefield for the next few days. The Germans succeeded in taking back half of the territory before the troops of the Red Army finally took possession of the contested ground.[17] The Soviet soldiers stayed in the cemetery for quite a few days; they lived in the mausela and buried their dead in that part of the cemetery, which later became the unified resting place of the Soviet soldiers. After 1956 the members of the Soviet army who died in the battle were buried in the same plot, mixed, undistinguished, with the dead of World War II. This is how those who defeated the revolution in 1956 could remain invisible among the multitude of the soldiers who died during the siege of Budapest in 1945.

On the recommendation of János Kádár, on September 7, 1956, the Politburo of the Hungarian Communist Party passed a resolution, as suggested by the would-be first secretary, "to bury comrade László Rajk in the Kerepesi Cemetery in a representative plot, reserved for the Communist martyrs. On the occasion of the funeral, the Budapest party committee should mobilize two to three thousand people."[18] Kádár, himself one of the show-trial victims in 1951, left prison in 1954, became rehabilitated, and became a member of the Politburo once more before the revolution broke out in 1956.[19] He who now presented the resolution on Rajk's reburial to the members of the Politburo had been present on the morning of May 30, 1949, at the closed meeting of the five highest-ranking members of the Politburo, when Rajk's imprisonment was decided.[20] Kádár, who shortly before Rajk's arrest succeeded him as the minister of the interior, together with the minister of defense (the deputy of the secretary general of the party), visited Rajk in prison (in a villa with a peculiar octagon-shaped room on Liberty Hill) to force him to confess.[21] According to the tran-

17. Krisztián Ungváry, *Budapest Ostroma* [The Siege of Budapest] (Budapest: Corvina, 1998), pp. 127–28.

18. Cf. Péter Sipos, *Gyászszertartás Budapesten 1956 október 6* [Mourning Service in Budapest, October 6, 1956], *História* (March 1989): 22–23.

19. Back in 1949, when Kádár was a member of the Politburo, the central secretariat of the party appointed him to oversee the first—at that time failed—Communist attempt to erect a martyr-monument, dedicated to "five great martyrs of the party" on a busy public square in one of the proletariat districts of Budapest. MOL 276/54/(Secretariat of the Hungarian Workers' Party).

20. Tibor Huszár, "Kádár János Rajk-perei" [János Kádár's Rajk Trials] (special issue: Who Was Kádár?), *Rubicon* no. 100 (June 2000): 13.

21. Péter Nádas, "Helyszínlelés," in *A Napló* [The Diary] 1977–1982, ed. Imre Barna et al. (Budapest: Minerva, 1990), pp. 24–37.

script of a secret tape of the meeting, Kádár, between two beatings—these are the breaks in the recording—did persuade Rajk; it was he who pressed Rajk to confess. It was he who gave the report on the investigation to the shocked members of the Central Committee at its closed session on July 11, 1949. He, who took part in the fabrication of the accusations, at the September 3, 1949, session, revealed to the Central Committee the proofs that meant to verify the accusation that Rajk—according to his self-confession—became a Western spy already during the Spanish Civil War, a police informer before World War II, and a Titoist who conspired to murder the leaders of the Hungarian party after 1945. It was also Kádár who later told the following anecdote: "The secretary general asked me to distract Rajk's attention on the day of his planned arrest, in order to prevent him from making phone calls, or notifying anybody. So I asked him to come up with me for a chess party to one of the villas of the party on Liberty Hill. When I heard the steps on the corridor, I looked at him and said, 'checkmate, comrade Rajk.'"[22]

He was there at Rajk's execution, when Rajk, with his last words, hailed Stalin and Rákosi, the Hungarian Stalinist leader, who played the central role in his doom. After the execution, the potentates, who watched their comrades being hanged, withdrew to one of the prison's rooms to celebrate and congratulate one another.[23] Cardinal Mindszenty, the archconservative archbishop of Hungary, another show-trial victim, was locked in

22. Ibid., p. 13. Kádár, like Lenin, played chess. (On the famous—and repeatedly doctored—photograph, "A game of chess in Capri, Italy, April 1908," Lenin plays chess with Alexander Bogdanov, who was soon to become his political enemy. Lenin was spending a week of vacation on Capri with the writer, Maxim Gorky, who is also in the picture. Bogdanov was expelled from the party in 1917, but his ideas on "Proletkult" became influential after the victory of the Bolshevik Revolution. "Gorky noted that Lenin, who lost the game, grew angry and despondent." Subsequently, some of the figures disappeared from the published versions of the photograph. Cf. David King, *The Commissar Vanishes: The Falsification of Photographs and Art in Stalin's Russia* (New York: Metropolitan Books, 1997), pp. 18–21.

Chess was not politically neutral in the Soviet Union. After 1924, when the Soviet team defeated France in the first-ever state-sponsored chess tournament, playing chess became considered as an act of loyalty to the regime. Cf. D. J. Richards, *Soviet Chess* (Oxford: Clarendon, 1965).

It was known that Kádár regularly played chess. After 1956 he closely followed the life of the chess association and appointed the chairman of the Reverence Committee to the headship of the Hungarian Chess Association.

23. Cf. one of Rajk's investigators, Márton Károlyi, who was with one of the co-defendants in his cell during the last hours and who was a close witness of the execution, in

one of the cells in the same prison when the execution was carried out. From the window of his cell he witnessed the execution that he later described in his autobiography together with the events that followed the killings:

After I learned that he had been hanged, my mind dwelt a good deal on Rajk's fate. For on that same October 15, 1949, I had had to watch an execution from my window, so that later I conjectured that he may at that time have been executed in the prisoner's yard. . . . There was a fairly large nail in my shoe, and I managed to pull it out. With the nail I broke some of the wires from the grating over the window, so that I could see out rather more clearly through the small gap. . . . Beneath the gallows stood a middle-aged man clad only in underwear. The hangman knotted the noose on the rope; the party of spectators [János Kádár among them] seemed to let that in no way diminish their good humor. But suddenly the babble of conversation stopped as the condemned man screamed: "I die an innocent man!" I spoke the prayers of absolution for him, and the execution was carried out.

There is nothing more depressing than a convict's funeral and a convict's grave. In many large cities there are well-cared-for cemeteries for dogs and cats with marble gravestones bearing tender sentiments; there are grave mounds, wreaths, ivy, hot tears, choking sobs. "We will never forget this beloved animal," the bereft owners say, and they mean it, for throughout their lives they will remember their grief. But nothing of the sort is accorded the prisoner when he closes his eyes and the noose is tightened around his neck. Neither his mother nor his wife and children will be informed of the time or place of his burial. No tears will be shed, no flowers strewn or prayers said over his grave. No stone or other marker will tell who lays there. Only the trumpet of the Last Judgment can reach such a grave. No one even sees the prisoner's grave.[24]

The next day Rákosi called Kádár. Kádár—according his later recollection—was rather gloomy. "Was it the execution that spoiled your mood?" asked Rákosi. "From the question I have instantly realized," remembered Kádár, "that immediately on the day of Rajk's execution, those who were with me there in the courtyard of the prison started intriguing and undermining my standing at Rákosi."[25]

---

a written confession describes the postexecution celebration in vivid details. Cf. Huszár, "Kádár János Rajk-perei," p. 19. One of the chief investigators of the trial, Vladimir Farkas, the son of the minister of defense, concurs to this account in his memoirs, published after 1989.

24. Jozsef Cardinal Midszenty, *Memoirs* (New York: Macmillan, 1974), pp. 150–51.
25. Quoted by Huszár, "Kádár János Rajk-perei," p. 20.

When in September 1956, three years after Stalin's death, and after the Twentieth Congress of the Soviet Communist Party, where Khrushchev, in his famous and secret speech revealed part of the Stalinist crimes, the Hungarian party, in the face of mounting pressure both from Moscow and from within the Hungarian party, decided to bury some of the most famous victims of the show trials, Kádár thought the party should mobilize two to three thousand people to have a decent crowd at the funeral. Instead, according to the *Paris Match*, three hundred thousand people were in the Kerepesi Cemetery on October 6, 1956. (See Figure 3.1.) Rajk and the three others who were hanged with him were found in a small forest not far from Budapest, where the bodies were carried a few years after the execution from the courtyard of the prison. On October 6, 1956, the bodies lay in state in front of Kossuth's Mausoleum and then were buried near the mausoleum in a plot reserved for the veterans and luminaries of the party. The bodies were moved later from here to the "Pantheon of the Workers' Movement." The 1956 Revolution in fact started from here; there was no way after October 6, 1956, to stop the unfolding events that led to the demonstration on October 23. The revolution started on the day of mourning and ended on November 4 when Soviet troops came back in. November 4 is now a day of mourning, the day of remembrance to the victims of the revolution and those of the postrevolutionary retribution.

*

At the August 9, 1957, meeting of the secretariat of the party, in the course of the discussion about the right bodies to inter in the "Pantheon," somebody asked why a certain person was included instead of his brother who probably had done much more to advance the cause of the proletariat. According to the answer the brother had to be left out, for he had committed suicide. (He killed himself in order to avoid being sentenced to death at one of the show trials.) It seemed that the definition of martyrdom depended "not upon the fact or manner of death, but upon the cause died for."[26] "I think that there should probably be a guideline somewhere that might state who can be considered a proper martyr," the secretary of the Budapest City Council said, expressing her hopes at one of the meetings devoted to the martyrological issue.[27]

26. David Loades, "Introduction," *Martyrs and Martyrologies: Studies in Church History*, vol. 30, ed. Diana Wood (Oxford: Blackwell, 1993), p. XV.
27. MOL M-Bp-1/1 PVB/67 (January 18, 1960).

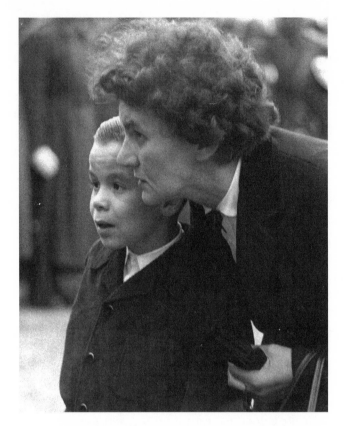

FIGURE 3.1. Mrs. Júlia Rajk with her son László Rajk at
the reburial of László Rajk Sr., October 6, 1956. MTI Photo
Archives.

Selecting the bodies was not an easy task. It turned out that the overwhelming majority of the veterans, worthy of consideration either in, under, beside, or near the "Pantheon" ended their lives either in Moscow or
in Budapest under circumstances that could not be considered normal for
a martyr: as accused of Communist show trials that ended with a death
sentence. (They were martyrs only in the sense the New Testament uses the
term "Martus": a legal witness.)[28] Compared to the number of victims of
the interwar Horthy regime, the Communists did a thorough job. Most of
those who miraculously avoided the gallows, either committed suicide

28. Cf. The entry "Martus," in *Theological Dictionary of the New Testament*, ed.
G. Kittel and F. Friedrich (Grand Rapids, MI: Eerdmans, 1964–76, 1983–85), pp. 474–508.

(like Sándor Zöld, state secretary in the Ministry of Interior, who not only took his life, but killed two of his children, together with his wife and mother-in-law) or were beaten to death (like the famous Social-Democrat lawyer and later minister of justice, who met his fate during his interrogation in the cellars under the secret police headquarters in 60 Andrássy Boulevard). Three out of the five members of the secretariat who discussed the issue of the proper Pantheon spent long years in prison, after having taken part (four of the five members)—as persecutors—at the show trials of their comrades, and they would in less than a year collectively give their consent to the death sentence of Imre Nagy. (Kádár was involved in the imprisonment of two members of the secretariat; one of them, Kállai, "found himself in prison on April 20, 1951, when the secretary general of the Hungarian Communist Party, in order to prevent 'a wave of suicide among prospective show-trial defendants' arrested him together with several other leaders of the party.")[29] Under these circumstances it was difficult to find the right words to be inscribed on the Pantheon's facade.

Probably it was one of the first works of Christian hagiography, deacon Pontius's *Vita et passio Cypriani* (St. Cyprian's life and passion), that formulated for the first time the theological and ethical maxim that the exemplary life (*vita*) of the saint is almost as important as the martyrdom (*passio*) suffered by Christ.[30] According to the original suggestion submitted to the secretariat of the party, the dark sentence "They Died for the People" would have been inscribed above the gate leading to the upper chamber of the Pantheon. Kádár, who chaired the meeting, had, however, serious concerns: "There is a problem here, comrades, with the word 'martyr.' What should we do with those, who were not killed by the enemy but died instead in a tragic way [killed by us]? Are they now the martyrs of the labor movement, or are they not our martyrs? In my view, comrades the bottom line is this: as long as these people were alive, they lived for the party. This is what should be clearly stated." In turn, the Politburo decided that instead of the inscription "They Died for the people," the text on the memorial should be "They Lived for Communism and for the People."[31] (See Figure 3.2.)

---

29. András Nyírő, ed., *Segédkönyv a Politikai Bizottság Tanulmányozásához* [Manual to the Study of the Politburo], Interart Stúdió (Budapest: Interart Stúdió, 1989), p. 288.

30. Cf. *A III-IV század szentjei* [The Saints of the Thirteenth-Fourteenth Centuries] (Budapest: Jel, 1999), pp. 13–37.

31. MOL 288. Fond. 5/83. ő.e. (June 17, 1958).

FIGURE 3.2. "They Lived for Communism and for the People." The Pantheon of the Working-Class Movement. Photo: István Rév.

Until the spring of 1914 the whereabouts of the corpses of the Hungarian Jacobeans—executed in 1795—was shrouded in mystery. The reactionary government of Francis I, fearing the action of the people who sympathized with the aims of the executed, buried them secretly, during the night, in unmarked graves at an undisclosed place. In 1914, the chief archivist of the Budapest City Archive discovered the description compiled by an engineer from the end of the eighteenth century that pointed at the exact place of the burial. . . . After careful archaeological excavations, in the outer ditch of the old military cemetery the bones of the martyrs came into daylight. Each of them was laid in a separate coffin the cut heads placed in-between the legs. A then young anthropologist, now a professor at the Budapest University, identified the remains. He published a detailed study, illustrated with photographs, about the excavation that was published during the time of the Hungarian Soviet Republic, in 1919.

After putting together the bones, the remains were placed in small wooden coffins, sealed, and "temporarily" stored on the corridor of the Budapest City Archive. . . . The plan was to bury them on the "Bloodfield" [*Vérmező*] on the Buda side, where the Jacobeans had been executed. The outbreak of the World War and the unfriendly attitude of the official authorities, however, prevented the burial from taking place.

In 1919, the Hungarian Soviet Republic declared the martyrs as its own dead and started the preparation for both the burial and the erection of a proper monument. Because of the short time, however [the Soviet regime lasted only for 133 days], there remained no time for executing the plans.

The counterrevolutionary period [that is, the Horthy regime of the interwar years, officially referred to in history textbooks as the *counterrevolutionary regime*] did not want to grant special graves at public expense to the remains of the dead. . . . In August 1926, seven boxes were buried in the Kerepesi Cemetery (the authorities did not even care to put the bodies into proper coffins) secretly, without any festivity, in the presence of just two officials.

In 1953 the Hungarian Rubber Factory, which was expanding at that time, claimed that particular part of the cemetery, so the graves were emptied. The boxes, containing the bones of the martyrs were placed in an empty crypt on the outskirts of the cemetery. They are still there today. The ashes were found after one and a half years of tiresome research by one of the retired general inspectors of the Hungarian Railways. He sent a memorandum to the Historical Institute, and representatives of the institute, including myself, in the presence of the director of the cemetery, and the retired railway inspector properly identified the remains.

After all these events it becomes the task of the People's Republic both to bury properly and to commemorate the bodies of the Hungarian Jacobeans, who suffered martyrdom one hundred and fifty years ago while fighting for bourgeois progress and national liberty. The People's Republic should bury them in the appropriate festive way and mark the graves with a memorial column. . . .

The martyrs are the dead of all those Hungarians who believe in progress, the dead of the whole country; this is why the party and the government should be in charge of the memorial. A committee should be created, the composition of which should be such that the names express the gratitude felt by present-day Hungary for the martyrs who died for the progress of mankind and national liberation.[32]

Kálmán Benda, the author of the memorandum dated in May 1959, was a highly respected historian, a specialist of the 1795 Hungarian Jacobean movement, and later the rector of the Calvinist University in Budapest. At the beginning of the 1950s he was fired from the Historical Institute but was permitted to work as an archivist, digging up the documents of the Hungarian Jacobean conspiracy. He sent his memorandum to the head of the Scientific and Cultural Department of the Central Committee, who in turn prepared a proposal for the secretariat to the party. The

32. MOL 288. Fond. 33/1959/12. ő.e.

recommendation repeated some of the key sentences of the original memorandum but suggested

the remains of the Jacobeans should be buried in publicly granted representative place in the Kerepesi cemetery. . . . A proper memorial should be set up in May 1960 on the occasion of the 165th anniversary of the execution of the Hungarian Jacobeans. The ceremony should be modest without the participation of the public, in the presence of an official committee. . . . At the time of the unveiling of the memorial, the press should inform the country about the finding of the remains of the martyrs, and the historical significance of their movement. The Presidential Council should grant to the retired inspector general of the Hungarian Railways, who played a central and selfless role in finding the bodies, "the Medal For Socialist Work."[33]

From an historical point of view, the Bloodfield would have been the appropriate resting place for the Jacobeans. The *Ordo Executionis*, signed by the royal legal director on May 19, 1795, ordered that the beheading should be carried out in public on the meadow under the royal castle in Buda. "From the Royal Legal Director, we have received the order of the Highest Royal Court concerning the wish of the Emperor and the King in connection with the execution that should take place on the 20th day of the present month of May, at 5 o'clock in the early morning, in Buda, beneath the castle, on the meadow of the captain of the castle," reported the chief constable to the deputy-lieutenant of Pest County on June 9, 1795.[34] And, in fact, "on the 20th at 5:30 in the morning, through the Vienna Gate, the five condemned, surrounded by 200 cuirassiers, were led to the meadow in the lower city, named after St. Christina, besides the old military cemetery, where a small mound had been created with the chair on top of it, for the condemned to receive the deadly blow, executed with wild force by the headsman."[35]

On April 27, 1795, the Highest Royal Court sentenced Abbot Ignác Martinovics to complete loss of his wealth, degradation (divesting his clerical office, that is, literally, stripping in public his ecclesiastical vestments),

33. MOL 288. Fond. 7/71. ő.e. (February 9, 1960).
34. In *Kálmán Benda-Judit Elek, Vizsgálat Martinovics Ignác szászvári apát és társai ügyében* [Investigation in the Case of Ignác Martinovics, Abbot of Szászvár and his Accomplices] (Budapest: Magvető, 1983), p. 403.
35. Letter by E. W. to Count István Illésházy. Pest, May 20, 1795 (*Kálmán Benda-Judit Elek*, p. 406).

and death. He had to witness the beheading of the four directors of his two secret societies before losing his own head, and as the conclusion of the execution, the headsman was ordered to burn the handwritten copies of the manifestos of the secret societies, together with the French, Hungarian, and Slovak versions of Rouget de Lisle's *Marseilles*.

Martinovics was thirty-nine years old when he met his fate. He studied philosophy and theology, according to the biographical sketch included in his "political last will" written before the execution, and he spoke ten languages (including Russian, Serbian, Latin, Greek, and Hebrew). He was a close friend and the traveling companion of Count Ignat Potocki, the enlightened Polish politician and one of Kosciuszko's closest allies during the Polish uprising; became professor of physics at the University of Lemberg; was appointed chemist of the court by Leopold II, the Habsburg emperor; and invented a new air pump, a tobacco-cutting machine, and a harvester. He published *Theoria Generalis* in 1880, a work of algebra, dealing with the most important contemporary mathematical problems. He traveled throughout Europe, was elected member of several European learned societies and academies, and corresponded with Condorcet, Priestley, Guiton de Morveau, and the like. Leopold II promoted him counselor to the court, and Martinovics became an agent of the secret police. Under the rule of Francis II, Martinovics fell out of favor and lost the confidence of the court. He organized two secret societies, "The Society of Reformateurs," and authored its manifesto, the *Catechismus occultae societatis reformatorum in Hungaria*, and "The Society of Liberty and Equality," and wrote its catechism in French, the *Catéchisme de l'Homme et du Citoyen par Democrite la Montagne, citoyen français*, using the pseudonym Democrite la Montagne.[36]

Martinovics came from an undistinguished family, started his career as a Franciscan friar, left the order, and remained a priest. He was a small, balding hypochondriac with a hunchback who looked like a miserable creature. He was also fascinating, charismatic, a womanizer, a great manipulator, a

36. Besides Rousseau's influence, the "Catechism" bore the marks of the French materialists, mostly Holbachs's, that of the *Almanach du père Gérard pour l'année 1792 by Collot d'Herbois* (which was known in German translation as *Haus und Dorfkalender de alten Vatters Gerhard, eines französischen Landmanns, für das vierte Jahr der Freiheyt. Nach Christi Geburt 1792*) and Rabaut de St. Etienne's *Precis de l'histoire de La Revolution francaise*. Cf. Kálmán Benda, *A magyar Jokobínusok iratai* [The Documents of the Hungarian Jacobeans], vols. 1–3 (Budapest: Akadémia, 1957), pp. 1016–17.

master of intrigues, a secret police agent, and an enlightened and dangerous provocateur who had epileptic seizures and who desperately tried to at-
tract attention. After his arrest, he immediately gave up all his real and
imagined collaborators; wrote inventive and imaginative memoranda to
the emperor from his cell; uncovered fictitious global schemes allegedly
planned by the *Convent*; pretended that Robespierre gave his consent to his
conspiracy; and reminded the emperor that "I had warned you that what
has happened would in fact happen."[37] He uncovered himself and his conspiracy and gave up the best minds and the bravest among his contemporaries in order to regain the trust of the court. He read the Moniteur regularly, was a shameless atheist, saw himself as the martyr of dark ages and
dark forces; he begged for pardon and died without remorse, after having
watched the beheading of four accomplices of his conspiracy.

The Jacobeans were finally buried in plot no. 11/1 beside plot no. 12
where the veterans of the party were buried. In July 1989, in the very last
days of the Communist rule, János Kádár ended up in the middle of the
very same plot, isolated from his comrades and the nearby graves. Although the Bloodfield, where the executions had taken place (this is the official name of the park), would have seemed to be the right place for the
Jacobeans, still, it would have been a somewhat unfortunate and risky
choice for the party. (See Figure 3.3.)

On March 16, 1972, in a conspiratorial apartment, a secret agent
handed over a report to one of the sublieutenants of the Department III/III
(the department of the secret police in charge of the so-called inner reaction, that is, dissidents) of the Ministry of the Interior. The report describes
the events that took place on the previous day on March 15, the anniversary
of the 1848 Revolution. The agent went up to the castle district in Buda to
become the witness of the secretly planned unofficial celebration by a group
of university students. "Already on my way up to the Castle hill, while
standing in the bus stop, quite a few people joined me," wrote the agent,
which leaves the reader with the feeling that the man had a decisive, although perhaps unplanned, role in the unfolding events. Up in the castle
there was already a small group, and when the agent discovered a police car
nearby, he went over to the police, asking for the arrest of a tall, blond
young man who seemed to be the organizer of the memorial gathering.

37. Minutes of Ignác Martinovics's Examination by the Investigation Committee of
the Court, 4 Vienna, September 2, 1794, in *Kálmán Benda-Judit Elek*, p. 249.

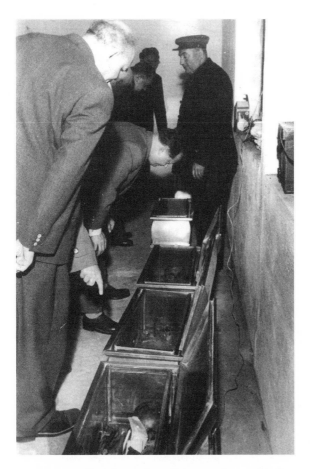

FIGURE 3.3.   Re-exhumation of the remains—with the
severed heads—of the Hungarian Jacobeans. Photo
Archives of the Budapest History Museum.

"The crowd, in response to the attempt of the police to arrest the young
man, became agitated and started singing. Subsequently, the police unit
forced the crowd to the stairs of the Fishermen's Bastion, where the demonstrators started shouting, calling the police the hit men of the Russians,
then the crowd started its way down to the Bloodfield," continued the report of the secret police agent.[38] (The agent should earn the trust of those
whom he is supposed to observe, and his efforts might lead him to the

38. Quoted by Kenedi, *Kis Állambiztonsági Olvasókönyv*, vol. 2, p. 86. The document that is referred to is most probably stored in the so-called Historical Office, the

front row of the crowd on its way to demonstrate against the regime, which employs such agents. In order to clear himself, the agent then uses the first opportunity to alert the police who, in turn, might provoke exactly the type of action that the presence of the agent was supposed to prevent. The presence of the agent amounts to a self-fulfilling prophecy. As Martinovics so succinctly wrote to the emperor, "I had warned you that what has happened, would in fact, happen.")

At the time of the incident and the report of the agent, the Jacobeans rested already in the Kerepesi Cemetery, in the vicinity of the "Pantheon of the Martyrs of the Workers' Movement." On the memorial of Martinovics and his co-conspirators, four misquoted lines from Petőfi's poem, "Vérmező" (Bloodfield) are inscribed. The Communists made use of the discovered Jacobean bodies. The history textbooks, used in high schools during the 1960s and 1970s, presented Martinovics, the agent of the court, and the Hungarian Jacobeans as part of the continual story of Hungarian progression, as the forerunners of the 1848 revolutionaries. The Jacobeans—according to the books—prepared the way for the spring of 1848 (which in turn was the forerunner of the spring of 1945, the victory of the Communists in Hungary).[39] The students, who decided to continue their forbidden demonstration in 1972 on the Bloodfield, had good reason to suppose that the Bloodfield was in historical vicinity to March 15 Square where Petőfi's statue looks over the demonstrators every year on the day when the 1848 Revolution was started.

Still, in 1960 the men of the Central Committee decided against the Bloodfield and deposed the Jacobean martyrs in the Kerepesi Cemetery. The

---

former secret-police records center. It is not clear from the text whether the document can be found in file V-156.043, V-159.241/1–7, or in V-159.297/1–2.

39. Already the First Hungarian Soviet Republic, during its 133 days, reached back to the Jacobeans. In early May 1919 the Hungarian Postal Service—under Communist leadership—decided to issue the first five of a new series of stamps, to express the *Weltanschauung* of the young Soviet Republic. The new stamps were issued with the portraits of Marx, Engels, Petőfi, Martinovics, and Dózsa (the leader of the 1514 Hungarian peasant war) with the semicircular text: Hungarian Soviet Republic. See László Surányi, *A Magyarországi Tanácsköztársaság bélyegkiadásainak és a Vörös Hadsereg tábori postájának története* [The History of Stamp-Publishing of the Hungarian Soviet Republic and that of the Field-Post of the Red Army] (Budapest: Akadémiai Kiadó, 1978), pp. 11–30, 63–105. Quoted by Boldizsár Vörös, *1848–49 történelmi személyiségei 1918–19–ben* [Historical Personalities of 1848–49 in 1918–19], in *Emlékezet, Kultusz, Történelem* [Memory, Cult, and History], ed. József Hudi and Páter G. Tóth (Veszprém: Laczkó Múzeum, 1999), pp. 47–48.

Bloodfield was stained not only with the blood of Martinovics and his accomplices but with bad associations as well. On May 24, 1957, while, as part of
the postrevolutionary terror, the summary courts tried and sentenced the participants of the 1956 Revolution, *Népszabadság*, the central organ of the Hungarian Communist Party, ran a sensational revelation, according to which

on 4 November 1956 [on the day when the Soviet army came back to Hungary to
defeat the revolution] the counterrevolutionaries were planning a "burial with
provocative aim" in order to bury their own dead on the Bloodfield. The eulogy
would have been presented by Archbishop Mindszenty, and the ceremony would
have signaled the beginning of a general anti-Communist "night of long knives."

According to the article, with the expressive title "White terror, for or
against," at the beginning of November 1956, the counterrevolutionaries
kept 2,929 Communist prisoners, and in line with their secret plans, the
execution would have taken place after the funeral of the counterrevolutionaries, on November 5 and 6.

The Hungarian National Radio reported on September 9, 1957, "The
counterrevolutionaries had prepared long death-lists during the final days
of the counterrevolution, and decided to execute the Communists on the
Bloodfield." The report also mentioned that during the night of November
3, 1956, the courtyards of some of the Budapest prisons had been strewn
with sawdust in preparation for the execution next dawn. This is what the
arrival of the Soviet troops was meant to prevent; this is why it was not
possible to wait any longer for the intervention.[40]

The Jacobeans were resting not only in the vicinity of March 15, but
there was some dangerous interference between their corpses and October 23
as well. Perhaps this played a role in the decision to bury them somewhere
else instead of in the most obvious place, the Bloodfield. The insightfulness
of the decision became justified retrospectively one more time. The secretariat of the No. III Department (the secret police) of the Ministry of the Interior, as part of its usual "daily information report," reported in June 1988:

Preparation by individuals belonging to the internal radical opposition groups, on
the occasion of the coming thirtieth anniversary of Imre Nagy's death shows that
the opposition forces want to turn the occasion into a large political demonstration. . . . Among the probable alternatives, opposition groups are contemplating

40. Kossuth Rádió 9/9 1957, 6:30 PM in Hungarian Monitoring Collection, Open
Society Archives (OSA).

the possibility of transporting a memorial by car to a selected point on the Blood-field and setting up the monument in front of a large crowd.[41]

(This did not happen. Instead, a symbolic monument, designed by László Rajk, was unveiled on June 16, 1988, in the Pére Lachaise Cemetery, in the plot donated by Jacques Chirac, then mayor of Paris.)

*

"We, who work on this sad and trying field of the division of labor, know better than anybody else the intense, wide, and everyday renewed public interest, filled with sincere emotions, that is expressed by the public, visiting the Pantheon of the Labor Movement," wrote the deputy director of the Funerary Institute of the City of Budapest in the introduction to the thin guide to the Pantheon.[42]

The mausoleum was completed by 1959, for the fortieth anniversary of the 1919 Hungarian Soviet Republic. It is not like the astonishing Lycian "home tomb" from chamber IV of the Sidon Necropolis that stands beside the "Alexander sarcophagus" in the Archaeological Museum in Istanbul and definitively does not resemble the sepulcher of the ruler of Caria, Mausolos, and his wife, Artemissa in Halicarnassus. We cannot see here what Pliny described: a tomb enlarged to truly heroic proportions and topped by an Egyptian pyramid. It is obviously different from the Church of Sainte-Genevieve that Quatremere de Quincy, the friend of Canova and David, following Mirabeau's death, transformed into the Pantheon of the great. And it does not recall a factory building, what Mayakovski dreamed of for Lenin, in order to evoke the notion of perpetual movement. And it is far from the remarkable constructivist funerary structure that Aleksei Viktorovich Susev built first of wood, then of stone on the Red Square for Vladimir Iliyich Ulianov, and above the entrance of which just one single word was inscribed: Lenin. Still, it is a remarkable "domatomorphic" con-struct.[43] It is a rather puritan, elevated wall covered by stone, but the wall is in fact a house, with two massive bronze doors that open to or close an

41. Kenedi, *Kis Állambiztonsági Olvasókönyv*, vol. 2, p. V.

42. Sándor Szerényi, chairman of the Reverend Committee of the Central Committee of the Party, ed., *Ismertető a Mező Imre úti temető Munkásmozgalmi Panteonjáról* [Guide to the Pantheon of the Labor Movement of the Imre Mező Avenue Cemetery] (Budapest: Fővárosi Temetkezési Intézet, 1977), p. 5.

43. Cf. Erwin Panofsky, *Tomb Sculpture: Four Lectures on its Changing Aspects from Ancient Egypt to Bernini* (London: Phaidon Press, 1992). Panofsky distinguishes between "anthropomorphic" and "domatomorphic," houselike monuments.

upper and lower chamber. The wall-house with the two chambers is a very distant commonplace reference to the "many mansions" in the Gospel according to John (John 14:2) and vaguely recalls the Pantheon de los Reyes in the atrium of the San Isidoro church in Leon, which King Ferdinando I built, by keeping in mind the close etymological relationship between the Latin *atrium* and the French *aitre*.[44] Despite the strange resemblance, there was not much in common between the walled garden of the "Pantheon of the Working-Class Movement" and the Early Christian notion of Paradise resembling a walled garden. There are three pylons in front of both sides of the wall with uninspiring Socialist-realist reliefs and a group of three figures in the middle, opposite the main stairs leading up to the wall and the doors.

There is strict order inside: the ashes of the "truly remarkable" personalities of the labor movement are housed in huge jars made by the famous Zsolnay *majolica* factory in the upper chamber; the bodies of those with the most heroic life stories, stored near to the doors, and the ashes of the less heroic "truly remarkable" in descending order further and further from the brass doors. In the lower chamber, once more in a strict martyrological order, rest the not "truly" but still "remarkable" martyrs.[45] On the pylons, marble plaques with the names and dates of birth and death of those veterans, who, although—as injustice of death—buried somewhere else, but under normal (?) circumstances would have a place in the Pantheon. Along the promenade leading to the mausoleum are the graves of the "most notable" martyrs who "earned a name in the movement," who were not cremated but buried in a coffin.[46]

In the mausoleum, that is, in the wall-shaped building, there was originally room for 365 urns, but until 1988 only 75 places became occupied. Today only 72 jars are filled: the families of three veterans moved their ashes to less representative but quieter places (following the example of "the heirs of Marshal Jean Lannes [who] were so outraged by the Pantheonization of Zola that they asked that their forebear's remains be transferred to the cemetery of Montmartre, well away from the writer's repugnant presence").[47]

44. Cf. Paul Binski, *Medieval Death Ritual and Representation* (London: British Museum Press, 1996), p. 74.

45. Szerényi, *Ismertető a Mező*, p. 10.

46. Ibid.

47. Mona Ozouf, "The Pantheon: The Ecole Normale of the Dead," in *Realms of Memory: The Construction of the French Past*, ed. Pierre Nora (New York: Columbia University Press, 1996), p. 343.

The first body buried along the promenade was the great Communist Freudian poet, Attila József, who was expelled from the party and committed suicide in 1937. He was brought here from plot no. 35, where he rested with his mother and sister. In 1963 his former wife was buried beside him in the Pantheon, but in 1994 the remaining members of the family decided to move the poet back to his mother's side. Today only the wife remains on the promenade with the veterans of the party. László Rajk found a third (but once more just temporary) resting place on the promenade, when, in the course of the completion of the Pantheon, his body was moved from the vicinity of the Kossuth's Mausoleum. However, when Kádár, the active participant of his execution, as the last act of the falling Communist regime, was buried nearby in 1989, Rajk's son took the bodies of his parents and moved them a few hundred meters away, in the vicinity of the Mausoleum of Count Károlyi, the first president of the Hungarian Republic in 1918.[48]

Even for the naive or completely ignorant visitors, there was something utterly wrong about the Pantheon of the Working Class. The almost uniform date of death on one of the pylons (1937, in ten out seventeen cases) leaves the uninformed perplexed. Along the alleys and in the veterans' plot there were too many bodies who died relatively young at the end of the 1940s and beginning of the 1950s (András Szalai 1917–49; György Pálffy 1909–49; Tibor Szőnyi 1903–49; and György Angyal 1911–49; István Ries 1885–1950; Sándor Zöld 1913–51, respectively), and there were too many names on the gates of the wall and on the pylons, honoring people who were obviously not buried there, who, for example, survived the carnage of the Spanish Civil War but then died in the Soviet Union in the late 1930s; others who were obviously not the victims of the Hungarian anti-Communist terror but who had to die somewhere else at the hand of their own comrades.

The gravestone of the former minister of the interior, Sándor Zöld, in itself would be enough to raise uncomfortable feelings in the unsuspicious visitor. There are five names on the stone: Dr. Sándor Zöld, 1913–51; Mrs. Dr. Sándor Zöld, 1916–51; Widow of Sándor Zöld, 1880–1951; Sándor

---

48. The act of Rajk's son recalled Mirabeau's de-Pantheonization: when Marat's body entered the Pantheon through the main entrance, the remains of the first great dead of the French Revolution were slipped out through the side door. (Marat, later on, was moved too.)

Zöld Jr., 1943–51; Anna Zöld, 1945–51—the minister, his wife, his mother, and his two small children. The eight- and six-year-old children are here, together with their parents and grandmother in that part of the cemetery reserved exclusively for the martyrs. It would be difficult to argue that they are not the martyrs *of* Communism (although, it is quite obvious, that, at least the children, did not "live for Communism and for the people"). In order, perhaps, to straighten the case, Sándor Zöld has a plaque on one of the pylons, with his name and the date of his birth and death. He is meant to be buried twice: once together with the members of his family, whom he murdered, before he killed himself, and once alone, as the veteran and martyr of the party. This is not surprising: materiality, that is, the concept that a "person was not a person without body" was evidently not a major concern for the developers of the Communist Pantheon.[49]

The "Guidebook to the Pantheon of the Working-Class Movement of the Imre Mező Avenue Cemetery" provides short biographies of not only those who are actually buried in and around the "Pantheon" but even of those who are present just in their names. Keeping in line with the inscription above the door to the wall-shaped Pantheon ("They Lived for Communism and for the People"), the biographical sketches resemble clumsy encomia, highlighting not a good death but a good life—especially since some of the panegyrics remained completely silent about the death of the martyrs. Twenty-four biographies provide only the year of death of those whose life ended in the Soviet Union either in 1937 or in 1938. In these biographies there is no mention of the cause of death, nor even death itself, just the last occupation or job of the deceased. These are the Hungarian Communists who perished in the purges. There is one exception: Lajos Magyar, a journalist and sinologist, one of the leaders of the "Oriental Secretariat" of the Komintern, who, according to the guide, allegedly died on July 17, 1940. Magyar, who studied the "Asiatic mode of production" and used the term long before Karl Wittvogel popularized it in his "Oriental Despotism" in 1957, immigrated to the Soviet Union after the defeat of the 1919 First Hungarian Soviet Republic. He was arrested and sentenced because it was too easy for the Stalinist leadership to presume interference between "Oriental Despotism" as applied to Chinese history and Soviet reality of the early 1930s. Lajos Magyar perished in the Gulag,

---

49. Cf. Walker Bynum, *Resurrection of the Body*, p. 11.

but—despite the precise date of his death in the Pantheon—his wife has never learned where, how, and when he had actually perished.[50]

The Pantheon of the Working-Class Movement, besides being the resting place of all sorts of figures, who had once belonged to "social progression," whatever that meant, and that of the Communist henchmen, their victims, and the relatives of these victims, is an assemblage of empty graves without bodies, plaques that refer to persons who were buried somewhere else, or whose resting place is unknown. There is great affinity among the dubious corpses, which held attraction for each other. This is a mausoleum of missing bodies: uninhabited graves, empty urns, and ill-referring plaques. There is no concern here for material continuity, no preoccupation with "I am not 'I' unless my body," and contrary to the notion that "it is certainly today true that considerations of self and survival take the body with impassioned seriousness," it is fairly obvious that this is not what was on the mind of the pantheonizers.[51]

The Pantheon with the known but empty graves, with the names of sometimes evidently dubious but elevated dead, was the corollary of the unknown grave of the executed prime minister of the revolution. Pseudo-graves in the "Pantheon," without real bodies or real martyrs, and the half-dead (not *semimortuus* but *semianimus*, who cannot die) who wander who knows where, whose bodies had been thrown in a ditch, who are outside consecrated ground and thus treated as nonpersons, relate to each other.[52] The unknown grave, the unspeakable crime, the unmentionable true martyr is part of the construct of the Pantheon of (in some cases) real graves of unreal martyrs.

Had folk wisdom prevailed, then corpses in the Pantheon would have bled to accuse their murderers. For the less naive and more knowledgeable visitors, it was obvious that victims and their executioners are buried side

---

50. The memoirs of Blanka Péchy, Magyar's former wife, the celebrated actress of the Salzburger Festspiele, mentions only that Magyar was arrested in December 1934, was sentenced for ten years in prison, and died sometime in exile, somewhere in Siberia (Blanka Péchy, *Regény* [Novel] [Budapest: Magvető, 1963]).

51. Walker Bynum, *Resurrection of the Body*, pp. 15 and 17, respectively. In the epilogue of her book, Bynum expresses her strong confidence in the survival of medieval doctrines: "Yet for all its incoherence and self-contradiction, the doctrine of resurrection has been of enormous consequence in shaping assumptions *we still hold* concerning personhood and survival. Much about *our current Western notions of the individual* has taproots in medieval discussions of the ontological significance of body" (p. 341; emphasis added).

52. Cf. ibid., p. 204, n. 14.

by side in or around the mausoleum, that it was the executioner who designed the place, who selected the bodies, who was the guardian of the fate both of the living and the dead. However, sometimes it is not absolutely clear whether it is a victim or an executioner who rests in a grave: some of the later victims started their career as executioners, while some of the later executioners in the Pantheon spent long years in prison before consolidating their position—at least, temporarily.

The post–1956 executioners could not do without the promiscuous arrangement. The Pantheon was constructed as "A Short Course," this time, not about the history of the Bolshevik Party, but, obviously, about the 1956 Revolution. Nothing shows more obviously the close relationship between the construction of the Pantheon and the urge to do something with the story of the 1956 events than the fact that on the day following the execution of Imre Nagy, on June 17, 1958, the Politburo had no more urgent issue to discuss than the proposal of the Martyrs' Sepulche Committee about the proposed list of those who would be interred in the Pantheon.[53] It was meant to be a *Biblia pauperum*—an expression first used by Pope Gregory the Great. Diderot reasoned that images were the literature of the poor—or a parahistory of the "counterrevolution": easily conceivable, neatly arranged in the proper context.

In accordance with the official understanding and propaganda of the causes of the so-called 1956 counterrevolution, developed by the Temporary Central Committee of the party already in December 1956, the counterrevolution had four distinct but still related causes: the injustices and "mistakes" of the pre-1956 Stalinist "cult of personality"; the work of the internal "counterrevolutionary" reaction; the external "imperialist" intervention; and the activities of Imre Nagy's group, which "took its criticism outside the party and into the streets, where reactionary elements were able to join in. . . . This fraction of the party opposition, which failed to provide a positive program for correcting the mistakes, one-sidedly attacked only the party, and did not distance itself from reactionary forces."[54]

The veterans, the members of the internationalist brigades of the Spanish Civil War, together with Hungarian Communists in illegality, who fought in Germany, Czechoslovakia, France, and even in the United States,

53. MOL 288/5/83.
54. The *1956 Hungarian Revolution: A History in Documents* (Budapest: CEU Press, 2002), pp. 460–63.

are here to demonstrate the uncompromising fight against the imperialists worldwide. They were moved here to remind the visitor that imperialism has always been the enemy of Communism, that the Hungarian Communists, in different historical moments and geographical places, and under different historical conditions, always had to fight, and they did fight—and not only in Hungary—the external enemy.

Unlike in the case of the victims of the Stalinist purges—where not even the fact of death is mentioned—the biographies of those who died on Hungarian soil, and typically in 1949, end with the laconic *epitheton ornans*: "became the victim of lawlessness." Hungarian victims of the show trials were needed to substantiate another element of the official version of the causes of the 1956 counterrevolution: the so-called cult of personality and the "lawlessness" that went with this deplorable practice, that annoyed the working people, and that made even some of the most loyal and well-seasoned Communists critical; this is what the internal and external reaction was supposed to be able to exploit. In order to strengthen their interpretation, for the leaders of the restored Communist Party, some of them executioners before 1956, others, victims of the Stalinist injustices, it was unavoidable to include some of the defendants of the Stalinist show trials from Hungary. The most prominent and least forgettable home-killed victims had to have a place among the special dead. It was unavoidable, though, not to mention that it was sadly not the class enemy who killed them. But there was neither political nor historical need to refer, even in a shy way, to the circumstances under which the accused of the Moscow purges ended their lives, although they were also needed for construction of the Pantheon: in their absence, some of the most important former Communist personalities would have simply disappeared from sight.

Most of the important and less-important leaders of the 1919 Hungarian Soviet Republic were built into the Pantheon, either in body or, typically, by name, as most of them had been buried somewhere else, mostly in unknown graves in the Soviet Union. The 19ers could not be left out, even though their bodies remained somewhere in the Gulag. Before 1956, before the Twentieth Congress of the Soviet Bolshevik Party, it would have been embarrassing to celebrate the Hungarian Soviet Republic too loudly and visibly, while most of its executed leaders were not yet rehabilitated in the Soviet Union. The role 1919 played before 1956 was simply to remind the country to the fictitious continuity of the Communist rule: what happened after World War II in Hungary and in Eastern Europe was not without autochthonous precedent. By pointing at March 21, 1919, when the Communists took over in Hungary, the post–World War II Communists proudly recalled the fact that Hungary was the first country that successfully followed the example of the Bolshevik Revolution. Every schoolbook carried the photograph of Tibor Szamuely, the head of the security forces, standing together with Lenin in Red Square. (Szamuely—whose body the Ministry of the Interior so desperately tried to find at the end of the 1950s in Austria—went on an adventurous mission and flew to Moscow to ask for military help from the Bolsheviks. He watched the May Day celebration together with Lenin in Red Square, when the famous photo was taken.) Instead of Béla Kun, the real leader of the short-lived 1919 experiment, who was either executed or died in prison in Moscow in 1939, Mátyás Rákosi, "Stalin's best disciple," the secretary general of the Hungarian Communist Party, a relatively minor officer of the Hungarian Soviet Republic, was presented retrospectively in the history books of the late 1940s–early 1950s as the towering figure of 1919.

The situation dramatically changed right after 1956. The Twentieth Congress of the Soviet Party, with Khrushchev's secret speech about Stalin's crime (this was a desperate, although unsuccessful attempt, followed by Stalin's physical removal from the mausoleum, to get rid of Stalin's shadow, his political body, the embodiment of the Soviet regime, that loomed much larger than life over the Soviet leadership), cleared the ground. What became so important in the aftermath of the 1956 Revolution was not so much the construction of Communist historic continuity, but the opposite: the alleged continuity, throughout the twentieth century, of the counterrevolutionary forces, against which the Communists had to wage relentless war.

After the defeat of the 1956 Revolution, the returned Communists were searching for the appropriate frame to make the events comprehensible both for themselves and for the defeated country. The atrocity that took place in front of the Budapest party headquarters during the days of the revolution—the execution, the hanging of the Communist defenders of the building—was the bloodiest, most spectacular, and the most photogenic event, which held the promise that 1956 could be inscribed in the memory as a genuine anti-Communist bloodbath. On June 16, 1958, on the very day when Imre Nagy, on Kádár's order, was hanged in the courtyard of one of the Budapest prisons and buried in an unmarked grave, the Party Committee for Canvassing and Propaganda submitted its proposal to the secretariat of the party on the suggested way to celebrate the fortieth anniversary of the First Hungarian Soviet Republic on March 21, 1959.[55]

A few photographs that survived the 1919 anti-Communist atrocities, from the time of the white terror that followed the defeat of the Soviet Republic, offer striking similarities to the scenes of the October 30, 1956, siege of the party headquarters in Budapest and the hanging that took place after the capture of the building. This was a chance discovery, and photos of the hanging of agrarian leaders of Somogy County, near Lake Balaton, from August 1919 found their way into the so-called *White Book* published about 1956 by the Communists, as the antecedent of the execution of the Communists in 1956.

Sándor Latinka, the head of the *Directorium*, the county Soviet, the leader of the local land-occupation movement, was one of the best-known victims of the local white terror. He was hanged in the woods, and his grave, despite the efforts after 1956, has never been found. After 1956 Latinka was turned into an emblematic figure: the worker who did not hesitate to help the peasants, who organized the movement to occupy the land of the local "feudal" landowners, who, instead of distributing the land, understood the voice of the time and organized agricultural cooperatives. He took up arms against the foreign intervention, became a soldier of indomitable courage, and was killed in the most sinister way by the white terrorists. His name was inscribed on the first pylon of the mausoleum; a play, a musical, a film were made of his exemplary life; streets, factories, agricultural cooperatives, and schools were named after him. He became the ultimate white-terror victim, the proper companion to the Communists hanged in the streets of Budapest in 1956.

The 1919 veterans were present in the Pantheon as blood witnesses, to testify about the continuity of the counterrevolution that broke into the daylight from its subterranean existence whenever there was a chance to take revenge on the Communists. Although I could not find a single document that would have proved that the Pantheon was meant to be an illustration to the official interpretation of the 1956 counterrevolution, for those who carefully inspect the graves, the stones, and the arrangement, it

55. MOL 288/5/87.

is obvious that—perhaps not quite intentionally—this was the real agenda. Although it has never been explicitly stated, 1919, the short-lived Communist experiment, and especially its aftermath, became the Archimedean point for the Communist reading of the 1956 events.

*

Besides providing a sufficiently dark resting place for the martyrs and serving as the stage and background of the catafalques at the time of important Communist burials, the wall had another, fairly obvious but implicit function: behind the wall, in plot no. 21, rest still those whom the secretariat of the party back in 1957 decided to cover and segregate by "horticultural methods." These are the "counterrevolutionaries," the innocent passers-by, the children shot in the streets during the revolution, all those who could not have been exhumed without major annoyance. The Communist martyrs were, however, duly exhumed and moved to the Pantheon that in turn served as solid wall to make plot no. 21 completely invisible. The Pantheon finally distinguished between "our dead" and "theirs."

The only remaining difficulty now is to decide who is ours and who is theirs. "The chief character of any memorial, one which lent its validity, was stability and permanence."[56] But after 1989, horticulture took things in its own hands. The Pantheon is still in place, unlike Dimitrov's Mausoleum in Sofia which was finally blown up after at least three unsuccessful attempts in August 1999, but the alleys leading to the wall and the wall itself are slowly being covered over by weeds, and stunted plants move the loosely connected stones farther apart. Whereas in the Middle Ages tombs provoked both memory and action and offered the opportunity of good works for the praying living,[57] this site resembles the abandoned city, where Maugli met the old, fangless cobra in Rudyard Kipling's *The Jungle Book*. What was meant originally as a *domus eterna*, an eternal residence, a resting place for the remarkable dead, now speaks about the old truth of *sic transit gloria mundi*. Names have been erased from the plaques on the pylons, (eleven plaques are completely broken) as if some inhabitants of upper and lower chambers had decided to move to another address in another world. The contours of removed gravestones, like the Rajk's missing grave, along the alleys are still recognizable, as the relatives in haste took the remains of the veterans of the old regime somewhere else, to a less-recognizable part

---

56. Binski, *Medieval Death Ritual*, p. 71.
57. Cf. ibid., pp. 71–74.

of the cemetery. The Pantheon is visibly abandoned; in its decay, it turned into its own monument.[58]

The three huge figures standing in front of the middle of the wall were originally intended to represent the unified "retrospective" and "prospective" program of the Pantheon.[59] A male figure on the left, who can barely stand, with his head deeply lowered, probably was meant to stand for a tortured figure, who would not be on his feet, save the strong arm of the erect worker in the middle, staring firmly into the future, giving a strong helping hand to the martyr of the anti-Communist terror. A strong, robust, female—were she not so visibly hesitant, she would be a close relative of Vera Mukhina's 1937 "Collective Farm Woman," on top of an eight-storey-high tower of the Soviet pavilion at the International Exhibition of Arts, Crafts, and Sciences in Paris—with a small shawl that covers her hair, is looking for support on the right side of the strong worker in the middle, who embraces her: she cannot decide whether to look back to the left side and mourn the tragic state of the falling martyr, or look into the future, following the gaze of her conscious comrade, and place her trust in the inevitable, the surely coming final victory of the working people.[60]

The program was both retrospective—the long, tragic but heroic ordeal of the movement and its firm supporters—and prospective—the coming triumph already on the horizon. The Pantheon, with the graves of the carefully selected many (from different, artificially connected periods of the labor movement), the architectural and sculptural composition, with the strict economy of spatial hierarchy, both around and inside the wall, was presented as a narrative, based on, recited by, and illustrated with the bodies of the dead. As if we found ourselves in a late and very provincial

58. "You come upon the ruins of the abandoned cities, without the walls which do not last, without the bones of the dead which the wind rolls away" (Italo Calvino, *Invisible Cities*, trans. William Weaver [London: Vintage, 1997], p. 76).

59. On the "retrospective" and "prospective," see Panofsky, *Tomb Sculpture*, p. 16. According to Panofsky, in the pre-Christian era, tomb structures represented the *cursus vitae*, the biography of the dead, while Christian grave monuments fixated the eye of the living on the future, on heaven, on salvation.

60. "The 'Worker and Collective Farm Woman,' by Vera Mukhina, has the right to be considered an epoch-making work of art, expressing the content and the most advanced ideals and tendencies of our age. . . . World art had never seen popular images of such striking grandeur" (*Isskustvo* no. 5 [1947]: 16; quoted by Igor Golomstock, *Totalitarian Art in the Soviet Union, the Third Reich, Fascist Italy and the People's Republic of China* [London: Collins Harvill, 1990], p. 132).

Saint-Denis, the house of the royal tombs, and hence the producer and the guardian of the *Grandes Chroniques de France*.

The decaying wall, slowly conquered by nature, in front of—or depending on the perspective, behind—the newly emerging post-Communist Pantheon, has no real meaning and most probably does not arouse strong sentiments in the public of the cemetery. It would have been difficult for the first post-Communist conservative government after 1989 to exhume the dead Communist bodies and to destroy the Pantheon. The conservative government made substantial real and symbolic investments to prove its Christian, especially Catholic, loyalties, and for a government with arch-traditional Christian values, it would not have been easy to start with digging and moving the dead. The Pantheon behind the massive stonewalls in the Kerepesi Cemetery remained largely insulated against protest: it was not too visible, and the public did not have to confront the Communist bodies every day. The Pantheon of the Working-Class Movement is unlike the Lenin Mausoleum in Red Square in front of the Kremlin Wall, in the heart of Moscow, or Dimitrov's huge white stone mausoleum, built in just six days and six nights in 1949 in the former royal gardens in Sofia, right in the center of the city at the most important intersection of the Bulgarian capital.[61]

After having been displayed in public for forty-one years, Georgi Dimitrov, one of the founders of the Bulgarian Communist Party, and the hero of the 1933 Leipzig trial—when he was accused by the Nazis for

61. Ilya Zabarsky, the son of Lenin's and Dimitrov's mummifier, describes the circumstances in his memoirs:

On 2 July 1949 Georgi Dimitrov, head of the Bulgarian Communist Party and former leader of the Communist International, died in Moscow. . . . A special train, similar to the one that had taken Lenin's body to Tiumen [when it was evacuated during World War II and was stored throughout the War in the two-storey building belonging to the local school of agriculture], was hired to take Dimitrov's corpse back to Sofia, and my father and I went with it. . . . When we reached Sofia we were surprised to find Dimitrov's Mausoleum ready, for he had not been dead more than a few days. This monument has been built in the capital's main square and, except that it was smaller and white in color, was rather reminiscent of Lenin's Mausoleum. Rectangular in shape, on top was a platform from which the Bulgarian leaders, like their comrades in Moscow, would review the parades that took place in Sofia on 7 November and 1 May each year. (Ilya Zabarsky, with Samuel Hutchinson, "Lenin's Embalmers" [London: Havrill Press, 1998], pp. 173–75)

having set the Reichstag, the German Parliament, on fire—was cremated and buried beside his mother in July 1990. The official guard, who patrolled the sepulcher so long as Dimitrov's body rested there, disappeared, and the white walls of the building became covered with graffiti. Unlike in the case of the former headquarters of the Communist Party, about fifty meters from the mausoleum, which became the target of violent, popular attacks after the collapse of the regime, Dimitrov's Mausoleum was spared destruction, especially so long as the body stayed inside the walls and kept violence away. After the removal of the mummy, the building and the site around it became the locus of political protests, youth festivals, rock concerts, and happenings, and the Bulgarian National Opera started a regular summer program at the site, by turning the rock podium at the mausoleum into an opera stage.

The citizens of Sofia slowly made peace with the empty building that has lost its original function and its symbolic place. By the time the government could muster enough determination to take a radical stand in 1999, according to a public opinion poll, "66 percent of the citizens of Sofia wanted the mausoleum to be preserved. Twenty-four percent wanted to preserve the monument as it was, while 42 percent wanted to rebuild and re-adapt it. Only 34 percent answered that they wanted the mausoleum to be destroyed."[62] In spite of its central locality, both on the physical and ideological landscape, by the time of the final political decision, the mausoleum became purged from guilt, politically and symbolically neutralized; its history became largely invisible and inactive.

In June 1999, after having the building completely whitewashed, the government surprisingly announced that the mausoleum would be destroyed. (The planned visit of Bill Clinton that took place in November 1999, probably played a role in the final and unexpected decision.) Despite the intensity of the explosive (300kg ammonites) used during the first two attempts, the building was just slightly damaged. According to the deputy prime minister, Bozhkov, "Everything encounters difficulties—democracy building, the political changes, the destruction of the mausoleum."[63] Despite the sepulcher's resilience, its demolition was completed by September 8.

62. Nikolai Voukov, "The Destruction of Georgi Dimitrov's Mausoleum in Sofia: The Dissimilitude Of An Ideological Resemblance" (Mimeo, 1999), p. 2, n. 2. The description of the fate of Dimitrov's Mausoleum was largely based on Nikolai Voukov's essay.

63. *Demokratsia*, August 25, 1999; quoted by Voukov, "Destruction of Georgi Dimitrov's Mausoleum in Sofia," p. 9, n. 12.

But only the visible part of the mausoleum has disappeared. What had been invisible before remained. According to the Bulgarian daily, *Demokrazia*:

The refrigerating system remained in the basement under the mausoleum. The camera with the expensive refrigerating installation, which some years before was preserving the mummy of Dimitrov, would remain, sealed in the basement after the destruction of the upper part. . . . No decision was taken concerning the water power station with two big and four small electricity suppliers. According to T. Dechev, the chief of the destruction activities, "the small power plants under the mausoleum could produce power for two living quarters of average size in Sofia". . . . The tunnels, which linked the mausoleum with the nearby buildings of the National Bank, the Party House, the Houses of the State Council and the National Gallery [the former Royal Palace] were also preserved under the ruins.[64]

*

On Sunday, December 31, 2000, on the last Sunday morning of the millennium, when I visited the Pantheon under bloodless sunshine, instead of the *Grandes Chroniques*, it looked more like a dim chronicle that "wishes to tell a story, aspires to narrativity, but typically fails to achieve it. . . . It does not so much conclude, as simply terminate. It starts out to tell a story but breaks off in medias res, . . . it leaves things unresolved."[65] The life of the Pantheon, together with the fate of living and dead Communists, came to a sudden, unexpected end in 1989. The chronicler, who would continue the story, is not around anymore, and besides, it seems, there is no story to tell. The Pantheon simply stopped existing; its dead are mute and without the hope of any meaningful function: they cannot form the body of any future historical recital. The bodies and the whole construction froze in time, which contracted into a point without dimension. The dead do not make sense.

Behind the wall, however, there is life. Plot no. 21, the one that had been surrounded by "horticultural techniques" after 1957, has been resurrected. The wall remained a demarcation line; now it does not hide what is behind, but hides itself, its front side and what is in front of the wall: the alleys with the ruins of the Pantheon. The bushes are gone, and a careful garden-design took over in plot no. 21: another new sacred resting place is

64. Ibid., pp. 12–13.
65. Cf. Hayden White, "The Value of Narrativity in the Representation of Reality," *The Content of the Form: Narrative Discourse and Historical Representation*, ed. Hayden White (Baltimore, MD: Johns Hopkins University Press, 1987), p. 5.

in the making. "Their dead" became ours: the victims of the street fights, the innocent passers-by, the children shot accidentally during the revolt, the ones, who after 1956 had been called "the counterrevolutionaries," became the heroes and the martyrs of the post–1989 brave new world. The old gravestones remained in the plot with the old inscriptions ("you disappeared suddenly, without warning, there was no time to say good-bye"), but new uniform, flat stones were placed on the surface, with the names of all the dead in this part of the cemetery. In 1998 a new memorial was unveiled: the tablets with crosses on top of them, made of pink stone, imitate folk gravestones from small village churchyard cemeteries, with dates inscribed on them: October 23 (the first day of the revolution); October 24 and 25 . . . and the last one, November 4. The cross is broken on the last stone, and there are two lines beneath the date: "Remembering 4 November, the date of the Bolshevik stab in the back."

There is a small, grassy parcel between the back of the wall and the resurrected plot no. 21. This part of the cemetery is officially designated now as plot no. 57. It was a no-man's land between the Pantheon and the plot surrounded by bushes where the "counterrevolutionaries" were buried during the time of the resistance in 1956. After 1989 the newly formed 1956 veterans' associations (the "Association of Former Political Prisoners"; the "World Association of Hungarian Freedom-Fighters"; the "Hungarian Freedom-Fighters' Association"; the "Association of Former Deportees"; the "World Federation of Certified Freedom-Fighters"; and so on and so forth), with tens of thousands of newly discovered veteran members, decided to bury their dead in a specially selected part of the cemetery, near, as near as possible, to plot no. 21. (Plot 21 is full, so there is no place for the newly arriving and newly discovered self-proclaimed anti-Communists.) These associations are the mirror images of the former Communist "Partisan's Association" that was established after World War II, with tens of thousands of alleged former partisan members in a country where the illegal Communist Party during the war had seventeen [?] registered members. (Naturally there was not only collaboration but guerrilla fighting as well in Hungary, with the participation of a few dozen partisans trained in the Soviet Union but mostly, with the involvement of non-Communist anti-Fascists who were not entitled to membership of the Partisan Association after the war.)

In plot no. 57, most of the gravestones carry not two but three dates: besides the dates of birth and death, 1956 is inscribed in the middle: András Sóskuti 1930–1956–1991; Klára A. Vass 1922–1956–1997 or Mrs. József Kis-Bakos, née Mária Szil-Arany 1914–1956–1999. Sometimes, besides the two biographical markers (the birth and death dates), 1956 is carved on the middle of the cross. The date in the middle is intended to prove that the dead person is not an ordinary one, but somehow earned the right to rest in this special place, behind the wall, contiguous to the emerging new pantheon in plot no. 21. In fact, the dead in the newly opened plot no. 57 intend to form a unified space together with plot no. 21: the new symbolic center of the cemetery adjacent to Kossuth's Mausoleum. Besides the self-proclaimed special dead, sometimes their relatives also strive for out-of-the-ordinary treatment by right of birth. Under the name of Mrs. József Kis-Bakos, nee Mária Szil-Arany, there is another inscription: the name of the still alive Ferenc Kis-Bakos, 1934–. His entitlement to plot no. 57 derives not only from the fact of being probably the son of Mrs. Kis-Bakos, who had whatever connection to the 1956 Revolution, which she survived, but at the bottom of the gravestone there are two lines, which meant to strengthen the case of both the mother and her son: "My mother taught me to pray for and love my beautiful country *in Hungarian*" (emphasis added). We are not in the Middle Ages, when the dead haunt the living; it is the living who haunt the dead.[66]

Post Scriptum

John Reed, the author of *Ten Days that Shook the World*, one of the founders of the American Communist Party, personified by Warren Beatty in the 1981 film *Reds*, the husband of the journalist Louise Bryant, who, after Reed's death married William Bullitt, Roosevelt's first Moscow ambassador, was present at the burial of the martyrs of the 1917 October Revolution in Moscow.[67] The 238 dead of the ten days of street fighting in Moscow

---

66. Cf. Binski, *Medieval Death Ritual*, p. 21.

67. Bullitt, who was born in 1891, served between 1933–36 as the U.S. ambassador in Moscow. In 1919 Woodrow Wilson sent him on a mission to the Soviet Union where he became acquainted with Lenin. After his return to the United States he worked for Paramount Pictures in Hollywood and probably met Eisenstein there. He moved to Paris, befriended F. Scott Fitzgerald and Ernest Hemingway, and published a novel on American socialists (*It's Not Done* [New York: Harcourt, Brace and Co., 1926]). From 1925 for more than a decade he regularly visited Freud who analyzed him in Vienna. Freud was willing to coauthor with Bullitt a study on Wilson (*Thomas Woodrow Wilson: A Psychological Study*

were the first special dead who were buried at the Kremlin Wall. Reed—who would not long after be buried at the Wall himself, as probably the only American who was placed at the heart of the Bolshevik regime—was among the mourners who had to buy tickets in order to attend the ceremony. Reed reported back to the United States about this first special funeral.[68]

[Boston: Houghton Mifflin, 1967]; it was published after the death of Wilson's widow). Bullitt helped and persuaded Freud to leave Vienna after the Nazi occupation. George Kennan worked with him in Moscow and, as he wrote in his memoirs, he was proud of the ambassador (Cf. G. Kennan, "Memoirs 1925–1950" [New York: Pantheon, 1967]), who, at the time of the famine, was famous for his extravagant parties in the Soviet capital. On April 23, 1935, Bullitt organized his "Springfest" in the building of the American embassy on the Arbat. The ambassador had one thousand tulips brought over from Helsinki; he rented out wild animals, bears and giant parrots among them, from the Moscow zoo, and everybody, those who in the following months and years were to be executed, and their future executioners too, were invited and treated well with caviar, salmon, French champagne, and Russian piroshki at the huge party (cf. Ch. W. Thayer [one of the secretaries of the embassy], *Bears in the Caviar* [Philadelphia, PA: Lippincott, 1950]). Bukharin was there, together with Radek, one of the leaders of the Comintern; all the highest military leaders, Tukhachevskii, Egorov, among them; the most famous people of the Russian theater, Meierhold, Tairov, Olga Lepeshinskaia, the celebrated prima ballerina of the Bolshoi Theater, Bullitt's mistress and, most probably, NKVD agent; and Mikhail Bulgakov, the writer.

We know from the diaries of Bulgakov's wife, Jelena, that Bulgakov became spellbound by the "style russe" of the ball and the crowd of future executioners and their victims—the mix of evil, high society, and the soon to be dead. The majority of Bullitt's guests were dead in a few months' time, and their executioners soon followed the fate of the victims. Bulgavkov was one of the very few surviving guests when he composed the last chapters of his famous novel, *The Master and Margarita*, which would be published in Russian only in 1967—the year when Bullitt and Freud's book on Wilson is published in the United States (J. Bulgakova, *Dnevnik Eleny Bulgakovoi* [Elena Bulgakov's Diary] [Moscow: Knizhnaia palata, 1990], p. 95). Bullitt's ball most probably served as the model for the twenty-third chapter of the *Master and Margarita*, "Satan's Great Ball," one of the most enigmatic texts of twentieth-century Russian prose. According to some knowledgeable and influential Bulgakov experts, Woland, the Satan, the "foreign consultant," the mover of the plot in the *Master and Margarita* was modeled after Bullitt. Cf. Alexandr Etkind, *A Lehetetlen Erósza. A Pszichoanalízis Története Oroszországban* [The Eros of the Impossible. The History of Psychoanalysis in Russia] trans. László Bratka, Ilona Kiss, Miklós M. Nagy, and Katalin Szőke (Budapest: Európa Könyvkiadó, 1999). Etkind, in his intriguing book, devotes a long chapter to the complicated relationship between Bulgakov and the eccentric, seductive American ambassador: see Etkind's chap., "The Ambassador and the Devil: William Bullitt in Bulgakov's Moscow," pp. 518–66.

68. Cf. Catherine Merridale, *Night of Stone: Death and Memory in Russia* (London: Granta Books, 2000), p. 122.

On April 22, 1978, at 2:43 PM, a secret burial allegedly took place at the most sacred burial site of the Soviet Union, at the Kremlin Wall, not far from Reed's (and Stalin's) grave. A small box of bones was tossed into a ditch and hastily covered by a thin layer of soil, not far from the only subway exit to the Kremlin, the Aleksandrovskii Sad (Alexander Garden). The ditch had been dug as part of ongoing construction work at the wall, and a few days later, when the work was probably finished, the ditch, covered by soil, disappeared. Almost nothing marked the inexpert ritual. Almost nothing, as according to an article, published in the dissident paper *Novoe Russkoe Slovo-Russian Daily-News*; the burial, in fact the service held before the event at the Kremlin Wall, was filmed in a Moscow apartment.[69]

Mikhail Makarenko, a Russian/Romanian Jewish anti-Communist activist, supposedly organized the burial. He was born under a different name, which he changed into the more Russian-sounding Gomgorskii. As a child he fled to the Soviet Union, where, at the age of eleven, he joined the Red Army. Later he changed his name to Gershkovich, and after he married L. S. Makarenko, he took his wife's name. He served in the Soviet army during the Korean War, undertook all sorts of manual labor, studied restoration, collected artwork, lost and regained his name (became Hershkovich for a short time) and Soviet citizenship, became an in- and outpatient at different psychotherapeutic institutions, and for a short time, became the director of a small gallery in Akademogorsk, the Soviet academic settlement in Novosibirsk, Siberia, where he showed works of early Russian avant-garde, and unofficial Soviet art, before the gallery was closed down in 1973 as a consequence of a planned Chagall exhibition—which, allegedly, would have provided the first opportunity for the painter who had emigrated after the revolution, to return to his home country. He wanted to use the small museum "for the rehabilitation of the titans." Makarenko—in between his other activities—spent eleven years in prison and in the Gulag and was threatened by forced psychiatric treatment. A group of prominent French intellectuals—Eugene Ionesco, the playwright; Pierre Emmanuel, the poet; Vercors, the novelist, among them—signed an appeal on his behalf. In 1978 he emigrated to the West where he organized *Memento—The Society for the Research of the Problems of Culture and Man Under Totalitarianism* and testified before the U.S. Congress about the involvement of forced

<hr />

69. Andrei Sedykh, *Zametki Redaktora* [Editorial's Note], Tuesday, January 18, 1983, pp. 5–6.

labor in the construction of the large Siberian pipeline. He left behind in the Soviet Union a 106-page typewritten autobiography, *Iz Moei Zhizni* (From my life), from which I have compiled this biographical sketch.[70]

It seems that Makarenko was the initiator of the "Red Terror Victims Memorial Day" on September 5, 1972, to remember the day when, in 1918 Sovnarkom RSFSR, the ruling body of the Soviet Union, signed the decree "Upon the Red Terror" that unleashed the decades of terror upon the peoples of the Soviet Union. The first celebration, according to Makarenko's own account, took place in the Gulag, in camp #VS-389-36, near Kuchino on the Chusova River.[71] Makarenko has stated on several occasions and in numerous *samizdat* writings that the anniversary became a regular annual demonstration against the terror. According to a piece published in the *Evroipeiskie Vedomosti* (European Herald), #1, September 1990, Solzhenitsyn gave permission to the Western printing of his *Gulag Archipelago* on September 5, 1973, as a gesture of solidarity on the day of the anniversary.[72] In Makarenko's description:

On the eve of September 5, in the evening, when darkness approached, we began to gather one by one in the half-built barrack. In order not to be found by searching camp administration, we have put the blankets on the windows of the barrack from inside in order for it to seem uninhabited from the outside. There were thirty-six participants representing all nationalities and religions to be found in the camp.

In the dark, we took stand along three walls of the barracks. In front of the fourth wall, on the white linen we have created a symbolic grave—several buckets of secretly brought soil. This grave symbolized the brotherly grave of the millions. Between the grave and the wall we put several rolls of barbed wire. . . . In the middle of the barrack on the box turned upside down, we put a clean towel and candles of three sizes on it.

The oldest among us, Evgenii Prishliak, lit the biggest candle—one for the millions perished—and put it on the very top of the grave. After that, everybody had to put candles for their relatives and close friends who perished in camps and prisons. I did not expect that: almost everybody present came up to the box and, some took just one, others five, six, and even eight candles. A minute, and the whole grave

70. *Materialy Samizdata*, issue 41/73, November 2, 1973. HU OSA 300/80/7/7.

71. Makarenko's samizdat article in the samizdat collection of the Open Society Archives. "My ne Proshchaem" [We Do Not Forgive], AC #3065. HU OSA 300/85/9.

72. Vera Genisaretskaia, *Pokoites' v Mire* [Lay in Peace], in *Evropeiskie Vedomosti* no. 1 (September 1990): 4.

was burning with candles. Those who put their candles last, burnt their hands—there was almost no place left on the grave, and the hands were trembling.[73]

Makarenko apparently decided to organize a symbolic secret but real burial of the remains of some of those who perished at the construction of the Belomor-Kanal (the White Sea–Baltic Sea canal), one of the best-known and most infamous forced labor projects of the Gulag system.[74] The bodies of the prisoners, tens of thousands of them, were not properly buried, but rather were thrown into a huge common grave between the eighteenth and nineteenth canal locks; the place is still a marsh, without any inscription and with barbed wire all around. According to one source, Makarenko remarked that 48 percent of the inmates in the camps along the canal were between the age of fourteen and twenty-four.[75]

73. In ibid., p. 4. Quoted by Dasha Shkurpela, "Mikhail Makarenko" (Mimeo) (Budapest: Central European University, 2001), p. 5.

74. On the Gulag system and on the construction of the Kanal in particular, cf. "The Gulag," online exhibition of the Open Society Archives and the "Galeria Centralis" (www.osa.ceu.hu/gulag). The "BBK" *Belomorsko-Baltiiskii Kanal imeni Stalina* (The Stalin White Sea–Baltic Sea Canal) was built in just twenty months, between 1931–33. At least 126,000 prisoners took part in the construction, and tens of thousands of them died in the course of the forced work. The canal, which, due to the ice and the harsh weather, is closed for at least six months of the year, is 227 km long, longer than either the Suez or the Panama Canal. On board the steamship *Anokhin*, Stalin toured the artificial waterway at the time of the opening and expressed his deep disappointment on the sight of the shallow and narrow canal. He ordered another, bigger one to be built, but the plan remained unrealized. At the end of 1932, on the suggestion of Stalin or the OGPU (the supervisory authority of the Gulag system) a so-called writers' brigade was formed, with the participation of 120 writers, to write the history of the construction. The work ("The History of the Construction of the Stalin White Sea–Baltic Sea Canal") was based mostly on collective field-trip experience of the participating writers (Alexei Tolstoi, Kataev, and Viktor Shklovksii among them). The work was published in 1934 and banned in 1937, after most of the writers became victims of Stalinist purges. The book was reprinted in 1998. Maksim Gorkii acted as the general editor. Bulgakov was invited to take part of the collective work but politely refused. Viktor Shklovsky, perhaps the most important Russian formalist literary theorist, the author of "On the Theory of Prose" (published in 1929) took a personal trip, in order to free his older brother, the noted dictionary editor, who was a prisoner on the construction site. He managed to assist in the release of his brother, who could not survive his next arrest. When questioned by an OGPU officer, "How do you feel here?" Shklovsky allegedly answered, "Like a live silver fox in a fur store." Cf. Cynthia A. Ruder, *Making History for Stalin: The Story of the Belomor Canal* (Gainesville: University Press of Florida, 1998), p. 58.

75. Report by Jim Anderson, "Dissidents Secretly Entomb Victims at Kremlin Wall," Munich, March 31, 1980, CND/UPI, p. 1.

All the sources that report the search for the remains and the burial rely on Makarenko's personal account. It is difficult to verify the description provided by either samizdat or the published Western accounts, because their only source is Makarenko's own testimony, in which the small expedition "struggled through forests and marshes, escaping highways and large settlements, secretly passing the guard towers, exhumed the bones and hiked back to Moscow."[76] Supposedly, Makarenko planned the secret burial to be held on September 5, on the Red Terror Victims Memorial Day, but because of the hunt of the KGB that could have arrested him at any moment, he decided to get rid of the bones as soon as possible, and he chose April 22, Lenin's birthday, the birthday of the person who signed the decree of the red terror.[77] Makarenko and the small group of dissidents who emerged from the metro station at the wall of the Kremlin presumably managed to complete their special funeral in haste, despite the fact that the wall was guarded and patrolled by the KGB day and night.

A film was made—or so it is said—about the religious service held in a Moscow apartment before the illegal funeral.[78] According to later recollections, besides the memorial service, the film shows the banks of the canal, covered by snow, the taiga, and the Kremlin walls with the Troitsk Tower. Anderson cites Makarenko, who said that as all the prisoners had died without blessing or communion, they wanted to offer a solemn memorial to those who had perished. First an old rabbi read the Kaddish, and then two orthodox priests delivered the ritual of the burial service, at the end of which one big and sixty-seven small candles were lit for all the dead, whose number—according to Makarenko—amounted to sixty-seven million.

Petr Starchik, a dissident songwriter who dedicated many of his songs to the victims of the red terror, claimed presumably in an interview to have taken part at the service:

76. Cf. Sedykh, *Zametki Redaktora*, with a lead "Ostanki Zhertv Krasnogo Terrora Pohoroneny u Kremlevskoi Steny" [The Remnants of the Red Terror Victims Are Buried Near the Kremlin Wall], published in *Novoe Russkoe Slovo* (Russian Daily News), Tuesday, January 18, 1980.

Cf. Shkurpela, "Mikhail Makarenko," p. 8. According to Sedykh, "The KGB tried to contact or contacted Makarenko through his son-in-law, W. Murashov, saying that 'if the bag with the bones were to be thrown away,' they would let Makarenko leave the USSR [at these times the KGB was in search of Makarenko who was lost from the sight of the agency]" (ibid., p. 6).

77. Cf. Genisaretskaia, *Pokoites' v Mire*, p. 5.

78. Cf. ibid., p. 4; and Sedykh, *Zametki Redaktora*, p. 5.

Everything had to be done quick, and for several days I was running around, trying to persuade different priests. Only Nikolai Pedashenko agreed. We knew each
other before. . . . He was very ill when I came to see him, and although he was not
able anymore to go out to the street, he agreed with joy, and said that to hold such
a service was the dream of his life. I do not even know how he managed to conduct the whole service. And it seems to me that this was his last service, as soon
after he died. He held the service with such an inspiration as if it were a holiday
for him. I do not remember a mourning service as happy and joyful as that one
was. It was a miracle.[79]

Citing Makarenko, UPI reported, "The KGB has managed to obtain
a copy of the film [from Makarenko?], and several dissidents shown in the
film have been subsequently arrested."[80] The film disappeared. Memorial,
the Gulag archive in Moscow, has no information about its existence.

79. Genisaretskaia, *Pokoites' v Mire*, p. 4; and Shkurpela, "Mikhail Makarenko,"
pp. 9–10.

80. Anderson, "Dissidents Secretly Entomb Victims," p. 2; quoted by Shkurpela,
"Mikhail Makarenko," p. 11.

4

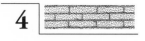

Holy Days

On October 7, 1957, not long before the first anniversary of the outbreak of the revolution, the Executive Secretariat of the Budapest Party Committee held its regular meeting. One of the secretaries, burdened by the weight of the difficult political situation, and her responsibility in guiding her comrades in the right direction, started with a

theoretical question on which we have to take a stand. In view of the fact that we came away from the building exactly one year ago, we should commemorate the anniversary. The only question is whether we should have the commemoration on October 30, or on November 4? I would prefer the 30th but other comrades would rather choose November 4. I think that we should organize the commemoration on the 30th, as this day is not only the sad anniversary of the defeat of the Budapest Party Committee, the symbol of the loss of the building and the battle, and the evacuation of the headquarters, but also a reminder of a glorious fight and the fact that Communists took up arms against the counterrevolution. . . . In my view, the only remaining question is this: Commemorating, but how? Should there be a large rally or not? Should we decorate our heroes with medals on that day or rather on November 7?

Another secretary raised concerns:

The Central Committee has already worked out the plan for a big centrally organized rally for November 4. If we decided to organize a rally on Republic Square [where the headquarters of the Budapest Party Committee was located; today it is the headquarters of the Hungarian Socialist Party, the former Communist Party]

on November 4 too, this would not be wise as it is almost impossible to organize two big rallies on the very same day. But there is another question before us here: If we go ahead with the rally on the 4th, could another one still be organized on October 30?

Somebody else had rather different concerns: "It is true that October 30 is the first anniversary of the attack and the bloodshed, however November 4 is the anniversary of the beginning of victory, since the new government was formed on that day. November 4 would and should become an important date in the history of all the Hungarian people. We should have it on that day!"

But others were of a different opinion: "We have martyrs," as one of the functionaries recorded in a matter-of-fact way, "whom we should honor every year. We cannot repeat what happened during the years before 1956: that we remained silent about important anniversaries year after year, for example, 1919 [the First Hungarian Soviet Republic]. . . . In my view there should be a smaller commemoration on October 30, and a real rally on November 4."[1]

Another functionary reminded the gathering that "it has emerged that there should be no rally on the 30th, but rather the unveiling of a memorial plaque on the wall of the Budapest party headquarters with the names of all our martyrs." A former racing driver, a future deputy minister of transport, supported the idea of the rally on the 30th; however, he had a question to raise: "Will there be a rally on November 7 this year, on the anniversary of the Great October Revolution?" (One should remember that in November 1957 the fortieth anniversary of the Bolshevik Revolution was approaching. As the Orthodox Church in Greece, Romania, and Russia had adopted the Gregorian calendar only in 1923, the revolution that—according to the Gregorian calendar—had taken place and was commemorated in

1. Béla Kun, the leader of the Soviet Republic, perished in a Stalinist prison, a victim of the purges. His name was barely mentioned before the Twentieth Congress of the Soviet Communist Party, before the rehabilitation of the victims of the Stalinist show trials, before 1956. When, in the post-1956 Communist historiography, the 1956 Revolution was reframed as a counterrevolution, it was described as another outburst of the constantly present threat of the "white terror" that had defeated Béla Kun's First Hungarian Soviet Republic. In order to situate the 1919–20 white terror, the Hungarian Soviet Republic, together with its leader, had to be rehabilitated. The fortieth anniversary in 1959 was a demonstrative commemoration when the Soviet Republic became firmly located in the continuity of the working-class movement.

November, was remembered and referred to as the Great October Revolution. This confusion aggravated the already voluminous problems, as 1956 became referred to by the surviving participants in Hungary as the "October Revolution.") The answer was: "No, no rally on the day of the Bolshevik Revolution this year." Then instead of a centralized demonstration, the race-car driver suggested several smaller decentralized rallies at the district level. A cautious female functionary, however, warned the participants at the meeting: "We cannot turn October 30 into a day of rejoicing; our duty is rather to honor our fallen martyrs." A well-known hard-liner came up with yet another alternative:

Serious thought should be given to the idea of organizing some sort of military parade on November 4 on the former Stalin square, where comrade Kádár will address the masses. [This is the square where, until October 23 of the previous year, the gigantic statue of Stalin had towered. The monument was destroyed as one of the first acts of the uprising. In October 1957, remnants of Stalin's boots still stood on the pedestal.] In this case we could hold a rally on October 30 and mobilize at least fifty thousand people for the military parade. People like military parades.

But another figure, who until this moment had sat silently in the corner, expressed serious concerns regarding a massive military demonstration: "I do not agree with the plan for a military parade. Because of the approaching anniversary the atmosphere is somewhat tense in October anyway. People are waiting for something to happen. The military parade is not without serious risks; it could be fatally misunderstood."

At the end of the long discussion the comrades agreed that since they did not have reliable information about the latest and true intentions of the higher leadership of the party, they could not and would not make any final decision, but instead would ask the leadership of the party to communicate its ideas, after which the Budapest Party Committee would act accordingly.[2]

A year before, on October 30, 1956, armed groups belonging to the noncentralized revolutionary forces had attacked the premises of the Budapest Party Committee. A cruel and bloody skirmish ensued, in the course

2. MOL BB. 1. Fond. 11957/8. ő.e. The document was published in Kenedi, *Kis Álambiztonsági Olvasókönyv* [Small National Security Textbook] (Budapest: Magvető, 1996), pp. 9–12. I have quoted from the original. There are slight differences between the original typewritten version and the published one.

of which tanks sent by the Ministry of Defense to help out the defenders of the building went over to the side of the attackers and ruined the building almost completely. Twenty-five defenders were killed, and when the headquarters surrendered and truce-bearers carrying the white flag stepped out of the building into the square, they too were massacred and their bodies hanged in disgrace.

This was the most significant and bloodiest anti-Communist atrocity during the twelve days of the revolution.[3] "The real content of October 23, its substance, was expressed on October 30. That which the 23rd had still tried to cover . . . came to light on the 30th. . . . The essence of October and November 1956 was revealed in the clearest way on that day. . . . On the 30th reality broke forth from beneath appearances," wrote the official Communist chronicler of the counterrevolutionary events of the square.[4] For the historian of the counterrevolution, October 23 actually happened on October 30. The reformist, humanist, anti-Stalinist slogans of the 23rd, the day of the beginning of the revolution—according to the Communist reading—functioned only "to disorient the students" who organized the demonstration on that day. What the march from Petőfi's monument to

3. David Irving, the noted Holocaust-denier (see the ruling and the opinion of Justice Gray in the case *David John Cawdell Irving v. Penguin Books Limited, 1st defendant, Debora Lipstadt, 2nd defendant,* on April 11, 2000. The High Court of Justice 1996–I-1113. Queen's Bench Division), in his "Uprising! One Nation's Nightmare: Hungary 1956" argues that "what happened in Hungary in October 1956 was not a revolution but an insurrection. . . . It was truly a movement of the masses bound by one common hatred of the old regime" (p. 5), the leaders of which were Jewish.

When researching his book, Irving had asked for help from the Hungarian Communist authorities. According to the testimony of the documents stored in the former party archives, the Hungarian party leadership, after much hesitation, decided to help the well-known right-wing British historian. The Communist ideologues sensed that the book by the anti-Semite author could strengthen the official Communist interpretation of the 1956 uprising, namely that it was a right-wing counterrevolution. Irving did what was expected of him: the central thesis of his thick and well-researched book was that, as the overwhelming majority of the Communist leaders before 1956 had been Jews, the 1956 Revolution was an anti-Jewish, hence anti-Semitic event. At the beginning of the book, Irving provides a "Who's Who in Hungary," in which he identifies as Jewish most of the Communist leaders and the reform-Communist leading personalities of the revolution. The name of the person in the "Who's Who" is usually followed by the laconic statement: "Jewish." Irving provides a long, detailed, and emotional description of the massacre on Republic Square, based mostly on Ervin Hollós and Vera Lajtai's officially approved *Köztársaság tér 1956* (Budapest: Kossuth, 1974).

4. Hollós and Lajtai, *Köztársaság tér 1956*, pp. 226, 227, 318.

the statue of General Bem, the Polish military leader of the 1848 Hungarian Revolution, allegedly tried to accomplish was nothing other than to defend Socialism from itself, only to correct the mistakes, to rescue the idea from the excesses of the "Stalinist cult of personality," argued the Communist apologist. (According to the original plans for the demonstration, János Kádár, who after his rehabilitation in 1954 was the secretary of the largest working-class district of Budapest, would have had to speak at Petőfi's statue. He chose not to.)

The practice of postdating that is at work here is the mirror image of the debate on the 30th versus the 4th (the 23rd that happened in fact on the 30th, while the 30th in fact took place on November 4). After 1956, whenever the Communists wanted to prove the brutality of the "counterrevolution" (as 1956 was to be invariably defined in Communist historiography), and emphasize the merciless anti-Communist nature of the events, they always referred to "Republic [Köztársaság] Square." "*Köztársaság Square and other similar atrocities*" became the *epitheton ornans* of the "white terror."

On October 30, 1957, following the tiresome and cautious discussions of the Executive Committee, a rally was held on the square. It was the first and last big rally on that day after 1956, as from 1958 onward the remembrance was held strictly on November 4, when the Soviet army came back in 1956, and not on the day when the party headquarters fell. The commemoration followed a rigid ritual: wreaths were laid on the memorial tablet and later at the foot of the huge monument erected in the middle of the square in memory of the martyrs; there were short speeches and then the dignitaries proceeded to the National Cemetery, not far from Republic Square in Mező Imre út (named after one of the truce-bearers, a secretary of the Budapest Party Committee, who was shot and tortured on October 30 in the square) to lay wreaths at the Pantheon of the Martyrs of the Workers' Movement, and finally decorated the Memorial of the Soviet Heroes on Liberty Square, which still stands today in front of the American Embassy, just under the window of the late Cardinal Mindszenty, who had received political asylum in the embassy on the morning of November 4, 1956.

With one single exception—on the occasion of the tenth anniversary in 1966—Kádár, the secretary general of the party, never attended the memorial services. Until 1965 not even the Central Committee of the party officially took part in the ritual, except for the first secretary of the Budapest Party Committee, who was customarily a member of both the Central Committee and the Politburo. In 1960, an extraordinary memorial ceremony was held on October 30 to mark the unveiling of the monument to the gigantic, falling, but even in defeat victorious, *heroes*, on Republic Square (interred today in the "Sculpture Park"), but according to the decision of the Politburo only five hundred "representatives of Budapest's working class" were allowed to be invited.[5] In 1965, the chairperson of the "Reverence Committee" of the party wrote a confidential memorandum to the secretariat in which he repeated the question:

Annually on the fourth of November the Budapest Party Committee, the Ministry of Defense, the Ministry of the Interior, the Communist Youth Organization and Hungarian Association of Partisans lay wreaths at the graves and at the mausoleum of those outstanding fighters who fell victim to the counterrevolution. This commemoration is covered by the press, the radio, and television every year, and on each occasion many people ask the question: Why does the Central Committee not take part in a commemoration that has such national significance? This is the reason why we suggest that on November 4 every year two comrades selected by the Central Committee should participate in wreath-laying at the monument and in the cemetery.[6]

In response to the suggestion, on October 26, 1965, the Central Committee decided to delegate two of its members to take part in the celebrations.[7]

*

Choosing between October 30 and November 4 was not the first difficult official calendrical decision that the rulers of Hungary had to face. In 1897, three years after Kossuth died in exile and his corpse was brought back and buried in Hungary, and thirty years after the 1867 Compromise between Austria and Hungary, Kossuth's son Ferenc, a member of parliament, proposed in the House an official celebration on March 15, the day when in 1848 the anti-Habsburg revolution broke out in Pest. March 15, 1898, was to be the fiftieth anniversary of the day when censorship was abolished, the free press was born, and the people rose against both Habsburg absolutism and feudal institutions. March 15 was remembered as the symbolic date of freedom and liberty, and although the revolution was a bloodless victory in 1848, twelve years later in 1860, when students tried to

5. MOL 288. Fond. 5./206 ő.e. (October 25, 1966).
6. MOL 288. Fond. 22/1965./1/ő.e.
7. MOL 288. Fond. 7./246 ő.e. (October 26, 1965).

commemorate the anniversary of the event unofficially by organizing a celebration in the National Cemetery, the police fired into the crowd at the gate, killing a law student. From that year onward it became obvious that March 15 could not be the official anniversary of the revolution but the day of opposition, a day that belonged not to the authorities but to the street. This is what Kossuth's son—a member of the opposition in parliament—wanted to rectify when he proposed an official holiday instead.

For his father, Lajos Kossuth, who was the head of the revolutionary government, it was April 14—rather than March 15—that had significance worthy of remembrance. Already in 1849, in a letter written to his wife, he expressed his amazement over the fact that people were willing to commemorate the first anniversary of March 15, when "besides some noise in Pest, nothing else happened." (Kossuth was not in Pest on that day in 1848, and was not one of the radicals of the revolution. Later on, he allegedly said, "Although, I consider Pest the heart of the country still, as a lawmaker, I will not follow its lead.")[8] For him the day of the dethronement of the Habsburgs, and his proclamation of the Decree of Independence, a year later on April 14, 1849, in the Great Church of Debrecen in eastern Hungary was the day significant enough to deserve commemoration.

Between the Scylla of March 15 and the Charybdis of April 14, the government proposed the middle-of-the-road date: April 11. In the end, the Law V. of the year 1898, signed by Emperor Francis Joseph, proclaimed April 11 a national holiday. On that day, fifty years earlier, in 1848, Ferdinand, then Habsburg emperor—threatened by the news of the revolution in Pest—had sanctified the "April Laws," whereby feudal institutions were practically abolished in Hungary. (This was the orderly, legal satisfaction of some of the demands of the revolution, still strictly within the framework of the Habsburg monarchy.) When the "April Laws" were later proclaimed in the Hungarian Parliament in Pozsony (now Bratislava in Slovakia), Prince Francis Joseph was present for the occasion. Later that year Francis Joseph became emperor; precisely because it was not he who had promulgated those laws, his future acts were not bound by the word and signature of his uncle, so he could take up arms against the revolution. In 1897 the same Francis Joseph, who in 1849 not only defeated the revolution but also ordered the execution of its leaders, was still sitting on the throne.

8. See Imre Szvák's remark in parliament on March 12, 1898, in *Diary of the Sessions of the Hungarian Parliament.*

The introductory words of the *Jubilee Almanac*, published for the fiftieth anniversary of the "April Laws," proclaimed, "It is mutual love and affection that connects the Hungarian nation to her monarch. And the nation is happy and grateful that she can celebrate the great anniversaries of her history in harmony with her Ruler, by expressing her faithfulness and obeisance to him. This is exactly how we feel when celebrating the joyful jubilee of our fight for freedom."[9]

"When choosing one from among the great days of that Spring that lies fifty years behind us, we cannot select any other day than the one when the word became incarnate," enthused the rapporteurs of the draft parliamentary petition (appointed by the government), justifying their choice of April 11.[10] "According to the Justice Committee of the parliament, as "true patriotism equals respect for the law," the day when the ruler enshrined the law with the signature of his royal hand in April 1948 is the only appropriate date for celebration and remembrance.[11] Kossuth's son Ferenc, who belonged to the opposition, disagreed: "According to the spirit of the constitution, although signing a law is the privilege of the monarch, it is a constitutional royal duty as well, since the king has no choice but to sanctify the will of the nation. . . . And we should venerate the memory of that ruler who lost his crown precisely because of his constitutional duty."[12] There were deputies (in the opposition) who asked: Why should the nation be reminded of the fact that it had a king who had to abdicate for what he had done in the spirit of the Law, promulgating the April Laws on April 11, 1848? Somebody else reminded the House that the act of sanctifying actually took place on April 14, 1848, not on April 11, so that the dethronement of the Habsburgs in 1849 coincided, in the most unfortunate

9. Quoted in György Gyarmati, *Március hatalma a hatalom márciusa* (Budapest: Paginarium, 1999), p. 24.

Jubilee, or the ceremonial anniversary related to the life cycles of monarchies, was a popular ritual, especially in the last two decades of the nineteenth century. Cf. Eric Hobsbawm, "Mass-Producing Traditions: Europe, 1870–1914," in *The Invention of Tradition*, ed. Eric Hobsbawm and Terence Ranger (Cambridge: Cambridge University Press, 1992), pp. 281–82.

10. Appendix to the document no. 360 of the Hungarian Parliament (March 8, 1898).

11. Gyula Zsigárdy, March 11, 1898 (Diary of the Sessions of the Hungarian Parliament).

12. Ferenc Kossuth, March 11, 1898 (Diary of the Sessions of the Hungarian Parliament).

way, with the day of the royal signing in the previous year.[13] ("Perhaps this is just a typographical error; but on this original copy, which was printed in the printing press of the parliament, and which I hold in my hand, I see April 14 as the date of sanctification," argued Géza Polónyi, a disputatious member of the House.)[14]

Easter, the center and starting point of all Christian holidays, unexpectedly seemed to offer a way out of the difficult calendrical dilemma.

This year—as a probable consequence of pure chance, but more probably by the grace of God—April 11 will fall on Easter Monday. Hungary is the land of Saint Stephen. Hungary is clearly a Christian state in the sense that people following other faiths, for example even the Jews, have already assimilated to such an extent that they celebrate Christmas Eve as much as we Christians do. So they too would accept my proposal. As I see it, if we celebrate the fiftieth anniversary of our liberty on April 11 this year, and if, by the Grace of God, April 11 falls exactly on Easter Monday this year, I would like to suggest enshrining it in Law: that in the future, in all the years to come, this country will not celebrate on April 11 but on Easter Monday. To remember its liberty, from now on, the nation would hold its National Holiday on Easter Monday every year.[15]

13. Géza Polónyi, March 11, 1898 (Diary of the Sessions of the Hungarian Parliament).

14. On March 14, 1898 (Diary of the Sessions of the Hungarian Parliament).

15. Gedeon Rohonczy, March 12, 1898 (Diary of the Sessions of the Hungarian Parliament).

The logic of the argument was similar to that presented by Zalmar Shazar, a member of the Knesset, the Israeli Parliament, and the minister of education and culture, in the course of debate on the right date to celebrate the independence of the state of Israel. In opposition to arguments that called for a fixed date in the sense of the Gregorian calendar, Shazar stated, "I can't imagine how it is possible to introduce this holiday according to a different system and a different spirit and concept different from those which we are accustomed to celebrating the Israeli holidays" (Knesset Record, "Arisal [Independence] Day Law, 1949"; quoted in Donald Handelman, *Models and Mirrors: Towards an Anthropology of Public Events* [Cambridge: Cambridge University Press, 1990], p. 290, n. 6). What has a fixed location in the Gregorian calendar varies from year to year in the Jewish ceremonial cycle; the difference can be a matter of weeks.

As Romme reminded the Convention, there are two ways of beginning the year: it may begin either with a season or with an historical event. But the [French] Republican reformers were spared this uncertainty, for it was their own history that had named the season. There was no need to argue for very long over the respective merits of equinox and solstice: the Republic had been declared on the precise day of the autumnal equinox. Romme's report stresses this miraculous simultaneity over and over again: "on

(According to contemporary accounts, on March 15, 1898, the day of the fiftieth anniversary of the revolution—which did not become the official holiday—the mob, hired by the government, provoked bloody street fighting in order to prevent peaceful celebrations by the citizens of Budapest.)

*

It was unimaginable that nothing should be said or done on November 4, 1957, or on the same day in any other year, until the Fall in 1989. The uprising in 1956 would not have been defeated without the Soviets; in fact it was only the Soviets who could suppress the revolution. It was the Soviet leadership that, after some hesitation, chose Kádár as its *Gauleiter*. On November 2, 1956, he found himself in Moscow, escorted by Soviet officers and officials to the GUM department store to buy a pair of shoes for himself, in which he could appear in front of the Soviet leadership.[16] "My personal impression," said Kádár on November 11, 1956, "is that the Soviets did what they did out of a strong sense of duty."[17] By simply celebrating the crushing of the so-called counterrevolution on November 4, the commemoration of the military victory would have equaled constantly reminding the country of the victors, the foreigners, the invaders, "the Soviet Army *temporarily* stationed in Hungary," and later on, "the South Division *temporarily* stationed in Hungary" (the euphemism remained in use until the middle of 1991, when the last Soviet soldiers finally left the country). To remember the foreign victors on November 4 would have inscribed in the memory of the country, year after year, the fact that the Kádár government was a puppet regime.

"To withdraw the Soviet troops would be desirable," stated Kádár at the November 11, 1956, meeting of the Provisional Central Committee of the Hungarian Socialist Workers' Party. "Politically it would be highly desirable. After some time we would have to sit down anyway in order to discuss the

---

that very day," the sun illuminated both poles at once and the flame of liberty illuminated the French nation. (G. Romme, *Rapport sur l'ere de la République* [Paris: Imprimerie nationale, n.d.]; quoted by Mona Ozouf, *Festivals and the French Revolution*, trans. Alan Sheridan [Cambridge, MA: Harvard University Press, 1988], p. 160)

16. Viacheslav Sereda and János M. Rainer, eds., *Döntés a Kremlben 1956* [Decision in the Kremlin 1956] (Budapest: Institute of the 1956 Revolution, 1996).

17. Protocol of the Meeting of the Temporary Central Committee of the HSWP on November 11, 1956, in *A Magyar Szocialista Munkáspárt ideiglenes vezető testületeinek jegyzőkönyvei* [Protocols of the Temporary Leading Bodies of the Hungarian Socialist Workers' Party], vol. 1, November 11, 1956–January 14, 1957 (Budapest: Intera Rt., 1993), p. 28.

issue of the withdrawal, and as far as the outlook is concerned, there is no question that sooner or later the troops should be withdrawn from the territory of Hungary. But for this to happen, we need our own force."[18]

At the 1956 December 2–3 meeting of the Provisional Central Committee of the Hungarian Socialist Workers' Party, János Kádár, in his political assessment, concluded, "The fourth cause of the events [that is, the 1956 counterrevolution], and at the same time *the most important moving force*, was international capitalist imperialism. . . . The real basis of the counterrevolution—perhaps one can say this with confidence—was probably not in Hungary. . . . The basis was abroad."[19] If international capitalist imperialism was the most important force behind the counterrevolution, it was no wonder that the Hungarian Communists were unable to deal with it alone; under such circumstances it was understandable that foreign help was needed to undo the counterrevolution that had been organized from abroad. Still, even under such a description, November 4 was an uncomfortable date for a regime that claimed that it represented the overwhelming majority of the country, in the name of which it had come back to power.

The overwhelming majority, however, had clearly done nothing to defend the Communists during the days of the uprising; it had done the opposite. One of the most urgent issues the Communists had to address after the Soviet troops reinstated them in power was how to reconcile their claim to have received public support with the facts: the active anti-Communist opposition, or at best the passivity of the majority of the civilian population and indeed of the armed forces during the uprising.

As early as its December 1956 meeting, the Central Committee came forth with the idea that the majority of the workers had been trapped: they went into the streets on October 23 in order to force the Stalinist leadership to correct its mistakes, to strengthen the achievements of Socialism, but the internal and external forces of reaction exploited the opportunity and manipulated the naive demonstrators.[20]

18. Ibid.

19. Protocol of the Meeting of the Provisional Central Committee of the HSWP on December 2–3, 1956, in ibid., p. 139; emphasis in original. According to the draft resolution, the most important proof of the role of imperialism was "the admission by Allen Dulles, the head of the American spy organization, that he knew about the Hungarian uprising in advance" (ibid., p. 215).

20. At this point I have decided to look for the verb "to correct" in a Hungarian-English dictionary, hoping that instead of "correct" I will be able to find a more suitable

From the point of view of the equilibrium of forces, the peculiar characteristic of the situation was that the forces faithful to the People's Republic and to Socialism commanded a clear majority even in the most critical periods but were on the defensive. The supporters of the counterrevolutionary restoration, in spite of the fact that they were in a minority position, attacked from all possible directions and managed to show great activity.[21]

For the historians of the counterrevolution, the slogans and the aims of the early days of the revolution testified to the strength and rootedness of Socialism in Hungary. While in 1919, when defeating the First Hungarian Soviet Republic, Admiral Horthy was able openly to resort to counterrevolutionary rhetoric and ideology, in 1956,

as a consequence of the strength of the Socialist forces, the counterrevolution had to wear a mask. . . . This is how the great carnival was prepared and gradually expanded. At a carnival, as we know so well, people usually wear masks. Before the masses of young and simple people, the real face, the real intentions, was covered by well-prepared masks. On Republic Square, on October 30, the hour of the black carnival arrived. And one could witness the moment when the counterrevolution threw away its mask.[22]

When the reactionary groups tried to divert the movement from its original aim, the majority immediately turned passive. Those who were passive, who did not resist the counterrevolution, were retrospectively presented as the supporters of Socialism: nonaction, in the face of counterrevolutionary manipulation was in fact understood as a vote for the Communist regime. The passive ones were waiting presumably for help, for the Soviets to come, for something to happen. As the majority remained passive, that is, covert partisans of Socialism during the uprising, the argument for majority support was supposedly well grounded and verified.

Despite this formula, November 4 in itself could never have legitimized the restored order. By remembering the martyrs who died on October 30, five days later, on November 4, the fact of Soviet intervention could be moved into the background, and the repression of the uprising

---

synonym. On page 1070 under "kijavít" (correct) I found the following expression: "[text] he corrected/altered/changed 56 to 58." The author of the dictionary, László Országh, had a minor role to play in 1956. (Imre Nagy was hanged in 1958.) László Országh, *Magyar-Angol Szótár* [Hungarian-English Dictionary], 2nd rev. ed. (Budapest: Akadémiai Kiadó, 1963).

21. Hollós and Lajtai, *Köztársaság tér 1956*, p. 76.

22. Ibid., pp. 231 and 197, respectively.

could be presented as a direct reaction to the brutal killing of the truce-bearers in front of the headquarters of the Budapest Party Committee. In this way, the defeat of the revolution immediately followed, even in the narrow chronological sense, the massacre; one followed (from) the other. "The 'revolutionary center' came into being *almost* immediately after the massacre on Republic Square," wrote the Communist chronicler.[23]

We now know that the so-called revolutionary center was set up not only by the Kremlin but *in* the Kremlin, when Khruschev, in a friendly way, placed his heavy hand on Kádár's shoulder and appointed him prime minister of Hungary on November 2, 1956, in Moscow.[24] The use of the "loose chronological catch phrase," *almost immediately* serves to fill both the temporal and spatial gaps separating the massacre from the defeat of the revolution by foreign arms. One of the locus classicus—and earliest—of this type of chronological displacement is the narration of Assurbani-pal's campaigns against Elam and Babylon. In edition "A" of the annals of Assurbanipal, the scribe used the formula *ina umesu*, "at that time" "in or-der to link the separated portions of the narration [in order to link an ora-cle with the alleged immediate fulfillment of the prophesy]. . . . Actually, this ambiguity is intentional. The scribe's technique—according to careful textual analysis—implies an artificial linking of time frames. The use of a vague linking phrase such as *ina umesu* to cover up chronological inexacti-tude is attested elsewhere in the Assyrian royal inscriptions," writes a stu-dent of chronological displacement in the Bible.[25] Unlike the Assyrian case, in Hungary the stake is only a few days and even that in a flatly secu-lar sense; still, the use of "almost" functions here "'as a kind of prophetic future' in the sense that events that had not yet occurred are spoken of as if they had already come to pass."[26]

The purposeful chronological ambiguity presents the crushing of the revolution as a story of crime and punishment. There is real chronological urgency here to narrow the temporal distance; the right temporal se-quence, the appropriate before-and-after needs to be firmly in place. The

23. Ibid., p. 312; emphasis added.

24. Cf. Sereda and Rainer, *Döntés a Kremlben 1956*.

25. David A. Glatt, *Chronological Displacement in Biblical and Related Literatures*, Society of Biblical Literature, Dissertation Series, no. 139 (Atlanta, GA: Scholars' Press, 1993), pp. 24–25.

26. Ibid., p. 54.

Communist chronicler struggles to establish continual connections, to give a measure of plausibility to a chronologically and thus historically implausible explanation. Temporal displacement functions to eliminate the spatial distance (geographical, political, and historical) between the two squares: Republic Square in Budapest and Red Square (with the Kremlin above it) in Moscow.

Until the very end of Kádár's rule, in spite of a very few imperfectly covered up traces, it was one of the official secrets that on November 2, 1956, Kádár was taken to Moscow, that his "revolutionary worker-peasant government" was formed in the Soviet capital, while the radio proclamation that was broadcast on the 4th, allegedly from the Hungarian provincial city of Szolnok, had in fact been taped back in the Kremlin. After having participated at the meeting between Imre Nagy and Andropov, the Soviet ambassador (later head of the KGB and secretary general of the Soviet party), on November 1, when Hungary announced her withdrawal from the Warsaw Pact (with his consent), Kádár disappeared from the building of the Hungarian Parliament, so mysteriously that even his wife genuinely knew nothing of his whereabouts.[27] Kádár resurfaced only behind the advancing Soviet tanks after November 4.

(The foundation myth of the post–1956 Hungarian government resembles in certain important respects the foundation myth of the post–World War II Polish Communist regime. Polish Communist historiography claimed that the so-called July Manifesto, which was considered the foundation document of the Polish Communist state was issued in Lublin on July 22, 1944. Incidentally at that time, Lublin was controlled by the anti-Communist Polish Home Army, the representatives of the exiled Polish government in London, while the Communist-controlled Committee of National Liberation arrived on Polish territory from the Soviet Union only a few days later, on July 27, 1944, and even at that later time, at Chelm and not at Lublin. The manifesto was unfortunately and most probably produced and issued while the committee was still in Moscow, but the fact was kept falsified for the next forty years.)[28]

27. Cf. *1956 A forradalom kronológiája és bibliográfiája* [The Chronology and Bibliography of the Revolution] (Budapest: Századvég Atlanti Kiadó, 1956-os Intézet, 1990), p. 63.

28. Cf. Andrzej Albert, *Najnowsza historia Polski 1919–1980* [Contemporary History of Poland] (London: Puls, 1991), pp. 434–36.

Inside and in front of the Budapest party headquarters, it was Hungarians and not Soviets who gave their lives to defend Socialism in 1956. They, and not the foreign soldiers (who also suffered significant losses), were the Communist martyrs who were officially remembered every year on the very day the invaders came, and not on the day when those Hungarian Communists had been killed. Events were not only covered up, but time became compressed: retribution (almost) immediately followed the massacre. There is a clear desire here to overcome any possible *temporal vacuum*, to bridge any possible—however narrow—chronological gap, to establish firm succession, and to mix up consecutiveness with consequence—post hoc, *ergo propter hoc.* The use of connectives, like *almost,* when reporting the alleged succession of the events, the consciously confusing choice of the date of commemoration and the locus of the celebration (November 4 at the scene of the events of October 30) implied an attempt to compensate for the embarrassing rupture of direct causal connection and chronological sequence. The past is rearranged by redistributing the dates that make up the chronology. The links that bind the successive events in the new chronology reveal the meaning of history—or at least, so it is felt.[29] The desire for this strong connection between events aims not only to reduce "the aberrant chronological elements" but also to eliminate them firmly, decisively, and irretrievably from the story.[30]

*

In 1966, after some hesitation, the secretariat of the Communist Youth Organization—following the example of the "Revolutionary Festivals," the continual narrative of the French Revolution, the revolutionary "days"— proposed and then decided to introduce "Revolutionary Youth Days." The real intention behind the proposition was to emphasize "the continuity and unity of the tradition of national liberation struggles and the revolutions, by connecting the 1848 national liberation struggle with the First Hungarian Soviet Republic of 1919 and the liberation in 1945."[31]

29. Cf. Patrick Nerhot, *Law, Writing, Meaning: An Essay in Legal Hermeneutics* (Edinburgh: Edinburgh University Press, 1992), esp. pp. 78–87.

30. See Michel De Certeau, *The Writing of History* (New York: Columbia University Press, 1988), p. 89.

31. An analoguous Romanian case is the 1984 attempt to re-present the 1784 Horea and Kloska uprising as a revolution and prefiguration of both Romanian independence and Communism. See Katharine Verdery, "Historiography in a Party Mode: Horea's Revolt and the Production of History," in Katharine Verdery, *National Ideology Under Socialism* (Berkeley: University of California Press, 1991), pp. 215–55.

Overemphasizing the revolutionary traditions, reinterpreting every national, antistatist (that is, anti-Habsburg) uprising of distant history as prehistory, as part of the prehistory of the Communist revolutionary tradition, had already backfired once in 1956. On October 23 the students marched from Petőfi's statue to the monument of General Bem, and every year after that even the rigid, half-hearted official commemorations on March 15 were unavoidably full of 1956 reminiscences—not to mention the unofficial commemorations by dissident groups on that day every year. To empty out both the original and the acquired possible senses of the Ides of March, the young Communist functionaries proposed to present it as a stage in the eschatology that led to the ultimate fulfillment of historical destiny—April 4—when the Soviet troops liberated Hungary from the German Fascists in 1945 and laid the foundation of the People's Republic and the Communist takeover. The present unfolds along the axis of time, punctuated with important dates, worthy of mention and celebration, that explain the real meaning of the present, which in turn gives significance to those special dates from the past.[32] From 1967 onward (this was the tenth anniversary of the birth of the post–1956 new Communist Youth Organization, and the fiftieth anniversary of the Bolshevik Revolution), the "Revolutionary Youth Days" were carefully organized. The secretariat of the organization even suggested that "the Minister of Culture and Education should order that from the 1966/1967 school year onward the schools should hold the Easter break between March 15 and 21 [irrespective of the actual date of Easter]."[33]

A holy day commemorates "essentially unique, incommensurate experiences," but the effort to bring March 15 under control turned and reduced the unique into one element in a succession of commensurate entities.[34] "The before and after of an event"—Reinhart Koselleck reminds—

32. "So August 10 completed the inaugural event of July 14 . . . and fulfilled the meaning of July 14. . . . The Revolution's past must be taken in hand and declared to be irreversible. . . . In order to bring the Revolution to an end and remove from the future its threatening uncertainty, the most urgent task was, therefore, to decide on the narrative of the Revolutionary events. . . . Removed from the whims of time, projected into the eternity of discourse, the Revolution would discourage men both from challenging it and from wishing to continue it" (Ozouf, *Festivals and the French Revolution*, pp. 173 and 168, respectively).

33. MOL 289. Fold. 4/209 (1966), p. 17.

34. Cf. Simon de Vries, "Time in the Bible," in *Concilium: International Journal for Theology*, ed. David Power, special issue of "The Times of Celebration" (Edinburgh: T. and T. Clark, 1981), pp. 3–13.

"contains its own temporal quality which cannot be reduced to a whole within its longer-term conditions."[35] But this is exactly what the young Communists were after: to force a new temporal quality on March 15, to regularize it, to correlate it, and to present thereby a story of succession, three subsequent dates, representing three springs, the earlier always being the preparation for the later. By the help of the closeness of the dates, the hope was to show the close causal relationship of the three subsequent historical events. As if the actors of the former events had a subliminal foreknowledge, as if they had been the agents of the future to come: the real meaning, the fulfillment of the sequence thus became evident only after the final date: the victory of the Communist revolution.[36]

"Continuity" is the word that the original document emphasized; a date (especially an earlier date) has no intrinsic meaning in itself: it is merely an anticipation, an announcement, a promise, which becomes decipherable only from the vantage point of the end of the tale. Fortunately enough for the organizers, the chronological and holiday cycle coincided: March 21—the anniversary of the declaration of the Soviet Republic in 1919—followed (from) March 15, while April 4 followed (from) the previous anniversaries. The calendar followed the intentions of Communist historiography. March 15 became thematically de-centered; Communist salvation was put in the thematic center instead.

In 1971 the youth organization went one (more) step further. Instead of March 15, the conventional starting date of the commemorative sequence, the propaganda department suggested February 23, the fifty-third

35. Reinhart Koselleck, "Representations, Event Structure," in *Futures Past*, ed. R. Koselleck (Cambridge, MA: MIT Press, 1985), p. 110.

36. "For example, if an occurrence like the sacrifice of Isaac is interpreted as prefiguring the sacrifice of Christ, so that in the former the latter is as it were announced and promised, and the latter 'fulfills' (the technical term is *figuram implere*) the former, then a connection is established between two events which are linked neither temporally nor causally—a connection which is impossible to establish by reason in the horizontal dimension (if I may be permitted to use this term for a temporal extension). It can be established only if both occurrences are vertically linked to Divine Providence, which alone is able to devise such a plan of history and supply the key to its understanding. The horizontal, that is the temporal and causal, connection of occurrences is dissolved; the here and now is no longer a mere link in an earthly chain of events, is simultaneously something which has always been, and which will be fulfilled in the future" (Erich Auerbach, *Mimesis: The Representation of Reality in Western Literature* [Princeton, NJ: Princeton University Press, 1953], pp. 73–74).

anniversary of the birth of the Soviet army, as the festive beginning. From that date on, the spring commemoration-series went as follows: March 8 (International Women's Day); March 15; March 21 (the anniversary of the First Soviet Republic); April 4 (the Soviet liberation of Hungary); April 12 (the anniversary of Gagarin's space voyage, the "Day of the Cosmonauts"); April 22 (101st anniversary of Lenin's birth); April 23 (seventy-fifth anniversary of the birth of Máté Zalka, internationalist officer in the Spanish republican army in the Civil War, later on a victim of Stalin's show trials in the Soviet Union); April 24 (the international day of youth fighting against colonialism and neocolonialism); May 1; May 8 (Victory Day in Europe).[37] (In this sequence, even spring—the symbolic focus of the anniversaries— lost its unique quality: February 23—at least until 1971—had been considered by both astronomers and meteorologists as a date still unquestionably in winter. It is true that even Easter—so closely associated with the arrival of spring—had sometimes been celebrated before the arrival of spring—at least in the strict, astronomical sense of determining the seasons.)

*

In the Eastern and Central European countries under Communist rule, Easter ham was served for dinner on Saturday evening; thus was the Lenten fast broken. For the majority of people, especially for children, this culinary practice was the source of both numerical and eschatological confusion. If the Resurrection, the advent, the coming of the Savior and of the spring, took place on the third day, two days after the Crucifixion, and Jesus was crucified, according to the Gospels and the adherents of the Dominican Pascha, on Good Friday, which is two days before His resurrection, why should people celebrate the Resurrection on the next day, on Saturday evening? Why on a Saturday, which is the special day for the Jews and which immediately follows Good Friday, thus contradicting the *triduum*—the three-day celebration—and the chronology of the story of the Lord's Passion?[38] Why not eat the Easter ham for breakfast on the third day, on the Lord's Day, on Sunday, on the first day of the Christian week—

37. MOL 289. Fold. 16/16 (1971), pp. 42–46.
38. "The anomaly of chanting, in broad daylight, 'This is the night in which Christ burst the bonds of death' is matched only by the misunderstanding and lack of appreciation of the faithful. The triumphant Alleluja is intoned with the observance of Good Friday barely past" (Frederick R. McManus, *The Ceremonies of the Easter Vigil* [Paterson, NJ: Anthony Guild Press, 1953]; quoted by John Allen Melloh, "Revising the Holy Week and Easter

which had replaced Saturday, the Jewish Sabbath—since 321 AD, the time of Emperor Constantine?[39]

The answer to this unsettling question started to emerge only after the Fall of Communism, when longer and longer Saturday night vigils (night watches) are gradually replacing the processions held on late, uninspiring Communist Saturday afternoons. Although the Easter vigil, as a nocturnal activity, was already suffering a serious decline as early as the eighth century, the Christian churches in the Communist countries were in a special position.[40] They could not expect believers to expose themselves, under the watchful eyes of the secret services, to long, heroic, tiresome stays in the church until dawn (until cockcrow, the traditional hour for the sacramental consumption of the vigil) on Easter Sunday morning; they were happy to be able to organize short processions around the local church, and to persuade their parishioners to show up despite the close scrutiny of the Communist authorities.[41] After the short procession the be-

---

Rites," in *Passover and Easter: Origin and History to Modern Times*, ed. Paul F. Bradshaw and Lawrence A. Hoffman [Notre Dame, IN: University of Notre Dame Press, 1999], p. 216).

Although the description was not specifically directed to the deficiencies of the Easter ritual in Eastern and Central Europe, this is an appropriate characterization of the situation that prevailed in that part of the Christian world during Communist times.

Although it explicitly ran against Orthodox canon, a common practice of the church in the Ukraine was to reschedule the ritual blessing of Easter food for the afternoon of Holy Saturday. The rescheduling served "to prevent bustle and crowding in churches, and to provide the possibility to have Eastern food blessed even for those who could not stay in the church through the vigil and the Easter Mass" (Nataliya Slikhta, "Church Life Under Soviet Rule: A Study on the Experiences of the Ukrainian Exarchate Between Two Local Councils (1945–1971)" [Mimeo], p. 206).

39. "By the time that the Christian liturgy had begun to take shape (second century), the Sunday Eucharist was preceded by a vigil service of Scripture readings and psalms. In this must be seen the origin of the Easter Vigil service, one of the striking celebrations of Easter in both East and West; from being a weekly observance the vigil has turned into an annual one at Easter only. As it is now constituted in the Roman Catholic missal, this vigil consists of the blessing of the new fire (a practice introduced during the early Middle Ages); the lighting of the paschal candle; a service of lessons, called the prophecies; followed by the blessing of the font and baptisms and then the mass of Easter. . . . This pattern is quite primitive and, in its principal elements, can be traced to the 3rd-4th century" ("Easter," Britannica Online *http://www.eb.com:180/cgi-bin/g?DocF=micro/184/21.htm*).

40. Cf. Melloh, "Revising the Holy Week and Easter Rites," esp. pp. 214–25.

41. It is true that since, at least, the late Middle Ages, as "a remarkable reversal of the earliest traditions of Christianity, the Easter vigil itself became the least well-attended

lievers rushed home to sit down to the festive dinner and eat the Easter ham. Everything had to happen in a hurry; there was no time to wait until Sunday, and the Resurrection arrived.

After 1989, however, partly as a reaction to the changes, and more so as a compensation for their past, more and more new converts, born-suddenly-again Christians undertaking longer and longer fasts—in church, visibly, in the company of other like-minded sinners—decided to follow the renewed strict rule of the church. ("The entire celebration of the Easter Vigil takes place at night. It should not begin before nightfall; it should not end before daybreak on Sunday. This rule is to be taken according to its strictest sense.")[42] And they stayed an uncomfortably long time in the

---

liturgy of the whole season, and what is more, for the convenience of the clergy, in the course of the Middle Ages it was moved back from Saturday night to Saturday morning, with the result that the drama of the Easter candle shining in the darkness was lost in the brightness of the daylight" (Paul F. Bradshaw, "Easter in Christian Tradition," *Passover and Easter: Origin and History to Modern Times*, ed. Paul F. Bradshaw and Lawrence A. Hoffman [Notre Dame, IN: University of Notre Dame Press, 1999], p. 5).

The Protestant Reformation of the sixteenth century got rid of the Easter vigil as part of the reformed liturgy of Easter. The liturgy under the Communist regimes showed new visible marks of the necessary compromises the church had to accept. But what is more important and more revealing is the zeal with which the church, in the former Communist countries, decided to stick to recovered and tiresome ancient practices after 1989, as a compensation for the previous compromises.

Whenever the preeminent feast of Easter coincided with May Day celebrations, the Ukrainian Orthodox clergy deliberately rescheduled the religious ceremony to allow believers to participate at the official public demonstrations.

> Diocesan administrators seemed not to worry about this coincidence and without objections complied with the demand of the plenipotentiaries to schedule services over the Holy Week and Easter for inappropriate time (early morning or early afternoon).

In the formulation of the higher Orthodox clergy in the Soviet Union, the coincidence of Easter and official May Day celebrations was a visible sign of the unity between the church and the Soviet people. According to the text of the sermon delivered by Fr. Melnykov in the church of Berdinansk, during the Holy Week of 1967: "Brothers and sisters! Orthodox! In a few days we will celebrate Holy Easter, which is linked to May Day celebrations. This close unity of two popular holidays is blessed by God and professes our [i.e., the church's] inseparable link with our people. God bless our eternal friendship with our people! Thank Jesus Christ!" (Slikhta, "Church Life Under Soviet Rule," p. 207)

42. See The Catholic Liturgical Library, Circular Letter Concerning the Preparation of the Easter Feasts—Easter Sunday. (http//www.catholicliturgy.com/documents/easter7shtml). "It should be stressed that Easter Vigil is celebrated during Easter night, and . . . it is one single act of worship" (ibid.).

church, taking part in the Easter vigil that nowadays usually finishes well after midnight.[43] In the early, primitive Christian liturgy, which followed the
Johannine chronology, the Passover night watch, the vigil, was extended to
cockcrow of Nisan 15, probably in part to delay the time of rejoicing until
after the termination of the feasting of the Jews.[44] While according to early
Jewish reckoning of the day—which is typical of cultures that follow a lunar
calendar—the day begins with sunset, the Greeks, who followed a solar calendar, counted the days from dawn to dawn.[45]

After the collapse of the Communist regimes, the Catholic Church
decided to follow painstakingly the minute details of the Stations of the
Cross, as if trying to clean itself of all the impurity of collaboration that
had been attached to it during the time of the Communist regime.[46] The
church—returning in this respect to its early roots and practices—emphasized the historicity of the Redemption. The positivist adherence to and
the literal representation of the alleged chronology of the events in Jerusalem could be seen as the counterpoint to the failed transhistorical eschatology of the Communist ideology.[47] As part of the pretentious post-

43. Following Pope Pius's encyclical, *Mediator Dei*, in November 1947 a movement
started inside the hierarchy of the Roman Catholic Church, in order to restore the proper
status of the Easter night vigil. In February 1951 *Dominicae Resurrectionis Vigiliam* was issued by the Congregation of the Sacred Rites for the nocturnal celebration of the vigil. This
was still an optional rite, but at the end of 1955, "the Restored Rite of Holy Week," reestab-
lished the compulsory nightly celebration of the vigil. Cf. Melloh, "Revising the Holy Week
and Easter Rites," p. 217. Eastern Orthodox churches never fully abandoned the ceremony.

44. See Thomas J. Talley, *The Origins of the Liturgical Year: The Liturgical Press* (Collegeville, MN: Liturgical Press, 1991), esp. pp. 1–77.

45. See G. J. Whitrow, *Time in History* (New York: Oxford University Press, 1988),
esp. Appendix 3: "The Calculation of Easter," pp. 190–93; and Talley, *Origins of the Liturgical Year*, pp. 13–18.

46. "The origin of the problem of the dating of Easter can be traced back to the
Babylonians. The rituals performed by the king-priest, particularly at the New Year Festival,
were regarded as the repetitions of divine actions and were meant to correspond exactly in
time as well as in character with the rituals on high. From this primitive idea sprang the belief that it was important to celebrate Easter at the correct date, since this was the crucial
time of combat between God (or Christ) and the Devil, and God required the support of
his worshippers to defeat the Devil" (Whitrow, *Time in History*, p. 32).

47. This compulsive obsession with the historicity of the salvation could be seen as
a return of early Christian efforts. Cf. "The phrase *sub Pontio Pilato* in later credal formu-
lae," in Talley, *Origins of the Liturgical Year*, p. 13. "Thanks to the 'historicism theory' of
Gregory Dix in particular, the development of Holy Week has often been explained as the

Communist self-torturing, the fast is now extended almost until dawn on Easter Sunday, the time of the sacramental and presumably historically faithful consummation of the vigil.[48] Obviously, the church did not pay attention to the warning of Kepler, who, at the Diet of Regensburg in 1613, said that "Easter is a feast and not a planet. You do not determine it to hours, minutes, and seconds."[49]

The churches, however, for all sorts of reasons have treated Easter as if it were a planet and have insisted on determining the exact hours of both feast and fast. In 1997 at a consultation organized by the World Council of Churches in Aleppo, Syria, it was stated, "Churches in the East and West celebrate Easter, the Resurrection of Jesus Christ from the dead, on two different dates in most years. It has long been recognized that to celebrate this fundamental aspect of the Christian faith on different dates gives a divided witness and compromises the churches' credibility and effectiveness in bringing the Gospel (good news) to the world." The consultation recognized that the differences in calculating the exact date of Easter were not due to fundamental theological differences; instead, "in the Middle East and Eastern Europe, where Christian Churches have lived with the challenge of other religions and materialist ideologies, loyalty to the 'old calendar' has been a symbol of the churches' desire to maintain their integrity and freedom from

---

result of post-Nicene preoccupation with Jerusalem, whose 'liturgically minded bishop Cyril, was fixated on the liturgical commemoration of historically holy events at the very holy places where they once occurred. From Jerusalem as a pilgrimage center, then, these commemorations spread to the rest of the church and tended to shape the way this week was celebrated elsewhere" (cf. Gregory Dix, *The Shape of the Liturgy* [London: Dacre Press, 1945], pp. 348–53). Referred to by Maxwell E. Johnson, "Preparation for Pasha? Lent in Christian Antiquity," in *Passover and Easter: The Symbolic Structuring of Sacred Seasons*, ed. Paul F. Bradshaw and Lawrence A. Hoffman (Notre Dame, IN: University of Notre Dame Press, 1999), p. 38.

48. According to the old Quartodeciman observance, the consummation of the Eucharistic meal was postponed until dawn. "It seems likely that [this choice] has its roots in watching and waiting for the predicted return of Christ to complete his work of redemption, just as Jewish tradition expected the coming of the Messiah to be at Passover time" (Paul F. Bradshaw, "Origins of Easter," in *Passover and Easter: Origin and History to Modern Times*, ed. Paul F. Bradshaw and Lawrence A. Hoffman [Notre Dame, IN: University of Notre Dame Press, 1999], p. 85).

49. H. Nobis, "The Reaction of Astronomers to the Gregorian Calendar," in *Gregorian Reform of the Calendar*, ed. Coyne, Haskin, and Pederson (Vatican City: Pontifica Academia Scientarii, 1983), p. 250.

the hostile forces of this world."[50] The World Council proposed to unify the calculation of the precise date of Easter and celebrate it on the very same day starting in the year 2001, both in the West and the East. In 2001, Easter fell on the very same day according to the calculation of both the Western and the Eastern Churches. However, the decision remained on paper.

Some of the churches surrounded by "the hostile forces of this world" stuck to the "old calendar," knowing that the old algorithm with which the dates used to be determined has already been replaced by more rigorous methods of calculation. Easter, in turn, even in very small communities, for example in villages in Transylvania, has been celebrated by people belonging to different denominations on different dates. Before the Council of Nicea, in 325 AD, as a consequence of calendrical divergence, different Christian communities observed Easter a whole month apart.[51] The villagers have witnessed two Calvaries, one following immediately the other in the same commemorative cycle; each claiming adherence to the unique temporal moment. In view of such experiences, the question of the flexibility of dates seems to be unavoidable: How far can a date, a feast, a holiday, a commemorative moment, *temporal locus*, be stretched? Where is the threshold beyond which a date loses its genuineness, its ability to relate directly or indirectly to the event that it is meant to commemorate?[52] For as M.-J. Chenier remarked, a historical festival "cannot reasonably be amalgamated with another and celebrated at a different time from its own."[53]

*

50. World Council of Churches, Press and Information Office, March 24, 1997. ("Astronomical observations, of course, depend on the position on earth," conceded the participants of the consultation, "which is taken as the point of reference. Therefore it is proposed that the basis of reckoning be the meridian of Jerusalem, the place of Christ's death and resurrection.")

51. Cf. Eviatar Zerubavel, "Easter and Passover: On Calendars and Group Identity," *American Sociological Review* 47 (1982): 285–86.

52. "It is initially natural chronology that provides the framework within which a collection of incidents join into an event. Chronological accuracy in the arrangement of all elements contributing to an event is, therefore, a methodological postulate of historical narrative. Thus, for the meaning of historical sequence, there is a *threshold of fragmentation* below which an event dissolves. A minimum of 'before' and 'after' constitutes the significant unity which makes an event out of incidents. The content of an event, its before and after, might be extended; its consistency, however, is rooted in temporal sequence" (Koselleck, "Representation, Event, and Structure," p. 106).

53. M.-J. Chenier, *Rapport sur les fêtes du 14 juillet et du 10 août* (Paris: Imprimerie nationale, Year IV); quoted in Ozouf, *Festivals and the French Revolution*, p. 164.

On May 3, 1791, under the rule of Stanisław August, the Polish Assembly of the Estates, the "Four Years Sejm" enacted Poland's first written constitution. In 1919, following World War I, when Poland finally became independent once more, May 3, Constitution Day, became an official state holiday, one of the most important holidays of Piłsudski's interwar regime. Following the Communist takeover, immediately after the end of World War II on Polish territory, the new Communist authorities recognized the opportunity created by the temporal closeness of Constitution Day on May 3 to May Day, May 1.[54] In 1945 the Ministry of Information and Propaganda ordered a proper balance to be kept between the celebrations of the two close dates, as "it must be understood that May Day is the day of unification of the nation under a democratic government, based on the most progressive principles, while May 3 expresses the same ideas based on a deep national tradition."[55] In 1946 the anti-Communist opposition tried to use May 3 celebrations for demonstrations against the new regime, and in response, the authorities decided to give up their efforts to fuse the two dates into a continuous, seamless three-day celebration.

54. In fact, the affair that led to the "Haymarket incident" that gave birth to International Workers' Day, took place not on May 1 but on May 3, 1886, in Chicago.

In 1884, the Organized Traders and Labor Unions passed a resolution stating that eight hours would constitute a legal day's work from and after May 1, 1886. The resolution called for a general strike to achieve that goal. . . . The heart of the movement was in Chicago, organized primarily by the anarchist International Working Peoples' Association. . . . On May 3, 1886, the police fired into a crowd of strikers at the McCormick Reaper Works Factory, killing four and wounding many. Anarchists called for a mass meeting next day in Haymarket Square to protest the brutality. . . . After the meeting a bomb was thrown at the police, killing one and injuring seventy. Police responded by firing into the crowd, killing one worker and injuring many others. Although it was never determined who threw the bomb, the incident was used as an excuse to attack the entire Left. . . . Anarchists in particular were harassed, and eight of Chicago's most active were charged with conspiracy to murder in connection with the Haymarket bombing. . . . Despite a lack of evidence . . . they were sentenced to die. . . . Four were hanged on 11 November 1887. . . . One of them committed suicide. The remaining three were finally pardoned in 1893. . . . Emma Goldman, a young immigrant at that time, later pointed to the Haymarket affair as her political birth. (see l.gaylord@m.cc.utah.edu)

55. Archiwum Akt Nowych w Warszawie Archive of New Acts in Warsaw (AAN), MiP (Ministry of Information and Propaganda) mf 28.689,52. The following analysis is based largely on an unpublished MA thesis by Izabella Main: "The Celebration of Polish National Holidays by the State and the Church between 1944 and 1980." The thesis was written under my supervision at the History Department of the Central European University, Budapest, 1997.

When in 1946 the May 3 celebration in Kraków turned into a bloody demonstration against the Communist state, the authorities decided to terminate the holiday.[56] May 3 was canceled as an official holiday, and in 1947 the so-called Week (later on "Days") of Education, Book, and Press was introduced instead, starting on the old Constitution Day, on May 3. (During the interwar years in Hungary, May Day was celebrated as the "Feast of the Birds and Trees.") In 1967 the official party newspaper referred to the Days as a regular commemoration, with an already long and substantial tradition: "When we look into the annals of the twenty long years' tradition of the Days . . . ," and so on. The next year, in 1968, the Days started to closely resemble the extended Revolutionary Youth Days in Hungary, since the celebrations were linked up to the twenty-fifth anniversary of the Polish People's Army, the 150th anniversary of Marx's birthday, the twentieth anniversary of the Polish United Workers' Party, the fiftieth anniversary of KPP (the old Polish Communist Party), and the fiftieth anniversary of Polish Independence. In 1971, the Days were linked to the twenty-fifth anniversary of the victory over Fascism, the seventy-fifth anniversary of the farmer's movement, the 100th anniversary of Lenin's birthday, and the twenty-fifth anniversary of the liberation of Warsaw.[57] As Mona Ozouf remarked in connection with the French revolutionary calendar: "Throughout . . . one senses the need for overdetermination: every choice must be capable of being justified several times over, either by a return, in the history of the Revolution, of encounters and coincidences or by harmony with nature."[58] The combined richness of these chronological fragments offered a chance to impress the population, to provide a sense of explanatory force, and to compensate for the evident lack of any causal connection among the isolated happenings.[59] The dates evidently "no longer

56. Cf. Jan Kubik, *The Power of Symbols Against the Symbol of Power: The Fall of Solidarity and the Fall of State Socialism in Poland* (University Park: Pennsylvania State University Press, 1994), pp. 207–14.

57. Main, "Celebration of Polish National Holidays," p. 18. Naturally there was no mention of the fact that this happy coincidence of dates was the consequence of the decision of the Soviet Army High Command to watch from the other side of the Vistula River for long weeks while the Germans killed almost all the members of the Home Army who took part in the Warsaw uprising and ruined the city completely.

58. Ozouf, *Festivals and the French Revolution*, p. 166.

59. Calendrical overdetermination was part of the Fascist quest for temporal regeneration in Italy as well. "Thus March 23 Youth Day, commemorated the founding of the *Fasci*; April 21, Labour Day, the founding of Rome; May 24, Empire Day; the entry of Italy

had any reality, they had only signification."[60] In the absence of autochthonous historical processes, what these events and dates exemplified, signified, or were supposed to stand for were deeply problematic.

In 1655, the Polish king Jan Kazimierz dedicated the Kingdom of Poland to the Virgin Mary, to express the gratitude of his nation for the miracle that had saved the shrine of Częstochowa on Jasna Góra, the sanctuary of the holiest Polish icon, the Black Madonna, from the Swedish army of Charles Gustavus.[61] In 1890 the Vatican gave its official blessing to the celebration and commemoration of the Black Madonna on April 1. In 1908 the church moved the holiday to the first Sunday of May, and after independence in 1918, the Polish Episcopate decided to link the holiday of the Queen of Poland to the Constitution Day holiday on May 3.[62] The Vatican confirmed the decision in 1923. (In 1930, the holiday of Mary, Queen of Poland, obtained a special liturgy.) So the state holiday of the constitution and the religious festivities of the Virgin Mary were celebrated on the same day. In the interwar period the officials of the state participated in the church celebration on Jasna Góra.

After the establishment of the Communist regime, and even after the official abolition of the commemoration of the constitution, the Catholic Church continued celebrating May 3 as the holiday of the Queen of Poland, reminding believers and the other citizens of the country of the close connection between the two anniversaries—the secular and the religious, one of them mostly invisible and unmentionable—that fell on that day.

---

into the First World War; September 20, Italian Unity, the incorporation of Rome into the Kingdom of Italy; October 28, the Fascist Revolution, the March on Rome" (Herbert Schneider, *Making the Fascist State* [New York: Howard Fertig, 1928], pp. 223–30; quoted by Roger Griffin, "'I Am No Longer Human. I Am A Titan. A God!' The Fascist Quest to Regenerate Time" [written-up version of a talk given in November 1998 at the Institute of Historical Research at *http://www.history.ac.uk/projects/elec/sem22.htm*]).

60. Auerbach, *Mimesis*, p. 116.

61. After the forty-day siege of the Jasna Góra Monastery, the Polish king made a solemn vow: the blessed Virgin should henceforth be venerated as "Queen of the Crown of Poland." Cf. Oskar Halecki, *A History of Poland* (New York: Roy Publishers, 1956), p. 159.

62. "Stress was laid on 'the perfect agreement existing in the history of the French Revolution between the time of the foundation of the Republic and that of the acceptance of the Constitution'—and the possibility, therefore, of celebrating on 1 Vendemiaire two anniversaries in one" (N. Parent-Réal, *Motion d'ordre tendant à faire consacrer, par la fête du 1er vendémiaire, l'accord parfait qui existe dans l'histoire de la Révolution française* [Paris: Imprimerie nationale, Year VII]; quoted in Ozouf, *Festivals and the French Revolution*, p. 161).

In 1956, the primate of Poland, Cardinal Wyszyński, who was still interned by the Communist authorities, announced an unprecedented nine-year-long preparation for the Millennium of Polish Christianity. The first act of the Novena was the renewal of King Kazimierz's oath, committing Poland to the Virgin Mary, on May 3, 1957. From 1957 onward, the "Vows of Jasna Góra" were repeated every year during the Novena on the first Sunday following May 3 in every parish of the country. The culmination of the nine-year-long commemoration was the new coronation of the Virgin Mary on May 3, 1966. Cardinal Wyszyński, acting as the pope's legate, dedicated the country "in servitude to Mary, the Mother of the Church for the sake of church freedom in the country and the world. . . . Pope Paul VI later called this act a 'second christening of Poland.'"[63] At the end of the ceremony, Wyszyński proclaimed:

In the face of the totalitarian threat to the nation . . . in the face of an atheistic program . . . in the face of biological destruction, a great supernatural current is needed, so that the nation can consciously draw from the Church the divine strength that will fortify its religious and national life. Nowhere else is the union of Church and nation as strong as in Poland, which is in absolute danger.[64] Our "temporal theology" demands that we dedicate ourselves into the hands of the Holy Mother, so that we may live up to our task.[65]

The Polish Marian myth, similar to the Hungarian church-state doctrine of the *Regnum Marianum*, served to strengthen the position of the Catholic Church and to suspend the separation of state and church.[66]

63. Andrzej Micewski, *Cardinal Wyszyński: A Biography* (San Diego: Harcourt, Brace, Jovanovich, 1984), pp. 265–66; quoted by Kubik, *Power of Symbols*, p. 113.

64. The formula "the Church in Danger" recalls the debate in the House of Commons between 1702 and 1704, when Tory members of the House, following the passage of the so-called Toleration Act, argued that the growing number of Dissenters and Non-Conformists had placed the church in danger. Cf. *The Parliamentary History of England* (London: T. C. Hansard, 1810), vol. 6, p. 509.

65. Micewski, *Cardinal Wyszyński*, pp. 266–67; quoted by Kubik, *Power of Symbols*, p. 113.

66. *Regnum Marianum*, the land of the Virgin Mary, refers to the myth according to which Saint Stephen, the first Hungarian king, in 1038 AD, on the day of his death offered the country to the Holy Mother. The myth played an important role in the interwar years, when the conservative, extreme right-wing Hungarian government turned the doctrine into the central legitimizing factor of the counterrevolutionary regime. On the occasion of the Millennium of Hungarian statehood and the Catholic Church, the conservative government of Hungary, by reversing the separation of church and state, used St. Stephen's day (August 20, 2000) to resurrect the dogma. At the beginning of 2000, St. Stephen's "holy

(At the beginning of the year 2000, responsible Hungarian state officials, among them the government commissioner for the millennium, suggested "temporarily suspending the separation of the state and church for the time of the millennium.") The Marian myth was (is) in the service both of faith and of a political and theological doctrine: it reaffirms and points in the direction of a nonsecular state, announces the claim to moral and political authority of the church. Long after the end of the Novena, in a letter, dated in June 1980, the Polish Episcopate stated, "The purpose . . . was to obtain the help of the Holy Mother in the moral renewal of the Nation. . . . The Holy Mother was to support personally the great undertaking of spiritual renewal of the whole of society and our fidelity to the vowed oaths, which bind us forever."[67] On the occasion of the coming millennium, Cardinal Wyszyński said, "O Mother, we will not leave Calvary, for You are there, and since You stand there, the Cross and the Calvary are for us simply power, victory, and joy. In the age-long journey of the Nation this power has survived. Is it not an indication for us, who look for strength for the next millennium, that we should rely only on such powers that have survived and defeated time?"[68] However, the emphasis on the extratemporal in the sermon does not exclude the possibility of concrete historical references.

Besides doctrinal formalism, there is a historical narrative attached to the holiday of the Queen of Poland. When after 1918 the church decided to move the holy day to May 3, the feast of the Virgin became intimately connected to the holiday of the first Polish constitution. Besides this historical connection, the holiday of the "Queen of the Crown of Poland" in itself is rooted in more or less specific historic events: in 1655 the Swedish army broke a truce with Poland and virtually swept away the Polish army. . . . "Only a miracle could save the country, and one did. Jasna Góra monastery unexpectedly resisted the enemy. After a forty-day siege, Polish soldiers carrying the Holy Icon—the icon of the Black Madonna of Czestochowa—with them into the battle forced the Swedes to retreat for the first

---

crown" was transferred to the building of the parliament, and on August 20, as part of the "holy saint's right-hand" procession, St. Stephen's alleged relic was brought to the parliament ("so after a thousand years the holy right-hand could meet the holy crown").

67. Published in *Krzyż Nowohucki* no. 2 (1980); quoted by Kubik, *Power of Symbols*, p. 110.

68. Stefan Wyszyński, *Wielka Nowenna Tysiąclecia* [The Great Novena of the Millennium] (Paris: Societé d'Editions Internationales, 1962), p. 63; quoted by Kubik, *Power of Symbols*, p. 115.

time during the war. After this victory, King Jan Kazimierz made the solemn vow."[69]

The historical "arch-event," however, probably would not have been enough to consolidate the holiday. What is commemorated is both the anniversary of the original vow and the memory of the long tradition of subsequent commemorations. In 1863, for example, a priest who was involved in the anti-Russian uprising designed an insignia, an oval with the Black Madonna in the middle of the badge. The design became the emblem of independent Poland, and even Lech Wałęsa, the leader of the Solidarity Trade Union and the future president of post-Communist Poland, wore the same badge. The icon was crowned with the papal crown three times, in 1717, 1910, and at the time of the Millennium of the Polish Statehood and the Church. In this way, May 3 could combine doctrine with concrete historic events (victory over the Swedish army, the oath of the king, the baptism of Prince Mieszko, the foundation of the Christian Polish state) together with the commemoration of past commemorations and their effects. Figural meaning (more or less), detailed historical specificity, eschatology, doctrinal formalism, legends, and historical narrative support each other in the service of an acceptable, that is, an "authentic," holy day. It is really as if, when events took place in the distant past, the future was already there: as if Mieszko's christening had taken place under the guardianship of the Queen of Poland, and several military victories over the Tartars and the Turks, before the middle of the seventeenth century, had been made possible by Our Lady's divine intervention. Temporal superimposition contributes to an extrahistorical continuity that allows the commemorative community to see the connection between the present, the present commemoration, and its prehistory. Despite the time reversals, chronological inexactitude, and mixed-up chronological order, theology is still rooted in historical temporality.

The Communist authorities for their part set up a special Commission for the "Celebration of the 1,000 Years of Polish Statehood" and originally decided to schedule the celebration in 1965—instead of 1966, which the church had already reserved—as this was the twentieth anniversary of the "return of the Western territories" (there was complete silence about the Eastern territories, which became part of the Soviet Union after World

---

69. Halecki, *History of Poland*, p. 159; quoted by Kubik, *Power of Symbols*, p. 109.

War II).[70] The state at first decided not to compete directly with the church but to carve out its own space for secular celebrations.

In 1966 the church started the commemoration on April 9, the anniversary of the christening of Mieszko, the prince of the Piast dynasty who was baptized with his court in 966. (His son, Bolesław Chrobry, was crowned in 1025.) The state, having abandoned its original plan to celebrate in 1965, decided to challenge the church head on and opened the official celebrations on April 14 of the same year, on the twenty-first anniversary of the crossing by the Soviets of the Odra and Nysa rivers, which became Poland's western border after World War II. In 1966 May Day celebrations lasted longer than usual, extending into the beginning of the Days of the Book and the Press, which in turn took place on May 3–17.[71] On the day of the Virgin Mary (and that of the constitution) the state organized a ceremony in Katowice (Silesia) to celebrate the forty-fifth anniversary of the Third Silesian Uprising with a pledge of loyalty to Socialism (competing with and imitating the vows of Jasna Góra).[72] On June 21, 1966, on the eve of the anniversary of the bogus Lublin Manifesto of 1944, issued at that time by Polish Communists who were still on Soviet soil, the government held a special ceremonial session in the Sejm, the Polish Parliament. Prime Minister Gomułka, in a speech entitled "The Destiny of the Polish Nation Is Forever Linked with Socialism," justified the date of the special session:

We chose July 21, the eve of the twenty-second anniversary of the Manifesto of the Polish Committee of National Liberation, as the most fitting day for the Sejm session, precisely to lay emphasis on that inseparable link that joins Poland's present-day Socialist reality with that which was the best, the most noble, creative, and patriotic in her past. The past twenty-two years are not only the most recent part of the history of Poland, but, at the same time, crown the road traversed by the Polish nation through history towards freedom and progress.[73]

During the first official visit of the Polish pope, in June 1979, the Jasna Góra vows were once more renewed in Częstochowa. In his speech, Pope

---

70. *Tajne Dokumenty. Państwo-Kosciół 1960–1980* [Secret Documents. State-Church, 1960–1980] (London: Aneks, 1996), pp. 213–23, 234–46.

71. Ibid., pp. 196–97.

72. Main, "Celebration of Polish National Holidays," pp. 22–29.

73. Władysław Gomułka, "The Destiny of the Polish Nation Is Linked with Socialism for Ever," *Polish Reports* nos. 7–8 (1966): 3; quoted by Kubik, *Power of Symbols*, p. 114.

John Paul II defined national identity with reference to the role of Virgin Mary: "The history of Poland . . . can be written in different ways. . . . But if we want to know how this history is reflected in the hearts of the Poles, we must come here. We must put our ear to this place. We must hear the echo of the Nation's life in the Heart of its Mother and Queen."[74] The intimate connection between church and state, the Black Madonna and the constitution, faith and history had been reaffirmed.

On November 11, 1920, the first official celebration of the Polish Day of Independence took place. On that day, back in 1918, Marshal Piłsudski had arrived in Warsaw, securing his control over the country during the next few days. Every year up to the outbreak of World War II, the leaders of the state and the Catholic Church attended the celebrations together. During World War II, under occupation, secret celebrations and masses for the Fatherland were conducted in the churches on that day.

In 1944, after the liberation of Poland, the Communists decided to keep celebrating Independence Day, but according to the official newspaper of the party, it was the Bolshevik Revolution of 1917, rather than Piłsudski's military successes, that had played the decisive role in attaining independence: for the Bolsheviks had recognized the right of Poland to become an independent state.[75] The Polish Communists obviously discovered that, just as in the case of May 3, the anniversary of the old constitution, there was a possible temporal substitute for Independence Day on November 11 as well: while in the former case the natural substitute seemed to be May 1, in the latter case November 7 served as the nearest surrogate—the Communists hoped that it was near enough.

The following year, in 1945, the Communist authorities decided to cancel the official celebrations altogether: "November 11 will no longer be Independence Day . . . the new Independence Day will be the date when Poland's new freedom started."[76] From that year on, the official party newspaper published press commemorations of independence on November 7, the anniversary of the Bolshevik Revolution, instead of the 11th of the same

74. Kubik, *Power of Symbols*, p. 142.
75. *Życie Warszawy* 25 (November 11, 1944); quoted by Main, "Celebration of Polish National Holidays," p. 33.
76. Marshal Rola-Żymierski's statement at the debate in the Council of Ministers on May 8, 1945. Archiwum Akt Nowych w Warszawie, PRM, 5/1097.

month.[77] In 1954 the Polish prime minister, Józef Cyrankiewicz, reminded the country that "those were historical days in November, *1917* when Polish independence was proclaimed."[78] (The majority of Poles however, most probably still remembered that Poland was to become an independent state only a year later, in 1918. The prime minister—even if the misdating was simply a slip of the tongue—was obviously trying to fill the year-long gap between the Bolshevik Revolution and the proclamation of Poland's independence.)

Rather than Piłsudski's takeover on November 11, 1918, the Communist emphasis was placed more and more on another date, November 7, 1918, when the so-called Lublin government was formed. This new element served as an added reason for the Communists to move the celebration four days back, to have it coincide with the anniversary of the Bolshevik Revolution. In 1947 the Polish press singled out those Bolshevik documents that, according to the Stalinist interpretation, had led to Poland's independence: *The Decree about Peace* (November 7, 1917) and *The Declaration of the Rights of the Nations of Russia* (November 11, 1917). Despite the fact that the so-called Lublin government was proclaimed on November 7—although, unfortunately in 1918 and not in 1917—there was a minor problem with it that the Communist historiography tried to ignore: the Lublin government at the very end of World War I was in fact an initiative of the independent Polish left: of the Polish Socialist Party and the two Polish Farmers' Associations, and not of the Communists. The Lublin government issued a manifesto to the Polish people that emphasized two main goals: the revolutionary changes in Europe *and* Polish independence leading to a democratic and parliamentary republic. The Polish Communist Party (SDKPiL) did not participate in the Lublin government; in fact, it opposed it, claiming, "the idea of an independent Poland [is] a hinge around which the forces of social reaction and enemies of the working class are concentrated."[79] But after World War II the Communists had different historical recollections and decided to include the Lublin government among the precursors of the Polish Communist state.

---

77. Cf. *Życie Warszawy* and *Trybuna Ludu* in 1947–51, 1957, 1959, 1960–66, 1969–80, respectively.

78. *Życie Warszawy* 266 (November 11, 1954), p. 2; emphasis added.

79. See Albert, *Najnowsza historia Polski*, pp. 21, 28, 32, 33, 35, 40, 47, 60, 61.

The Lublin government had another role to play in the new anniversary cycle, as it could be connected to the so-called Lublin Manifesto (unfortunately proclaimed not on Polish soil but in Moscow on July 22, 1944) issued by the Polish Committee of National Liberation (the so-called New Lublin Government) and even to the new Stalinist constitution of Communist Poland, which was not-so-accidentally ratified on the same day, July 22, in 1952. In this ingenious way the focal point of the most sacred of Polish secular holidays (May 3, the [old] Constitution Day and November 11, Independence Day) became November 7, a definitively non-Polish holiday, the anniversary of the revolution in Russia, traditional archenemy of Polish nationalism, the revolution of the Bolsheviks, who later on the basis of the Molotov-Ribbentrop pact had taken away Poland's eastern territories.

The force of Communist gravity pulled the holy days out of the orbit of the Polish national commemorative cycle, which was originally based on well-known, accepted (more or less), concrete, tangible, and visible sites, icons and relics, and stories built around those very sites, figures, heroes, deeds, dead bodies, and events. Neither the heroes nor the sites, although they have allegedly played such a decisive role in shaping the course of Poland's fate, were Polish any longer. The concrete dates and the sense attached to those dates were no longer under Polish jurisdiction. Those who were to celebrate these new holidays as their own could not experience the dates proposed by the Communists as relevant to their own history. The potential participants in the commemorations had absolutely no imaginable, meaningful, sensory relationship with the events that had purportedly taken place on the proposed new dates. The proposed events had no acceptable relevance to the perceived, received, inherited history of those who were supposed to celebrate them.

Historical acceptance that is related to a certain sense of connectedness can be helped by the realization of past experience (this is what the Germans call *Vergegenwärtigung vergangenen Erlebens*).[80] The commemorator is most probably in need of a certain depth of actual historical detail—the concrete description of the action cycle—that will make the connection between his or her present and the remembered past at least plausible. In the absence of any obvious both direct—even sensory—and deep sym-

---

80. Cf. Hans Ulrich Gumbrecht, "Versuch zur Antropolgie der Geschichtsschreibung," *Formen der Geschichtsschreibung. Theorie der Geschichte*, ed. R. Koselleck, H. Lutz, and J. Rüsen, vol. 4 (Munich: Deutscher Taschenbuch-Verlag, 1982), pp. 495–501.

bolic connection between the proposed special event and the historical "sense" of contemporaries, the anniversary cannot have the ring of a holy day. "If a truth is to be settled in the memory of a group it needs to be presented in the concrete form of an event, of a personality, or of a locality," concluded Maurice Halbwachs his study *The Legendary Topography of Gospels in the Holy Land.*[81]

As they [the guests at the traditional Jewish Passover Seder] eat the matzoth and drink the wine, all males are required to recline on the left side—for this was the position of free men at Roman banquets—but the festive celebration of freedom is qualified by the eating of bitter herbs and, traditionally, by the injunction to show some sign of hurry or anxiety in order to reenact the flight from the pursuing Egyptians. For the entire meal is an acting out of the exodus story, as well as a commentary upon it, in order to fulfill the commandment that the events be experienced as though they were your own or rather that you speak of them to your child as your own personal history. And your child in turn must make your history his own. . . . In what is thought to be the oldest part of the Passover ritual, the matzoth is uncovered and held aloft, while the following words are recited in Aramaic: "This is the bread of affliction that our fathers ate in the land of Egypt." . . . At the moment of elevation in the Seder, historical time is drastically foreshortened; the distant past is made so intensely present that it lays claim to the material world here and now. . . . In the Jewish ritual, historical distance is continually reinvoked even as it is abrogated by the act of eating what is imagined as a piece of history. And the piece of history remains crucially what it always was—a piece of bread baked in a certain way. There is no transformation of its substance; on the contrary, history suffuses the object and passes into the body of the celebrant precisely to the extent that it is what it appears to be, in a plain and literal sense. Hence the claim to a direct personal experience of the bondage and liberation is at once confirmed and qualified in the sentence, "This is the bread of affliction that our fathers ate in the land of Egypt."[82]

81. Published in M. Halbwachs, *On Collective Memory*, ed. Lewis Coser (Chicago: University of Chicago Press, 1992), p. 200. But Halbwachs adds, "In order for recollections of the life and death of Christ and of the places through which he passed to endure, they had to be made part of a doctrine. . . . In order for the abstract idea of expiation to become something other than an aspiration, so that one would believe in it as one would believe in a historical truth or a fact of experience, it was necessary that it claim to belong to a living and to human testimony" (ibid., p. 200).

82. Stephen Greenblatt, "The Mousetrap in Memory of Louis Marin," *Shakespeare Studies* 35 (1997): 3–6.

"There [in the festival] the child will come and read the names and glorious deeds of the heroes, there their souls will be imbued with love of country and a taste of virtue"

Thus the feast of the Seder, as an exercise in mnemonics, requires and facilitates not only commemoration but also reexperience: by physical, bodily gestures, remembering, memorializing the suffering, and what the Lord did for the Jewish people, and at the same time, remembering the commentaries on that event by famous rabbis, together with the long tradition of the act of celebration. The feast, as Jan Asmann remarked, "besides its other functions, serves to turn past into tangible present."[83] The Seder therefore has several historical and sociotemporal layers, and each helps the participants to commemorate but also to perform, helps each of them to live through the remembered events unaltered. This invariance is an essential element of the acting out of sacred memories.

During medieval times, the strict and rigid fixing of the Seder ritual was "as if to say that messianic deliverance was conditional on punctilious ritual perfection. . . . On that night they were redeemed [in the past] and on that night they will be redeemed in the future."[84] Acting out the required commemorative ritual served not only as a mnemonic technique, focused on the past, not simply as a ritual replication, but also as an effective means of active intervention in the affairs of the present and the future. Commemoration has an actualizing function and component. Cooperation, in the form of active remembering, was required in the auspicious hour, in order for the foretold future to arrive. The Easter liturgy, likewise, was meant to be "more than a series of commemorations of past events recalled to mind": it was considered as the "means whereby the worshipers participate in the saving events."[85]

If the ability to relate both in a literal and figurative way to concrete events of the past (filled with historical details) was not only an important element of one's historical consciousness but also the precondition of active symbolic participation in bringing about the events of the future, then

---

(F. A. Daubermesil, *Rapport au nom de la commission chargée de présenter les moyens de vivifier l'ésprit public* [Paris: Imprimerie nationale, Year IV]; quoted in Ozouf, *Festivals and the French Revolution*, p. 317, n. 18).

83. Jan Assman, *A Kulturális Emlékezet* [Cultural Memory] (Budapest: Atlantisz, 1999), p. 53.

84. Cf. Lawrence A. Hoffman, "The Passion Meal in Jewish Tradition," in *Passover and Easter: Origin and History to Modern Times*, ed. Paul F. Bradshaw and Lawrence A. Hoffman (Notre Dame, IN: University of Notre Dame Press, 1999), p. 20.

85. J. Gordon Davies, *Holy Week: A Short History* (Richmond, VA: John Knox Press, 1963), p. 65; quoted by Melloh, "Revising the Holy Week and Easter Rites," p. 227.

those anniversaries that cannot provide temporal reexperience of the past cannot achieve commemorative status either, and thus cannot help in the perception that participation would contribute to bringing about the desired future.[86]

Even the inattentive observer had to acknowledge at a certain point that there were fatal calendrical, chronological, and commemorative flaws in the Polish Communist operation: it was more than a mere chronological coincidence that on exactly November 11, 1980 (on the day when independence had been commemorated in pre-Communist times and when it would be commemorated once more after the collapse of the Communist regime), *Trybuna Ludu*, the official Communist newspaper, had to report the official registration in court of *NSZZ Solidarność* (the Solidarity Trade Union), which in the next decade was to play such an important role in reestablishing the traditional Polish national holidays.

Besides the suspicions of the population—the majority of which was increasingly alienated by the policy of the regime—there were generic problems with the Polish Communist commemorative cycle: (1) the holy days that the Polish Communist regime inherited from the interwar period were difficult to fill with meaningful, plausible, and chronologically acceptable concrete counteractions, which (2) could have appropriate figurative meaning in fulfilling historical destiny from a Communist perspective.

In order to turn the dates into acceptable holidays, which the people could relate to, the dates would have had to be filled by "reality," that is, "timely," real, narratable events, that the majority could have regarded as part of their prehistory. The version of the past that the Communist authorities offered to the population was not fit for "semiotization," that is, could not be used, could not be filled with reason and relevant meaning; it could not become the object of remembering.[87] By contrast, for the holidays to become useable for the Communist authorities, they would have had to fit into the Communist eschatology and function as announcements of the future. But the Communist impresarios failed to cover the traditional national or religious holy dates with sufficiently close internationalist ones (May 3 with May 1 and November 11 with November 7) as

---

86. Historical consciousness as an experiential process, "Erfahrunsprozess." Cf. Hans Ulrich Gumbrecht, "Das In vergangenem Zeiten Gewesene so gut erzahlen, als ob es in der eigenen Welt ware," in Gumbrecht, "Versuch zur Antropolgie der Geschichtsschreibung," pp. 485–513, esp. pp. 503–6.

87. Cf. Assmann, *Moses the Egyptian*, p. 291.

they were not able to prove convincingly that events that had allegedly taken place on these days were related to Polish national history in a chronologically persuasive and symbolically important way. The Communist narrators did not succeed in building a seamless chronology by demonstrating the historical authenticity of the suggested substitutes.

*

Easter is probably the most persuasive and successful example of complex commemorative substitution. What is commonly referred to as Passover (*transitus*—as Origen understood it) was probably rooted in two separate festivities: a springtime sacrifice by nomadic shepherds and a Canaanite agricultural festival of the Unleavened Bread. (The memory of this is still in Mark 14.21: "the first day of the Unleavened Bread.") At least from the time when Jerusalem became the sole sanctuary of the nation, Passover became considered as the festival of Israel's redemption from slavery in Egypt. And according to rabbinical teaching, Passover was also associated both with the creation of the world and with the expected coming of the Messiah.[88]

Early texts like the *Epistula Apostolorum*—probably written in the second half of the second century—suggest that "the Christian observance was a gradual modulation of the Passover."[89] Christianity, like the Jewish tradition, adhered to the obligation of telling a story that, in both cases, starts with degradation (the Egyptian servitude in one case, and the Crucifixion, in the other) and ends with praise (for the redemption from Egypt, and the Resurrection of Christ). In the Christian version, naive realism and minuscule adherence to detailed historicity went hand in hand with, indeed were dependent on, springtime nature festivities. In the Johannine version the Passion took place on Nisan 14 in the course of the preparation for the Passover. According to the Julian calendar, in the year of Jesus' passion, Nisan 14 fell on March 25, which coincided with the spring equinox of the Julian calendar.[90] (In England, even in the eighteenth century New Year's Day was on March 25.) By placing the spring equinox on a day that is associated in the rabbinical teachings with the creation of the world, the emphasis of the Christian celebration shifted "from memorial of the death

---

88. See Talley, *Origins of the Liturgical Year*, esp. pp. 1–70.

89. Ibid., p. 5.

90. Ibid., p. 10. *De solstitiis et aequinoctis*, a Latin work written presumably after the fourth century, "no longer views the coincidence of the Julian equivalent to 14 Nissan [March 25] and the established date for the spring equinox as accidental, but makes the equinox itself the occasion of the passion" (ibid., p. 11).

to celebration of the resurrection."[91] This shift of the meaning attached to the celebration was also manifest in the growing importance of the Sunday observance, which was associated with the day of resurrection. The Resurrection of Jesus overwrote the memory of the deliverance from Egypt and the creation of the world. And this took place most probably gradually, while at least occasionally the connection between Passover and natural phenomena and natural feasts was strengthened.

It would perhaps be misleading to view the gradual shift in the meaning and temporal location of the passage as an attempt to explain natural phenomena. "Myths often think *with* natural objects; they are almost never about them. Their focus is not on the genealogy of things but on the topography of relations. . . . The season may serve as an experimental medium for thinking about issues such as periodicity, regularity, transformation, and the like. This is, above all, an intellectual activity that need not be equated with agrarian concerns or fertility cults."[92]

91. Ibid., p. 11. According to other authorities, in the early days of the church, in Asia Minor, the Passion was commemorated, while in the West, especially in Rome, the Resurrection was celebrated. Cf. William Dugmore Clifford, "A Note on the Quartodecimans," *Studia Patristica* 4 (Berlin) 79 (1961): 411–21. Melito of Sardis, who, however, was most probably an adherent of the Quartodeciman tradition, in his *Peri Pascha* (About Easter), dated around 165, wrote, "This is he who in the virgin was made incarnate, on the cross was suspended, in the earth was buried, from the dead was resurrected, to the heights of heaven was lifted up" (*Peri Pascha* 70). The English translation of Melito of Sardis's text is in Raniero Cantalamessa, ed., *Easter in the Early Church* (Collegeville, MN: Liturgical Press, 1993), p. 43.

92. Jonathan Z. Smith, "A Slip in Time Saves Nine: Prestigious Origins Again," in *Chronotypes: The Construction of Time*, ed. John Bender and David E. Wellbery (Stanford, CA: Stanford University Press, 1991), p. 71; emphasis in original. "The mistake of Mannhardt and the Naturalist School was to think that natural phenomena are *what* myths seek to explain, when they are rather the *medium through which* myths try to explain facts which are themselves not of a natural but a logical order" (C. Levi-Strauss, *The Savage Mind* [Chicago: Chicago University Press, 1966], p. 95; quoted by Smith, "Slip in Time Saves Nine," p. 71; emphasis in original).

"'On that very day,' the sun moved from one hemisphere to the other and the people from Monarchical government to Republican government. Romme lists the significant coincidences that emerged from this encounter between the history of men and that of the stars. Furthermore, autumn is the season of blessed abundance; even the Egyptians celebrated the emergence of the earth out of chaos at that time. . . . Certainly the Revolutionary calendar would be the work of men, but of enlightened men, men following 'the natural course of things'" (Ozouf, *Festivals and the French Revolution*, pp. 160–61).

"Equally, May Day played a major part in the development of the new socialist iconography of the 1890s in which, in spite of the expected emphasis on struggle, the note

However, not everybody shares the view that it was the result of a gradual modulation that Easter became distinguished from Passover. According to Eviatar Zarubavel, "the Church made deliberate efforts to dissociate Easter—mainly by calendrical means—from Passover."[93]

In a letter attributed to Constantine the Great, the Roman emperor wrote, "It appeared an unworthy thing that in the celebration of this most holy feast we should follow the practice of the Jews. . . . For we have in our power, if we abandon their custom, to prolong the due observance of this ordinance to future ages. . . . Let us then have nothing in common with the detestable Jewish crowd."[94] From these words almost naturally follows the scholarly reasoning:

In order to guarantee that Easter would never coincide with Passover, the church determined that it would always be observed on the Sunday following the full moon which coincides with, or falls next after, the vernal equinox. Given that the full moon has no significance whatsoever in Christianity, it is quite obvious that the only reason for insisting that Easter be observed on the Sunday following a full moon was to segregate it temporally from Passover and, thus, totally to *dissociate the ecclesiastical calendar from the Jewish calendar.*[95]

Although this interpretation contradicts the "gradual shift" view, it is possible to reconcile slow modulation, leading to the Nicaean resolution in 325 AD, with the church's attempts to establish its own unique identity and to promote segregation of Christians from Jews. Zerubavel remarks:

Note, however, that the goal of establishing an Easter cycle that would be *totally* independent of the Jewish calendar has never been achieved. Rather than remain entirely solar, like the Julian—and, later, Gregorian—calendar within which it has essentially been anchored, the ecclesiastical calendar has had to incorporate some awareness of the lunar cycle, and especially with regard to its principal festival, a most ironic reminder of some fundamental Jewish principle. . . . In order to make sure that it would never coincide with its original precursor, the Church has com-

---

of hope, confidence and the approach of a brighter future—*often expressed in the metaphors of plant growth*—prevailed" (Hobsbawm, "Mass-Producing Traditions," pp. 284–85; emphasis added).

93. Zerubavel, "Easter and Passover," p. 285.

94. Eusebius Pamphilus, "The Life of Constantine," in Vol. 1 of 2nd Series: *Nicene and Post-Nicene Fathers of the Christian Church*, ed. Philip Shaff (Grand Rapids, MI: Eerdmans, n.d.); quoted by Zerubavel, "Easter and Passover," p. 287.

95. Zerubavel, "Easter and Passover," pp. 287–88; emphasis in original.

mitted itself to moving it from one date to another every year. Thus, ironically, by trying so hard to dissociate the ecclesiastical calendar from the Jewish calendar, it has only managed to immortalize its awareness of—as well as actual dependence on—the latter.[96]

Zerubavel feels it is *ironic* that Easter immortalized the Jewish feast, and even the traces of dependence of the date of Easter on the date of Passover. Zerubavel, however, fundamentally misses the point: the historical authenticity of the story of Christ's Passion is inseparably dependent on the Jewish feast. (According to the synoptic gospels Jesus sends his disciples to prepare the room for Passover: "I have earnestly desired to eat this Passover with you before I suffer" [Luke 22.15]. And according to John, the Crucifixion takes place on the day of the Passover, and Jesus is in fact the "Passover lamb," whose bones cannot be broken; this is why the soldiers are unable to break Jesus' leg [John 19.32–36, and so on].) Faithfulness to alleged historical details, which implicate the Jews, aims at establishing both historical authenticity and symbolic, eschatological authority. Easter would not make sense without the reminder of Passover, the feast in Jerusalem, the Last Supper, the disciples around the table. Halbwachs expresses similar convictions in his *Topography*: "The Christian collective memory could annex a part of the Jewish collective memory only by appropriating part of the latter's local remembrance while at the same time transforming its entire perspective of historical space. . . . Hence two linked exigencies which were at the same time contraries."[97] Passover is not simply erased, covered, but it is exploited, turned around, made use of; it

96. Ibid., p. 288.

97. Halbwachs, *On Collective Memory*, pp. 215 and 216, respectively. Halbwachs elaborates this idea in the following way:

> Those parts of the Gospel that give the account of the last days of Christ, of his death and resurrection, take us to another location, namely to Jerusalem, in Judea; that is, to a city and a region where, before Christianity and outside its purview, there were at every step places that already had been commemorated, that were associated with ancient memories of Jewish history as told in the Old Testament. . . . The Christianity of the Sermon on the Mount might have remained a moral outlook (if, by the way, it could have subsisted in this way) but it would never have been elevated to the rank and power of a religion if it had not incorporated some essential elements of the Jewish religion that were fused with the history of the Jewish people. . . . This history and indeed this religion could have been imposed on the first Christians, who lived within a Jewish milieu, only if it came from a conspicuously Jewish background. (Ibid., pp. 212–15)

is perfectly recycled. The ecclesiastical calendar, thus, had to incorporate awareness of the lunar cycle.[98]

Having tied the date to the combination of the solar and moving lunar cycle, to the spring equinox, the historical narrative is tied to natural phenomena, chance events embedded in the laws of nature, providing the aura of inevitability to the story.

98. Not everybody shares the view that the Jews are, "in a certain sense our elder brothers," as Pope John Paul II, following Saint Paul, formulated the relationship at the occasion of his visit to the Synagogue in Rome. Cf. Carlo Ginzburg, "Pope Woytila's Slip," in *Wooden Eyes, Nine Reflections on Distance* (New York: Columbia University Press, 2001), pp. 173–80. Following the work of David Daube, a British scholar, who, in 1966 published a thin book in London with the title, *He That Cometh*, Israel J. Yuval, the radical historian of Jewish medieval history argues that the Jewish Seder and the Christian Easter celebrations are but two polemical variants that grew out of the same root, early Judaism. According to this radical revisionism, each side might have had strong theological and liturgical influence upon the development of the other. From this perspective one cannot claim that Christianity was an offshoot of Judaism; in fact, both were replacements of the defunct paschal sacrifice after the destruction of the Temple in 70 CE. Yuval, in an interesting, philologically dense but not entirely persuasive paper, that, among other sources, analyzes two important Christian tracts with the same title, *Peri Pascha* by Melito of Sardis and Origen, argues that "the parallel development of two different narratives of a similar nature, meant for the same festival and introduced by two rival groups who lived alongside one another, ought to be discussed in a comparative manner." It was not only Christianity that tried hard to detach itself from the Jewish origins but

> a similar process of denial is evident in the early components of the Passover Hagadah. . . . The Hagadah is equally a response to the challenge of a rival Christian interpretation of the festival. . . . Both Christianity and Judaism developed parallel "Passover eve liturgies" featuring story-telling and commemorating. . . . The Jewish view that sees Judaism as always influencing Christianity, but never the other way around, is theologically grounded, based on the assumption that Judaism is the mother-religion of Christianity. But early Christianity and tannataic Judaism are two sister religions that took shape during the same period and under the same conditions of oppression and destruction. There is no reason not to assume a parallel and mutual development of both religions, during which sometimes Judaism internalized ideas of its rival rather than the other way around. (Israel J. Yuval, "Early Jewish-Christian Dialogue," in *Passover and Easter: Origin and History to Modern Times*, ed. Paul F. Bradshaw and Lawrence A. Hoffman [Notre Dame, IN: University of Notre Dame Press, 1999], pp. 98–124)

Daniel Boyarin's *Dying for God: Martyrdom and the Making of Christianity and Judaism* argues along similar lines: "We need to speak of a twin birth of Christianity and rabbinic Judaism as two forms of Judaism, and not of a genealogy in which one—Judaism—is parent to the other—Christianity" ([Stanford, CA: Stanford University Press, 1999], p. 2; cf. especially "Introduction: When Christians Were Jews: On Judeo-Christian Origins," pp. 1–21).

It seems to be important not to lose sight of the fact that parallel with the strengthening of the natural elements at the base of Christ's story, the importance of historical concreteness remained, as the use of the formula *sub Pontio Pilato* in the credo shows. In a sense, the weekly eucharistic observance on the first day of the week, on the day of the sun, celebrating the Resurrection of Christ, was also meant to emphasize the historicity of the feast: "The accommodation of the annual celebration to the structure of the week—the termination of the fast on the day of the resurrection, and the extension of the fast so as to begin on Friday, the day of the crucifixion—contained the seeds that would eventually yield the refraction of the single mystery of redemption into a series of commemorations of discrete historical moments in that mystery."[99]

Augustine, in De Trinitate (IV.5) wrote, "For he is believed to have been conceived on the 25th of March, upon which day he also suffered; so the womb of the Virgin, in which he was conceived, where no one of mortals was begotten, corresponds to the new grave in which he was buried, wherein was never man laid, neither before him nor since. But he was born, according to tradition upon December the 25th." According to the fourth Gospel, as I have already mentioned, the Crucifixion took place on Nisan 14. Some authors, among them Tertullian in *Adversus Iudaeos*, identified Nisan 14 with March 25 of the Julian calendar in the year of Christ's Passion, and that date coincided with the spring equinox in the Julian calendar. In the framework of this chronology, beginning and end meet: Jesus was conceived and crucified on the same day, on the spring equinox. His first coming in the flesh, coincides with and is dependent on the date of his death. Besides, the coincidence is closely tied to natural phenomena: Jesus' birth is nine months after the spring equinox, while the date of his death is on the winter solstice. (It is probable that here too we are confronted with a modulation of a rabbinical tradition, which identifies the dates of the birth and death of the patriarchs on the same day.) These dates stand in close connection with the conception of St. John, who was conceived at the autumnal equinox and born at the summer solstice. The death of the Savior is connected to his conception; suffering, tragedy, to hope, to the expectation of his coming, so death relates to birth, to the first coming in the flesh nine months later, on December 25, to the arrival of

99. Talley, *Origins of the Liturgical Year*, p. 39.

the sun at the winter solstice, and that is an affirmation of the hope in his second coming, the final *parousia*.

*

Now I would like to tell a story of dis-identification; instead of acceptance, organized rejection. What follows is a successful counterexample; instead of covering history, this is the story of chronological uncovering. This story is about consciously, officially dismantling a holiday, of emptying out a date, stripping away and taking back all the reference to reality that had been invested in it in the first place. I hope that the lessons of the story will help me to get nearer to the confirmation of a proposition. Michelet, in the chapter, "Prise de la Bastille, 14 juillet 1789", in his "Histoire de la Révolution Francaise" informed his readers "that 'still today' the key to the Bastille was stored in an iron cabinet in the archives of the French National Assembly." Reading Michelet, Hans Ulrich Gumbrecht remarked that according to historical pragmatics, a historical narrative should be able to demonstrate that "the thematized world of the past is metonymically present in the world of the recipients through certain objects."[100] What Gumbrecht most probably meant was that evocation of the past, in order to be successful and acceptable, should be able to demonstrate the existence of a connection between the narration of the past events and surviving traces (sites, objects, ruins, relics, recovered names, dates, and so on) of the narrated events. In the absence of such verifiable surviving reference to reality, dates cannot acquire privileged status or become holy days; instead they fall easily into oblivion.[101]

When the symbol of the Bastille was missing, people complained: Is it not true that this festival would have been more interesting if [there were] . . . in place of those columns and those insignificant canopies, a simulated Bastille that could have been stormed! This is what has just been done at Chartres. . . . It is thus that, through the magic of the arts, events depicted life-size leave a profound and lasting impression.[102]

---

100. Gumbrecht, "Versuch zur Antropolgie der Geschichtsschreibung," p. 491.

101. "Throughout the eighteenth century, thinkers from Locke to Hume had maintained that belief must be constantly given new impetus by the force of present impressions; by linking the memory of great events of the Revolution to periodic spectacles, it was believed that those events could be saved from gradually lapsing into unbelief. . . . By transporting the past into the present, the historical rite conferred the virtues of the former upon the latter" (Ozouf, *Festivals and the French Revolution*, p. 167).

102. Le patriote français, 28 Messidor, Year VI; quoted by Ozouf, *Festivals and the French Revolution*, p. 319, n. 49.

According to the first paragraph of the "Tenth Executive Order with the Status of Law of the year 1950," April 4 is "the commemoration of the Hungarian people's never ending gratitude, love and friendly and allied fidelity to her Liberator and Hero, the Soviet Union, the Guarantor of her Independence, the Chief Guardian and Strongest Champion of Peace, and April 4 should be the Feast of the Glorious Soviet Army and that of the Teacher and True Friend of Progressive Mankind, the Great Stalin." The Hungarian history books of the Communist era remembered April 4, 1945, as the Day Of Liberation, the day when the Soviet army cleared Hungary of the last Fascist German soldier. April 4 became Hungary's National holiday, her Independence Day, her official *quatorze juillet*.

In the late 1980s, Hungarian Communists started to behave as if it had not been history (the coming of the end of Communism), but rather historical antiquarianism that forced them to give up one of their last strongholds. In 1988, in the weekly *Hungarian Youth*, the then director of the Historical Institute of the Hungarian Socialist Workers' Party stated that in the light of the latest archival research, "we now know two things for sure: that it was not Battonya that was the first Hungarian village to be liberated in the course of World War II, and that it is not April 4 that is the day of the complete liberation of the country from the Nazis. April 4 is in fact April 13."

The historiographical withdrawal had certain "antiquarian" antecedents. In 1982, two experts in scientific socialism published a well-researched paper in which they claimed, on the basis of documents allegedly found in the archive of the Military Research Institute, that "it seems most probable that despite the popular belief, it was not the village of Battonya that was first liberated by the advancing Red Army."[103]

The director of the Museum of the Military Academy, in an interview he gave in April 1989, went even further: "I would like to say that the first Hungarian settlement to be liberated cannot even be found in Hungary. It is in Northern Transylvania, in the valley of Uzd. At that time the borders of Hungary crossed the Carpathian Mountains—why should one deny this? I count the first Hungarian villages from there. I want to be precise, so I start with the Trianon borders."[104] Now it is true that Hungary,

103. Mihály Korom and György Zielbauer, "Magyarország felszabadulásának megindulása" [The Beginning of the Liberation of Hungary], in *Tudományos Szocializmus Füzetek* 67 (1982).

104. Ignác Ölvedi, in *Magyar Hírlap*, April 1, 1989.

as Germany's closest ally, invaded northern Transylvania in 1940 in order to recapture some of the territory that had been given to Romania in 1920, as part of the Trianon Peace Treaty. But the military expert could even have suggested Naples as the first liberated Hungarian settlement, on much the same grounds, for Hungary captured Naples not once but twice, in the middle of the fourteenth century. A few days before the legal Fall of Communism, just before the first post-Communist democratic election, the military officer had realized that the time for not-so-covert nationalist discourse had arrived once more.

The historical situation became somewhat confusing in retrospect, not only in southeastern Hungary from where the Soviet army was advancing in 1944, but even on the northern borders of the country, where Nemesmedves, the village allegedly liberated last on April 4, could be found. In a rather cryptic article published in March 1989, a historian argued that "the latest historical research has proved beyond any doubt that there were armed clashes on Hungarian territory as late as April 11. In the light of the latest scientifically available evidence, the last village cannot have been Nemesmedves; thus, Hungary was not liberated on April 4."[105]

Even before Communism was over in Hungary, the location and the date of both the first and last liberated settlements, thus the historically exact date of the Communist national holiday, had been successfully undermined: all ties between the date of the holiday and the references on which this date had been based, had been loosened. A few months before the changes, the Communists, although still in charge, had to realize that there was no chance of keeping April 4 in the national calendar together with October 23, the day when the anti-Soviet revolution broke out in Budapest. (By the end of the Communist period, it was obvious that the regime had no power to prevent the inclusion of that date in the national holiday cycle.) It was unimaginable to create a new commemorative cycle out of April 4, June 16 (the day of Imre Nagy's execution and reburial), and October 23. There is no temporal, causal, or omnitemporal connection between these dates. The days of April 4 were obviously numbered. There was nothing left for the regime to do except to try to keep up appearances: to prove that the problem with April 4 was purely chronological, that is, that nothing remarkable had actually happened on that particular day: it was an archival,

---

105. György Zielbauer, in *Reform*, March 10, 1989.

archaeological mistake. The political withdrawal was dressed up as an advance of positivist scholarship.

After all the historical arguments had been put forward, a new question arose: On what date should the country remember the liberation? If—as a consequence of the indeterminacy of the past—either April 11 or 13 were taken as the unquestionable anniversary (but which of the two?), this would amount to retroactively extending the period of Hungary's alliance with Nazi Germany by a few more days. Even if the liberation of the country had taken place on April 4, Hungary would still undeniably have remained Germany's last ally. And who would have wanted to extend this shameful period by a few more days in the wake of the fiftieth anniversary of the end of World War II? In an interview on April 1, 1989, one of the researchers from the Institute of Party History drew the inevitable conclusion: "Moving the anniversary a few days ahead, would be tantamount to strengthening the undifferentiated thesis of the 'last ally.'"[106]

One of the obvious alternatives would have been December 21. On that day in 1944, the Provisional Assembly formed the provisional government in Debrecen, in the very same church where the Habsburgs had been dethroned and where Kossuth had read the Proclamation of Independence on April 14 back in 1849. The provisional government was still a coalition administration in which the Communists played an important, although minor role; the government declared war on Germany, recruited Hungarian soldiers who fought together with units of the Third Ukrainian Front, and helped the Red Army to liberate Austria. This seemed to be a perfect date on the eve of the introduction of the multiparty system, a few weeks before the scheduled first post-Communist democratic elections. The date was almost perfect. Almost, but not quite: it had one, just one, fatal flaw: December 21 was Iosif Visarionovich Stalin's birthday. In the spring of 1989 it was difficult to imagine the Hungarian Socialist Workers' Party suggesting that the date of Stalin's birthday should be declared a national holiday.

The chief officer of the "Young Guard" (the paramilitary unit of the Communist Youth Organization) made a suggestion at the very last minute: on March 31, 1990, he came up with the idea of moving April 4 forward to May 9, Victory Day in the Soviet Union (not to May 8, which was Victory Day in the West). In this way, as he said, "We would save ourselves

---

106. Karoly Urban, in *Magyar Hírlap*, April 1, 1989.

from the disgrace of having lost the war. We would be able to turn defeat into victory, and celebrate together with the victors . . . as one of them."[107] Unfortunately, between April 4 and May 9, 1990, the Communists lost the election and with them, Hungary has finally, irreparably lost the war.

April 4 is no longer a national holiday. The number of those who have vague memories of the military parades, the speeches, and the celebrations shrinks every year. Nobody demonstrates; nobody remembers the date. After 1989, when the Red Army became remembered more as the army that occupied Hungary until 1991 than as the army that liberated the country in 1945, it would have been impossible to refer to April 4 as the "Day of Liberation." Last year, perhaps even the year before, I completely forgot it myself. Only my son, who has an exceptionally good memory for dates, and who remembers them from the time he was two years old, asked me, "Do you know what date it is today? Do you still remember April 4 at all?"

April 4 has disappeared almost without a trace. What lies at the root of its extinction is not just the present weakness of the small Hungarian Communist Party, which does still celebrate, but other dates: July 6, when János Kádár died, and May 1, International Workers' Day. The handful of self-conscious Communists cannot stage a commemoration on April 4, as the concrete reference of the day, and also "the figurative realism" that was once evoked by it (if it was ever there) has been successfully undermined. World War II as such became problematic and politically sensitive after 1989, after the Fall of Communism. The notion of liberation—from Nazi occupation by the Soviet Red Army—was difficult to reconcile with the anti-Communist legitimization of the post-Communist regimes. At the beginning of the 1990s the new governments of the former Communist countries tried hard to defend themselves from the accusation of past collaboration and to clean up the historical record of the previous decades. The most obvious argument was to state that the post–World War II decades in Central and Eastern Europe were not part of "authentic national history," as the nations of that part of the world were under foreign occupation; Communism was introduced from the outside by the occupiers. Occupation and liberation did not go together.

When in 1986, after the fortieth anniversary of the end of World War II, *Pravda*, the official paper of the Soviet Communist Party, initiated

107. József Lestak, in *Magyar Hírlap*, April 1, 1989.

a public debate about the possibility of establishing a "Day of Commemoration," in memory of the victims of World War II, 43 percent of the respondents opted for June 22, the day when Nazi Germany attacked the Soviet Union in 1941. June 22 is a powerful chronological landmark, standing for the starting point of the epic of the Great Patriotic War, which chronologically comprised the German-Soviet (that is, Fascist-Communist) conflict (according to Soviet historiography, the essence of World War II), which was formally part of World War II. The Great Patriotic War is framed by "strong dates": June 22 and May 9, Victory Day in Russia, the inevitable outcome of and the punishment for the Nazi attack in Soviet historiography. Some of the most embarrassing Soviet episodes of World War II—the Molotov-Ribbentrop pact, the occupation of the Baltic states, the Western Ukraine, and Belorussia, and the Katyn massacre—took place before June 1941 and so lay outside the 1,418-day temporal framework of the Great Patriotic War.[108] As it is the Great Patriotic War—and not World War II—that is commemorated in post-Soviet Russia, memory here is still shielded from some of those embarrassing elements that make the anniversary of the war so difficult to commemorate in the other Eastern and Central European countries.

Victory Day, the so-called VE Day, falls on May 8 in America and Western Europe, in contrast to the May 9 celebration in Russia. On May 7, 1945, in Reims, General Jodl signed the document of the surrender of the German forces in front of General Eisenhower. The surrender was to come into effect on May 8. During the night of May 8 to 9, the final signing of the unconditional surrender took place in Berlin in front of Marshal Zhukov, the leading general of the Red Army. Soldiers of the Nazi garrison in Prague were still fighting on the final day of the war, May 9, the traditional date of the widely televised Soviet military parades on Red Square in Moscow. Despite the one-day-late victory day, the wreath-laying ceremony at the tomb of the unknown soldier at the Kremlin Wall, together with a similar ceremony at Lenin's Mausoleum earlier on the same day—linking the Bolshevik Revolution with victory over Fascism—customarily took place on the previous day, May 8, in other words on VE Day in the West.[109]

108. Cf. Andriy Chernevych, "Victory Dates: Shaping the Memory of the Great Patriotic War" (Mimeo, 2000).

109. Cf. Andriy Chernevych, "The Wreath-laying Ritual to the Tomb of the Unknown Soldier at the Kremlin Wall" (Mimeo, 2000).

Choosing between May 8 and 9 as the authentic end of World War II or "the last military operation of Soviet troops in the war," as the *Soviet Military Encyclopedia* phrased it, is not a purely academic question.[110]

According to the official Soviet version, presented in the five-volume *History of the Great Patriotic War*, Prague was liberated by the tank divisions of the First and Fourth Ukrainian Fronts, which fought together with the First Independent Czech Tank Brigade. The military units entered Prague on the morning of May 9, 1945, in order to give support to the Communist-led uprising in the city. Still, after the "velvet revolution" of 1989 until the collapse of the Soviet Union, a tank stood on a pedestal in Prague, which was allegedly the first Soviet armored vehicle to have entered the city, driven by Senior Lieutenant Ivan Goncharenko, who was killed on the morning of May 9, 1945, when his tank was severely damaged. According to Communist memory, the grateful inhabitants of the city asked the Soviet authorities to donate the tank to Prague as an eternal reminder of the sacrifice of the Red Army. Goncharenko's tank was almost Michelet's key to the Bastille: the nearly genuine material connection between the narrated and commemorated event, and the present—as it was presented by the propaganda department. (Eventually, the Soviet military decided not to donate the damaged "T-34," but offered the more advanced "NS-2" instead. This more sophisticated version—the roughly authentic relic—stood on its pedestal in a busy Prague street until 1991 as the tangible reminder and proof of the Soviet military victory and the Soviet liberation of Prague.)[111] The Supreme Soviet even established a medal "For the Liberation of Prague," which was awarded to all the participants in the battle.[112]

"Prague was really liberated by foreign troops, after all," confirmed an American war correspondent, who was in the Czech capital from May 8, 1945. But, he continued, "not by the Allies, who did not arrive until the shooting was over, but by 22,000 Russian outlaws wearing German uni-

110. *Sovietskaia Voiennaia Entziklopediia* [Soviet Military Encyclopedia], vol. 5 (Moscow: Voenizdat, 1978), p. 496.

111. Cf. A. Krushinskis, "Dva Tanka" [Two Tanks], in *Pravda*, May 2, 1991, p. 5. Krushinskis mentions that after the Czechoslovak Velvet Revolution, in the course of the withdrawal of the Soviet army from Czech territory, in 1991 one of the tanks of the Soviet army, a "T-72," caught fire and exploded, killing more than twenty Soviet soldiers in the accident.

112. Cf. Nataliya Shlikta, "The Day of the Liberation of Prague and the 'Vlasov Phenomenon': The Problems 'Under Discussion'" (Mimeo, 2000), p. 4.

forms."[113] Those Russians in the German uniform were members of the First Division of Lieutenant-General Andrei Andreievich Vlasov's Russian Liberation Army (Russkaia Osvoboditiel'naia Armiia). Vlasov was chief military advisor to Chiang Kai-shek in China in 1938–39, fought bravely at Kiev at the beginning of World War II, played an important role in the defense of Moscow, and was one of the commanders of the Volkhov front in June 1942, before being captured by the Nazis. Despite these accomplishments, the official Soviet history of the Second World War, published in 1961, makes only a one-line reference to Vlasov and only in connection with his treachery and cowardice that caused the loss of the 2nd Shock Army on the Volkhov Front.[114] After his capture, General Vlasov cooperated with the Nazis, who appointed him to the leadership of KONR, the Committee for the Liberation of the Peoples of Russia (Komitet Osvobozhdeniia Narodov Rossii) and that of ROA, the Russian Liberation Army. "Although he was barely mentioned in the Soviet Union, his name became synonymous with the figure of the traitor, and in popular perception the term *vlasovets* meant traitor, defector."[115] According to some of the deeper and more substantive analyses of Vlasov's activities, he offered his services to the Nazis, who contemplated the idea of organizing the approximately one million Soviet prisoners of war potentially able or willing to be drafted into the Wehrmacht and the SS, in one Russian unit under General Vlasov.[116] Actually ROA forces were not deployed by the hesitant Germans, and the only armed incident in which Vlasov's army—although without Vlasov himself—took part occurred at the very end of the war, when upon "its arrival in Czech territory, the First KONR Division entered upon the most dramatic single episode of the entire history of wartime Soviet opposition."[117]

On the basis of published descriptions, including the documentary film on Vlasov's activities (*The Twice Accused General*), it is not easy to

113. Cf. George Fischer, *Soviet Opposition to Stalin: A Case Study in the Second World War* (Cambridge, MA: Harvard University Press, 1952), p. 102.

114. Cf. Catherine Andreyev, *Vlasov and the Russian Liberation Movement: Soviet Reality and Emigré Theories* (Cambridge: Cambridge University Press, 1987), p. 10.

115. Cf. Shlikta, "Day of the Liberation of Prague and the 'Vlasov Phenomenon,'" pp. 11–12.

116. Cf. George Fischer, *Soviet Opposition to Stalin* (Cambridge, MA: Harvard University Press, 1952); Nikolai Tolstoy, *Victims of Yalta* (London: Corgi Books, 1979); Andreyev, *Vlasov and the Russian Liberation Movement*.

117. Fischer, *Soviet Opposition to Stalin*, p. 100.

reconstruct what actually happened: most probably, ROA tried to surrender to the advancing American army units, before the Red Army could capture them. The leaders of the Prague uprising, faced with desperate SS resistance, asked for military help, and the First Vlasovite Division, stationed on Czech territory and led by General Buniachenko, felt that it would be expedient to do something that would impress the Western Allied command and so decided to support the uprising, especially in the light of the inevitable and dramatically approaching final German collapse. According to a recent and serious Russian analysis, Vlasov was against any military confrontation with the Germans.[118] Still, the Russian Liberation Army entered Prague and helped the uprising, the leaders of which, together with the surprised inhabitants of Prague, were not quite sure where the help had come from. According to Fischer, "The Vlasov troops were given a jubilant reception by the populace, who were evidently never quite sure just who their saviors were—an understandable confusion resulting from the spectacle of Russian-speaking soldiers in German-type uniforms savagely opposing the SS forces."[119] Fischer's description is verified by the documentary on Vlasov's fate, which shows cheering crowds greeting the advancing First Division in the streets of Prague.[120] Not only the Czechs but most probably the fighting SS units were surprised to be confronted by soldiers wearing German uniforms. "A captain of General Eisenhower's staff, in charge of an armored scout column which had been sent ahead to discover what was happening in Prague . . . was very surprised to see the German uniforms of the 1st Division."[121]

The Americans told the Vlasovites that the demarcation lines had been agreed upon between the American and Soviet staffs, and according to the agreement, the Red Army would enter the city. When the National Council, the resistance leadership, learned who it had received help from, it demanded either the unconditional surrender of Vlasov's army to the Soviets or their immediate withdrawal from the city. The Vlasovites understood their hopeless situation and left Prague, probably as early as May 7 or

118. S. V. Ermachenkov and A. N. Pochtariev, "Poslednii Pokhod Vlasovskoi Armii" [The Last Campaign of the Vlasov Army] *Voprosy Istorii* 8 (1998): 98–99.

119. Fischer, *Soviet Opposition to Stalin*, p. 101.

120. *Vlasov. Dvazhdy prokliatyii general* [Vlasov. The Twice Accused General], doc. film (60 min.), written, edited, and directed by I. Betke and P. Sergeev, 1995 SFB WDR, 1995 RGTRK "Ostankino," "Lentefilm."

121. Andreyev, *Vlasov and the Russian Liberation Movement*, p. 75.

at the latest in the morning of the 8th.[122] On their way through to the American lines, they became involved in skirmishes with both the retreating Germans and the advancing Soviets, thereby guaranteeing that Prague would be liberated by the inhabitants themselves.[123] The German garrison in Prague surrendered at 4:00 PM on May 8, probably at a time when Vlasov's soldiers had already left the city but before the arrival of the first units of the Red Army.[124] Despite the German surrender, other SS units entered the city and when the first Soviet soldiers, Senior-Lieutenant Goncharenko in his T-34 among them, arrived next morning in Prague, there was still scattered fighting in the city.

In accordance to the Yalta agreement, Soviet citizens on foreign territory, including Vlasov's soldiers, were repatriated to the Soviet Union. On August 12, 1946, Moscow Radio broadcast a communiqué that stated that the Military Collegium of the Supreme Court of the USSR had sentenced Vlasov, together with ten of his closest military subordinates, to death and that the sentences had been carried out.

After the defeat of the 1968 Prague Spring, when the Soviet army, together with divisions from some other Warsaw Pact countries, invaded Czechoslovakia and Soviet tanks rolled once more through the streets of Prague, "Goncharenko's tank" acquired a new meaning: the armored vehicle on the pedestal belonged to and reminded people of the invaders, the occupiers, and clearly not of the liberation, in which the tank, offered as a relic, had definitively not taken part. The fake, tangible relic created a clear new connection between the Soviets and the present. This was the time when the official Soviet version of the liberation of Prague was publicly questioned for the first time in Czechoslovakia since World War II.[125] In

122. Ermachenkov and Pochtariev, "Poslednii Pokhod Vlasovskoi Armii," p. 99.

123. Or, according to a slightly different version:

Now came the news of the unconditional surrender of Germany; Buniachenko requested and received authority from the provisional (patriotic?) Czech Government for his Division to evacuate the city westwards. Fearful of losing such choice victims, the Communists attempted to encircle Prague and prevent their egress. In this confused state of affairs the KONR men found themselves once again allied with Germans similarly trying to avoid capture by the Red Army, and with the aid of two companies of *SS Panzerjager* troops they smashed their way through the cordon. . . . Inadvertently, by preventing a clash between the SS and the Red Army, they had saved the city of Prague from becoming a battlefield. (Tolstoy, *Victims of Yalta*, p. 370)

124. Ermachenkov and Pochtariev, "Poslednii Pokhod Vlasovskoi Armii," p. 99.

125. Shlikta, "Day of the Liberation of Prague and the 'Vlasov Phenomenon,'" p. 8.

1991 the tank was removed, disappeared from sight, and for the first time Prague did not celebrate on May 9 but on the 8th instead. However, what is celebrated nowadays is not the liberation of Prague but Victory Day, the end of the Second World War.

It is highly probable that the German garrison in Prague capitulated before the entry of the Red Army to the city, but it would be hard to exclude the possibility that scattered fighting continued until later that day, May 9. However, even today it would not be easy to commemorate an event in which Stalin's former soldiers, fighting on Hitler's side, played a significant role. In 1993 a cross was unveiled in the Prague cemetery of Olkhov, on the common grave of the approximately twelve hundred ROA Vlasovite soldiers who died in Prague. The inscription on the cross reads, "We died for our and your liberty."[126] Senior-Lieutenant Ivan Goncharenko is buried nearby, also in the Olkhov Cemetery.

The Soviet Communists can still commemorate November 7, despite the fact that most of the popular historical images we have of that day come from Eisenstein's fictive reconstruction in his film, *October*.[127] The date when the outbreak of the Bolshevik Revolution is remembered still has enough reality-reference, and a potent enough image of action cycle, to tie the figure strongly to the temporal order.[128]

126. Ibid., p. 20.

127. Eisenstein's film in turn was a recreation of Nikolai Evreinov's spectacular reenactment of "The Storming of the Winter Palace" on the third anniversary of the October Revolution. With one thousand soldiers and sailors Evreinov staged a nocturnal mass spectacle in front of more than one hundred thousand spectators. Eisenstein had not been in the city during the time of the Bolshevik Revolution, nor did he see Evreinov's spectacle on Palace Square in Petrograd; his reconstruction was based on the film of Evreinov's theatricalization of history. "The crowd shots in [Eisenstein's film] may be familiar to those who have never seen *October*, because they are the first of several sequences from the film that have subsequently been used as documentary film material" (Richard Taylor, *October* [London: British Film Institute Publishing, 2002], p. 32). On "The Storming of the Winter Palace," see also James von Geldern, *Bolshevik Festivals 1917–1920* (Berkeley: University of California Press, 1993), pp. 199–207.

On the shooting of *October*, Viktor Shklovskii, the formalist literary theoretician, remarked, "The Revolution has taken into its care museums and palaces that it does not know what to do with. Eisenstein's film is the first rational use of the Winter Palace. He has destroyed it" (quoted in Taylor, *October*, p. 13).

128. "'Invented traditions' have significant social and political functions, and would neither come into existence nor establish themselves if they could not acquire them. . . . Yet it also seems clear that the most successful examples of manipulation are those which

In the absence of firm or firmly established temporal place, however, the referred event ceases to remain an event; it no longer has any reality and might degenerate into a mere sign. And commemorating a sign, instead of an event, is an overambitious expectation. In order for a date to became an occasion for meaningful commemoration—it seems—the figural interpretation, the *demonstration* should be reconciled with the *presentation* of a (at least seemingly) verifiable uninterrupted historical sequence of events. "An event taken as a figure [should] preserve its literal and historical meaning."[129]

*

The problem with October 30/November 4 was that the former event happened only *almost* on the latter date. The impresarios of the commemoration were not able to protect "the maintenance of the basic historical reality of figures against attempts at . . . allegorical interpretation."[130] Partly as a consequence of the chronological inexactitude, it was just too obvious that the events of October 30 happened on that very date and not on the day of the Soviet intervention. In the meantime, between October 30 and November 4, 1956, Kádár, as a member of the Nagy government, first dissolved the old Communist Party, then founded a new one, voted for Hungary's neutrality, agreed with Hungary's leaving the Warsaw Pact, and greeted the uprising as a revolution. He did all these things after October 30, after the massacre on Republic Square. As a consequence of the intervening events, October 30 could not be convincingly presented as coincident with November 4. In this case, *almost* was too much; despite the mere four-day difference it was still too far away from October 30.

The forced nature of the association was revealed by the clumsy ritual: the commemoration on Republic Square, with the recollection of the martyrdom of the defenders, who had died rather than surrender (although the truce-bearers, carrying the white flag, were just attempting to negotiate the conditions of surrender when they were killed); the laying of

---

exploit practices which clearly meet a felt—not necessarily a clearly understood—need among particular bodies of people" (Hobsbawm, "Mass-Producing Traditions," p. 307).

This is Hobsbawm's most clearly stated explanation of how so-called invented traditions come into being and are kept alive. As my text shows, I feel his argument leaves the core of the issue unanswered.

129. Auerbach, *Mimesis*, pp. 195–96.
130. Ibid., p. 196.

wreaths both on the memorial plaque and on the graves in the Pantheon of the Heroes of the Working-Class Movement in the nearby cemetery; and ending the stages of the celebration on Szabadság tér (Liberty Square), right in the center of the city, in front of the American Embassy, by laying a wreath at the memorial of the Red Army.

The Soviet memorial was erected in 1948, in gratitude for and in memory of the liberation of Hungary from the Nazis during World War II. No new memorial was set up after 1956 to remember the Soviet help in crushing the "counterrevolution." Holding commemorative ceremonies at the World War II monument on November 4 made it possible to equate the counterrevolution with the Nazis, the acts of the counterrevolutionaries with the terror of the Fascists, and at the same time made it unnecessary to set up a new monument with an inscription that would have reminded people of the role the Soviets had to play in 1956. In this case 1945 simply overwrote 1956 on the column: 1945 covered 1956.

On July 28, 1989, the Central Committee of the Hungarian Socialist Workers' Party discussed a suggested statement concerning "The Day of National Reconciliation." On June 16 Imre Nagy was reburied; on July 6, János Kádár died.[131] The text suggested that as a symbol of the chain of events between October 23 and November 4, 1956, the country should commemorate October 23 as "the day of reconciliation."[132] "On that day," in the new reading of the Hungarian Communists,

a popular uprising broke out against a regime that had become alienated from the people, as a consequence of the deep offenses suffered by national sovereignty. . . .

131. The date June 16 is incidentally "Bloom's Day," the celebration of June 16, 1904, when Leopold Bloom took a journey through the streets of Dublin between 8 AM and 2 o'clock the next morning in James Joyce's *Ulysses*. The date, June 16, is Leopold Bloom's birthday; Bloom's grandfather and father, Rudolf Virag (later Rudolph Bloom), were both born in Szombathely, western Hungary.

132. October 23, by the way, marks another anniversary as well. Dr. John Lightfoot, a contemporary of James Ussher, archbishop of Armagh, the famous chronographer of the seventeenth century, in his opus, *A Few and New Observations on the Book of Genesis, the most of them certain, the rest probable, all harmless, strange and rarely heard of before*, published in 1642, set the beginning of the world at exactly 9 AM on October 23, of the year 4004 BC. Lightfoot, the vice chancellor of Cambridge, worked hard to match the exact date of the Creation—based on a peculiar reading of the Old Testament—with the start of the academic year at Cambridge. Cf. Peter James, *Centuries of Darkness: A Challenge to the Conventional Chronology of Old World Archaeology* (New Brunswick, NJ: Rutgers University Press, 1993), p. 6.

The renewing Hungarian Socialist Workers' Party sees October 23 as the symbol of the movement for Democratic Socialism, for national sovereignty, for comprehensive and deep reforms. . . . We bow our heads before those too, who, led by good intentions, and their conviction, by fighting on the other side, became the victims of fighting or atrocities.[133]

A long and heated discussion preceded the passing of the resolution. The debate started in fact immediately after Nagy's reburial. At the previous meeting of the Central Committee a plan was put forward to set up "a joint national votive memorial," inspired by the Spanish example after Franco's death and to organize an international conference on October 23 with the participation of "Spanish, Greek, Portuguese, and probably Uruguayan and Brazilian [*sic*] official delegations." At the same time there was a preliminary proposal to name October 23 as "the day of the martyrs."[134] The final statement of reconciliation proposed October 23 as a "national day of remembrance," October 30 as the "day of the martyrs and victims," and October 31 as "the anniversary of the formation of the Hungarian Socialist Workers' Party."[135] "Perhaps the members of the Central Committee have noticed that among the proposed days there is no mention of November 4. We wanted to show up two roads, the two directions in which the original events might have led: one that led to a compromise, the other that contained no possibility of a compromise; roads that were still open on 31 October in 1956"; that was how the secretary in charge of agitation and propaganda explained the strange silence around November 4.[136]

November 4 could not have a proper place in this new succession of dates for at least two reasons: this time it was not enough to remain silent about the foreign intervention, not to remind the country of the role played by the Soviets, of the suppression of the revolution. Even the cover of the date, October 30—as later developments made it obvious—ceased to have an acceptable place in the chronology. The party could not have its

133. In 1989 Proceedings of the Central Committee of the Hungarian Socialist Workers' Party, Budapest, 1993, pp. 1403–4.

134. Ibid., pp. 1241, 1244.

135. Both Imre Nagy and János Kádár were among the seven founding members of the Hungarian Socialist Workers' Party. The day stands for their joint efforts, their "action in concert," their close relationship (which they surely had but definitively not in this sense). The 1989 Proceedings . . . , pp. 1347–48.

136. Ibid., p. 1350.

own partisan martyrs when it aspired to become the initiator of collective national dates of remembering.[137] (Later somebody discovered this consequence as well.) In the absence of the other side, there cannot be either October 30 or November 4, not even November 4 understood as October 30.

"A date is a member of a class," stated Levi-Strauss.

These classes of dates are definable by the meaningful character each date has within the class in relation to other dates which also belong to it, and by the absence of this meaningful character with respect to dates appertaining to a different class. . . . A historical date, taken in itself, would have no meaning, for it has no reference outside itself. . . . The code can therefore consist only of classes of dates, where each date has meaning in as much as it stands in complex relations of correlation and opposition with other dates. . . . The dates appropriate to each class are irrational in relation to all those of other classes.[138]

If there are antinomical positions, "irregularity" of dates, then—contrary to what Michel De Certeau thinks—it does not "suffice that one of the terms of the conflict be classified as past."[139] Then the past should be recreated by a new successivity, proper historical continuity "in which the links have an explanatory meaning."[140]

After a close reading of the proposed text, a member of the Central Committee with an eye for hermeneutics pointed out the obvious contra-

---

137. "The problem of the Hungarian 1956 could be and should be solved immediately by accepting Georg Lukács's formula, according to which the Hungarian 1956 could not be simply defined either as counterrevolution or as revolution but should be characterized as an uprising. In Lukacs's view the characteristic of an uprising that distinguishes it from both a revolution and a counterrevolution is the fact that an uprising does not have a clear aim. If we succeeded in having the party accept this formula, then both the scholarly research on 1956 and the debate of opposing views about it would become unhindered. It would be possible to reach an agreement to the effect that 1956 had both revolutionary and counterrevolutionary currents." This is how the philosopher and the expert of the so-called Asiatic mode of production, Ferenc Tőkei, tried to reconcile the opposing views (Proceedings, p. 44).

Lukács was a member of the Nagy government, so he was expelled from the party after 1956 but was readmitted some years later, when he arrived at the conclusion that "even the worst Socialism was better than the best of Capitalism." Lukács, when having formed his views about the 1956 "uprising," had most probably been heavily influenced by Albert Camus's *L'homme révolté* (originally published in 1951).

138. Lévi-Strauss, *Savage Mind*, pp. 259–60.

139. De Certeau, *Writing of History*, p. 89.

140. See Patrick Nerhot, *Law, Writing, Meaning: An Essay of Legal Hermeneutics* (Edinburgh: Edinburgh University Press, 1992), p. 89.

diction in the statement: "Here is this sentence: 'We bow our heads in front of those . . . on the other side.' But in the context of the text, *we* are in fact *the other side* as well."[141] If everybody fought for Democratic Socialism, for the sovereignty of the nation, for deep reforms, then we are the heirs of everybody on all sides, on both sides, then we are both on this side and on the other one (if the other side had any meaning at all). We shot at ourselves while defending ourselves from ourselves, and either we are the Soviets too, or both of us (that is, we) were invaded. The secretary in charge of agitation and propaganda agreed: "Yes, by deleting 'the other side' in fact, we are able to strengthen the number and position of those who stood up for Socialism."[142]

At this point a member of the Central Committee proposed the logically obvious:

I would leave October 30 entirely out of the picture. The anniversary of the attack against the party headquarters is an internal business. What we want to create is a national holiday, but this one cannot be anything but a memory of the Hungarian Socialist Workers' Party and of the Communist movement. What happened on Republic Square cannot become an affair of the state, but remains only the memory of the party.[143]

The director of the Institute of the Party and the Party Archive (he was one of my history professors at Budapest University) drew the historical conclusion of the proposal:

Why is October 23 the right solution? . . . What did our current possible partners and adversaries [the new opposition parties that were being formed in July 1989] say in the past decades? They said that [in 1956] they had not fought against Socialism, but they had wanted, so to say, to correct Socialism. What they said in 1956 is no different from what we want to say today. If—according to the suggestion—October 23 became "the day of renewal of the People's Democracy" then this would make it obvious that we support the most valuable traditions of our nation. . . . In this way we will be able to create *continuity* for our own present history.[144]

The new succession creates *temporum certitudo*, not only the certainty of times but also the certainty of fixed dates. The unmediated cardinal

141. Proceedings, p. 1359.
142. Ibid., p. 1377.
143. Ibid., p. 1368.
144. Ibid., p. 1362; emphasis added.

numbers, with the smallest possible distance in between the dates, erase the appearance of interpretation and refer to what Barthes described in a different context as "concrete reality."[145]

In this reading, Kádár and Nagy together were the founders of the Hungarian Socialist Workers' Party, Kádár (the executioner) continued the work of (his victim) Imre Nagy, there is no break on November 4, and now (after the reburial in July 1989, when new parties are being formed) the party continues to follow their direction.

Although the members of the parliament would have liked nothing more than to have their lunch break, the speaker of the House proposed discussing just one more item on the agenda before lunch: "Reparations for violations of the law following the 1956 *popular uprising*" and "Reparations to those who were interned or resettled by force after 1956". . . . After lunch the program of the parliament became jam-packed, and the time wasted [*sic!*] with the general debate about reparations and rehabilitation could not be regained until the late evening hours. . . . Still, the members of the parliament accepted the proposed bill both in general and in details.[146]

In such a way, after lunch, did the last Communist parliament, by a summary decision and without examining individual cases, rehabilitate almost all the victims of the postrevolutionary terror—except for some of the major leaders of the revolution, like Imre Nagy, who were rehabilitated later, as the result of seemingly proper court proceedings.

Between this decision and dinner, the members of the parliament decided that October 23 would not become a day of rest and a national holiday as the "day of reconciliation." Instead, a national referendum should be held to determine which anniversaries should become national holidays. Following this decision, the plenary session of the last Communist parliament "burst into long and loud applause when the prime minister announced that the proclamation of the Republic is planned for the morning hours of 23 October 1989, right in front of the parliament building."[147] One hundred forty-one years after Lajos Kossuth proclaimed the dethronement of the Habsburgs in the Great Church of Debrecen, on October 23, 1989, before Communism and the People's Republic stepped off the

145. Roland Barthes, "The Reality Effect," in his *The Rustle of Language* (Berkeley: University of California Press, 1989), p. 146.

146. *Népszabadság*, October 21, 1989, p. 4.

147. Ibid.

scene, the Republic was proclaimed from the balcony of the neogothic/baroque Hungarian Parliament.

Two days later an invitation was published in the major newspapers: "We inform the inhabitants of the country that the Hungarian Republic will be proclaimed on Kossuth Square at noon on Monday, October 23, 1989. We cordially invite each Hungarian citizen and foreign guest to this festive occasion." At the same time the organizers of the first, open, public commemoration of the 1956 Revolution wanted to address the crowd also from the balcony of the parliament. The speaker of the House insisted, however, that the balcony could be used only by high representatives of the state and offered something lower, the steps of the parliament instead, the place where Count Károlyi had proclaimed the Second Republic, after the end of World War I, following the dissolution of the Austro-Hungarian monarchy on November 16, 1918.

At the very time when the first officially tolerated commemoration after 1956 was taking place in the streets of Budapest, from the balcony of the building of the parliament—the same balcony where the hesitant Imre Nagy appeared, following the popular demand in the evening of October 23, and addressed the crowd as "comrades" (see Figure 4.1); but "we are no comrades" came the immediate response from below, and after a few seconds that appeared as eternity, the bespectacled man, who looked much older than his age, decided to start once more (he did not know yet that what he started was not a speech but the revolution), this time as "ladies and gentlemen"—from the same neogothic balcony, a former Communist ambassador to the Soviet Union and later to (East) Berlin, a former hardliner secretary of the Central Committee, who by chance happened to be the speaker of the parliament, and who, as such, according to the constitution, at the moment of the proclamation of the Republic, became its first provisional president (and who, later on, would become a born-again nationalist, populist member of the parliament of the new Republic), proclaimed the Hungarian Republic. (See Figure 4.2.)

The leaders of the People's Republic tried hard to find an acceptable place for October 23 in the emerging new cycle of holidays: instead of giving in to history, they decided to make history, to proclaim the new form of state and point at the inevitable and heavy coincidence. The last Communist government and the vanishing old parliament hoped that the proclamation of the Republic would overwrite the recovered memory of the revolution. The calendrical inversion recalls deep-rooted strategies: "The most

FIGURE 4.1. Imre Nagy addressing the demonstrators from
the balcony of the Hungarian Parliament, October 23, 1956.
MTI Photo Archives.

efficient way of erasing a memory is by superimposing on it a counter-
memory. . . . The Christians followed the same principle by building their
churches on the ruins of pagan temples and by observing their feasts on the
dates of pagan festivals."[148]

At the turn of the millennium, however, a decade after the sacrifice
of the People's Republic, on the still fiercely contested day of October 23,
when thousands of elderly self-proclaimed new veterans, "Certified Members" of one of the mushrooming "World Federations of Hungarian Freedom Fighters of the 1956 Revolution" swarm on to the squares of Budapest
and the cemetery on the outskirts of the city, where the executed prime

148. Assmann, *Moses the Egyptian*, pp. 58–59.

FIGURE 4.2. Mátyás Szűrös, the interim president of the Republic, addressing the crowd from the balcony of the Hungarian Parliament, October 23, 1989. MTI Photo Archives.

minister, together with the executed revolutionaries rest, still loudly demonstrating against the Communists, the former Communist ambassador from the former Soviet Union and the former East Berlin is probably the only person in Hungary (except perhaps a few historians, like me) who heroically still remembers October 23 as "The Day of the Republic."

5

A Rule of Law

A legal case that had been under consideration for seventy-three years was closed on November 28, 1994, in an open session of the Supreme Court of the Hungarian Republic. The Supreme Court upheld the death sentence brought against Mihály Francia Kiss in 1957 for war crimes and other criminal acts by the Council of the People's Tribunal of the Supreme Court of the Hungarian People's Republic. The Supreme Court reexamined the case at the appeal of Francia Kiss's bereaved daughter. According to the criminal code, since a claimant may make such an appeal only once and since there may be no appeal to a decision made by the Supreme Court in such criminal cases, this legal procedure, which was initiated in the summer of 1921 and which continued with interruptions until the end of 1994, was finally closed.[1]

In August 1921 Albert Vári, assistant royal prosecutor, and Péter Kovács, prosecutor, were directed by the minister of justice to undertake an investi-

1. Naturally, the white terrorist's was not the longest legal procedure. According to the records: "When the State of Israel was established and the Supreme Court inaugurated in Jerusalem, dozens of Christian clerics implored President Smoira to allow the Supreme Court, as the successor of the Great Sanhedrin (the Supreme Jewish Court of antiquity), to retry Jesus Christ and thereby rectify the injustice caused to him" (see Asher Maoz, "Historical Adjudication: Courts of Law, Commissions of Inquiry, and 'Historical Truth,'" *Law and History Review* 18, no. 3 [fall 2000]: 1). The president of the Supreme Court sent the request to the state attorney, who in turn started extensive research, the result of which was published in the book *The Trial and Death of Jesus* (New York: Harper and Row, 1967).

gation of murders and other atrocities committed in the region between the Danube and the Tisza rivers in 1919 and 1920. The investigation, however, was interrupted when Governor Horthy—who came to power after the defeat of the 1919 First Hungarian Soviet Republic—granted a general amnesty to those who committed crimes out of "patriotic fervor" between 1919 and 1921. This clemency was granted primarily to paramilitary detachments and was especially directed to the countless murders committed by Iván Héjjas's so-called supplementary gendarmerie after the summer of 1919. During the prosecution's investigation in 1921, only one charge was brought against Mihály Francia Kiss (despite the fact that his name arose in connection with a number of crimes) in the case of the murder of a trader from Pusztamérges, Vilmos Kalmár, in the woods at Orgovány on June 6, 1920. The victim's relatives brought the charges against the defendant. Mihály Francia Kiss never denied committing the crime, but, though the evidence indicated murder and robbery rather than "patriotic fervor," the government's amnesty brought an end to the prosecution.[2] (Afterward, a remarkable instance occurred in which the judge said, "God bless you, Mihály!" to the departing defendant, who then threatened to kill his accusers.)[3]

On May 13, 1947, after the end of World War II, Budapest's People's Tribunal delivered a murder conviction in the case of Iván Héjjas and company (in fact, due to Iván Héjjas's absence, Zoltán Babiczki and company were convicted). Mihály Francia Kiss, defendant no. LXII in the case, was sentenced to death by hanging in absentia.[4]

The lawyer of eight of the defendants on trial submitted a petition debating the political nature of the crimes. According to the lawyer, "If forces arising are under such great stress that they believe they can achieve their goals only through the introduction of violence, terror, and struggle, a revolution is born. Acts, especially violent acts, carried out in the interest of achieving such a revolution may be considered to be of a political

2. Budapest Főváros Levéltára [Archives of the City of Budapest] (BFL) B. XI. 1798/ 1957–9 (BFL–VII. 5.e/20630/III/49), p. 17.

3. Office of the Attorney of the City of Budapest (BÜL) 638/1957 (BFL 1798/57/I). When I was a small child, I heard this story several times from my grandmother. She remembered the incident vividly, as it had happened at the time when my grandfather, for his involvement in the 1918 Revolution, and in the subsequent Soviet Republic, had been sentenced to five years in prison. When my mother was born, my grandfather visited her in the hospital, accompanied by two prison guards.

4. Besides Francia Kiss, Ivan Héjjas, the chief of the supplementary gendarmerie, was sentenced to death in absentia.

204 A Rule of Law

nature."[5] Thus, according to the defense lawyer, only revolutionary acts are political in nature.

The Dictatorship of the Proletariat, which achieved power through the use of violence and was only able to keep power through violence and terror, had already fallen on August 1, 1919. By autumn 1919, and in 1920, there was no longer any need for acts of a political nature to overturn the existing state and the social and economic order. By that time the counterrevolution had succeeded, and the regime served by those accused in the Orgovány case was already in power. The motives and reasons for the actions carried out in Orgovány were not the desire or attempt to achieve political goals, but rather revenge![6]

Governor Horthy's amnesty of November 1921 was for those who committed acts of "patriotic fervor"—in other words, acts with political motivation and (at least on paper) not common crimes. However, Dr. Nagy, the defense lawyer—keeping in mind the fact that the statute of limitations was lifted exclusively in the case of crimes with clear political motivation or crimes against humanity—attempted to show that the acts committed by the accused "were common crimes, as is proven by the methods with which they were carried out . . . and also proven . . . by the fact that they were accompanied by theft, robbery, and other means of extorting money."[7]

In its accusation, the People's Tribunal had originally referred to Act VII of 1945, according to which "crimes are to be punished and are declared not to have reached the statute of limitations, in which human lives were taken in 1919 and the times following, and which were left unpunished over the twenty-five years following the counterrevolution due to Amnesty Decree No. 59 391/1921.I.M., passed on November 3, 1921, and due to the sympathy shown by the authorities responsible for punishing these criminal acts, sympathy which went beyond even the bounds of Amnesty."[8] (The legal reasoning cited here is identical to the logic of the so-called Zétényi-Takács legal draft of the Hungarian Parliament, which recommended after the collapse of the Communist regime in 1991 that the statute of limitations had not been reached for certain types of crimes not

5. Népbíróság iratok [Documents of the People's Court] (Nb), IV. 131/1947 (BFL-VII. 5e/20630/I/49), p. 6.

6. Népbíróság ügyészségi iratok [Documents of the People's Court, Documents of the Prosecutor] (Nü), IV. 131/1947 (BFL-VII. 5e/20630/I/49), pp. 6–7.

7. Nb, IV. 131/1947 (BFL-VII. 5e/20630/I/49), p. 7.

8. Nü, 13672/5. Sz. 1946 (BFL-VII. 5e/20630/III/49), p. 1.

punished for political reasons during the decades of Communist rule in Hungary, as the statute should be counted from a point in time following the fall of the Communist system—in fact, from the time when the first democratically elected post-Communist government came into office in May 1990.)

The appeal in the case of Héjjas's detachments came before the appellate court, the National Council of People's Tribunals (NCPT), which brought a sentence on November 25, 1948. The NCPT for its part decided that the incidents under question in the case could be considered war crimes under different paragraphs—under Parts 11 and 5 and Parts 13 and 2—and this is why the statute of limitations did not apply to them. The National Council stated that the decree, which brought the people's tribunal into existence and which later became law, had been formulated "so that as soon as possible, punishment would be meted out to all those who were the cause of, or participated in, the historic catastrophe which struck the Hungarian People."[9]

This passage in the law quoted by the People's Tribunals refers to World War II as the historic catastrophe and specifically to the Fascist Arrow-Cross rule of 1944. The reasoning of the National Council, therefore, created an immediate connection between the acts carried out by detachments some twenty-five years before in 1919 and the reign of Szálasi's Arrow-Cross forces in 1944:

It is a commonly known historic fact that following the fall of the Dictatorship of the Proletariat of 1919 . . . which made a heroic, revolutionary attempt to liberate Hungary's repressed working classes and other social strata and to establish a Socialist economic and political system, our homeland fell into a dark age of counterrevolution and white terror, followed by the Horthy-type reactionary system of consolidation, that logically—that is, with unavoidable consistency and as if by law—led to the servile affiliation with Italian-German policies, which eventually led to the evil and insane intervention in World War II, and finally, in 1944 poured the filthy, murderous flood of Arrow-Cross rule onto our people and our nation, a rule whose terrible acts and destruction of human lives and material goods were in proportion, scale, and methods beyond human comprehension. . . . It is, therefore, an unquestionable historical fact that the multiple and typical crimes discussed in this case, whether committed directly by Héjjas's detachments or under

---

9. Népbíróság Országos Tanácsa [National Council of the People's Court] (NOT) II. 727/1947/9 (BFL-VII 5e/20630/I/49), p. 4.

their direction or inspiration, were spawned in the filthy, deadly swamp of the coun-terrevolution, from whence they draw their bestial power and outrageous nature.[10]

In its charges in 1947 the public prosecutor had already established that the crimes of the accused had arisen from the "national-Christian the-ory" of the 1919 provisional counterrevolutionary government in the pro-vincial city of Szeged.

It was this Idea from Szeged which Miklós Kállay [then prime minister] referred to in 1943 in his unfortunate speech as a theory predating the idea of National So-cialism by more than a decade, and yet being essentially identical to it and having a major influence on it. This Idea from Szeged was one which even Adolf Hitler had to admit was his inspiration. This Idea from Szeged was the first sprout of the enormous tree of Fascism.[11]

The reasoning behind the accusation treats Hitler and Szálasi as if there had been no other historical alternative to Fascism after 1919; events that followed the logic of history had to lead to 1944, then to 1947, and finally to the courtroom where these events and their consequences were being discussed. Thus the executioner, Mihály Francia Kiss, was in fact already a member of the Arrow-Cross in 1919, long before the party was set up, and perhaps even then knew of Hitler—in contrast to those who in 1889 failed to notice that an infant called Hitler had been born. In fact, in its view of history and its style, the logic of the court is not at all far from the views of George S. Berkeley, who, in discussing the suicide of Prince Rudolf and his lover, Marie Vetsera, in his book *Vienna and its Jews*, notes, "The other event of special significance to the Vienna Jews that occurred in 1889 passed unremarked by almost everyone, Jews and Gentiles alike. Three months after Rudolph's death, in the border village of Braunau, a son was born to Alois and Klara Hitler."[12]

*

10. NOT, II. 727/1947/9 (BFL-VII 5e/20630/I/49), p. 4.

11. Nü, 13672/5sz/1947 (BFL-VII. 5e/20630/49), p. 1. It is an undeniable fact that while in the German Parliament, the Reichstag, in 1924 only 6 percent of the members be-longed to the NSDAP, the National Socialists, and half a year later their representation fell to 2.4 percent; in the Hungarian Parliament, until 1926 more than 10 percent of the mem-bers belonged to radical right-wing, anti-Semitic parties.

12. George E. Berkley, *Vienna and Its Jews: The Tragedy of Success* (Cambridge, MA: Madison Books, 1987), p. 87; quoted in Michael Andre Bernstein, *Foregone Conclusions: Against Apocalyptic History* (Berkeley: University of California Press, 1994), p. 18. In opposi-tion to such apocalyptic reasoning, Arthur Danto remarked, "No one came to Mme. Diderot

Georg Lukács, the once well-known Marxist philosopher, was a People's Commissar in the government of the First Hungarian Soviet Republic. After the defeat of the Hungarian Soviet regime he fled to Vienna, where in 1920 he published a short article in the Communist émigré newspaper *The Proletariat*. In his short essay, "The Social Hinterland of the White Terror," Lukács condemned the right-wing Social Democrats who were unable to distinguish between different kinds of dictatorship and terror on their class basis. Lukács was preoccupied by the unleashed white terror in Hungary and the fate of his fellow Bolsheviks who, unable to escape, fell victim to the terror. He felt it necessary to try to provide a theoretical distinction between the merciless red terror of the defeated Soviet Republic, based on necessity and the iron laws of history, on the one hand, and the pointless and doomed ongoing terror of the whites, on the other.

"What is the red terror?" asks Lukács, a not-so-academic question at the beginning of his analysis.

It is the institutional form of the unflinching and forceful will of the proletariat class in power, which aims at getting rid of all the obstacles (the counterrevolution, sabotage, corruption, chain-commerce) in its way to Socialism. . . . As the natural development of the society . . . inevitably leads to the victory of Socialism, the resistance of the counterrevolution will naturally weaken, which in turn would lead to the softening of the red terror. . . . The white terror, however, becomes necessary for the oppressing classes, when they are forced into defense against the proletariat; when in the course of their desperate resistance they win a battle, and desperately, using all available means, they try to give the *appearance of permanence to this necessarily transitory victory*. . . . The white terror is the Holy Alliance of the oppressing classes against the proletariat. . . . The only ground of common interest of these classes is the preservation of the *abstract possibility* of preserving oppression and exploitation. . . . The white terror is the bloody and filthy, *abstract* expression of oppression. . . . [After the collapse of the Austro-Hungarian monarchy, for the post–World War I déclassé social strata] the *white terror became an end in itself*. . . . Unlike the terror of the proletariat, which, in the sure knowledge of its final and necessary victory, is defensive and human . . . the white terror is doomed to failure. . . . This is why it feeds itself, this is why *it is not a means but an end in itself*. This is why it carries in itself its own mortal disease. . . . The white terror is its own grave digger. . . . The oppressing classes, which are fighting among each

---

and said: 'Unto you an encyclopaedist is born'" (Arthur C. Danto, *Analytical Philosophy of History* [Cambridge: Cambridge University Press, 1965], p. 12; quoted by Bernstein, *Foregone Conclusions*).

other are not able either to rule or regulate or force it and turn it into their service. They cannot live without it, however the existence of the white terror undermines the fundaments of their survival.[13]

In addition to the link between Szálasi and Iván Héjjas (and the crimes committed by Francia Kiss in 1919), the prosecution found other direct links to Fascism. According to the prosecution's reasoning, the crimes committed by the detachments not only preceded but also served as a model for Hitler and the National Socialists. (To complicate the picture, it is unavoidable to mention that at the beginning of the 1920s the Hungarian extreme right in fact served as a model for the radical German right. Ludendorff himself wrote a letter to Admiral Horthy asking for support. Between 1920 and 1939 there were almost a dozen different parties in Hungary, which used the "Fascist" or the "National Socialist" adjectives in their names.)[14] The prosecutor also found proof of the detachment's historical roots and their defining role in the development of European Fascism in his introductory remarks, in which he discussed the biography of the former prime minister, Gyula Gömbös:

The organizer of the Horthyist National Army was in fact Staff Captain Gyula Gömbös who had served for some time in Croatia and who was well acquainted with the secret South Slav military organization called the "Black Hand," as well as its cover organization "Narodna Obrana." He established his own secret society, called the Etelköz Association (EKA), on this model. . . . This association attempted to realize the holy trinity of the Szeged Idea. EKA, under the leadership of its founder, who later became prime minister, was secretly in complete control of the whole country during the quarter of a century of Horthyist rule. Ministries, the parliament, social, political, and economic organizations were all merely puppets on EKA's stage.[15]

Thus, according to the public prosecutor, the crimes committed by the detachments were not merely a preview of what Hitler's theories and Szálasi's rule of terror were to bring, but in fact from 1919 on the members of the detachment—Héjjas, Mihály Francia Kiss, Gömbös, and the secret

13. Originally published on August 19, 1920, in György Lukács, *Collected Works*. *Történelem és osztálytudat*. [History and Class-Consciousness] (Budapest: Magvető, 1971), pp. 69–75; emphasis in original.

14. Cf. Krisztián Ungváry, "Kik azok a nyilasok?" [Who Are the Arrow-Crossers?], in *Beszélő* 8, no. 3 (series III) (June 2003): 58–68.

15. Nü, 13672/5sz.1947 (BFL–VII. 5e/20630/49), p. 2.

Fascists of the Etelköz Association—were in control of the country, "for only people who were, or who became members of EKA were allowed to play a serious role in politics in Hungary."[16] From the very minute of the defeat of the dictatorship of the proletariat onward, Hungary was in fact controlled by Fascists, who moved political players like puppets. By starting the story in 1919 with the defeat of the First Hungarian Soviet Republic, the court succeeded in presenting Fascists as primarily anti-Communists, as if Fascism had come into existence in the first place in order to challenge Communism. Without emphasizing 1919, it would have been more difficult to push the other targets, other victims, other adversaries of Fascism into the background.

In the reasons for its judgment in the appeal, the National Council of People's Tribunals also highlighted the fact that

the "Orgovány methods"—the binding with barbed wire, the gouging out of eyes, scalping, burying alive, and all the rest of the bestiality which is incomprehensible for a European—were, if not in extent, then at least in content, a true forerunner of concentration camps and gas chambers. The inhumane irresponsibility of the leaders of the detachments can only be compared with the leaders of S.S. bands and Fascist party units. . . . After the course of twenty-five years Héjjas's detachment made it possible for Sztójay's and Szálasi's regimes in 1944 to afford this country the dubious honor of calling the counterrevolution Europe's first Fascist system, and thus Hungary was brought to the judgment of the world after World War II with an even greater burden of sin and guilt.[17]

This is apocalyptic history, and an indictment is an appropriate genre for such a depiction of events. Methodologically, if not stylistically, the court's text is closely related to the flashback as it is used in film and fiction. The American literary historian, Michael Andre Bernstein, calls this technique "foreshadowing"—"a technique whose logic must always value the present, not for itself, but as a harbinger of an already determined future. . . . At its extreme, foreshadowing implies a closed universe in which all choices have already been made, in which human free will can exist only in the paradoxical sense of choosing to accept or willfully—and vainly—rebelling against what is inevitable."[18]

16. Ibid.
17. NOT, II. 727/1947/9 (BFL–VII. 5e/20630/I/49), pp. 6–7.
18. Bernstein, *Foregone Conclusions*, p. 2.

It is as if the prophecies of the Old Testament had referred to events in the New Testament, as if the former were merely prefigurations of the latter, as if at a higher level the New Testament, in its completeness, were to perfectly fulfill the promise of *praeparatio evangelica*.[19]

*

At the beginning of 1957 the police in Dunavecse village learned that (as was included in the text of the judgment of the Budapest Capital Court) "during the counterrevolution [of 1956] Mihály Francia Kiss appeared in the region of Szabadszállás in a Soviet-made Pobeda automobile and there met the president of the local counterrevolutionary National Committee. The investigation that followed showed that it was most likely that the person who called himself József Kovács of Bodakút and Mihály Francia Kiss were one and the same person."[20] On March 8, 1957, Mihály Francia Kiss was arrested and imprisoned. On March 22, 1957, in the Interior Ministry's Csongrád County police headquarters, Mrs. Jenő Rácz appeared and accused Mihály Francia Kiss of the kidnapping and murder of her brother, Vilmos Kalmár, in Pusztamérges in the summer of 1920. The mutilated upper body of the kidnapped trader had been found in the woods at Orgovány with other extremely mutilated and beheaded corpses. A suit had been brought against Mihály Francia Kiss in this case at the start of the 1920s, but the case had been dismissed due to the general amnesty granted by Admiral Horthy.

Budapest's Capital Court initiated a new suit in Mihály Francia Kiss's case. In contrast to the judgment of 1947, the Capital Court did not restrict its charge to "the crime of the illegal torture and murder of humans," but also found Francia Kiss guilty of "the production of one counterfeit identity card, the crime of the registration of false personal data in his identity papers, the attempt to commit a crime by using one counterfeit identity card, and the crime of concealing one weapon and bullet under his pillow." The court condemned him to death for all these crimes.[21] In the course of the trial the court found that the accused had taken part in the kidnapping, torture, and murder of sixty-six victims in twelve separate incidents. (See Figure 5.1.)

19. See Amos Funkenstein, "Collective Memory and Historical Consciousness," *History and Memory* 1, no. 1 (1989): 14.
20. B. XI. 1789/1957–9 (BFL-VII. 5e/20630/III/49), p. 19.
21. B. XI. 1789/1957–9 (BFL-VII. 5e/20630/III/49), p. 1.

FIGURE 5.1. Mihály Francia Kiss in court. MTI Photo Archives.

The court also found that the procurement of a counterfeit personal-identity card and the hiding of a pistol after World War II was proof that the defendant had not abandoned his criminal ways and that there was continuity in his ongoing criminal activities between 1919 and 1956: "In addition to the crimes committed by Mihály Francia Kiss in 1919 and 1920, he also committed crimes following the liberation of Hungary in 1945. . . . There can be no doubt that Mihály Francia Kiss was, and remains to this day, an individual with undeniable Fascist sympathies."[22]

This judgment placed an even greater emphasis on the continuity of Fascism in Hungary and on the vital role played by the white terror of 1919 in the development of Fascism worldwide. "[Francia Kiss was one of those] who represent the catastrophic political tendency which led to true Fascism, Nazism, World War II, the terrible and horrifying acts of the Arrow-Cross Party, and the deaths of hundreds of thousands of working people."[23]

22. B. XI. 1789/1957–9 (BFL-VII. 5e/20630/III/49), pp. 18–19.
23. B. XI. 1789/1957–9 (BFL-VII. 5e/20630/III/49), p. 5.

The Council of the People's Tribunal of the Supreme Court (which acted as the appellate court in the Francia Kiss case and which confirmed the death sentence reached by the first court) reversed the chronology of history in its judgment on August 9, 1957, by declaring that in 1919, the detachment already

rightly claimed that it was the predecessor and harbinger of Hitler's Fascism and Szálasi's reign of terror. . . . These Fascist-style acts of terror and the driving of the country into the reign of terror of open Fascism and World War II are links in a chain which are joined one to the other, just as the acts of terror and the heinous acts of the Arrow-Cross hordes are not merely related to the vandalism of October 1956 [the 1956 revolution] in form, but are a part of the bitter struggle of the former ruling classes. . . . The crimes committed by Mihály Francia Kiss, therefore, are to be considered war crimes, but not because the country could not be regarded as being in a state of peace when they were committed, as the court first suggested, but rather because they are part and parcel of the causes of the historic catastrophe which bestruck the Hungarian nation at the fall of the glorious Hungarian Soviet Republic [in 1919], with the twenty-five years of Horthy's Fascism, and directly led to and peaked with our role in World War II and to Szálasi's reign of terror.[24]

Such turns of phrase as "rightly claimed that it was the predecessor and harbinger of Hitler's Fascism and Szálasi's reign of terror" might make one think of what a German burger must have sounded like as he ran through town shouting, "The Thirty-Year War has just begun!"[25]

In 1957, however, the court felt it was its duty to find and prove the connection between the white terror of 1919 and the so-called second coming of white terror, the counterrevolution of 1956. The elderly white terrorist-murderer served as a link between 1919, 1944, and 1956; this link became one of the most important elements of the explanations of the outbreak of the counterrevolution in 1956:

[The] Fascist-type acts of terror initiated by Iván Héjjas and Mihály Francia Kiss, which grew in size and scope over time, became a seed for the worldwide move-

24. Nbf, II. 5123/1957/14 (BFL-VII. 5e/20630/49), pp. 2, 8–9.

25. Bernstein, *Foregone Conclusions*, p. 26. See also how Habermas formulated the same idea: "The sentence, 'the Thirty Years War began in 1618,' presupposes that at least those events have elapsed which are relevant for the history of the war up to the Peace of Westphalia, events that could not have been narrated by any observer at the outbreak of the war" (Jurgen Habermas, "A Review of Gadamer's Truth and Method," in *Understanding and Social Inquiry*, eds. Fred R. Dallymayr and Thomas A. McCarthy [Notre Dame, IN: University of Notre Dame Press, 1977], p. 346).

ment which is known everywhere as "Fascism" and which initially oppressed and destroyed millions of people and finally drove the whole world into the World War II Catastrophe [*sic*]. The Hungarian counterrevolution became a cradle for Fascism, and through the mutilation of human souls led in a straight line to the events which exploded in Hungary on October 23, 1956. . . . The detailed and well-established facts of the case are entirely recognizable in the acts of terror and mass murders committed by the Arrow-Cross in 1944 and are also clearly visible in the movements which were committed against the faithful sons of the Hungarian People's Republic during the counterrevolution after October 23, 1956. The sadistic murders, skinning of humans alive, cutting out of sexual organs, and similar acts committed in Orgovány, Izsák, and the region of Kecskemét in 1919 were not unknown to those who carried out similar murders in the Arrow-Cross's Party Headquarters in Budapest. The murderers of our executed and mutilated martyrs on Republic Square [in front of the Budapest headquarters of the Communist Party where the only truly bloody anti-Communist atrocity of the revolution occurred on October 30, 1956] and those who committed murders in front of the police department in Miskolc [another site of bloodshed during the revolution] used the same methods and carried out their acts with the same sadistic cruelty as Mihály Francia Kiss and his terrorist companions did in 1919. All of this makes it clear that the crimes committed by Mihály Francia Kiss and Iván Héjjas some thirty-eight years ago are closely connected to the latest round of vandalistic Fascist attacks which are to be found right through Hungarian history.[26] (See Figures 5.2 and 5.3.)

"Mihály Francia Kiss was one of the cruelest counterrevolutionaries of all time," indicated the court in its judgment of his guilt and the effects of his acts.

His crimes point the way down a lasting trail leading to the next horrors and were a cradle to the deformity that was later called Fascism. His behavior laid its stamp on the quarter of a century of rule by Horthy Fascism; it was to be found in the underground organization of the counterrevolutionary movement throughout the period of the building of Socialism, and this same spirit eventually exploded with elementary power in the horrible days of the rebirth of the counterrevolution on October 23, 1956. The seeds Mihály Francia Kiss and company sowed in 1919 grew into a terrible harvest in the days of the counterrevolution of 1956. The orgy of murder and blood roared identically in both periods, and the connection between the two is to be found in Mihály Francia Kiss and his spirit.[27]

26. B. XI. 1798/1957–9 (BFL-VII. 5e/20630/49), p. 8.
27. B. XI. 1798/1957–9 (BFL-VII. 5e/20630/49), p. 32.

FIGURE 5.2. White terrorists execute local officials of the 1919 Hungarian Soviet Republic. Photo Archives of the Hungarian National Museum.

FIGURE 5.3. Execution of Communists on Republic Square in Budapest, October 30, 1956. Photo Archives of the Hungarian National Museum.

Both photographs (Figures 5.2 and 5.3) were included, facing each other, in the *White Book*—the official Communist chronicle of the 1956 events.

Even without a deeper analysis of the text, it is clear that the evocation of white terror in 1956 was not merely a stylistic formula. Historical continuity was presented on both the positive and the negative sides in the court's judgment, for as the Capital Court had established in 1957, history was continual on the other side as well: "In October 1918 a proletarian revolution broke out in Hungary. The imperialist formation of Austro-Hungary collapsed, fell to pieces, and this initiated the process which finally, after decades and decades of hard fighting, led to the liberation of nations and eventually to the development of People's Democracies. This journey, however, was not an easy one."[28]

28. B. XI. 1798/1957–9 (BFL-VII. 5e/20630/49), p. 3.

According to the account of history given in the accusation, the advance of history was first interrupted by the white terror of 1919, which drove the forces of progress underground. After the victory of the Soviet Union and the working classes in 1945, however, the forces of Fascism hid underground and continued their work illegally (as had the "Black Hand" in the Balkans in its time), waiting for the moment when they could resurface. October 1956 brought the moment they had awaited. "The true character of October 23 was expressed on October 30 [the date of the siege of Communist Party headquarters on Republic Square in Budapest]. What was still hidden on October 23 came out into the light of day on October 30. On October 30 the hour struck for the beginning of the black carnival. We were witnesses when the counterrevolution took off its mask," wrote Ervin Hollós and Vera Lajtai, apologists and official historians of the post–1956 Communist restoration in Republic Square 1956.[29]

*

Ervin Hollós not only wrote but made history as well. As the head of the Political Department of the Budapest Police Headquarters, he was the initiator of the so-called gendarme-trials in 1958–59. At the time, as part of the postrevolutionary retribution, former members of the interwar gendarmerie were tried and sentenced. In December 1959 the chief military prosecutor sent a top-secret report to the Politburo of the Hungarian Socialist Workers' Party and to the minister of internal affairs. The account was part of the periodical reports the chief military prosecutor regularly sent to the Politburo about the ongoing procedures of the "counterrevolutionary cases." This time, however, the report did not deal with ordinary political trials, but with "criminal cases of Horthyist gendarme-officers and detectives of the former Political Police." The chief military prosecutor informed the members of the highest organ of the party:

Due to our former incorrect criminal policy, and due to the inefficiency of the investigative work during the years following the liberation of our country, numerous former police and gendarme-officers remained unpunished who had committed serious war-crimes. . . . On the basis of severe factual errors, discovered by the newly repeated investigations, we initiated new procedures in cases that had formerly been already tried by the courts.[30]

29. Kossuth Publishing House (Budapest: 1974), pp. 318 and 197, respectively.

30. MOL MDP-MSZMP files, Fond. 288/1959, file 46; quoted by Andás Mink, "The Culture of the Counterrevolution" (unpublished PhD dissertation at the History Department of the Central European University, 2002), pp. 29–30.

Hollós, in a book he published after he had been released by the political police, stated:

At the time of the counterrevolution probably the most staggering fact was the extremely high number of criminal elements at large. These people could not be released from prison, unlike the majority of ordinary criminals, as they had been at large throughout the whole period. . . . These counterrevolutionaries, terrorists, butchers with bloodstains on their hands had escaped well-deserved conviction. Those perpetrators who should have been tried and convicted already in 1945, or latest between 1948–49, by the time the Hungarian administration of justice had been purged of those rightist elements whose aim was nothing but to save the reactionaries and war criminals, could only be called to task after the defeat of the counterrevolution in 1958–59. These murderers should have been in prison instead; they formed the true reserve of the counterrevolution. The real crime of the [pre-counterrevolutionary] Rákosi-regime was that while excellent faithful soldiers of the labor movement had to serve long prison sentences for fabricated crimes, many of these bloody-handed gendarme-officers and murderers had lived undisturbed.[31]

As a result of Hollós's work as a political police investigator, twenty-eight defendants of the so-called gendarme trials—some, although not all of them, former gendarme-officers—were sentenced to death; another ten received sentences of life imprisonment.[32] Hollós and the regime carefully produced the evidence for the later historical accounts.

The Communist historical thriller *The Spearmen* by András Berkesi and György Kardos was written to illustrate and popularize the court's—and official Communist—theories. The book, which was reprinted nine times (it retained its popularity even after 1990) and was finally turned into a film, follows the story of one Major Ákos Rajnay (whose real-life model was István Korponay, a high-ranking officer of the interwar years, who, after World War II became a high-ranking leader of the Hungarian rightwing military emigration and most probably an employee of the West German and American secret services) from the time of his involvement in the white terror through the hibernation of the "Spearmen" in 1944 until their reawakening and reactivation in 1956. The Spearmen were a (real or

31. Ervin Hollós, *Kik voltak, mit akartak?* [Who Were They, What Did They Want?] (Budapest: Kossuth Kiadó, 1967), pp. 301–2.

32. Cf. András Kovács Zoltán, "Csendőrsors Magyarországon 1945 után" [The Fate of Gendarmes after 1945 in Hungary], in *Katonai perek 1945–1958* [Military Trials 1945–1958], ed. Imre Okváth (Budapest: Archives of the Historical Office, 2001).

fictional—who knows?) paramilitary organization that the authors based on the Communist interpretation of the Etelköz Association. The white-terrorist Iván Héjjas clearly serves in part as a model for Ákos Rajnay. The two authors present the counterrevolution as the outcome of the joint conspiracy of international imperialist intervention—this provided the justification for Soviet military intervention to help the Hungarian Communists—and the underground forces of the white terror. (According to the book, the Spearmen were left behind as saboteurs-in-hibernation by the German and Hungarian Fascists, who ordered them to hide themselves as ordinary and loyal citizens until the time arrived for an armed counterrevolutionary uprising.) The novel could not have been written without the active cooperation of the Interior Ministry, the secret service, and the Communist Party's Department of Propaganda and Agitation, for its authors clearly used forged, imagined, and classified documents about the Spearmen from the Interior Ministry's secret archives.[33] This was all the easier to assume, as the coauthors had both served in the ministry's military-political counterintelligence department before they began their writing careers.[34]

The Spearmen could be considered to be the official Communist interpretation of the counterrevolution. The historical thriller, the imagined underground conspiracy, is the appropriate genre of the Communist historiography of the counterrevolution: lacking hard evidence, it is only the internal logic of the fabrication that holds the elements of the official story together. The Wagnerian "leitmotiv" of the thriller is the continuity between

33. In fall 1997 all copies of the book were checked out from the Budapest Central Public Library.

34. According to the information General Béla Király was kind enough to pass to me, at the end of 1944, when the Soviet army was already in the country, he was approached by some of Szálasi's military leaders, who offered him the post of the chief of staff of the secret "Spearmen" organization. According to General Király, who had served in the Hungarian army from the 1930s and who in 1956 became the leading general of the revolutionary armed forces, the "Spearmen" was most probably an existing secret organization that came into being at the beginning of the 1920s and was active mostly in Transylvania, where it was engaged in intelligence operations and sabotage activities. The Fascist leadership hoped that the "Spearmen" would be able to perform the same functions in the back of the Soviet army. General Király, who became a member of the Hungarian Parliament after 1990, found the situation absolutely hopeless in 1944 and declined the offer. In his view, as a consequence of the advancing Soviet army, the "Spearmen," most probably, remained just an imaginary organization.

the 1919 and 1956 counterrevolutions, the reactivation of the hibernated old forces of black reaction on the eve of the counterrevolution. The book had an important function to fill in Hungary after 1956: at the time when no detective stories were published, when dull Socialist-realist novels— mostly translations from Russian—occupied the place of pulp fiction, an adventurous thriller could easily capture the imagination of the public, which did not have television yet, where the movies with just a few exceptions were politically correct, boring Soviet films. The Spearmen had enormous popularity, and thanks to the book, the official reading of the 1956 events could reach a mass audience.

My elementary school Hungarian literature teacher suggested that I read the book, and until 1995, when I started to work on an exhibition "The Representation of the Counterrevolution," I was convinced that the story of the arch-reactionary conspiracy had been the work of pure fiction. In the course of the work on the exhibition, we unexpectedly discovered in the archives the traces and a few objects of the 1957 traveling exhibition, "The Dreadful Deeds of the Counterrevolution in Hungary," organized by the Ministry of the Interior. On one of the panels, originally included in the exhibition, among the photographs of the most merciless counterrevolutionaries, one of my colleagues discovered a photo marked with a thick green arrow with a handwritten note: "A Kopjás," "The Spearman." There was a caption attached to the picture: "Department of Political Investigation, Police Headquarters, Győr-Sopron County—Minutes of Frigyes Beck's interrogation, Győr, 20 July 1957."[35]

Beck's files led to a strange story. He was arrested first in 1946 as a former Arrow-Cross Party activist, when he gave a detailed description about his activities during the war, including his participation in the infamous Novi Sad massacres in 1942–43, after Hungary attacked Yugoslavia and recaptured the former Hungarian territories. His confession was the first mentioning of the Spearmen conspiracy.[36] Beck, according to his recollection, had worked with the Soviet authorities and intelligence services already during the last months of the war, but the Soviets arrested him, as they found him not only an unreliable source but a habitual liar as well. After his arrest in 1946 he most probably started to work for the Hungarian secret services, but in 1951 he was arrested once more, on charges of

35. Archives of the Historical Office (AHO) V—1411883. Frigyes Beck case, p. 18.
36. AHO, file no. V-84039, pp. 13–16.

having forged identity papers that meant to prove that he worked for nonexistent secret agencies. He was sentenced, left prison in 1956, and during the revolution worked as a medical doctor in the provincial city Győr, although he had not been trained as a doctor. In 1957 he was arrested, this time as a counterrevolutionary, and was sentenced to eight years. He worked as an informer in prison. (As one of the organizers of an alleged prison revolt in 1961, he received an additional nine years.)

"I started to deal with the 'Kopjás' [Spearmen] movement at the Military Intelligence in the summer of 1949," wrote Berkesi, one of the coauthors of the Spearmen novel in his confession in 1953. At that time the future writer served his ten-year sentence in prison for charges of forgery and abuse of power. Probably his case was a minor follow-up show trial of the Rajk case, although one cannot exclude the possibility that in his case the original charges had been based on verifiable criminal evidence.[37] He was convicted in 1951 and rehabilitated in 1954.

He became a *mouton de prison* and in 1953 prepared an extensive report on the alleged Spearmen conspiracy, most probably in large part based on his conversations with one of his cell mates. In September 1957 Berkesi published an article in *Népszabadság*, the daily of the party, with the title "I Volunteer as a Witness."[38] In the article, which was in a sense the draft of the future Spearmen novel, Berkesi describes how he spent four years as an innocent Communist, together with real criminals and enemies of the state, in prison. He argues that the majority of his inmates were real enemies of the People's Republic, an assertion proved during the days of the counterrevolution when the overwhelming majority of the former prisoners supported the counterrevolution, while only a tiny fraction of the former inmates took arms in defense of the Communist regime. Those who, even after the long years in prison, decided to defend Communism, testified by their act that they had been innocent victims of the pre–1956 show trials; whereas those who chose to help the counterrevolution proved retrospectively that they had been guilty of political crimes and had not been the victims of show trials. The very small number of former prisoners who fought on the side of the Communists in 1956—in Berkesi's imagination, and here he speaks as the spokesman of the restored regime—confirmed that only the minority of the political prisoners had been sentenced on the

37. AHO, file no. V-142778, the Berkesi file.
38. "Tanúnak jelentkezem," *Népszabadság*, September 7, 1957.

basis of forged evidence. According to Berkesi, the enemies of the state did not hide in prison that they had always been stark enemies of the People's Republic, and they "tried to overbid each other in their quest to prove the seriousness of their clandestine activities."

Berkesi gives a detailed classification of the prison community. The openly anti-Communists, the former war criminals, white terrorists, gendarme-officers, and members of the interwar military intelligence belonged to the first group. The second group consisted of members of the different post–1945 conspiracies (most of them framed, imagined complots). The alleged agents of the Western secret services (even agents who worked for these services during World War II, at the time when Hungary was Hitler's ally) and presumed supporters of the Hungarian émigré organizations, together with the members of the Spearmen comprised the third group. The so-called right-wing Social Democrats formed the fourth part of the underground prison world. In Berkesi's "testimony" these groups, under the leadership of the József Kővágó, mayor of Budapest between 1945–47, formed the "Alliance of Political Convicts" already in prison and prepared for the counterrevolution and the execution of the Communists. In Berkesi's account these enemies of the People's Democracy played the central role during the days of the counterrevolution.

In 1945 the Soviet army captured a group of Hungarian soldiers who supposedly had taken part in a parachute operation, in order to leave future anti-Communist partisans in the back of the Soviets. The Soviet Military Court in Baden, Austria, tried their case and sentenced the soldiers for ten to fifteen years' imprisonment and deported them to the Gulag. After Stalin's death in 1953, those of the group who survived received amnesty and came back to Hungary.[39] After their return the Hungarian secret services started a secret surveillance operation and kept these people, almost six hundred of them, under constant observation for decades. Quite a few of the former Gulag inmates became recruited as informers. Most of them moved to the countryside and managed to find meager jobs, if at all. Their very unimpressive life fueled the suspicion of the authorities, who conjectured that the inaction of the former Gulag prisoners was just the sure sign of their skillful mimicry. The Hungarian secret authorities, under the in-

---

39. Kopjás "object" dossier. These are surveillance documents. AHO, file no. O-14851.

fluence of the Spearman fantasy, treated them as the embodiment of the Spearmen, the ultimate proof at last of the existence of the one-time clandestine organization. Although they had been rehabilitated in the Soviet Union already in the middle of the 1960s, the Hungarian secret services continued their surveillance until 1972.[40] Their sad fate proved the success of the writer's imagination beyond the pages of his book.

According to the restored post–1956 Communist regime, the white terror of 1919—as depicted in the accusation of the People's Tribunal, and in the judgment by the people's court of 1947—was a precursor to Fascism, or rather was Fascism in its original form that, via underground organizations, as the Spearmen, following the victory of Communism after World War II, eventually led to 1956. Thus the counterrevolution of 1956 was closely connected to and rooted in Fascism. By using this historical theory, an immediate link was found between 1919, 1944, and 1956. Mihály Francia Kiss symbolized the logic of historic continuity in a person. Even though some alleged witnesses saw the former white terrorist driving a Pobeda automobile to a meeting with the president of the local National Council, the old mass murderer who hid in a field watchman's shack on the great Hungarian plain from 1945 until his arrest in 1957 could not have convincingly claimed to have taken an active part in the terrible crimes of the counterrevolution. A stronger, more direct link was needed.

On March 14, 1957, eight days after Mihály Francia Kiss's arrest and two days after the publication of news of his detention, however, the official daily of the Communist Party *Népszabadság* printed a story under a headline typed in bold: "Mihály Francia Kiss's Offspring Arrested." The story gave an account of how Béla Francia, the "offspring" of the infamous white terrorist (the exact relationship between the two was obscured by an imprecise noun) was arrested for his role in breaking into a grocery store with other common criminals during the days of the counterrevolution. Béla Francia was to be sentenced to four years in prison. (After 1963 he was rehabilitated, for he had ironclad proof that he could not have been on the scene when the store was broken into. It was also proven that he was in no way related to Mihály Francia Kiss. He was not even an "offspring" of the man's family. He merely—to his very bad luck—bore almost the same family name.) Béla Francia's arrest, the report about it, his trial, and his

40. Cf. Mink, "Culture of the Counterrevolution," pp. 328–39.

condemnation provided the missing link to the tale that began in 1919. If the white terrorist himself was humanly incapable of carrying out the long list of horrible deeds in 1956, his offspring was not: blood is thicker than water (even blood on a murderer's hands).

In the course of the trials Francia Kiss became the archetype of the Fascist: the Fascist who had been there at the beginning of all things, who had hidden and survived underground (as the Black Hand had under the name Narodna Obrana). In all that time he had not changed. He was just biding his time and waiting to do what he had done from the start—show the world the true face of Fascism. The crimes committed by Mihály Francia Kiss only gain their true meaning in the context of later horrible events, especially following 1956. According to the court's judgment, the anti-Communist had to be, by definition, a Fascist.

*

Fascists, before all things, were—in this reading—anti-Communists. The history following World War I was a history of constant, ongoing struggle between the forces of Communism and of Fascism—as the 1919 white terror clearly revealed. Fascism's true enemies were always Communists, even if its victims may have appeared to be others. The only true goal of Fascism was the destruction of Communism. Communism, for its part, was the only active, uncompromising, and organized arm against Fascism, the only guarantee against (the return of) the dark forces.

Miklós Horthy and the officers who massed around him proclaimed far and wide that the causes of the ruin of Hungary, of the 1919 revolution, and of the country's mutilation after World War I were the Marxist Socialists, or in other words, the Bolsheviks and Jews, whom they believed to be one and the same. Horthy himself, his friend, the German General Ludendorff, and his protégée [*sic*] Adolf Hitler, all fully believed the anti-Semitic and anti-Socialist book of trash, *The Protocols of the Elders of Zion*, which had been edited by the Russian teacher Nilush at the behest of the chief of the czar's secret police, the Okhrana, in 1903. After the Russian Revolution the book was widely disseminated throughout Europe by none other than Russian counterrevolutionary officers. One could say that it became a sort of bible for Horthy and the coattail politicians and officers who massed around him. In this spirit Gyula Gömbös, István Zadravetz, and their counterrevolutionary company in Szeged initiated the most unbridled propaganda and hate campaign against anything that could be called left-wing or—what was to them one and the same—Jewish.[41]

41. Nü, 1372/5.sz./1946 (BFL-VII. 5e/20630/III/49), p. 2.

The public prosecutor found it important to mention the fact that the anti-Semitism of the counterrevolutionary forces in Hungary was rooted in the work of the Bolsheviks' sworn enemy, the Okhrana, the czar's secret police, which was then disseminated throughout Europe by counterrevolutionary officers who worked against the Bolshevik Revolution. Horthy's friend's protégé, Adolf Hitler, also borrowed from this source, even if later than the leaders of the Hungarian counterrevolutionaries.[42] (Thus Hitler himself becomes Horthy's protégé.)

In its opinion in 1957, Budapest's capital court defined the essence of Fascism's anti-Semitism in an even clearer and more direct way:

The imperialist forces in every country recognized the danger posed to capitalism and the furthering of imperialism by the strengthening of the dictatorship of the proletariat, and this is why they felt that no means are too low to be used in the suppression of movements working toward the democratic transformation of the masses and to uphold the power of the upper classes. In working toward this goal, especially under the conditions that prevailed in Hungary at the time, they found that the most successful strategy would be to misdirect the class struggle into a religious conflict. Due to Austrian policies at that time, beside the conflict between nationalities that became sharper and sharper on the territories of the Austro-Hungarian Empire, it was especially the so-called Jewish question, which was constantly and carefully kept on the platter at all times by the governments of the monarchy. This religious contradiction was the one that was most useful over the course of time in suppressing every sort of democratic movement among the working class, because the loss of the War and the following events were ascribed to Hungary's Jews, and the attacks directed against leftists were also used to feed and fuel the hatred directed against the Jews.[43]

In this system of argumentation it was not the Jews who were the real victims. Quite the opposite: the insults they suffered served to "misdirect the class struggle into a religious conflict," to fool the "masses"; "the dubious characters who gathered in Szeged . . . openly propagated the claim

---

42. In fact, in June 1939 Szálasi, the leader of the Hungarian Arrow-Cross Party, after having read Alfred Rosenberg's "The Myth of the XXth Century," wrote the following critical note in his diary: "What the Jews have been doing for six-thousand years, now, according to Rosenberg, the Germans want to do six-thousand year later: racially grounded religion, racially grounded moral, intellectual and material life" (*Szálasi Ferenc börtönnaplója 1938–1940* [Ferenc Szálasi's Prison Diary 1938–1940] [Budapest: BFL-Filum, 1997], p. 111).

43. B. XI. 1798/1957–9 (BFL–VII. 5c/20630/III/49), p. 4.

that the Communists caused Hungary to lose the War and to fall apart, and that it was the Jews who invented Communism, and thus the entire policy of the counterrevolution was the uprooting by root and shoot of the power of the proletariat."[44] The counterrevolution—that is, Fascism, in the narratives by the court—associated Jews with Bolshevism to hide its true nature and work, which was, according to the Communist court, nothing other than anti-Communism and the struggle against the only protectors of the working masses. In other words, the Jews were useful for the Fascists only to disorient the workers, to fool them in order to suppress them by leading them in a false direction.[45] "Anti-Semitism, which cannot in theory be reconciled with Christian ideology, budded to such a degree in the practice of the Héjjas detachment and in its pre-Fascist cruelty, that it showed it was a worthy partner of the vandalism carried out by Fascism in the 1940s. Because of the association of the terms 'Jew' and 'Bolshevik' in their propaganda, every Jew was an enemy and, thus, to be destroyed."[46]

*

"It is a publicly known fact that the Hungarian and German fascists exceedingly humiliated the Hungarian Jews, robbed them of all their means of subsistence, and wiped out two thirds or perhaps three fourths of them with the sole justification that they were the enemies of Fascism and the spiritual ally of the democratic powers; that they wished and worked for the victory of the anti-Fascist Allied forces."[47] The National Office of the Hungarian Israelites issued this statement in 1946. Barely a year after the end of the war and the deportation of the Hungarian Jews, and in order to gain the confidence of the so-called Hungarian democratic forces (the Communists and their allies), the highest organ of the Hungarian

44. B. XI. 1798/1957–9 (BFL–VII. 5e/20630/III/49), p. 5.

45. "Those who spread anti-Semitism today, do this in order to misdirect the attention from the sabotage of the supporters of the pseudo-feudal order, the big capitalist and the reaction that is the cause of all our troubles today," argued Erik Molnár, the would-be director of the Historical Institute of the Hungarian Academy of Sciences, the would-be minister of foreign affairs and minister of justice in the 1950s, at one of the rare public debates held right after the war (Erik Molnár, *A zsidókérdés Magyarországon* [The Jewish Question in Hungary] [Budapest: Szikra, 1946], p. 16).

46. Nü, 13672/5. sz./1946 (BFL–VII 5e/20630/III/49), p. 6. Szálasi was against the deportation of the Jews. He wanted to force them to work in Hungary and have them as hostages in case of British-American bombings in the course of World War II. Cf. Institut für Zeitgeschichte MA 1541/1, 1.8., 324. 1943; quoted by Ungváry, "Kik azok a nyilasok?" p. 58.

47. The Archives of the Hungarian Jewish Museum. XXXIII-5/a/1.d. 8. file.

Jews felt it necessary to state: the tragedy of the Jews had not been caused by racism and anti-Semitism; their fate had been intimately connected to their conscious anti-Fascist commitment and their support of the Allied powers. Representing the wish of the majority of the survivors, the officials wanted to retrospectively present the Hungarian Jews as the victors of the war, instead of as the humiliated victims of Fascism.

The Press Service of the Hungarist Movement, the propaganda office of the Arrow-Cross Party in exile, issued an announcement in 1956 that essentially repeated the statement of the Hungarian National Jewish Office:

It is true that after October 15, 1944, when the Arrow-Cross took over, the Hungarists did not open the gates of the Budapest Jewish ghetto. The Jews were praying for the victory of the Soviets, and as an untrustworthy minority, similarly to the German, Italian and Japanese populations in the United States, they remained locked up. And if this was understandable in the belligerent United States, than why was this not acceptable in Hungary, which was not only a belligerent country but one of the theaters of the war as well.[48]

*

In Western Europe following World War II it was only a short time before a new history of the war, the myth of wholesale national resistance, was established.[49] In Europe's Soviet half, however, the Communist movement retroactively took complete control of resistance to Fascism. In the West—allegedly—only certain well-defined and marginalized figures and groups collaborated with the Nazis—that is, with the Germans—who, in this tale born not long after 1945, were primarily and almost solely responsible for the horrible crimes committed in World War II.[50] Germans stood accused by the court at the Nuremberg Trials, and the prosecution proved German responsibility. Thus the outcome supported this view of history. ("The aim of the Nuremberg Military Tribunal was to try 'the highest level'

48. *Fények és Árnyak Október idusán. A Hungarista Mozgalom Tájékoztató Szolgálata. 1956 október* [Lights and Shadows on the Ides of October. The Press Service of the Hungarist Movement. October, 1956].

49. "When the postwar quest for truth began, forms of resistance were in place of honor, forms of collaboration were being concealed" (Natalie Zemon Davis, "Censorship, Silence and Resistance: The Annales During the German Occupation Of France" *Litteraria Pragensia* 1, no. 1 [1991]: 21).

50. On the myth of nationwide anti-Fascist resistance in the West, see Tony Judt, "The Past Is Another Country: Myth, Memory in Postwar Europe," *Daedalus* (fall 1992): 83–118, esp. 90–108.

German war criminals.")[51] The Germans started World War II, and they robbed and murdered throughout Europe. The guilty were to be found among the citizens of Germany—a slowly disappearing country that effectively no longer existed, that was merely a group of zones of occupation, and that soon became two separate entities, attached to two separate worlds.

The Communist parties of Western Europe also played their own, not-so-insignificant role in the creation of the retrospective fiction of wholesale national resistance. Communist anti-Fascists could thus become members of the national majority, and even its avant-garde, for example in France and Italy. It is no coincidence, then, that the first draft of the Italian amnesty bill was prepared by the secretary general of the Italian Communist Party, Palmiro Togliatti, in 1946. Right until the end of the 1970s, and in some countries even up to the crumbling and collapse of the Communist systems at the end of the 1980s, there was hardly any attempt to carry out critical or self-critical analyses of the history of national resistance in the western part of the European continent.[52]

In Europe's eastern half only Communists were allowed to be anti-Fascists in histories that could only be written by Communists. Fascism—in Communist historiography—came into being in opposition to Communism, and the placement of someone other than Communists in the role of the victim was only a dirty trick on the part of the Fascists—a transparent attempt to fool the people, "nothing but a weapon of the ruling

---

51. M. Cherif Bassiuni, *Crimes Against Humanity in International Law* (Dordrecht: Martin Nijhof Publishers, 1992), p. 245.

52. "A silence of the Occupation days that persisted after the Liberation was silence about the Jews. It was not until the last number of the Annales of 1947 that two books on Jewish history were finally reviewed, and there was little more until two essays in 1957. The lack here was not so much practical as conceptual. In 1945, when Febvre proposed to Gallimard a grandiose seventy-seven volume inquiry on the state of France, 'Semitiseme et l'antisemitisme' were included under the rubric, 'Quelques virus,' but under the rubric 'Quelques forces,' where he had envisaged books on 'nourritures chretiennes' and on 'le protestant francais,' there were no books on Jews. Only around 1953 did he conceive of a 'bel ensemble' of three books: 'un protestant francais, un catholique francais, un Israelite francais.' What seems likely is that the category 'Jew' had been so powerfully filled with negative and exclusionary association during the Occupation that it took time, outside of the active world of Jewish scholarship, to establish it as a meaningful historical subject—even around the elevated and assimilating term 'Israelite'" (Davis, *Censorship*, p. 22).

class for the enslavement of the German working class," as East German history books taught.[53]

Új Élet (New Life), the weekly of the Hungarian Jewish community, echoed the official interpretation in an editorial written in October 1950:

When on 12 May, the door of the prison cell behind Eugene Dennis, the American Communist leader, was closed, a thick shadow was cast over all Jewish men and women: the shadow of the concentration camps, the darkness of the gas chambers. . . . This is how it started in Hitler's Germany and the end was the extermination of six million Jews. It was Hitler who proved beyond doubt the criminal connection between anti-Communist and anti-Semite hatred. The imprisonment of Eugene Dennis should remind all working American Jews of the lead editorial in *Army Talks*, the journal of the American military, in March 1945. The journal of the American army stated: Hitler and Mussolini directed their assault primarily against the Communists. The Communists are the principal enemies of Fascism.

Fascists tried to destroy Communists, who were presumably the only real adversaries of Fascism. (The explanation for the Molotov-Ribbentrop pact was confusing and opaque in history books printed after 1945. It was described as a sign and consequence of the Soviets' naive trust and their peace-loving character. The secret clause was never even mentioned, as it was impossible both historically and by definition for Communism and Fascism to be allies.) This is one of the reasons why Jews had to disappear from the list of the true victims of Fascism, and it is the explanation for the triangle inscribed in stone on a memorial at Birkenau to differentiate the political inmates there. This is why during the reign of the Polish Communist regime the text on gravestones at Auschwitz emphasized the murder of a highly inflated number of political inmates.[54] This is why in its issue on the twenty-fifth anniversary of the liberation of Auschwitz the Hungarian Jewish newspaper *Új Élet* reported: "The delegation waited by the gate to Auschwitz for József Cyrankiewicz [Polish], Prime Minister, to whose coat his former fellow political deportees pinned the symbol of political prisoners, the triangle with a red letter P."[55] This is

---

53. See Angelika Timm, *Jewish Claims Against East Germany: Moral Obligations and Pragmatic Policy* (Budapest: Central European University Press, 1997), p. 39.

54. See James E. Young, *The Texture of Memory: Holocaust Memorials and Meaning* (New Haven, CT: Yale University Press, 1993), p. 141.

55. *Új Élet*, February 1, 1960, p. 1.

also why the National Executive Committee of Hungarian Israelites was forced to make the following statement in 1951 during the Stalinist anti-Semite campaign:

There is not a single person of Jewish faith among the ranks of those who are being forced to leave the cities and resettle in the countryside at this moment, not a single person who is being deported because of membership to our denomination. In contrast to rumors, those being deported now were all filthy rich traders, factory owners, and landlords before the war, and enjoyers of Horthy's Fascist system—a system which is known throughout the world for its persecution of the Jews, and a system to which those being deported now gave their material and moral support before the catastrophe of World War II.[56]

In Eastern Europe the (memory of the tragedy of the) Jews fell victim to the ideological war between Communists and anti-Communist Fascists. Out of the 120 panels of the first official Hungarian exhibition in Auschwitz, prepared by the Museum of the Working Class Movement in 1965, only 10 showed documents related to the fate of the 437,000 Hungarian Jews who perished there. During the summer of 1944 there were days when the bodies of 18,000 Hungarian Jews were burned in the crematoria (the chimneys collapsed because of the extreme heat; new structures had to be designed to satisfy the unforeseen demand). There was not a single word about the thousands of the Hungarian Roma who were killed in the camp. Every third victim in Auschwitz was a Hungarian Jew, but the official experts who reviewed the script of the exhibition insisted on the inclusion of more documents, related to "non-Jewish Hungarian Communist anti-Fascists" and "more extensive coverage of the armed struggle of Communist partisans"; they suggested that more space should be devoted to the documentation of "the roots of Fascism in the 1919 white terror" and to "the present-day resurrection of Fascism in other parts of the world, including the war in Vietnam [*sic*]."

The Tel Aviv correspondent of Radio Free Europe noted during the Eichmann trial: "The governments of Eastern Europe are ready to help the Israeli government in preparing for the Eichmann trial, in case the trial aims to be more than merely an investigation of the crimes the one-time Nazis committed against the Jews." An Eastern European diplomat who gave an interview to the Radio Free Europe reporter emphasized that "the

56. *Magyar Nemzet*, July 17, 1951, p. 2.

people's democracies wish the Eichmann trial to shed light on all acts committed by all Fascists, including that of the neo-Nazis of present day West Germany."[57] In Communist historiography, the twentieth-century history of Fascism was continual not only from the beginning of the century up to World War II but even from the end of the war until the arrival of the final victory of world Communism. In a six-part article printed in a series in the Hungarian party's daily during the trial in Jerusalem, two mercenary pen-pushers, László Szabó and István Pintér, uncovered how Eichmann's Hungarian assistants allegedly became agents of the West German intelligence services and the U.S. Central Intelligence Agency after 1945 and thus were the direct link between the Endlösung and the anti-Communist manipulations of the West after the war.[58]

The officers of Hungarian anti-Fascist military units that were not under Communist control during World War II were not allowed to be members of the Partisan Union until the late 1980s. They were not awarded the Freedom Medal, granted to other members of the resistance. The activities

57. Open Society Archives (OSA) 300/40/12371.

58. "Dr. Höttl, The Champion of Survival," *Népszabadság*, June 25, 1961. On the wall of 22 Nádor Street there is a small marble plaque, in front of which I pass every day (Central European University, where I teach, is at 9 Nádor Street): "In memory of those young people who continued to fight for Hungarian freedom even after the bloody suppression of the Revolution." A small radical, anarchist party had the plaque put up after 1989, in place of another one that honored a secret police major, Imre Bojti, who had been killed in front of the building during the 1956 Revolution. Pintér and Szabó, two Communist journalists, published a small book in 1964, *Famous Criminal Cases of the Century*. In that book they asserted that Bojti, the ÁVH major, had been shot by the same two criminals, Zsigmond Sipos and József Erdész, who two weeks later, in November 1956, committed a double murder and robbery. The police caught them, and the court sentenced them to death. According to the journalists with rather dubious credentials, the two murderers were waiting for their execution with Mihály Francia Kiss—who had also been sentenced to death by that time—in the same prison cell. Erdész and Sipos, the two robbers and murderers, managed to escape, but a few days later the police succeeded in finding and arresting them. "Sipos and his accomplice ended up on the gibbet, just like Mihály Francia Kiss, the murderer of the 1919 white terror, who had also taken part in the preparations for the escape. Sipos and Erdész had promised to Francia Kiss that they would take him with them but at the end they decided to bind him hand and foot and leave him in the cell, as the characteristically looking seventy-year-old white terrorist would have increased the chances of detection" (*A század nevezetes bűnügyei* [Famous Criminal Cases of the Century] [Budapest: Minerva, 1964], p. 346). (Sipos and Erdész, with Francia Kiss, are buried in the Rákoskeresztúr Cemetery in parcel no. 301, together with Imre Nagy and the martyrs of the revolution.)

of the Görgey Battalion, KISKA, and the Buda Voluntary Regiment (non-Communist, anti-Fascist, armed resistance battalions) were scarcely, if ever, mentioned. Hungary's Communist historiography of Communist anti-Fascist struggle was not an exception in Eastern Europe. In Tito's Yugoslavia, "textbooks stuck to a dogmatically simplified dichotomy of 'revolutionaries' (i.e., the partisans) and 'counterrevolutionaries' (ranging from Croat *ustashe* and Serbian *chetniks* to native 'quislings' and 'bourgeois' governments in exile) reserving, of course, not just political legitimacy, but also the 'good' virtues and morals only for the first ones." Another typical tendency of the textbooks was "to 'de-ethnicize' World War II on Yugoslav soil, describing the events predominantly from a 'class-perspective' as a war between Communist partisans and all kinds of 'bourgeoisie,' thus ignoring the war's ethnic dimension and its character as a civil war. . . . According to the 'class-approach' it was the 'bourgeoisie' on all sides—the Serbian, Croatian, Slovenian—which was held responsible for the ethnic violence and the war crimes."[59]

In the German Democratic Republic, the Socialist United Party tied its legitimacy to the long fight between anti-Communist Fascism ("the highest stage of imperialism") and anti-Fascist German Communism. The Holocaust became "de-Judaized" in the GDR.[60] It was as if only Ernst Thälmann, the secretary of the German Communist Party, had been killed in Buchenwald, as if the victims of Fascism—in the memory of the GDR—were first and foremost Communists. The postwar exhibition in the Buchenwald concentration camp focused almost exclusively on political inmates, leaving the Jewish victims in the shadows, and not mentioning Roma, homosexuals, and others persecuted in the camp. Postwar individual guilt and responsibility for the past was absolved through this collective anti-Fascist Communist sacrifice. The GDR presented the confrontation between the Communist German Democratic Republic and the bourgeois German Federal Republic as a continuation of the war between Communists and (the "offspring" of) Fascism. In Bulgaria, in the war-crime trials initiated by the Fatherland Front, no distinction was made between those who actively col-

---

59. Wolfgang Höpken, "War, Memory, and Education in a Fragmented Society: The Case of Yugoslavia" (paper for the conference on "Remembering, Adapting, Overcoming: The Legacy of World War Two in Europe," New York University, April 24–27, 1997), p. 14.

60. See Timm, *Jewish Claims*, p. 40.

laborated with the Germans, the so-called friends of the West, and anti-Communist democrats.[61]

*

After the end of World War II both the perpetrators and the victims wanted to forget—to leave the terrible memories of their past behind. The Communist Party—which in the interest of enlarging its own anti-Fascist role, retroactively drove Jews out of the camps anyway—offered Jews a chance to abandon their Jewish identities while remaining anti-Fascists. A large percentage of the Central European—especially Hungarian—Jewry was thoroughly assimilated before the outbreak of the war. (According to the last census before World War I, 76 percent of Hungarian Jews considered themselves to be Hungarian.) Most Jews were confronted with their Jewish identity only at the moment they were forced to wear the yellow Star of David in the ghettos or in concentration camps. Jewishness for them did not mean much more than victimization, starvation, loss of human dignity, suffering, the loss of relatives, the gas chambers, and other barely imaginable horrors. Most of them were unable to do anything with their lately discovered Jewishness but naturally wanted to stand firmly opposed to Fascism.[62]

By contrast, the majority of the witnesses and perpetrators of genocide hoped that so long as they maintained the appearance of loyalty to the Communist system, they would be able to avoid being held responsible for their actions. The stigma of being "Hitler's last ally" and a "Fascist people" (depending on political needs, these titles could be applied either strictly to the members of the former ruling classes or to all members of Hungarian society) was constantly harped on in the rhetoric of the leaders of the Hungarian Communist Party. This served as a reminder and warning that if the need ever arose to punish people for their pasts, there was something to remember. The opponents of Stalinism, the defendants of the show trials in the 1940s and 1950s, were almost always accused of having been Fascists or collaborators, among other things, either before 1945 or after. During the

61. See Judt, "Myth, Memory in Postwar Europe," p. 91.
62. "What should we think of those so-called socialist Zionists, who would like to furnish the most developed form of society, the Socialist society, according to the laws of a semi-nomadic shepherd people? . . . The progressive way of solving 'the Jewish question' in Hungary cannot be anything else but the total assimilation of the Jews. This road is the only one that leads to democratic development and to the elimination of those facts [*sic*] on which anti-Semitic propaganda subsists" (Molnár, *A zsidókérdés Magyarországon*, p. 17).

course of the criminal prosecution of the 1946 pogrom in Kunmadaras (in which Jews, who had just survived the concentration camp, were killed), the prosecutor and the court transformed the case, which was a twentieth-century mutation of the medieval blood libel, into an antidemocratic and—naturally—anti-Communist Fascist conspiracy.[63]

For tribunals, especially for people's tribunals sitting in judgment over war criminals, *in extremis veritas*. The ghastly crimes committed by the mass murderer Mihály Francia Kiss—the torture and murder of at least sixty people—therefore understandably compelled the court to make use of historical statements, which suggested that something had happened even before it could have happened and that everything that happened later was already part of the past.[64] The need to construct and prove historic continuity in such a view of history—and the grave dangers inherent in this—were obvious in the first judgment of Mihály Francia Kiss's case, or rather in the reasons given for the judgment. An ambition to introduce continuity to the case compelled the court to develop an official reading of history that was fraught with dangers, especially for the restored Communist order after 1956, but that were not foreseen at the time.

It can probably be proven that the construct of 1956 as a counterrevolution is the key to the understanding of the history of the Kádár era. Through the optics of the counterrevolution, the period before and after 1956 can be seen in a unique perspective, and this view would even have surprised the official history writers of the period. The construct of the counterrevolution—in an unintended way—created continuity between the Stalinist era and the period following 1956. The problem that arose and that the leadership of the party had to deal with after 1956 was similar to the one that early Christian apologists faced when they argued for the uniqueness of the New Testament and its special status, while simultaneously trying to prove to heretics the continuity between the two Testaments, for both were given by the same pastor.

One of the officially produced reasons for the outbreak of the counterrevolution was found in the pre–1956 Stalinist system—the show trials,

---

63. See Péter Apor, "The Lost Deportations: Kunmadaras, 1946" (Master's thesis, History Department of the Central European University, 1996).

64. "Supersessionist theology necessarily reduces the predecessor text to an 'Old Testament,' whose independent significance is fundamentally annulled once it is construed as only the first stage of a process culminating in the annunciation of a 'new and more complete truth'" (Bernstein, *Foregone Conclusions*, p. 3).

which demonstrated the unlawfulness of the period; but an equally defining role was given to the permanently present, underground Fascist counterrevolution that continuously operated in secret from the time of the
white terror of 1919. In this narrative, the post–1956 Kádár regime continued the anti-imperialist, anti-Fascist struggle of the pre–1956 period: it protected the same values against the same enemy that had now committed
crimes against humanity in its attacks against Communism on three occasions—in 1919, 1944, and 1956. The enemy exists out of the present; it is
not part of the society: the people who revolted in 1956 represented the
past, just reenacted an atavistic opposition. The year 1956 was not an uprising of the dissatisfied people against the Communist regime; it was just
a replay of an old story with roots in the depth of darkness.

Paradoxically, continuity with the pre–1956 regime provided legitimacy for the restoration of the Communist system after the Soviet troops
defeated the 1956 Revolution. The public, especially after the 1963 amnesty
when most of those who survived the postrevolutionary terror were released
from prison, found that although those in power were mostly the same and
although the system did not deny its close connection to the period before
1956, still, life was easier to live and was less unpredictable and frightening
than it had been before; it was different, and yet the same. In comparison
with itself, the Kádár regime seemed better than itself; people felt that they
had to fear the regime less than they should have had to. Had the basis of
comparison been another country—such as neighboring Austria—or another political system and not a previous incarnation of the very same
regime, it would have been much more difficult for the Communists to legitimize their unconstitutional and arbitrary rule. Kádár blamed his predecessor for all the political mistakes that led to the outbreak of the uprising in 1956, and he distanced himself from this Stalinist predecessor, but at
the same time he emphasized continuity. This delicate balance between
continuity and discontinuity, in which the counterrevolution played the
key role, proved to be a stabilizing factor, even if, perhaps, stability was not
the initial historic and ideological intention.

This history of continuity, however, gave populist reformers in 1988–
89 a chance to say, like Imre Pozsgay, one of the newly emerged new breed
of populist post-Communist leaders, at the occasion of the opening of a reconstructed palace that had been turned into a luxury hotel, "the long decades of demolishing and destruction have finally come to an end." With

the help of one single sentence, any distinction between the pre–1956 and the post–1956 periods was torn down—the two eras simply collapsed into one undifferentiated continuous history of "demolishing" and "destruction." This enabled and encouraged people around and after 1989 to talk about "the long decades of Bolshevik rule of bloody terror" when referring even to the events of the late 1980s, a time when in reality there were no political prisoners in Hungary and the majority of the population spent most of its time making money by whatever means possible in the second economy, which was informally tolerated by the regime. When the final days of Communism arrived, nobody was ready to remember any differences between Kádár and anybody or anything that had preceded him. The "Kádár era" became extended backward and incorporated the whole pre–1956 Stalinist period as well. ("[A party] which was, and the [party] which is existing in the present, are the same [party] and not different.")[65] The history of continuity that originally ensured the legitimacy of the Kádár regime after 1956 proved to be one of the most important elements of its delegitimization in 1989. Communism in part fell victim to its own historical construction.

*

One of the important goals of the East European war-crime tribunals was to prove that, as a rule, anti-Communists became Fascists: anyone who was an anti-Communist is a Fascist. But the trials and Communist history writing had another aim as well—to prove the truth of historical trivialism: that all Fascists were anti-Communists. These two statements combined have had a significant impact on the formation of views about Communism after 1989. I believe that the history of the twentieth century, written by Communists—with the fight between Communism and anti-Communist Fascism as its focus—has proven to be a serious obstacle to the development of an intelligent, honest, critical, and self-critical debate about Communism after its fall in 1989.

65. Even if the post–1956 Communists had tried to distinguish themselves from the pre–1956 regime—as a consequence of the notion of *partes non moritur* ("the party never dies") this would have been almost impossible. As Justice Choke under Edward IV opined, "The chapter can have no predecessor or successor, because the chapter is perpetual, and . . . cannot die, any more than a convent or commonality; thus the chapter which was, and the chapter which is existing at present, are the same chapter, and not different: thus the same chapter cannot be a predecessor of itself, for a thing cannot be predecessor or successor to itself" (quoted by Ernst Kantorowicz, *The King's Two Bodies: A Study in Medieval Political Theology* [Princeton, NJ: Princeton University Press, 1957], p. 315).

"Representing Mihály Francia Kiss's daughter, Mrs. Gyula Mészár, 'The National Union of Former Political Prisoners' appeals against the judgment of the Budapest Capital Court [of 1957], because the appellant believes that during Mihály Francia Kiss's prosecution the torture and murder of humans was not verified." The legal counsel of the National Union of Former Political Prisoners appealed in 1994 to the Supreme Court arguing that Mihály Francia Kiss had been condemned to death by hanging in the course of a typical show trial and was accused of war crimes and executed by the Communist court after the 1956 Revolution merely because he was an anti-Communist. His crime was that he fought against Communism as early as 1919 and then throughout the whole of his life, just as the Hungarian army had when it attempted to stop Bolshevism during World War II at the Don River. The leaders and generals of that army, who fought as allies of Nazis, who were responsible for the terrible death of two hundred thousand people, drafted soldiers and Jewish labor-servicemen without arms and proper clothes among them, and who were then condemned for war crimes and crimes against humanity, had been rehabilitated by the Supreme Court of the Hungarian Republic after 1990.

In the formerly Communist part of the world, the rehabilitation of war criminals after 1989 is not unique to Hungary. The Croatian leader Ante Pavelic, the Serb Draza Mihajlovic, Bishop Stepanic of Zagreb, and the one-time leader of the Romanian Iron Guard, Antonescu, are among others who gained acquittal, or for whom serious attempts have been made to gain such acquittal. Similarly Miklós Horthy was given a (partially) official reburial with the participation of the members of the first post-Communist, right-wing government. So there is nothing surprising or exceptional in the fact that the National Union of Former Political Prisoners tried to gain rehabilitation for the mass murderer Mihály Francia Kiss. According to those who worked for the rehabilitation of such people, their common crime, the reason why they fell victim to the Communist system, was that they were all anti-Communists, just as the courts and historians after 1945 had indicated. The Communist judges deemed anti-Communists as Fascists in order to sentence them as war criminals. Those who tried to rehabilitate Fascists and war criminals after 1989, after the disappearance of Communism, did nothing more than take the logic of the Communists deadly seriously in order to use it as a reason for acquittal.

The genocide of the Jews was the only mass atrocity in history which was followed and concluded by an explicit, formal, judicial, and practical precedent-setting act of international judgment. . . . Furthermore, the legitimacy of the postwar liberal democratic order of the "West" was explicitly tied to this judgment. Auschwitz was then, on the level of juridical clarification, not only "settled" through the clear identification of perpetrators and victims. But in addition, it was transformed into the ground for a reorganized international order based on the principle of "freedom," allowing that order to appear "transpolitical" (especially in its constitution as "natural" opposition to "totalitarianism").[66]

For the West after 1958–59 and especially following the Eichmann trial, Fascism meant and slowly became equal with the Holocaust and Auschwitz. This was the crime and the name that had to be remembered and recalled so that it would never be repeated: for so long as the memory of this horror lasts (goes the assumption) it can be controlled, and we might be able to defend ourselves from ourselves. Memory—in this historiographic and political practice—is the force whereby distance can be created from crimes against humanity. The West committed itself to intervention in Bosnia only when the Western press began to write about the "Holocaust" and "genocide in Bosnia," when the unique crime was evoked whereby, in a paradoxical way, the unbearable situation suffered by the Muslims was posed as a denial of the uniqueness and singularity of the Holocaust. This historiographic and logical paradox was repeated in Rwanda, and this is why the successors to Nuremberg, the International War Crimes Tribunals, were established to bring judgment to these crimes. The memory of Auschwitz and Nuremberg has become an important part of the self-definition of Western democracies and one of the most important sources of internationally accepted human rights.

The strange silence surrounding the history of Communism after 1989, however, seems to suggest the belief that, unlike Fascism, Communism has finally and truly come to an end, and that there is neither the need nor the time to remember it, to face it, or to talk about it. A thing has come to an end that we, in any case, did not make, a thing for which we are not responsible. Just as was the case with the Germans, those nonexistent citizens of a nonexistent country, Communism was made by the Soviets, the already nonexistent subjects of the nonexistent Soviet Union. While before

66. Adam Katz, "The Closure of Auschwitz but Not its End," *History and Memory* 10, no. 1 (spring 1998).

1989, when talking about the occupying army, Hungarians referred to the Russian troops, now only Bolsheviks and Soviets are mentioned and remembered—people who cannot be found anywhere anymore.

In the East the Jews, the Holocaust, Auschwitz, and even Nuremberg have fallen victim to the historiographic and ideological battle between Communists and anti-Communists. The system after 1945 was not legitimized by resistance to Auschwitz, the absolute crime, but by the mythologized rhetoric of the continual struggle against anti-Communist Fascists. Before 1989, Nuremberg and the judicial prosecution of crimes against humanity and war crimes could only be a footnote in the history of post–World War II events. After 1989 in the former Communist world, Nuremberg is presented as the justice of the victors: the Soviet prosecutor of the Stalinist show trials; the memory of Katyn, for which the Soviet prosecutor Pokrovskii tried to blame the Germans; the argument of *tu quoque*, that the Soviets committed even more and even greater crimes than the Germans did—all these have been used to delegitimize Nuremberg.[67] After the Fall of Communism, the Nuremberg trials, the source and basis of international human rights, have become just as suspect in post-Communist countries as everything else that was once associated with the Soviets or Communism.

In the West, a wall built upon the ruins of Auschwitz grows ever more massive in an effort to protect humanity from itself: the international system of human rights desperately tries—sometimes hopelessly—to keep catastrophe at bay. In the East, however, the soft, crumbling construction of Communism promised false protection—before falling utterly to ruin itself— against the simplified danger of Fascism fashioned as anti-Communism. In the Communist reading of recent history, anti-Semitism and race hatred were just a mask on the face of Fascism that had nothing to do with its true nature. Race hatred and national and religious persecution in this interpretation are not defining characteristics of Fascism, which is why it is so easy to incite hatred in the eastern half of Europe today. Extreme nationalists, anti-Semites, and racists are not necessarily seen as Fascists—for this is what the East European history books taught. "An anti-Communist is Fascist," said the Communists; for anyone who does not want to be

---

67. On the connection between Nuremberg and Katyn, see Telford Taylor, *The Anatomy of the Nuremberg Trials* (New York: Alfred A. Knopf, 1992), esp. pp. 466–72.

stigmatized as Fascist nowadays in the former Communist world, it is easier to be a racist.

The collapse of Communism and the revelation of its crimes caught large groups in Eastern Europe unprepared: if, the essence of Fascism was its anti-Communist nature as taught by Communist historiography, then how should the post-Communist public evaluate the most determined adversary of the criminal Communist regime? After 1989 it was not only (the official history of) World War II that was lost but certainty about the true nature of Fascism as well. The return of anti-Semitic rhetoric and politics in the public sphere filled with anxiety those who had been taught that the iron curtain built by the Communist guards would prevent Fascism and anti-Semitism from returning. With the fall of the iron curtain and the Berlin Wall, these false promises were gone as well.

Those East Europeans who found themselves defenseless among the ruins left behind the suddenly departed Communists, discovered the Holocaust and the construct of Fascism as anti-Semitism only after 1989. The interpretation offered by the West seemed to provide the only available, ready-made alternative for the discouraged East Europeans.

As Ernst Nolte argued in his *Der Faschismus in seiner Epoche* published in 1963, there is strong affinity but probably no exclusively defining relationship between Fascism and anti-Semitism. On the eve of Hitler's coming to power, the percentage of Jewish university students was substantially higher in Germany than in the United States. Anti-Semitism, however repulsive and humiliating it is, most likely becomes a truly dangerous social problem when democratic institutions cease to function in a proper way. This is what will likely become palpable after the end of the twentieth century.

Words do not preserve their original meaning—as Péter Esterházy, the Hungarian writer, asserted, referring to the wonderful life of words. We should accept what we have, the meaning being what we ourselves produce. By today, for certain groups even in the former Eastern Europe, Fascism means and slowly equals anti-Semitism, although this emerging new understanding is not without grave dangers. If Fascism were understood exclusively as anti-Semitism, then even empty formal gestures to the memory of the victims of Auschwitz could be accepted as enough reassurance against the return of Fascism. Given the lack of precise original meaning of the term "Fascism," one can understand the sensitivity of those right-wing figures, who nowadays do not want to be labeled as Fascists in the former

Communist world, for most of them would not wish for another Holocaust, for the physical extermination of large ethnic or religious communities. Most of them merely hope for an ethnically clean, homogeneous society, for national redemption that might herald a new era after the long decades of a degenerate, unauthentic history.

Even in death, the suspicion to which Communism gave birth—and this is becoming less and less obvious and more and more difficult to recognize—makes it difficult for anyone to analyze the history of the past century and to utter words that mean what they mean and not what justices meant by them in their judgment in the Francia Kiss case.

On June 4, 1996, at 4:20 PM during parliamentary debate over the bill that proposed to enshrine in law "the memory of Imre Nagy, martyred prime minister of Hungary," Ottó Sándorffy, representative of the right-wing Small Holders' Party, took the floor:

It's not likely that the prime minister, who struggled against the cult of personality in all of its forms, would have liked to have been raised above his fellow martyrs, and isolate himself from other victims. (Applause from the ranks of the Smallholders' Party.) All other executed victims suffered the same injustice. This is why it is right and just to read their names, one after the other, together with the name of the martyred prime minister aloud to this House. The names of the 278 heroes and victims executed by the Communist dictatorship in retaliation following the 1956 Revolution and Freedom Fight: Géza Adamszky (Members of parliament rise.) . . . Tibor Földesi, Mihály Francia Kiss, Ferenc Franyó . . .[68]

68. *http://www.mkogy.hu/naplo/183/18300046.htm.* Francia Kiss is buried in parcel 301 of the Rákoskeresztúr Cemetery, where Imre Nagy rests.

6

Underground

The most famous photographs of the 1956 Revolution capture the moment when the soldiers and policemen who had been defending the headquarters of the Budapest Party Committee left the building. Faced by the superior force of storming revolutionaries, the defenders understood that further defense was hopeless and gave up the besieged headquarters. On their way out, at the very gates of the building, the defeated were received by deadly machine-gun fire. *Life* magazine carried a series of close-up pictures of the killing.

Life photographer George Sadovy's photo-report of the bloodbath became one of the most famous sequences of war photographs ever made, comparable only to such legendary pictures as the Hungarian-born Robert Capa's war reportage from the front during the Spanish Civil War.[1] When

Chapter 6 is a substantially revised version of "Underground Stories, 1: Nazi and Communist horrors at the 'House of Terror,' Budapest," published in *Storiografia. Rivista annuale di storia* 7 (2003): 27–70.

1. When *Picture Post*, the British journal, published an eleven-page photo-reportage of the Spanish Civil War in December 1938, it called the twenty-five-year-old Capa, "the best war photographer of the world" (*Picture Post*, December 3, 1938, pp. 13–24).

On September 23, 1936, the French journal *Vu* published a series of Robert Capa's pictures, among them one of the most famous war photographs ever taken, known as "The Death of the Militiaman," or "The Falling Soldier," that Capa shot on September 5, 1936, at Cerro Muriano (pp. 1106–7). In 1975 Phillip Knightly, a British journalist, published a book *The First Casualty: From the Crimea to Vietnam; The War Correspondent as Hero, Propagan-*

Life decided to publish a special issue devoted exclusively to the images of the revolution, Sadovy composed a narrative account to accompany his pictures:

The fighting really began to flare up. People were dropping like flies. . . . Now the ÁVH [the abbreviation of the Hungarian secret police] men began to come out. The first to emerge from the building was an officer alone. It was the fastest killing I saw. He came out laughing and the next thing I knew he was flat on the ground. It didn't dawn on me that this guy was shot. He just fell down, I thought. . . . Six young policemen came out, one very good-looking. Their shoulder boards were torn off. Quick argument. We're not as bad you think we are, give us a chance, they said. I was three feet from that group. Suddenly one began to fold. They must have been close to his ribs when they fired. They all went down like corn that had been cut. Very gracefully. Another came out running. He saw his friends dead, turned and headed into the crowd. The rebels dragged him out. I had time to take one picture of him and he was down. Then my nerves went. Tears started to come down on my cheeks. I had spent three years in war, but nothing I saw then compared with the horror of this. I could see the impact of bullets on clothes. There

---

dist, and Myth Maker (New York: Harcourt, Brace, 1975), which, for the first time, alleged that one of Capa's two most famous photographs—"The Falling Soldier"—had been staged (the other one is a GI landing on Omaha Beach on D-Day in Normandy). Richard Whelan, Capa's biographer (*Robert Capa: A Biography* [New York: Alfred A. Knopf, 1985]), after a time-consuming investigation ascertained that Capa—born as Ernő Endre Friedman in Budapest—had, in fact, photographed the death of "The Falling Soldier" during the battle at Cerro Muriano, on September 5, 1936. Whelan, relying on the testimony of an eyewitness, was able to identify the soldier in Capa's photographs (Federico Borrell Garcia, a twenty-four-year-old Republican volunteer from the village of Alcoy, near the city of Alicante). In his article "Proving that Robert Capa's 'Falling Soldier' Is Genuine: A Detective Story," written for *Aperture Magazine* (no. 166, spring 2002), Whelan reconstructed the probable chain of events, which led to Borrell Garcia's death and Capa's famous picture:

Capa encountered a group of militiamen . . . from several units—Francisco Borell Garcia among them—in what was at that moment a quiet sector. Having decided to play around a bit for the benefit of Capa's camera, the men began by standing in a line and brandishing their rifles. Then, with Capa running besides them, they jumped across a shallow gully and hugged the ground at the top of its far side, aiming and firing their rifles—*thereby, presumably, attracting the enemy's attention*. . . . Once Borell had climbed out of the gully, he evidently stood up, back no more than a pace or two from the edge of the gully and facing down the hillside so that Capa (who had remained in the gully) could photograph him. *Just as Capa was about to press his shutter release, a hidden enemy machinegun opened fire. Borell hit in the head or heart, died instantly and went limp while still on his feet, as Capa's photograph shows.* (Emphasis added; Whelan published a version

was not much noise. They were shooting so close that the man's body acted as a silencer.[2]

Sadovy shot several rolls of film on Köztársaság (Republic) Square, while covering the siege of the Budapest party headquarters, which, incidentally, before the end of World War II, had served as the headquarters of the *Volksbund*, the Nazi sympathizer association of Hungarian Germans. *Life* published dozens of his photographs, among them the four-picture series of the massacre of the ÁVH soldiers, most of them enlisted men without rank. (See Figure 6.1.)

In the first picture the six young men are crowded against the wall near their captured building. On the left side of the six-portrait photo, a very good-looking thick-haired blond sergeant (the only one with marks of rank on his shoulder), about twenty-six years of age, with a bloodstain on his face, is looking distrustfully ahead, slowly raising his arms. There are quite a few similar faces, typical of the 1950s, looking into Jean-Pierre Pedrazzini's camera on the pages of *Paris Match* from November 3, 1956, which carried Imre Nagy's retouched color photo, "l'homme de Budapest,"

---

of his *Aperture* article in the *American Masters* series of PBS. See *www.pbs.org/wnet/americanmasters*)

In Capa's biography, Whelan wrote, "To insist upon knowing whether the photograph actually shows a man at the moment he has been hit by a bullet is both morbid and trivializing, for the picture's greatness ultimately lies *in its symbolic implications, not in its literal accuracy* as a report on the death of a particular man" (Whelan, *Robert Capa*, p. 100; emphasis added). As the biographer was not able at that point to demonstrate the authenticity of the picture, he opted for the idea that for the evidential status of the document it was not an issue of how the picture was made, but rather what it wanted to communicate. A few years later, when additional information became available on presumed specific circumstances of Capa's shot, Whelan changed his strategy and was at pain to prove that Capa's famous photograph had not been faked, but rather was unquestionably authentic. Whelan did not realize that in the course of his painful efforts he claimed something much more serious: that Capa had personally been responsible for the fall of the "Falling Soldier." Whelan wanted to clear the photographer morally; he finally craved for a picture that did not just look like but was, in fact, a document; he now insisted on the specific circumstances of the specific event. For the sake of morality of specificity as opposed to the immorality of generalization, the detective-turned-biographer was ready to sacrifice Capa's integrity and implicate him in the killing of the most important figure in the history of war photography (see Maria Mitropoulos, "The Documentary Photographer as Creator," *http://www.media-culture.org.au/0108/Photo/htm*).

2. John Sadovy, "The Fighting Really Began to Flare up," in *Hungary's Fight for Freedom*, a special *Life* magazine report in pictures, 1956, pp. 26–45.

on its title page. *Paris Match* published a close-up of the massive crowd at László Rajk's reburial (a one-time member of the Internationalist Brigade in the Spanish Civil War) on October 6, 1956, just days before the outbreak of the revolution, with a number of similar open faces, so familiar from the *Life* series.

The top button of the sergeant's uniform, on the pages of *Life*, is unfastened; he is wounded below his left ear; he is like a hunted animal forced out of the depths of the forest, who now feels with utter certainty that he cannot be alert enough to counter what is surely about to happen to him. The next moment, the next picture was captured in the midst of a drift of bullets, the camera focused but unstable, Sadovy's hands visibly shaking; the faces are somewhat faded, as if the light had to penetrate through a translucent veil. The soldiers are taken aback, and "in a last instinctive gesture they try to ward off the bullets with the upraised hands."[3] The group of soldiers double up in pain on the third photo. They are on their feet at the very moment before crumpling. In the last picture they fall to the rubble-strewn sidewalk, just in front of the gate of the building they left a moment ago. The sergeant's body has already tumbled to the ground, his head suspended for a last unrealizable moment in the air, as if it did not quite want to believe what has happened to the body.

John Sadovy's pictures were published all over the world. *Correio de Manha*, the Rio de Janeiro daily, gave permission to the *Délamerikai Magyar Hirlap* (South American-Hungarian Herald), a right-wing Hungarian diaspora paper, which decided to republish the photos, but under the misleading title "This Is How the Russians Kill." The pictures found their way into the *White Book*, the official Communist version of the events of 1956, this time, naturally, as the ultimate proof of the extreme brutality of the "counterrevolution," the inhuman nature of the organized anti-Communist terror.[4] Although the world was convinced that in looking at the pictures they were watching the last seconds of humans who would be dead a moment later, three of the soldiers in Sadovy's photos, one of them the

3. Ibid., pp. 38–39.

4. Maire-Joze Mondzain, "La vérité est image mais il n'y a pas d'image de la vérité" [Truth Is Image, but There Is no Image of Truth], in her *Image, icone, économie. Les sources byzantines de l'imaginaire contemporain* (Paris: Le Seuil, 1966); quoted by Bruno Latour, "What Is Iconoclash; Or Is There a World Beyond the Image Wars?" in *Iconoclash: Beyond the Image Wars in Science, Religion, and Art*, ed. Bruno Latour and Peter Weibel (Karlsruhe, Germany, and Cambridge, MA: ZKM and MIT Press, 2002), p. 14.

FIGURE 6.1. John Sadovy's photo-series on the events on Republic Square, October 30, 1956. *Hungary's Fight for Freedom*, *Life* magazine, 1956. Copyright by *Time Inc.*

sergeant, miraculously survived. In the spring of 1957 *Népszabadság*, the official daily of the Communist Party, ran a series under the title "Those who Came Back from the Grave."[5]

Sadovy was not the only photographer on the streets of Budapest during the thirteen days of the revolution. *Time Inc.* itself had six correspondents and photographers in the city; four were held for a time by the Soviets; one was wounded, but all survived, together with John Sadovy. Jean-Pierre Pedrazzini, the twenty-seven-year-old *Paris Match* photographer, however, was killed on November 30 on Republic Square, while covering the events in front of the Budapest party headquarters. When he went down, according to eyewitness accounts, he handed over his camera and said to a companion, "Here, take a picture for me."[6]

Sadovy's photos were included in the authorized Communist version of the events on Republic Square, in *Köztársaság Tér 1956* (Republic Square 1956), first published in 1974. Ervin Hollós, who authored the book together with his wife, was in the building during the siege. Immediately after the defeat of the uprising, he became deputy head of the Investigation Department of the Ministry of the Interior, the agency in charge of investigating "the counterrevolutionary atrocities" during the 1956 events, among them the massacre on Republic Square. Later on, he changed his career and became the official historian of 1956, making good use of the confessions he had coauthored as the chief investigator of the "counterrevolution."

Besides the textual account, in order to situate the narrative and to inscribe the memory of the events as counterrevolution in an easily memo-

---

5. It emerged from the interviews that by having imitated that they were dead, the severely wounded and hospitalized soldiers somehow escaped the rage. *Népszabadság* followed their life for some years, and on the occasion of the anniversary of the siege, customarily, revisited them. After some years, however, they disappeared from public sight and became completely forgotten.

The soldiers have been rediscovered after the collapse of Communism, and one of the right-wing papers published a report about them. Contrary to the facts, the paper insisted that the Communists, in a sinister way, made use of Sadovy's photos by having presented them as if Sadovy had photographed the death of the young men, as if the soldiers had been murdered by the revolutionaries, when, in fact, they survived the massacre. From the post–1989 report it emerged that the Communist journalists had reasons to discontinue following the lives of the miraculously escaped soldiers. One of them became an alcoholic; another divorced and lived in deep poverty; all three of them became allegedly deeply disappointed and thought that the authorities abandoned them.

6. Henry R. Luce, editor-in-chief, "Foreword," a special *Life* magazine report in pictures (1956).

rializable localization system, *Köztársaság Tér 1956* provided an extensive photographic coverage of the events. The pictures came mostly from the pages of *Time, Life,* and *Paris Match.* With the help of the photographs the historians condensed the most important events, connected to specific locations—primarily to Republic Square—in order to guarantee that future memories would be tied to known and concrete localities.

The pictures were included in the official account in order to solidify the status of the massacre as an immovable event. Photography, so it seems, does not require mediation; it promises noninterventionist objectivity. As the image is not made directly by human hand—it is just mechanical reproduction of "reality," it is an action at a distance—it promises the immediacy of evidence, almost as if it were revelation.[7] It is not made, but seemingly brought forth and revealed, like an object found in the depth of an archive. It does not refer to or resemble reality, but instead, it stands for reality and takes the place of the original.[8] It is thus an appropriate medium to transform a particular event into a frozen document, into a sign.

After the revolution, the courts made use of this evidence, these photos, when identifying and charging those who had taken part in the massacre on Republic Square.[9] The images were used as *hyperfacts,* capable of referring to and revealing other, more fundamental, until-then-barely visible facts: the striking similarity of the bloodbath to other right-wing, anti-Communist incidents of the past. The images—when looked at from the right perspective—suggested their own frame: in this case, the counterrevolutionary nature of the event. In that frame, suddenly everything fell into place; the hidden came into light.[10] The status of noninterventionist "objectivity" of the photograph and its ability to reveal the hitherto unknown

---

7. On *acheiropoietic* images, images not by a human hand, like the direct imprint of God on the Holy Shroud in Turin, see Marie Jose Mondzian, "The Holy Shroud/How Invisible Hands Weave the Undecidable," in *Iconoclash: Beyond the Image Wars in Science, Religion, and Art,* ed. Bruno Latour and Peter Weibel (Karlsruhe, Germany, and Cambridge, MA: ZKM and MIT Press, 2002), pp. 324–35.

8. Cf. Bruno Latour, *Pandora's Hope: Essays on the Reality of Science Studies* (Cambridge, MA: Harvard University Press, 1999), p. 67.

9. Cf. Hollós and Lajtai, *Köztársaság Tér 1956,* p. 168.

10. "In 1898 Secondo Pia, a lawyer and photographer, was instructed to take the first photographs of the [Holy] Shroud. On May 28 he exposed two 20 x 23.5 inch glass plates, which he developed the same night. The photographs were said to have revealed something new and unexpected: on the negative there appeared a positive image. It showed the front and the back of a male body, bright on a dark background, apparently three-dimensional

do not contradict each other: Röntgen representation is capable of showing up what has been invisible for the human eye in a presumably empirically reliable, nonsubjective way.[11]

The book carried portraits of the most important Communist martyrs of the bloodbath as well, among them the three truce-bearers, who were massacred when they left the building with a white flag. Imre Mező, one of the secretaries of the Budapest Party Committee, carried the white handkerchief on a stick. It was supposed to show that the defenders had realized that it would be irrational to continue the fight. He was shot and then miraculously smuggled into a hospital, where he died. (The street that leads from behind the party headquarters to the National Pantheon—where he was finally buried—carried his name until 1989, when it got its original name back.) One of the other truce-bearers, a colonel of the army, was shot and hanged with his head down; the other soldier was hit by a burst of machine-gun fire and when he was down, his heart was cut out.

Köztársaság Tér 1956 took full advantage of the fact that slaying of the truce-bearers carrying a white flag was a familiar image for readers of Hungarian Communist history books. There was already a ready-made, available frame for the pictures: during World War II, before the siege of Budapest, two Soviet truce-bearers, who had been sent to negotiate the possibility of saving the city, were killed by the Nazis at the eastern and southwestern gates of the city. Both soldiers, Captains Steinmetz and Ostapenko, were given huge monuments at the entrances to the city during the Communist period, reminding the people of the cruelty of Fascism and the sacrifice of the Soviets. Captain Steinmetz's body was translated, that is, reinterred, under the pedestal of his statue in 1949. Both monuments were blown up during the days of the revolution, and both of them were recast in 1958. (After 1989 the sculptures were moved to the sculpture park, the "skanzen" of the memorials from the Communist pe-

---

as though lit from above. The brownish traces—hardly decipherable on the shroud itself—became a light and readable image. . . . The long history of the shroud suddenly appeared as a prelude. In retrospect it became the history of a code, unlocked only in the age of photographic reproduction" (Peter Geimer, "Searching for Something: On Photographic Revelations," in *Iconoclash: Beyond the Image Wars in Science, Religion, and Art*, ed. Bruno Latour and Peter Weibel (Karlsruhe, Germany, and Cambridge, MA: ZKM and MIT Press, 2002), p. 143.

    11. Cf. Loraine Daston and Peter Galison, "The Image of Objectivity," *Representations* no. 40 (fall 1992): 81–128.

riod, while the new anti-Communist historiography came forth with an alternative account, according to which one of the captains was shot by mistake from behind by the Soviets; the other, while drunk, drove his car into a ditch.) Before 1989, however, the history books did not miss the opportunity to point out the parallel between the two cowardly acts, as one of the most visible proofs of the fact that it was indeed Fascism that had been let loose during 1956.

*

At the beginning of the 1950s, five years after the end of the siege of Budapest, stories were circulating in the city about a strange platoon of German soldiers who emerged from the tunnels of Kőbánya in the outskirts of Budapest. The soldiers, according to the rumor, had gone into hiding at the end of the Soviet siege of the city, using the old and deep tunnels that had been built at the time of the Turkish occupation in the first half of the seventeenth century. During the siege the tunnels served as storage space for one of the German divisions, which accumulated large quantities of dried rations in them. The entrance fell in at the end of the war, and the members of the lost platoon lived on dried food for years, while they dug their way out of the underground labyrinth.[12]

On November 2, 1956, two days after the fall of the Budapest party headquarters, *Magyar Függetlenség* (Hungarian Independence), one of the revolutionary newspapers, revealed that after they stormed the building, the revolutionaries had found "large quantities of half-cooked pancakes in the kitchen, enough for considerably more people than those actually found after the siege, but the ÁVH-men [members of the secret police] mysteriously disappeared." When the number of the dead lying in the square was added to the prisoners taken by the revolutionaries, the sum total, including civilians, was less than one hundred. The number surprised the victors, who had assumed that hundreds of soldiers and policemen were quartered in the party headquarters, together with hundreds or even thousands of prisoners, women and children among them.

In the indictment of one of the post–Republic Square trials, the Budapest Military Court stated that before the siege, rumors had started circulating among the fighting groups about the underground prisons and casemates that lay beneath the party headquarters, and the hundreds or

12. Péter Gosztonyi, "A Köztársaság téri ostrom és a kazamaták mítosza" [The Republic Square Siege and the Myth of the Casemates], *Budapesti Negyed* 2 (March 1994): 16.

even thousands of freedom fighters who were held there.[13] On the morning of the siege, one of the revolutionary military leaders assured his men,
"We are absolutely certain that under the party headquarters there are several floors of underground cellar prisons, full of political prisoners, whom
it is our duty to free."[14] The so-called *White Book*, the official Communist
version of the events, claimed that in the days before the bloody battle,
horror stories had circulated in the city about thousands of prisoners who
had been suffering in the underground labyrinth for already ten years.[15]
One of the dailies wrote about medieval prisons, other organs about "the
torture chambers of the inquisition," "the secret of the tunnels under the
party headquarters," and "the mysteries of the Communist casemates."[16]

When the beleaguerers entered the building, they immediately tried
to make contact with the prisoners. The revolutionaries investigated the
cellars but found nobody. They searched for secret entrances that supposedly led to the underground labyrinth, and listened to noises and ham-
mering coming from below. Some of the occupants claimed that they had
heard cries from below, and later on *Magyar Nemzet* reported that on lift-
ing the receiver of the telephone in one of the empty offices, a member of
the occupying forces overheard an abruptly cut-off conversation between
an ÁVH officer and a guard from the underground prison, who anxiously
inquired about the outcome of the fighting. "Let us out! We are prisoners.
We want to live!" was purportedly heard from deep below. "How many of
you are there?" came the question from above. "Hundred and forty," arrived the barely audible answer from the depth of the bunker.[17]

When the fighting ceased, in the early evening of October 30, the
search began on the square. The revolutionary military units issued war-
rants for the arrest of those who might have taken part in designing the
underground structures and for the officials of the Budapest Sewage Com-

13. Budapest Military Court B. IV. 432/1958. sz; quoted by Hollós and Lajtai,
Köztársaság Tér 1956, p. 105.
14. Supreme Court of the Hungarian People's Republic. Tb. 46/1960/5. sz; quoted
by Hollós and Lajtai, *Köztársaság Tér 1956*, p. 111.
15. *Ellenforradalmi erők a magyar októberi eseményekben I. kötet* [Counterrevolution-
ary Forces in the Hungarian October Events], vol. 1 (Budapest: Information Office of the
People's Republic of Hungary, 1957), p. 22.
16. Cf. János Molnár, *Ellenforradalom Magyarországon 1956–ban* [Counterrevolution
in Hungary in 1956] (Budapest: Akadémiai Kiadó, 1967), p. 184.
17. *Magyar Nemzet*, November 3, 1956.

pany, who were supposed to know the secret entrance to the underground structures. The Hungarian National Radio repeatedly requested anyone who had information about the layout of the casemates to report, without delay, at the headquarters of the rescue operation. On next afternoon, General Béla Király, the commander of the revolutionary National Guard, appointed a lieutenant-colonel to head the drilling.

Some of the Western photographers, together with a few Western film crews, had stayed on the square even after the final fall of the building and took pictures of the search. One of the photos shows two men, probably from the National Postal Services, listening carefully to an aural detector placed at one of the manholes on the square. The National Geophysics Institute, at the request of the Headquarters of the National Guard, sent a cathode-ray oscilloscope, four Soviet made geophones, and one anode-battery with the necessary cables.[18] The National Guard ordered the Hungarian-Soviet Oil Exploratory Company to send drilling rings, boring tools, even drilling vans and a boring rig to the square. From the Oroszlány coal mines three boring masters were ordered to the city from the Zala oil fields, and experts with sophisticated equipment were sent to aid the explorers. (See Figure 6.2.)

To start, twenty-meter exploratory wells were drilled, but on November 3 the wildcat wells went even deeper than that. The government sent powerful excavators to the works, and one of the pictures, published in *Köztársaság Tér*, clearly shows the enormous ditch excavated by the machine used for the construction of the Budapest underground. The Budapest Sewage Company sent workers, pickaxes, shovels, ropes, and other supplies. After the unsuccessful attempts to find the entrance to the labyrinth from the cellars of the building, the explorers descended into the sewage system to find the mysteriously invisible underground prisoners. The scene, described by some of the newspapers, resembled to the setting of Victor Hugo's *Les Misérables*, when the former prisoner Jean Valjean carries in his arms the seriously wounded Marius through the labyrinth of sewers under restless, revolutionary Paris.

People who claimed to know the secret of the casemates came one after the other to help the searchers, who continued to work day and night. An engineer pointed at the elevator shaft, and the drilling started once more

18. Expert report; Supreme Court of the Hungarian People's Republic B. F. I. 461/1958/10; quoted in Hollós and Lajtai, *Köztársaság Tér 1956*, pp. 205–6.

FIGURE 6.2. Postal workers are searching for the underground prisons on Republic Square, November 1, 1956. Photo Archives of the Hungarian National Museum.

inside the building without a moment's delay. Somebody suggested searching for an armored door covered by concrete in the cellar; an iron door was blown in, but it did not lead anywhere; the newspapers searched for a mysterious woman who allegedly, for unknown reasons, knew the exact location of the entrance under one of the elevators that led to the sewers. Large crowds, hundreds of people, stayed continuously on the square, where two days after the end of the siege, several deep holes, on each side, were constantly being searched and deepened. High-powered floodlights illuminated the dark scene during the late autumn nights. In the meantime the cellars of all the neighboring houses were investigated, especially after a woman claimed that one of her relatives had been kept under one of the houses and then released and had reached the surface from beneath another building several hundred meters away.

The Budapest Police Headquarters informed the newly published daily *Új Magyarország* (New Hungary) that "the underground prisons were not built by the Budapest Party Committee but either by the Gestapo or, on the orders of the Gestapo, by the Buda Public Development Company during World War II. The Communists simply took over and made use of the structure that the Nazis had constructed." The supposition was made believable by the fact that the headquarters of the ÁVH, where the defendants at the Communist show trials were tortured and interrogated in the cellars, had been before the end of the World War II the headquarters of the Arrow-Cross Party, the Hungarian Fascists, who had tortured and killed Communists and Jews in the prisons of the building. "One of the exits from the air-raid shelters opened into a huge wine cellar under the offices of the by now nationalized former Public Buildings Design Company. As a consequence of nationalization, the company ceased to exist, so a thorough search has started in the archives of all the construction companies of the city to locate the design drawings."[19]

George Mikes, a London-based Hungarian émigré who worked for the BBC, claimed that the prisons could be reached only through a hidden entrance from either the cellars or from one of the boxes of the City Opera building, which stood opposite the party headquarters on the other side of the square. A captured ÁVH officer, who managed to mislead the explorers, had revealed the secret—according to Mikes's account. After days of self-sacrificing explorations, the rescuers had to give up the search, and the 154 prisoners—including Mikes—together with their captors, perished in the depths.[20]

The miners, oil workers, geometers, well drillers, acoustics experts, army and police officers, and members of the National Guard had to give up the search after four days, as the Soviet troops came back to Budapest early in the morning on November 4. The defeat of the revolution suspended the search; the mystery remained unsolved; the prisoners have never been found. The fact that they had not been found did not disprove the existence of the underground prisons, but instead the tragic fate of the prisoners.

*

In 1896, by the time of the millenary festivities (according to the original official historical version, the Hungarian tribes had conquered the Carpathian Basin in 895, but as most of the festive investment could not

19. *Új Magyarország*, November 3, 1956.
20. George Mikes, *The Hungarian Revolution* (London: Andre Deutsch, 1957), pp. 118–19.

be completed by 1895, the government, together with the Academy of Sciences, decided to revise the received historical wisdom and declared that the exact date of the millennium should be a year later, in 1896) the first underground on the European continent was opened in Budapest. The underground railway was officially referred to as the "crust-railway"; the tunnel ran under the surface, just a few steps down from the world above. It was a remarkable engineering achievement, the proof of the modernizing potential of the Austro-Hungarian monarchy, the pride of the city of Budapest even at the beginning of the twenty-first century.

On September 17, 1950, the Council of Ministers officially announced that as part of the First Five-Year Plan, the construction of the new Budapest subway should immediately begin. The building of the subway was meant to be the flagship construction of the Five-Year Plan, second only to the development of Stalin City, the pride of Socialist urban development, a Magnitogorsk-type Communist urban utopia with a mammoth steel mill, based on imported Soviet iron ore.[21] The decision of the Hungarian Council of Ministers came just a few months after the inauguration of the fourth and most lavish section of the Moscow metro, which was opened on the occasion of Stalin's seventieth birthday.

Construction began immediately at fourteen different sites of the city, and according to the plans, it was ordered that the first section should be completed in less than four years. At that time there was still no drilling shield in Hungary; it was mostly unskilled pick-and-shovel men, recruited from the countryside, who worked at the sites.[22] The first stroke of a hoe was reported in June 1950 at "work-site no. 6" under the building at 66 Rákoczi Avenue, right behind Republic Square. Soon more than five thousand people, including numerous miners, were working day and night in three shifts in the deepening holes, for, according to the plans, unlike the "Millenary underground" that runs just under the surface, the new Socialist metro was envisaged to operate deep under the ground.[23] Newspaper re-

21. On Magnitogorsk and the construction of the Communist urban utopia, see Stephen Kotkin, *Magnetic Mountain* (Berkeley: University of California Press, 1995).

22. János Kelemen, *A budapesti metro története* [The History of the Budapest Subway] (Budapest: Műszaki Kiadó, 1970), pp. 57–58.

23. Miners working at the construction of the underground railway received special coverage in the press. They were hailed as the real heroes of the construction, in part, as a restitution for their past, historical suffering. Ever since the publication of Frederick Engels's *The Condition of the Working-Class in England in 1844*, miners—especially young boys

ports frequently compared the technically inferior, old "cut-and-cover" underground, with the vertically superior, extremely deep location of the modern Socialist tunnels in progress. The unusual and unnatural depth of the tunnels became a source of speculation about the real but hidden function of the underground: the citizens of Budapest were convinced that the real purpose of the very deep tunnels was to provide air shelters for the nomenclature of the party in case of a nuclear incident. Even the official chronicler of the metro construction had to acknowledge in 1970 that it had been senseless to dig such deep tunnels under Rákoczi Avenue in the first half of the 1950s.[24]

The work strictly followed the script of the Moscow metro construction: "The Budapest underground express-train is being built exactly following the guidelines of the 87-volume plans of the world-famous Moscow metro," claimed an article on the plans.[25] Delegations of Hungarian engineers frequently visited the Moscow sites and took part in regular study tours, while Soviet experts worked at the construction sites with imported Soviet equipment. The reports proudly announced that the Budapest underground would resemble neither the outdated old Budapest underground, whose first passenger had been Emperor Francis Joseph himself, nor "the empty bleakness of hopeless functionality, which reminds the thousands of workers who ride the Paris metro of the daily drudgery of exploitation."[26] Without the plans that had been generously provided by the Soviet Union, it would have taken years just to complete the drawings for the planned metro, wrote the daily of the Hungarian Communist Party.[27]

The newspapers calculated the exact time that would be saved by traveling on this fast and deep marvel of Socialist technology. The workers

---

working underground—have been considered the most exploited social group of the proletariat (Frederick Engels, *The Condition of the Working-Class in England in 1844*, trans. Florence Kelley Wischnewetzky [London: George Allen and Unwin, 1892], esp. chap., "The Mining Proletariat," pp. 241–60.

24. Kelemen, *A budapesti metro története*, p. 50. The subway lines at certain sections under Pyongyang, the North Korean capital, run in hundred-meter depths.

25. "Földalatti Gyorsvasút 1954" [Underground Express Train 1954] *Világosság* (October 6, 1951).

26. József Révai, *Vita építészetünk helyzetéről* [Debate about the Present Situation of our Architecture] (Budapest: Architectural Department of the Association of Hungarian Artists and Applied Artists, 1951), p. 58.

27. "Épül a Földalatti gyorsvasút" [The Underground Express Train Is Under Construction], *Szabad Nép*, April 13, 1952.

of Budapest, by using the metro, instead of the crowded buses and street-cars (there were almost no private cars in the city at that time, only black-curtained Soviet limousines for members of the highest echelons of the party), would gain nine million working hours annually, equal to twenty-seven thousand full two-week holidays for the working people of the city to enjoy. During these nine million hours it would be possible for millions of people to watch more than four and a half million movies.[28] Besides, according to a popular science journal, the construction of the metro would greatly contribute to our knowledge of the ancient history of the city. The construction workers bring to light information that had remained buried for thousands, even hundreds of thousands of years under the city from the prehistoric times of Budapest, which the socialist regime had decided to uncover, bring up to the surface, and share with the working people of the capital.[29]

Not long after Stalin's death in 1953, the new Soviet leadership ordered the Hungarian Communist leaders to the Kremlin to announce the appointment of Imre Nagy as the new Hungarian prime minister. Rákosi, the Stalinist secretary general of the Hungarian party and chief architect of the show trials, remained in office. The new Hungarian government was strongly advised to follow the new Soviet example and slow down its over-ambitious investment plans, including unrealistic developments in heavy industry and infrastructure, and, in a country of extreme scarcity of goods, to channel part of the resources into production of consumer goods. In early fall of 1954, at the time when, according to the original plans, the first line of the new underground was to have opened, the citizens of Budapest noticed with surprise the sudden silence around the drilling towers at all fourteen building sites in the city. The thousands of workers who emerged from under the ground were sent away, mostly back to the countryside. The secretary general, when addressing the meeting of the Budapest Party Committee, explained, "We have decided to temporarily halt the construction of the underground, because the concrete, the glass, the iron, the steel that would have been used under the ground, are now needed on the surface for the construction and reconstruction of the public transpor-

28. Ibid.
29. "Budapest ősföldrajzát derítik föl a Földalatti gyorsvasút építői" [The Workers of the Underground Express Train Uncover the Prehistoric Geography of Budapest], *Élet és Tudomány*, May 28, 1952.

tation system above the ground, and for the building and renovation of apartment buildings for the well-being of our working people."[30] In the same newspaper, a professor of the Budapest Technical University pointed out that halting construction was in fact equivalent to continuing the project, as the preservation of the completed tunnels would substantially enhance their quality. At the same time, an escalator, ten meters long, originally intended for one of the metro stations, would be set up at one of the end stops of the pioneer railway, built for the children with Soviet help in the Buda hills, in order to help citizens of Budapest to familiarize themselves with this new technical innovation. By the time the construction of the metro was resumed and the first line completed, the people of the city would have learned not to fear this unusual means of transportation and would know how to use it.[31]

Some of the construction materials were shipped to eastern Hungary to help in the reconstruction of the flooded area around the Tisza River. The newspapers proudly announced that from the summer of the coming year onward, "the Budapest Horsemeat Factory would be able to use the refrigerating equipment which until now was employed under the ground to freeze the underground water in order to protect the tunnels from incoming floods."[32]

After the 1956 Revolution, the newspapers revealed not only the enormous waste that had accompanied the hasty and irrational work, but also the human cost that was paid during the four years of the works. Hundreds of members of the Socialist brigades suffered from "caisson disease" because, in the midst of the *stakhanovite* work contests, they had not enough time to acclimatize to the sudden change of air pressure when descending to the underground workings or coming up from the deep tunnels. A public hospital not far from Republic Square had to be transformed into a specialized "metro hospital" to treat the victims of the construction work.[33]

30. "Mi a helyzet a földalattival?" [What Is the Situation with the Underground Railway?], *Népszava*, September 29, 1954.

31. Ibid. (Conversation with Dr. Károly Széchy, Kossuth Prize-winning professor of the Budapest Technical University.)

32. "A Földalatti Gyorsvasút építéséhez használt gépek, berendezések a lakosság szolgálatában" [Machines, Equipment Used at the Construction of the Underground Express Train in the Service of the People], *Esti Budapest*, September 7, 1954.

33. "A földalatti-építkezés botrányának hiteles története" [The Authentic Story of the Scandal of the Underground Construction], *Népszabadság*, December 31, 1956.

In the end, the building of metro line no. 2 proved to be the longest-lasting underground construction project in the world. The metro is not only an important part of the transportation system of the city but also a huge air shelter that can accommodate more than two hundred thousand people about thirty meters under the surface, with its own independent electricity and water-supply systems, ventilation, and air-filtering equipment.[34] After the beginning of the initial construction work, during the darkest times of the cold war, in the midst of dramatic shortages, the citizens of Budapest were convinced that the tunnels housed huge food reserves, hospitals, special bunkers, logistical centers, and offices for the military and political leadership.

The belief in the existence of the secret underground tunnels was fed by sporadic unsubstantiated reports about the Moscow "Kremlin line (Metro-2)," the secret underground labyrinth that, allegedly, had been started on Stalin's order even before the outbreak of World War II. The first public report on the Metro-2 was published in the Russian newspaper *AIF* only in 1992, although a Pentagon publication had made the maps of the secret line public in the previous year.[35] The command center of the Civil Rescue Committee was supposedly built under the Sovietskaia Square. The Sovietskaia Station was abolished in 1979, when it was realized that the planned expansion of the Moscow metro would need an irrationally long detour as a consequence of the secret station. Before World War II a tunnel was built, wide enough for two passenger car lines that led to and from the Kremlin (the entrance, allegedly, was under the Spasskii Gate of the Kremlin). According to the published map, there is a line that runs from the Izmailovskii Park Station to Stalin's underground bunker. This is the route that Stalin is supposed to have used on his way to representative state rituals. According to Jurij Zaichev, an expert of the Metro-2 story, the secret metro line ran under Stalin's dacha in Kuntsevo, where a special bunker was constructed with a large study, the so-called Generalskaia, the venue for the meetings of the National Defense Council during the Great Patriotic War, and with a simple bedroom for the Generalissimo.[36]

The May/June 1997 issue of the *Bulletin of the Atomic Scientists* published Andrei Ilnitskii's *Mysteries Under Moscow*. Ilnitsky describes a group

34. Kósa N. Judit and Péter Szablyár, *Föld alatti Pest* [Underground Pest] (Budapest: Városháza, 2001), pp. 13–14.
35. "Military Forces in Transition" (Washington, DC: Department of Defense, 1991).
36. Cf. *www.metro.ru/metro2*.

of explorers, the "Diggers of the Underground Planet," who, starting in 1990, decided to systematically explore the "six, and in some places as many as twelve levels under Moscow." The "Diggers believe the powerful and in-accessible Russian capital—with all its special security departments—is vulnerable from below. . . . The current city government is aware of the possibility of an undeclared 'revolution' from below, and the problem of Metro security stays on the agenda at government meetings." Vadim Mikhailov, the leader of the "Diggers,"

thinks there may be evidence of Stalin-era executions in some passages under the city. Under Solianka Street, for example, there is a large inaccessible network of tunnels that may conceal a mass burial site. . . . Other Soviet secrets lie under Moscow, including a second ring of Metro lines built by Stalin on the outskirts of the city, but never used by the public. . . . Muscovites speculate that the ring was employed by the military to shuttle bombs around the capital.[37]

"Some people say there is nothing better than the Taj Mahal, but I know they're wrong. In the Moscow metro there's a Taj Mahal at each station." Thus Alexander Kaletski begins his *Metro: A Novel of the Moscow Underground*.[38] About three-quarters of the walls of the "Underground Palaces," as the official Moscow guide calls the metro stations, are covered by natural stone: coarse-grained pink marble from the southern shore of Lake Baikal; white marble from the deposits in the Ural Mountains, from the Altay, and from the Caucasus; black marble from Armenia; deep-red marble from Georgia; yellowish, green-gray, and brown shades and layers of spotted marble-type limestone from the Crimea.

Thanks to the unique decorative character of quartzite found in Kareliia (the only place where this material of a rich raspberry shade is extracted) the underground hall of Baumanskaia Station has a peculiarly solemn architectural style. Semiprecious stones may be found and seen at the oldest Metro stations in Moscow. These are pink rodonite and marble onyx. . . . Mayakovskaia Station is rightly considered to be the main architectural masterpiece of the Moscow metro. This is a station, which lies deep underground, and belongs to the first, the oldest line of the Moscow metro. The station was opened in 1938. A mock-up of the station was successfully displayed the same year at the International Exhibition in New York. . . . The vaulting of the central hall of Mayakovskaia Station has thirty-three mosaics

37. *Bulletin of the Atomic Scientists* 53, no. 3 (May–June 1997): 11–14.
38. (New York: Viking, 1985), p. 1.

based on cartoons by the famous Russian artist Aleksander Deineka. The theme of all mosaics is called "One Day of Soviet Skies." The light character of structures, emphasized by the sparkling bends of stainless steel, is shaded by red and pink shades of rodonite, a fine semiprecious stone.[39]

It was not only the master plan, the volumes of technical descriptions, the experts, the supervisors, and the technical equipment that came from Moscow, but the aesthetic and ideological program of the Budapest metro as well. As early as the summer of 1951, an exhibition was organized above one of the prospective metro stations to familiarize the citizens of Budapest with some of the planned works of art that were to have decorated not only the stations but the tunnels as well. The paintings, in golden and silver frames, were supposed to give a foretaste of the heroic and tumultuous frescoes and mosaics of the underground art.[40] A visionary journalist working for *Brightness* reported:

The soccer match is just over and the hundred-thousand-strong crowd is pouring out of the brand new People's Stadium. All the people in their Sunday dress are heading in the very same direction: to the colossal bright red-marble building, complete with a four-story-high green-marble cupola. The marble building, bathed in the Sunday sunshine, is covered with the famous greenish marble from Siklós and decorated by numerous fountains and sculptures cast from white chalk. . . . The rails are divided by green-marble panels decorated with huge mosaics that testify to the unparalleled sporting achievements of our people, the guardians of peace, the builders of the ever brighter future.[41]

As the "Moscow metro serves as the example in every possible respect for the Budapest Underground Railway, which will try to live up to the comparison," the aesthetic and ideological program of each station was organized around a specific propaganda theme reflecting the world high above.[42] The station at the People's Stadium would have emphasized the life of our sporting youth; the station beneath the Eastern Railway Station would have depicted and glorified the unbreakable alliance between the

39. *http://www.Moscow-guide.ru/Culture/Metro.htm.*

40. "Képkiállítás a Földalatti Építkezésénél" [Exhibition of Paintings at the Construction of the Underground], *Népszava*, July 25, 1951.

41. "Földalatti Gyorsvasút, 1954," *Világosság*, October 6, 1951.

42. "Milyen lesz a Földalatti Gyorsvasút állomásainak képzőművészeti díszítése" [What Will the Artistic Decoration at the Stations of the Underground Express Railway be Like], *Magyar Nemzet*, February 21, 1952.

working class and the peasantry, with miners and potato pickers in the center; the next theme elevated Socialist art, while the station under Stalin Square, "which will be the single most important among all the stations, where in the future, three metro lines will cross each other," should have illustrated "all the important historic events related to the Liberation of Hungary, and would express the eternal gratitude of the Hungarian People to our Liberator, the Great Stalin"; stations would have been devoted to the Socialist Constitution (ratified on August 20, on Saint Stephen's Day, so that the semireligious traditional Hungarian holiday would be eclipsed by the "Day of the Constitution and of the New Bread"); to the importance of the continual Hungarian progressive liberation movements; to the Hungarian People's Army, "the Guarantor of Peace in the World"; to all the progressive elements of Hungarian historical traditions; the station under Moscow Square would have presented the achievements of the First Five-Year Plan; and at the final station, under the Southern Railway Station, from where trains leave to Lake Balaton, the most popular holiday destination of the country, art would have been devoted to the theme of the state-sponsored holiday of the working people.[43]

*

To save Utopia from the evil forces of the surrounding imperfect world, Boris Groys, the Russian-born art historian, once argued, there is a strong need for clear-cut spatial separation. It is no accident that the majority of reports of utopian places come from travel accounts, from time travel, from islands, from a different time zone, or from a high plateau.[44] People, a workforce, building materials, and a certain infrastructure are all needed to realize a utopian vision, so a real desert is not the most suitable place for the undertaking. A habitable part of the world, by contrast, which has already been occupied by groups and communities of people, would certainly threaten the integrity of the utopian construct. The ideal place could be an uninhabited area, relatively near an inhabited place: this might offer the feasible location. To realize his utopian master plan, Peter the Great found an apparently suitable place: the marshes at the mouth of the Neva River, where, on morass he built his utopian Westernized world, Saint Petersburg.

43. Ibid.
44. Boris Groys, "A fölalatti mint utópia" [The Underground as Utopia], in *Groys, Az utópia természetrajza* [The Natural History of Utopia] (Budapest: Kijárat Kiadó, 1997), p. 35.

When the Soviet leaders decided to build the center of the Communist new world, they moved the capital from the swamps to Moscow. Groys recalls that the avant-garde artists and revolutionary theoreticians first proposed to lift the new Soviet capital into the cosmic sphere, well above quotidian life on earth. Malevich suggested planning and building so-called planits that would have helped mortals to float above the ground in the air. El Lisitskii's constructs would have stood on very long supporting legs, high above historic Moscow, while Velimir Khlebnikov, the poet, proposed that the inhabitants of Moscow should be provided with movable glass homes above the ground.[45] The problem with all the avant-garde visions was that they lacked deepness, depth in a literal sense.[46]

Stalin's ingenious solution was to open up layers for the Socialist utopia that had not been inhabited, or utilized before, that lacked the traces of tradition of the inherited, spontaneous, organic development. By exploring, excavating, and exploiting the underground, the planner became the sole master of the stone world under, and became able to design a sphere, which he alone could totally control. While under the ground, the subjects became absolutely dependent on the plan of the master, who controlled not only the entrances, the exits, and the artificial light (this was not Tomasso Campanella's *Civitas solis*) but also the form and rules of life of his subjects beneath the ground. As the description of the "Underground Palaces" guide showed, Stalin's metro (its official name was "Metro in Honor of Lenin's Name") was a vehicle of transportation not so much from one local, marble-

45. "But is there a real need for building in the air? 'Generally speaking,' no. But 'in this case'? We live in towns that were born before our time. The tempo and needs of modern life are already too much for them to cope with. We cannot raze them to the ground overnight and start again correctly from a clean slate" (El Lisitzky, *First Skyscraper near Nikitinsky City-Gate* [Moscow]; cf. *http://www.utopia.ru*).

46. Groys, "A földalatti mint utópia," pp. 37–38. One of the entries to the Lenin Mausoleum competition in 1925 proposed "a colossal monument, a tower . . . that should be of a height only accessible by the latest engineering technology. The dimensions of this monument should eclipse all the currently existing tallest buildings in the world. It should proudly soar above St. Basil's Cathedral [on Red Square]. If the proposed monument were the height of the Eiffel Tower, its constructions and its upward soaring would worthily symbolize the great leader, as an innovator and a revolutionary, and the contrast to St. Basil would be truly striking" (A. Gruzdinsky's entry; cf., Russian Utopia).

The "Russian Utopia: A Depository," a catalog prepared for the Venice Biennale, VI International Exhibition of Architecture, contains a rich collection of vertically ambitious avant-garde architectural plans from the 1920s and 1930s (A-Fond, Moscow, 1996).

covered station to another but to the subsequent stages of the Socialist utopia.[47] (See Figure 6.3.)

Socialist realism became the only tolerated program of representing the world at the time when the first metro line under the Soviet capital was opened. Social realism was definitively not a style of artistic representation but an officially sanctioned way of making the world (available). It stood in stark opposition to "bourgeois objectivism," with its (false) acceptance of the world's being resistant to our will. According to official Socialist critics: "bourgeois objectivism" aimed at faithful representation, "the presumed truth," thus acknowledging the difficulties of overcoming the natural and social laws of outside reality.[48] "Bourgeois subjectivism" was not considered to be a lesser danger, as it lacked the determination to change the world, and thus accepted the world as it was subjectively (and falsely) perceived.

Alexander Kaletski, in his sharply anti-Soviet autobiographical novel, acknowledged:

The Metro is a world in itself—in the winter it's warm down there, cool in the summer. And it's always sparkling clean. No Russian would dream of spitting on the metro's marble floor; he'd sooner spit on the coat of another passenger. When I walked along the spotless platform under the high romanesque ceilings, mosaics, and crystal chandeliers all around, my entire body took in the sparkle of the station—my eyes, the whiteness of the marble walls; my hands, the pleasing feel of nickel pools; my feet, the smoothness of the polished stone. Why the modernization of Russia started with the hanging of chandeliers beneath the earth I didn't know, but I did know that when I was underground, I felt free.[49]

47. The Central Line, however, turns into itself. "This line embraces the center of Moscow, drawing its one-hour underground circle which rings the heart of the city and connects all its nerves and arteries. . . . Throughout the day, jam-packed trains run along the Circle Line. There is no end to the river of people, as there is no end to the circle. Alcoholics worship this line. It's their haven—there's no need to worry about being dumped out or arrested at the last stop; they can keep on circling around and around until they sober up, and the best part is that the farther they go, the closer they are to where they started" (Alexander Kaletski, *Metro: A Novel of the Moscow Underground* [New York: Viking, 1985], p. 1).

48. See, however, Barnard Williams's *Truth and Truthfulness*: "The fact that there are external obstacles to the pursuit of truth is one foundation of our idea of objectivity, in the sense that our beliefs are answerable to an order of things that lies beyond our own determination" (Barnard Williams, *Truth and Truthfulness* [Princeton, NJ: Princeton University Press, 2002], p. 125).

49. Kaletski, *Metro*, p. 2.

FIGURE 6.3. Vladimir Favorski, Moscow Metro Station. *Sosialistinen realismi—Suuri utopia*, exhibition catalogue. Valkoinen sali, Helsinki, Finland, July 17–September 22, 2002.

(The underworld as the location of utopia is not a twentieth-century recognition. John Foxe, who studied law at Grays Inn in the 1520s, the author of the anti-Catholic "Acts and Monuments" [published in 1563], argued that Purgatory—the existence of which was so fiercely and lengthily defended by Thomas More, in his "The Supplication of the Souls"—could not be found anywhere, "unless it be in Master More's Utopia.")[50]

The theme of the secret metro line resurfaces in Groys's short essay as well:

People have long whispered about the existence of another, a hidden line, deep beneath the known ones; about a secret network, that forms a double, an underground Kremlin, where the Soviet leadership would hide to in case of war. . . . Russian nationalist circles maintain even today, that careful study of the plans of the Moscow Metro reveals the form of a Star of David, referring to the Jewish as-

50. Cf. Stephen Greenblatt, *Hamlet in Purgatory* (Princeton, NJ: Princeton University Press, 2001), pp. 250–51.

piration for the rule over the Russian capital. This theory is substantiated by the fact that it was Lazar Kaganovich, who led the construction work of the Moscow Metro under Stalin. . . . And Kaganovich was the only Jewish member of Stalin's narrow circle of Communist leaders.

(Lazar Moiseyevich Kaganovich, the one-time Kubany [Ukraine] shoemaker, is one of the most frequently mentioned villains on extreme anti-Semitic Web sites. The name of the longest-living member of Stalin's Politburo—he died in 1991 at the age of ninety-seven—is connected not only to the construction of the underground labyrinth under Moscow but also to the destruction of the enormous Cathedral of Christ the Savior at the back of Red Square.) "The Star of David might refer to the prefiguration of all utopian cities: the heavenly Jerusalem, built of stone, and devoid of vegetation."[51]

*

The archive of Radio Free Europe includes an odd collection known as the "Items." An "Item" is an interview made with freshly arrived emigrants from behind the iron curtain to the West, or with tourists: visitors, who, in most cases, had the mistaken notion that they were talking to either an interested former compatriot, a casual acquaintance, or with a Western journalist. It did not occur to the majority of the interviewees that they were talking to an employee or a contractee of an intelligence agency, who would write a formal official report in their native language, complete with an English summary and evaluation comments. The texts, arranged by subject headings, were used later on by the programmers working at the national desks of the radios. Before the collapse of the Communist regimes, most of the "Items" were destroyed by the radios, partly in order to protect

---

51. Groys, "A földalatti mint utópia," p. 44.

"You see," Salon went on, "I was born in Moscow. And it was in Russia, when I was a youth, that people discovered the secret Jewish documents that said, in so many words, that to control governments it was necessary to work underground. Listen." He picked up a little notebook, in which he had copied out some quotations. "Today's cities have metropolitan railroads and underground passages: from these we will blow up all the capitals of the world. Protocols of the Elders of Zion, Document Number Nine!" . . .

"If I follow you, then, there's a conventicle of Jews—some Jews, not all—who are plotting something. But why underground?"

"That's obvious! Any plotter must plot underground, not in the light of day. This has been known from the beginning of time. Dominion over the world means dominion over what lies beneath it. The subterranean currents." (Umberto Eco, *Foucault's Pendulum*, trans. William Weaver [London: Picador, 1989], p. 443)

the interviewees, who, despite the anonymous format of the documents (the initials or pseudoinitials of the interviewers, however, are always noted on the front page of the interview) might be recognized. Thousands of the "Items" from the national desks, however, survived the shredding and provide unique information for scholars of Communist times.

The "Items" form a weird collection. In some cases it is obvious, and we even have direct proof, that the interview is a product of pure fiction. As some of the interviewers were paid by the piece, the contractors tried to produce as many interviews as seemed acceptable. A well-known Hungarian writer and sociographer, who immigrated to London and worked for the radios, composed some of the interviews facing just his typewriter in the solitude of his study. In most cases, the tourist and especially the recent emigrant wanted to please the interviewer and said what was—according to his anticipation—supposed to be expected of him (the overwhelming majority of the interviewees were young or middle-aged men). The collection reveals the notions that the East European had about the supposed image of Communism in the West. It is also apparent that this circular impression was typically formed by having listened to the programs of Radio Free Europe, where, in turn, the programmers made use of the interviews when broadcasting anti-Communist propaganda to the East. The stories that were told in reply to the suggestive questions of the covert agents— who presupposed the obvious anti-Communist leanings of the refugees who were waiting for their residence permits or of the tourists who were stunned by all the commercial wealth of the West—testified to the effectiveness of the self-fulfilling prophesies of the Western propaganda based on the information distilled from the severely biased "Items."

Among the Hungarian "Items," under the subject "Resistance," there are a few interviews that explicitly deal with the storming of the party headquarters and the underground prisons. "Item" no. 1264/57 originates in Vienna (probably from one of the refugee camps), and according to the English summary, "Source comments on the chapter [of the official *White Book*] 'Attack Against the Headquarters of the Party Committee of Budapest.' He refutes the statement of the *White Book* that the underground of the headquarters did not exist."[52]

---

52. Fonds HU 300–40–4 Hungarian Information Items (Police and Security), Records of the Research Institute of Radio Free Europe/Radio Liberty. Open Society Archives (OSA), Budapest, Hungary.

The source, a forty-nine-year-old former journalist from Budapest, states that he had kept a diary during the days of the revolution and recorded all the noteworthy events. He was present when, after the end of the siege, the besiegers entered the building but were not able to find the entrance leading underground. On November 3, the journalist reported to a captain of the technical division of the army that he had found telephone and electricity cables, which lead beneath the building. On the orders of the captain, geophysical equipment was immediately shipped from one of the coal-mining districts, and by the help of a radio telescope the rescue teams were able to make contact with the 131 prisoners, who said that they had been forced to descend to the underground prisons from room no.3 in the party headquarters.

Forty of us from the investigation team searched the building from roof to cellar but were unable to locate room no. 3, as the rooms of the building, unfortunately, were not numbered. . . . We decided to return the next morning, on November 4, and to carry on with the help of explosives. In view of the start of the Soviet attack, however, we had no opportunity to revisit the site. According to the catering book we found in the building, the kitchen catered for 250 people, and this clearly proves the existence of the underground prison and the secret passage, through which at least one hundred members of the ÁVH could leave the building via the tunnel of the underground railway. The political prisoners, however, remained forever underground. The circumstances of the construction of the party headquarters substantiate my claim. The construction of the building started parallel with the building of the underground railway [*sic*]. [Before World War II the building served as the headquarters of the *Volksbund*.] A delegation of forty Soviet engineers arrived in Budapest to lead the construction of the tunnels, and not a single Hungarian engineer was allowed the see the full plan, they were shown only small segments of the complete master plan. All of us who worked at the construction [this is the first mention that the journalist had personally participated in the work] were completely convinced that we were not building an underground railway, but nuclear shelters, instead.[53]

"Item" no. 3169/57 also originates from one of the Austrian refugee camps, and the source this time is a thirty-two-year-old technician from Budapest. The title of the "Item" "Underground Railway in Budapest and Party Headquarters at Köztársaság tér" is the first mention of the assumed direct connection between the underground prisons and the underground

53. Ibid., pp. 2–3.

railway. The English summary remarks, "Source took part in the attempts to locate the underground rooms with technical equipment for eight days [the siege took place on October 30; the Soviet troops occupied Budapest on November 4]."[54]

"In order to see the story in a clear context, we have to go back to the construction of the Budapest underground railway," insists the technician.

At one point of the line, a detour was built in the direction to Köztársaság tér, but the tunnel did not turn back anywhere to the main underground line. . . . This work was headed by an ÁVH officer, whose cover name was Kovács. He was a local party secretary, but in order to mislead the workers, he had been expelled several times from the party. . . . This part of the tunnel was built mostly by prisoners sentenced to death, who, without exception, were executed later on. As it proved to be impossible to supply all the necessary workforce from among prisoners sentenced to death, a few of the construction workers survived, and when the works stopped after 1953, all of them were sent to far away workplaces in remote parts of the country. Some of them returned during the days of the revolution, and they were the ones who were able to provide precise information about the whereabouts of the detour line. . . .

After midnight, on October 29 [the siege took place on October 30], the investigators transported an aerial detector from one of the mines to the square, which enabled the search team to listen to the vulgar conversation of the ÁVH officers, the crying of the children, and the screams of the women. We could determine the direction of the tunnel, which lead to a spiral staircase beneath the royal box, now reserved for the secretary general, of the City Opera, on the opposite side of the square. . . . In a cellar we have accidentally discovered a telephone switch. One of the members of the National Guard happened to know the secret password, which enabled him to start a conversation with the ÁVH officers underground. The officers, believing that they were talking to one of their comrades, requested him to turn on the water tap and asked him about the outcome of the siege. Naturally, we did not tell them that the headquarters had fallen and the revolutionaries had occupied the building. . . . On the square, with the help of taping equipments, the military managed to capture ciphered messages coming from below the ground, but they were not able to decipher the secret code. . . . We decided that next day, November 4, we would break through the wall at one end of the tunnel of the underground railway, but at daybreak the Soviet troops arrived, and the search had to be stopped. . . . On that day the Soviet military occupied the building, and during the coming days, the rattle of firearms could be

54. Ibid.

heard from the direction of the party headquarters. . . . The Soviets imposed a curfew until seven in the morning, but when I ventured into the street, immediately after the end of the curfew, I saw corpses every morning, children and women among them, lying flat on their faces in the square. In my estimate, during the next two weeks, about one hundred bodies were collected from the square after the end of the nightly curfew. Obviously, these were the people who had been kept underground.[55]

The text shows how the uplifting, bright—although artificially lit—utopia of the Stalinist underground was turned into the image of hell. The mirror image of the cellars under the party headquarters is also featured among the "Items." An interview that originally came from the Vienna News Bureau on September 2, 1957, describes, as the title phrases, "How the *White Book* Was Put Together."

According to the source:

The fighting was still going on in Budapest, when, in the former headquarters of the ÁVH, in 16 Jászai Mari Square [this building—commonly referred to as the "White House"—after 1956 became the Ministry of the Interior, and later on, until 1989, was occupied by the Central Committee of the party], or precisely in the cellars of the said building, the idea of the *White Book* that would uncover the counterrevolution was born. Please do not fool yourselves: this was not a cold, unfriendly, and dirty coal cellar, but a basement equipped with all imaginable comforts, an ample quantity of foodstuffs, hoarded in the "operation officers' shelter," three levels below the ground. Only their uniform distinguished those who stayed in this luxurious cellar from the rats. These rats with a human figure were the employees of the Political Department of the National Police Headquarters and their relatives. . . . The only resistance these "heroes" were able to think of was heroically resisting the temptation to leave the secure cellar and face up to the revolution.[56]

Following the depiction of the scene, the interviewee then gives a detailed description of the "curly dark hair," "the thin stature," and "the characteristic nose" of the rats, in whose mind the idea of the *White Book* was born. These characteristic people understood that with the help of real-life documents it would be impossible to prove to the world, and to the UN, that the "Hungarian Revolution was neither the Revolution of the People, nor the Revolution of the Hungarian Youth but that instead, it was the 'Horthyist-Fascist' mob, financed by counts, barons, bank directors and

55. Ibid., pp. 3–5.
56. Ibid.

the United States that wanted to overthrow the most glorious achievement of the twentieth century: the people's democracy."[57]

The source insists that the photographs included in the *White Book*, among them the pictures of the massacre on Republic Square, in front of the Budapest party headquarters, were fakes, doctored photographs prepared in the safe and secluded cellar, three floors underground, in the building of the "Headquarters of the ÁVH."[58] The ÁVH officers of characteristic appearance retouched the pictures in the depth of their well-appointed cellar, to turn the barbarity of the Communist secret police into sinister accusations against the Hungarian revolutionary youth.[59]

*

In 1992 the first post-Communist conservative government commissioned a two-part film-report on the underground prisons from the Hungarian National Television (the only television channel at that time in the country). The investigative film-report was aired in early March 1994, shortly before the parliamentary elections, as part of the so-called Unlawful Socialism series of the Hungarian television.[60] By that time the popularity of the first post-Communist conservative government—which had been in office since May 1990—was fading dangerously, and all the polling agencies predicted a Socialist victory and even an absolute Socialist majority in the upcoming elections.

As part of the transition from one-party rule, in 1989 the Hungarian Socialist Workers' Party reinvented itself as the Hungarian Socialist Party and had to divest itself of a large number of its former buildings, the head-

57. Ibid., p. 2.

58. "Images offering evidence that contradicts cherished pieties are invariably dismissed as having been staged for the camera. To photographic corroboration of the atrocities committed by one's own side, the standard response is that the pictures are a fabrication, that no such atrocity ever took place, those were bodies the other side had brought in trucks from the city morgue and placed about the street, or that, yes it happened and it was the other side who did it, to themselves. Thus the chief of propaganda for Franco's Nationalist rebellion maintained that it was the Basques who had destroyed their own ancient town and former capital, Guernica, on April 26, 1937, by placing dynamite in the sewers (in a later version, by dropping bombs manufactured in Basque territory) in order to inspire indignation abroad and reinforce the Republican resistance" (Susan Sontag, *Regarding the Pain of Others* [New York: Farrar, Straus, and Giroux, 2003], p. 11).

59. Fonds HU 300–40–4, OSA, p. 3.

60. *Pincebörtön* [Cellar Prison], two-part, 120-min film, directed by Zoltán Dézsy, MTV (Hungarian Television), Budapest 1992–94.

quarters of the party, the White House of the Central Committee, among them. The newly baptized party moved its central offices to the former headquarters of the Budapest Party Committee, the huge building that stands on Republic Square. After the first democratic elections in 1990, the Socialist Party ended up with a tiny block of seats in parliament. The election was won by a conservative, right-wing conglomerate, which had as its primary aim to reestablish the continuity of Hungarian history and to carry on from where "authentic Hungarian national history" had been artificially interrupted. The conservative Hungarian Democratic Forum, led by a failed historian, argued that from March 19, 1944, when German troops came to occupy Hungary, the country had lost its sovereignty, which was regained only at the moment when the first post-Communist democratically elected government was sworn in. Hungary, consequently, could not be held responsible either for the Holocaust or for the Gulag; the Germans and the Soviets, respectively, were to blame.

Practical considerations played the most important but not the only role in the decision of the Socialist Party to move its central offices into the former Budapest party headquarters on Republic Square: this was the largest party property in Budapest besides the White House, the former Central Committee building. The Socialist Party was not in a position to hold on to the White House: its location was too prominent at the moment of the transition; it stands beside the Danube, near the Parliament, and is too visible from everywhere in the city. The party wanted to normalize itself and project the image of a modest, almost invisible political organization, which detests privileges.

The reburial of the executed prime minister of the 1956 Revolution was the single most important representative event of the transition. It was the resurfaced memory of the postrevolutionary terror that proved to be decisive in delegitimizing the Communist rule. When in 1990 the successor party moved to the scene of the bloodiest and most visible anti-Communist atrocity, it moved not only to the scene of merciless slaughter but also to the location on which the counterrevolution was "made up." The scene recalled the atrocities that might have justified the postrevolutionary Communist "justice." The party could evoke its victims, its victimhood, its own pain in the face of the post–1989 discourse of nationwide suffering and mourning. In 1990 the enormous monument dedicated to the "Victims of the counterrevolution" still overwhelmed the square; the windows of the new central offices looked at the memorial; the new party headquarters incorporated the monument, the plaque at the entrance, the notion of the place.

Footage from the newsreels shot on Republic Square during the days of the revolution introduced the two-part film, with aerial detectors, microphones in the manholes on the square, the work of the excavators, and the twenty-meter-deep holes all over in front of the building. The film director interviewed participants from both sides, those who had been present at the siege and contemporaries who had worked either in different party offices or for the secret police in buildings, which, without exception, had underground cellars. A former typist, who worked at the Ministry of the Interior, in the White House after 1956, recalled a frightening experience. One evening in 1959, when she went down to the cellars to shred some papers, she discovered that the walls were covered by a characteristic brownish color up to her chest. To her horror, she immediately realized the possible cause of the discoloration: it could not be anything but dried human blood, she reasoned. She remembered the stories about a gigantic mincing-machine next to the shredder in the cellar. The mouth of the mincer—in the stories—was connected to the sewage system, which in turn opened to the Danube. (The White House stands on the embankment of the river. It is the same building where the curly-haired officers were busy retouching the photographs.) The typist, wearing a wig, facing away from the camera—she supposedly still feared the Communists—recalled the bathtubs full of acid that provided the alternative technology to obliterate all traces of the prisoners.

In April 1993 the film crew commissioned a study by the National Geophysical Institute. The experts were requested to analyze the profile of the soil in front of the headquarters of the Socialist Party. The study discovered strange "anomalies" in the ground: the antitypy (toughness of material) of the soil was higher at a depth of 30–40 meters than nearer to the surface. Strangely enough—concluded the professional analysis—the "anomaly" was observable especially beneath the pedestal of the huge memorial, which had been built at the beginning of the 1960s in memory of the defenders of the Budapest party headquarters. At this point the crew ordered oil drillers to the square, who arrived with sophisticated equipment: drills fitted with diamond bit heads.

On the back of the pedestal of the memorial, which weighed several tons and was dedicated to "The Victims of the Counterrevolution," there was a small iron door, which instantly aroused the curiosity of the film-makers. The drill with the exceptionally tough diamond bit was immediately positioned behind the door, and drilling started without delay through the strange opening. After days of work and fourteen meters of unhindered drilling through the clay bank, the apparatus hit something solid; probably concrete. When the bit was pulled out, it was discovered that the mysterious material had eaten up the diamond. The result was the same after the second and the third trial: the diamond head always became seriously damaged. In the meantime the mighty sculpture was removed and shipped to the outskirts of the city, to the "sculpture park," the ghetto of Socialist memorials, where the dead sculptures await the last judgment.

The intangible concrete material under the ground supplied the *argumentum ex silentio*, or "the evidence of things unseen," as Saint Paul formulated (Heb. 11:1), the proof based on silence, with which the film concluded.[61] The anomaly, the inconclusiveness that prevented the continuation of the search, provided the solid material that was hard to refute: something must be there in the depths of the blood-soaked soil, which, even after long decades, keeps the secret that everyone knows. At the elections, the Socialists

---

61. A classic example of a proof firmly based on silence or on void is the trial of General Tomayuki Yamashita in October–December 1945 in Manila, the Philippines. The United States Military Commission in Manila, and later on the Supreme Court of the United States, sentenced General Yamashita, "the Tiger of Malaya," to death by hanging, for unlawfully disregarding and failing to discharge his duty as commander to control the acts of members of his command by permitting them to commit war crimes and not preventing the atrocities from taking place. Yamashita most probably was not able to take action against the crimes, which members of the Fourteenth Army Group of the Imperial Japanese Army in the Philippine Islands committed in the final phase of the war in the Philippine theater. As one of the dissenting Supreme Court justices expressed in his opinion: it was not alleged that General Yamashita had any knowledge of the crimes, which the military under his command had committed. He could not have any knowledge of what went on in the last phases of the war, since the advancing U.S. army successfully disrupted the communication between his command and the fighting troops. As Justice Frank Murphy has put it, "To use the very inefficiency and disorganization created by the victorious forces as the primary basis for condemning officers for the defeated armies bears no resemblance to justice or to military reality" ("re: Yamashita, 327 U. S. 1"; quoted by Aryeh Neier, *War Crimes: Brutality, Genocide, Terror, and the Struggle for Justice* [New York: Random House, 1998], pp. 230–31). For General MacArthur, who affirmed the death sentence, the ultimate proof was Yamashita's silence, his lack of communication, the nonexistence of any document to the contrary. On Yamashita's case, cf. *Law Reports of Trials of War Criminals*, selected and prepared by the United Nations War Crimes Commission, vol. 4 (London: HMSO, 1948), Case No. 21.

won an absolute majority; the conservative Hungarian Democratic Forum got 14 percent of the votes.

It was not the film that did not quite work but the figure and the dystopia of the cellar prison. Above (or beneath) Stalin's underground—the utopia of both the underground movement and that of the Underground—the post–1989 anti-Communists superimposed the underground cellar. It proved to be difficult, however, to tie the Socialist Party to a representative, intense, compressed counterfigure of its past. Unlike the gas chamber of Auschwitz or the Gulag of Siberia, which although tied to more or less concrete locations, denote a horrifyingly complex and wide-ranging historical figure, the underground prison is not sufficiently unique, nor does it seem to be capable of evoking and denoting a whole historical epoch beyond itself. The notion of the dungeon is more conveniently tied to medieval castles, the torture chambers of the Inquisition, or to the tourist attraction of the *Maison des Esclaves* on Gorée Island, a short boat trip across Dakar in Senegal, than to the location and notion of terror during Communist times.[62]

Despite everything we know of the cellars of the Lubyanka Prison in Moscow (where, among thousands of other prisoners, Raoul Wallenberg was detained), the Communist regime cannot be evoked by a shorthand reference to the underground prison, in contrast to Auschwitz, which—at least in the West—unequivocally recalls Fascism, human horror, vulnera-

---

62. According to the tourist guides, tens of thousands of slaves were gathered, incarcerated, and then shipped from the dungeons of the Slave House in the eighteenth and nineteenth centuries. However,

> despite the name, it's unlikely that the *Maison des Esclaves* was used to hold many captive slaves, apart from those who "belonged" to the merchant. . . . In fact some historians have pointed out that although the island was a vital trading center and strategic port, and an important slave culture existed here, Gorée itself was never a major shipment point of slaves. . . . Of the 20 million slaves who were taken from Africa, only 300 per year may have gone through Gorée. Even then, the famous doorway [of the dungeons] would not have been used: a ship could not get near the dangerous rocks and the town had a perfectly good jetty a short distance away. . . . The historians who refute Gorée's connection with slavery are anxious to avoid accusations of revisionism, and emphasize that many millions of slaves were taken from West Africa in the most appalling circumstances. . . . But they see the promotion of Gorée as a site of significance to the history of slavery as a mere commercialism base on distortion, a cynical attempt to attract tourists who might otherwise go to Gambia's Jufureh or the slave forts of Ghana. Gorée's fabricated history boils down to an emotional manipulation by government officials and tour companies of people who come here as part of genuine search for cultural roots. (David Else et al., *Lonely Planet West Africa*, 4th ed. [1999], p. 792)

bility of human beings, and not just the Nazis. "Why has Auschwitz be-come the universal exemplum with the stamp of eternal perpetuity in the European consciousness that embodies the whole world of Nazi concen-tration camps, together with the universal shock of the spirit over it, and with the mythical site, which should be preserved in order for the pilgrims to visit, like the Mount of Golgota?" asked Imre Kertész in one of his es-says. What makes Auschwitz so perfect, asked the survivor of Fascism and Communism?

All truly great parables should be simple. And in Auschwitz, good and bad do not merge even for a single moment. . . . The picture is not distorted by a shade of alien color; the color, for example, of politics. The spirit of the narration here should not struggle with the fact that innocent—exclusively from the perspective of the movement, innocent—otherwise true-believer Nazis had been locked in Auschwitz; this story is not complicated by such a fact. . . . Auschwitz is fully ex-plored, and in turn, it is both spatially and temporally a closed and untouchable structure. It is like a carefully prepared archaeological find. . . . And we know all spatial segments of the story. . . . It stands in front of us as the Apocalypse, as one of Edgar Allen Poe's, Kafka's or Dostoevsky's horror stories, narrated with uncom-fortable details; its logic, its ethical horror and ignominy, the excess of torment, and the horrible moral of the story, which the spirit of the European narration cannot leave behind, all these details are well known.[63]

The right-wing historians and propagandists had no choice: the film had to be made. The world, the history that the Communists had created around Republic Square, the continual deadly battle of the twentieth cen-tury, in fact of modern times, between Fascism and Communism, the white terror versus historical justice, Republic Square as just another in-stance of the white terror of 1919 and of 1944, could not be undone without revisiting the underground, without arguing that what happened on the Square had been justified. By holding up the underground, by bringing it to light, they could hope that the whole Communist historical construct, the world that the Communists made, could be undermined. Republic Square was the Archimedean point of the Communist interpretation of history, which the cellars could be expected to make both historically and morally untenable.[64]

63. "Táborok maradandósága" [The Perpetuity of Camps], in Imre Kertész, *A száműzött nyelv* [The Exiled Language] (Budapest: Magvető, 2001), pp. 49–51.

64. After the Socialist Party came back to power, in October 2002 the chair of the party announced that the party would change its name to "Social-Democratic Party" and

The "Historical Office," which was set up by the Socialist-Liberal coalition government after its first election victory in 1994, moved out of the cellars of the Ministry of the Interior to its new premises in 1999. The "Historical Office" is an archive that holds mainly the documents of just one department of the former Communist secret services, previously stored in the Records Office of the Ministry of the Interior, located in the cellars of the ministry. This is the so-called III/III Department which, before 1990, was in charge of internal intelligence. The department, similarly to the practices of the East German Stasi and the Romanian Securitate, employed tens of thousands of formal and informal informers. By the time the office moved into its new building, the Socialists, together with their Liberal coalition partner, had lost the 1998 elections, and a new, fresh, radical right-wing, nationalist government had taken over. As part of the celebrations of the opening of the new archives, an exhibition was organized in the cellar of the "Historical Office."

The exhibition consisted of a reconstruction of an underground prison, allegedly from one of the former buildings of the Central Committee of the Communist Party. The building and its cellars featured in the 1994 television series. The exhibition presented a video, shot a few weeks before the opening, in early 2000, which showed the disused cellar with water up to waist-level. A tube was included among the objects on show, and the caption explained that the tube had been used for the ventilation of the cellar. The advisor of the prime minister, who opened the exhibition, and who previously had proposed a revisionist concept for the Hungarian part of the Auschwitz exhibition—which implicated, as a counter-image of the former Communist Hungarian exhibition in Auschwitz, the Communist leaders of the 1919 First Hungarian Soviet Republic (most of them Jews) for the Holocaust, the tragedy of the Hungarian Jews—called the attention of visitors to the probability that poisonous gas or a substance that could modify the functioning of the prisoners' consciousness might possibly be blown in through the tube.[65]

The reconstruction was the first attempt to show the underground to the public, to invite the visitors to experience it, to believe it by seeing. Real

would move out of its present building on Republic Square, in order to leave the tragic past behind, and emphasize the long road the party had traveled since the transition in 1989.

65. Cf. András Mink, "A Történelmi Kádár" [The Historic Kádár], *Budapest Review of Books* (spring 2002): 17.

presence provides the ground of eyewitnessing. The two-part film on television could not offer a tangible experience: despite the footage from the 1956 newsreels, it did not quite have the feel of a historical documentary. It was too openly politicized, it was shown too close to the upcoming elections, it was just like another movie, which had nothing serious to do with our present. A reconstruction in a real-life cellar, however, promised to produce at least the effect of the real thing that nobody could fail to take seriously: the concrete historical object, like the key to the Bastille, stored under glass in the museum.[66]

*

Whoever has visited Budapest before knows that one of the most beautiful boulevards in the capital is Andrássy Boulevard. The tree-lined street, with lavish villas and stately apartment buildings, connects downtown Budapest to Heroes' Square. It was named after one of the Austro-Hungarian Empire's greatest Hungarian statesmen, Count Gyula Andrássy. The Neo-Renaissance building at 60 Andrássy Boulevard was designed by Adolf Feszty in 1880. It is also notable that the twentieth-century terror regimes, the Nazis and Communists, both decided on a villa located on this boulevard for their executioners' headquarters. The fact that both regimes chose 60 Andrássy Boulevard as the scene of torture and interrogation, speaks for itself.

This was the first paragraph of the introduction to the "House of Terror" on the Web in January 2002, still before the completion of the House.[67] According to the marble stone at the entrance of the building, "the inspiration" behind the idea and the fulfillment of the House of Terror, was the very same person, "the chief advisor to the prime minister in affairs related to history [*sic*]," who had inspired the reconstruction of the underground prison in the Historical Office. The original introduction of the House (as a result of professional and public outcry, coming mostly from the left of the political spectrum, the Web site of the House has been slightly altered since) asserted, "During World War II Hungary found itself in the middle of the crossfire between the Nazi and Communist dictator-

---

66. The Catholic Church had also experimented with finding a concrete location for the entrance to Purgatory. The cave in the abbey at Lough Derg in Donegal County in Ulster became an important pilgrimage site, as the entrance to the world of the betwixt-and-between. Cf. Henry Jones, *Saint Patrick's Purgatory: Containing the Description, Originall, Progresse, and Demolition of that Superstitious Place* (London, 1647); Greenblatt, *Hamlet in Purgatory*, pp. 75–76, 93–101.

67. *http://www.terrorhaza.hu.*

ships.[68] On March 19, 1944, the Nazis occupied Hungary and raised the representatives of the extreme right, unconditionally faithful to them, into power. The new, collaborating Hungarian government did not guard the life of its citizens with Jewish origin any more."

Historical statements—to paraphrase Ian Hacking—"are words in their sites. Sites include sentences, uttered or transcribed, always in a larger site of neighborhood, institution, authority, language."[69] The words about the recent tragic history of Hungary are uttered in the House of Terror, and the site was supposed to provide authority for the historical events under description. The chain that connects the self-description of the House of Terror with the documented traces of the past is irreversible and not uninterrupted: moving backward from the narrative through surviving historical records, individual brute facts, and isolated events, one cannot arrive at the "total historical context" (in the sense of John Austin's "total speech act context") of 1944. The contours of the sunken world that glimmers through the story presented by the House are essentially different from what—after a professionally responsible and accurate study—comes through the historical documents. There is no *real situation* behind the text—this is just text; words, compromised by the site, by the House, that in turn, as an illustration of the possible consequences of the looping effect, is compromised by the words that the House was meant to authorize.[70]

Linguistically it would have been possible for Hungary to fight against both the Nazis and the Communists; it would have been imaginable—in a linguistic sense, outside the frame of Hungarian history—for Hungary not to have been Germany's last and one of its first allies; it would have been conceivable not to have had anti-Jewish legislation already from the early 1920s onward. The execution of the Jews could have been postponed until after the arrival of the Germans, and even the official Hungarian authorities would have had the option of not having actively and eagerly participated in the deportation of more than five hundred thousand Hungarian Jews. The House of Terror and the story it tells were presented as the embodiment of concrete, tangible, historically situ-

68. Archived on January 31, 2002. Cf.: András Mink, "Alibi terror-egy bemutatkozásra" [Alibi Terror—On the Occasion of an Introduction], *Népszabadság*, February 20, 2002.

69. Ian Hacking, *Historical Ontology* (Cambridge, MA: Harvard University Press, 2002), p. 68.

70. Cf. Latour, *Pandora's Hope*, pp. 122–27.

ated horror, as the only conceivable story to tell. The terror, however, it was meant to evoke was but fictional.

The villa at 60 Andrássy Boulevard had been the "House of Faith," the headquarters of the Arrow-Cross Party before World War II, and the Communists, partly for symbolic reasons, decided to move the headquarters of the secret police into the very same building. After the war, at the beginning, Fascist war criminals were kept and interrogated in their former House of Faith. Where Jews and Communists had been tortured and killed before 1945, their torturers and interrogators were tortured and interrogated after the defeat of Nazi Germany and its Hungarian ally. (Not all the war criminals were taken to Andrássy Boulevard. Some of the perpetrators, who had been captured in Germany and deported back to Hungary, leaders of the Arrow-Cross Party among them, ended up in the cellars of the Military Intelligence, in the present building of the Central European University where I teach. When we purchased the building in 1992, the prison cells were still in the cellar, with the spy holes in the doors.) (See Figure 6.4.)

The Arrow-Cross leaders and war criminals were soon replaced in the cellars by the political opponents of the emerging Stalinist political system, critics of its oppressive measures, innocent scapegoats, and by more and more former Social Democrats and former Communist comrades of the consolidating regime. All the victims of the show trials spent time in the cellars, under the ÁVH headquarters; László Rajk, the former Minister of Interior, and later on, his interrogator and successor, János Kádár as well. Following the Stalinist logic of the exercise of power, most of the people who at one time occupied leading positions and upper-floor offices at the secret police, ended up in the cellars of the same building: they either knew too much, became too powerful rivals, or grew "dizzy with success"; a slot had to be filled at the upcoming public show trial; the history of the past, of the illegal movement had to be rewritten in the light of the needs of the ever-changing political situation; the alertness, the level of mobilization of the country had to be maintained under the circumstances of the cold war.

The defendants of the show trials, without exception, were accused of having collaborated with the secret police of the interwar regime, during the time when the Communists were underground. Following the example of the history of the Bolshevik Party in the Soviet Union, the underground movement was considered to be not only the womb of future victorious Communist parties but also the proof of the sacrifices by which the Com-

FIGURE 6.4. Ferenc Szálasi, leader of the Hungarian Arrow-Cross Party, in prison, in the cellars of the present-day Central European University. Open Society Archives.

munists deserved their later and necessary victory. In the Communist histories illegality was described as something inherently superior, especially when compared with the "collaborationist," "revisionist," "reformist," and "treasonous" practices of the legal Social Democratic parties. Those formative chapters in the histories of the Russian, Chinese, German, Romanian, and Hungarian Communist parties are memorable and glorious because the founding fathers had to operate in extremely dangerous circumstances, under the constant threat of being exposed or uncovered. Underground, the members of the illegal party operated in precarious proximity to secret agents who tried to recruit, to bribe, to blackmail, and to break the moral backbone of the activists of the movement. An irrefutable sign of the permanent danger was the high number of recruited agents and that of those Communists who after being detected were sentenced to death or to long years in prison. As the rules and methods of illegal activity between the wars were distilled from the hard-learned lessons of the victorious Bolshevik Party, any mistake that led to exposure could not be anything but the effect of particular human weakness. Exposure could only be the consequence of the presence of agent provocateurs in the ranks of the underground movement.[71] The scripts of the show trials, the alleged treasons, did not undermine the apotheosis of the underground movement; one story was dependent of the other.

During the show trials at the end of the 1940s and the beginning of the 1950s, the former Communist leaders in the dock were accused of having signed secret pacts with right-wing and Fascist secret services, of having been recruited into the ranks of the counterintelligence agencies, of having collaborated in giving up the illegal members of the party. The heroic stories from the period of illegality, in the authorized versions of the Communist history books, highlighted the weakness and meanness of the accused. "The only question for us here is whether you are just a wretched devil who has fallen prey to the enemy, or you have been a conscious and stubborn enemy of our movement from the very first moment on, when you set foot in the working class movement. This is the only question you must answer," asserted Kádár when, as minister of the interior, together with the minister of defense, he went to interrogate Rajk.[72]

On May 18, 1951, it was Kádár's turn. The interrogation in 60 Andássy Boulevard was secretly recorded, and the minister of defense, with whom on June 7, 1949, Kádár had interrogated Rajk, listened to the loudspeaker in the adjacent room. "What do we call what you did in 1943? [Kádár, who was the secretary of the illegal party at that time, following the instructions of the Komintern, had dissolved the illegal party in order to reorganize it under a new name] . . . It is called class-treason," answered the broken Kádár, after long hours of psychologically cruel interrogation. "What kind of role did you play in dissolving the underground party?" "My role was conscious." "Conscious what?" asked the interrogator, a lieutenant colonel of the ÁVH, incidentally the son of the minister of defense, who was secretly listening

71. "'The Party can never be mistaken,' said Rubashov. 'You and I can make a mistake. Not the Party. The Party, comrade, is more than you and I and a thousand others like you and I. The Party is the embodiment of the revolutionary idea in history. . . . History knows her way. She makes no mistakes'" (Arthur Koestler, *Darkness at Noon*, trans. Daphne Hardy [1940; rpt., London: Vintage, 1994], pp. 40–41).

72. MOL M-KS 276.f. 62/2 ő.e. Cf. László Varga, ed., *Kádár János Bírái Előtt Egyszer fent, egyszer lent 1949–1956* [János Kádár in Front of his Judges. Once Up, Once Down 1949–1956] (Budapest: Osiris-Budapest City Archive, 2001), p. 159.

from the adjacent room. "Conscious class-treason," conceded Kádár. "Why were you in the movement in the first place? . . . What role can such a person play in the movement?" "I was recruited by the secret police. . . . Already in 1933 I was recruited; after my arrest, I had to sign."[73]

Andrássy Boulevard is now part of UNESCO's World Heritage. Most of the palaces along the boulevard were built around the same time, in the last decades of the nineteenth century, during the *Gründerzeit* of the Austro-Hungarian monarchy. Around the completely gray façade of the House of Terror (even the glass of the windows is painted gray) the architect designed a black metal frame. The idea of the so-called blade-walls, which isolate the House from the adjacent palaces probably, came from New York, where Marcel Breuer detached the Whitney Museum of American Art from the neighboring building along Madison Avenue by means of the same design tool. Around the roof, as part of the black frame there is a wide perforated metal shield with the word "TERROR," inscribed backward, the five-pointed star and the arrow-cross. When exactly at noon, the sun is supposed to shine through the perforation, the word "TERROR" and the signs of autocracy hypothetically cast a shadow on the pavement. The presumed "Darkness at Noon" harks back to the Hungarian-born Arthur Koestler's Nicolas Salmanovich Rubashov, the most famous fictional Communist show trial character: the illegal Communist activist turned captive in Communist prison cells. The roof of the House of Terror points at what is under the ground: the cellar. (See Figure 6.5.)

After the German invasion, the short and blood-thirsty Arrow-Cross rule began. . . . In 1945 Hungary was brought under the sway of the new conqueror, the Soviet Union. The Hungarian Communists who arrived in the Soviet tanks, in contrast to the short-lived Arrow-Cross rule, settled down for the long run. One of their first acts was to take over 60 Andrássy Boulevard, in order to signal to everybody that the moment of revenge has arrived. But that moment lasted but for very long painful years. . . . The museum wants to become a memorial dedicated to all those people who fell victim either to the Arrow-Cross terror, which lasted for a few months, or to the decades long Communist rule.[74]

The contrast between the duration of the Nazi and Communist rule (short months versus long decades) figures at least four times in the brief

---

73. The Interrogation of János Kádár [May 18, 1951] MOL M—KS 276. f. 62/63.ő.e. Reproduced in Varga, *Kádár János Bírái Előtt Egyszer fent, egyszer lent 1949–1956*, pp. 215–39.

74. *http://www.terorrhaza.hu* (archived on January 31, 2002).

FIGURE 6.5. The "blade walls" of the House of Terror, Budapest. Photo: János Szentiváni.

text, as if the Arrow-Cross never intended to settle down until the end of times ("resurrecting the thousand-year kingdom"), as if it had been meant just as a short intermezzo, in contrast to the devious and conscious Communists, who wanted to rule for long and painful decades. Incidentally, the text does not mention that there was a sort of connection between the coming in of the Soviets and the end of the Arrow-Cross rule.

When the Hungarian Communists arrived from the East in the safety of the foreign armored vehicles, they immediately signaled that the "moment [although a very long moment] of revenge has arrived." The text stipulates that the Communists who came in with the foreigners (so they, just like the Nazi mercenary Arrow-Cross, could not have been proper natives) settled in the House of Faith in order to take revenge for what the

Nazis had done to them, that is, to the Jews. The members of the ÁVH, the vanguard of the Communists, the Communists who were brought back by the conquerors, were Jews, who wanted to take revenge for the Arrow-Cross rule, and punished Hungary, the whole country for what had been done to them (by the German Nazis).

The Hungarian Communists who came back with the Soviets from Moscow, in fact had suffered not so much as Jews from the Nazis but as Communists from the Stalinists purges. The Hungarian Communist movement was decimated in Moscow, and most of those who survived the purges had suffered long years of persecution either in the Gulag or in Soviet prisons, or were subjected to humiliating disciplinary measures. If they had felt the need for revenge, the appropriate target of that revenge would have been their fellow Communists, who had denounced their comrades to the Soviet secret agencies back in Moscow. It would thus be more plausible to attribute the Hungarian Communist show trials, rather than the anti-Communist atrocities, to the urge "to signal that the moment of revenge has arrived."

Hungary—according to the introduction of the House—had tried to protect its Jews from the Germans, but the Bolsheviks—from whom Hungary had tried to save the blind West during World War II—with the help of their Hungarian agents let the Communist terror loose for more than four decades.

The *Sondereinsatzkommando Eichmann*—the deportation experts who came to Hungary with Adolf Eichmann after the German occupation in March 1944—consisted of less than two hundred people. The guarantee of success could not be but the collaboration of the Hungarian authorities. . . . As the events of the next months proved, Eichmann's original calculation had been well founded. . . . The mass deportation of the Jews from the countryside started early in the morning on May 15 in Sub-Carpathia, and ended on July 8–9 with the transportation of the Jews around Budapest. In fifty-six days [!]—according to German documents—437,402 Jews were deported by 147 trains, with the exception of fifteen thousand, to Auschwitz.[75]

This is what—contrary to the claims of the House—the archival records testify.

75. "Gábor Kádár—Zoltán Vági-Krisztián Ungváry, Hullarablás. A magyarországi zsidók megsemmisítése" [Robbing the Corpse. The Economic Annihilation of the Hungarian Jews], vol. 3 (unpublished manuscript, Budapest), pp. 159–63.

The secret police used the building until 1956 as its headquarters. The extremely cruel Communist terror stopped at the end of the 1950s with the final act of the postrevolutionary retribution, the execution of more than two hundred people (even a child among them) who were sentenced to death for their participation in the 1956 Revolution. After the beginning of the 1960s no one was sentenced to death for political reasons, and following the 1963 amnesty most of the imprisoned participants in the revolution were freed. The story of the House, however, is carved from one solid piece: it is the story of undifferentiated terror from the moment of the German occupation until the summer of 1991, when fifty-seven years later, the Soviet army left the territory of Hungary.

The building on Andrássy Boulevard is infamous for what has always been its invisible part to the public: the underground prison cells.[76] That which could not be seen was known to almost everybody. Even before the collapse of the Communist regime, the majority of the adult population of the country had heard horror stories about what went on in the cellars. The notion of the building and knowledge about its prisons were not divisible. The longest part of the introductory text to the House describes the prison and torture cells under 60 Andrássy Boulevard, where the resistance of the accused was broken, where a large number of them died already under interrogation, where the inmates had to suffer "the most horrible tortures one can possibly envision."

*

Out of the twenty-seven rooms of the House of Terror dedicated to the double history of terror, two and a half rooms are devoted to the history of the Arrow-Cross times. The exhibition starts with the story of "double occupation":

Hungary emerged from World War I on the losing side. Once part of the Austro-Hungarian Empire, she had possessed a territory larger than Italy or England. However, under the terms of the Treaty of Trianon which settled the war, the empire was carved up, reducing its territory by two-thirds. . . . At that time the focus of

---

76. One of my parents' best friends, István Gyöngyössy, a show-trial victim himself—he was sentenced to nine years at one of the follow-up trials of the Rajk case—after having been rehabilitated, became the director of Chemokomplex, a foreign-trade company in the 1960s. He has his office on the second floor in the building at 60 Andrássy út. Once he interviewed somebody for a job, who when entering in his office, said, "I have already been in this building, but four floors below."

politics was the implementation of a peaceful territorial revision. . . . In the mid-1930s, Hungary found itself in the crossfire of an increasingly aggressive Nazi regime in Germany as well as a menacing and powerful Soviet Union. First allies then enemies, the Nazi and Soviet dictatorships began a life-and-death fight to create a new European system of client and subordinated states, where there was no room for an independent Hungary. After the outbreak of WWII, Hungary made desperate attempts to maintain its fragile independence and democracy and maneuvered to prevent the worst: Nazi occupation. Significantly, Hungary managed to resist occupation until March 19, 1944, in the fifth year of the war. On June 26, 1941, air raids bombed the city of Kassa in Hungary. Reports at that time indicate that it was the Soviet air forces which carried out the attack. . . . Regent Horthy announced Hungary's participation in the war against the Soviet Union. . . . Until the Nazi occupation in 1944 Hungary had a legitimately elected government and parliament, where opposition parties functioned normally. . . . With the cooperation of the puppet Hungarian authorities appointed by the Nazi occupiers, the National Socialists began their assault on Western Civilization's value structure through the horrific and so-called final solution program. With record speed, the Nazi experts of Jewish persecution, the *Judenkommando*, began to round up and capture Hungarian Jews and on May 15, 1944, the deportation trains began running. In a period of two months, 437,402 Jews from the Hungarian countryside were sent to forced labor or extermination camps in the Third Reich. On August 27, 1944, Soviet troops crossed the Hungarian border. The country became the scene of life-and-death clash between the Nazis and the Soviet Union. The short, yet extremely brutal Nazi occupation during World War Two was then replaced by two generations of occupation of the Soviet Union. Hungary's sovereignty came to an end on March 19, 1944. For more than four decades, Soviet occupation troops remained on her territory. The last Soviet soldier left Hungary on June 19, 1991.[77]

The tourist, walking in the maze of the House of Terror, while reading the syntactically inaccurate sentences and looking at the photographs (some of them—but we do not know which of them—are "real," that is, contemporary, war—or documentary photographs; others are pseudo-documentaries or fictional reproduction) is not able to see through the (sub)text.[78] The upset visitor does not know that "the peaceful territorial

77. In each thematic room in the House of Terror there is a flyer, published in Hungarian and in English, which provides a narrative interpretation for the exhibition in the particular room. The quoted text comes from the English version of the flyer in the "Double occupation" room, in fact the first room of the exhibition. In this chapter I cite the text as it appears in the official flyer. I have not changed the spelling of the text either.

78. "A photograph is supposed not to evoke but to show. That is why photographs, unlike handmade images, can count as evidence. But evidence of what? The suspicion that

revision" meant that Hungary, in exchange for its support for Nazi Germany got back part of the lost territories from Hitler (as a consequence of the "First Vienna Decision" on November 2, 1938, still before the outbreak of World War II, and that of the "Second Vienna Decision" on August 30, 1940). Most of the visitors have not heard of the so-called *numerus clausus*, passed by the Hungarian Parliament already on September 26, 1920 (!), which restricted the number of Jewish students at the universities. The so-called first Jewish law, which radically restricted the number of Jews in the public sphere and professional occupations, was passed by the parliament in May 1938, before the outbreak of the war. The "second Jewish law" had already been ratified before the German troops attacked Poland in May 1939, and the Nazi Nuremberg legislation became internal Hungarian law as a result of the "third Jewish law" in August 1941, which forbade mixed marriage between Jews and non-Jews.

Hungary took part in the war on Hitler's side not in order to resist Communism in advance, in order to "save the blind West from the menace of Bolshevism," but for territorial gains. Hungary, as Hitler's ally, attacked Yugoslavia before Hungary's formal entry into the war. The Soviet military did not threaten Hungary during the interwar years. Hungary declared war not only on the Soviets, but also on Canada, New Zealand, South Africa, Australia, Great Britain, and the United States.[79] At the end of the passage,

---

Capa's 'Death of a Republican soldier'—titled 'The Falling Soldier' in the authoritative compilation of Capa's work—may not show (one hypothesis is that it records a training exercise near the front line) continues to haunt discussions of war photography. Everyone is literalist when it comes to photographs" (Sontag, *Regarding the Pain of Others*, p. 47).

79. As maintained by the contemporary anecdote, when, in the name of the Hungarian Kingdom, the Hungarian ambassador handed over the document on the declaration of war, the U.S. Secretary of State remarked, "It was most certainly a hard decision by His Royal Highness, your King." Whereas the ambassador noted, that although Hungary was a kingdom, she had no king. "Then who is the head of the Hungarian state?" asked the surprised secretary. "Admiral Horty is the Regent of the Kingdom," was the historically correct answer. "Don't you think then that your navy could be in grave danger during such a war?" came the sympathetic question from the secretary. "Let me remark," responded the pedant ambassador, "that although Regent Horty is an admiral, Hungary does not have a sizable navy, in fact, Hungary, momentarily, does not even have a sea." "What happened to your sea, if I may ask?" continued the polite conversation with the underinformed secretary. "We lost it after the Great War to Italy," was the enlightening reply. "Then Italy should most certainly be your enemy in the ongoing war," concluded the secretary of state. "Pardon me, Sir, but Italy is our ally," sounded the matter-of-fact answer. . . . And in such a way the friendly chat went on for quite a long time.

the Wagnerian leitmotiv of the "short, yet extremely brutal Nazi occupation" versus "the two generations of occupation of the Soviet Union" duly returns.

It was Admiral Horthy who, after the German occupation, appointed Germany's puppet government. It was the regent who handed over power to the leader of the Arrow-Cross. Had the Hungarian army not committed horrific war crimes in the Ukraine and in the Soviet Union, had Hungary not remained Hitler's last ally in the war, it would have been difficult for the Soviet Union to occupy Hungary and set the Communists in power after the war. But there are no perceptible syntactic differences between historical and fantastic sentences.

Under the section on "Hungarian Nazis" (by using the term "Nazi," instead of "Arrow-Cross," the flyer wants to stipulate that the Hungarian Fascists, who in 1939 had the electoral support of almost one million—about 20 percent of the votes—were in fact not really Hungarians) the text states, "The Germans defended Budapest as a fortress, which gave the Soviet Army a long and brutal fight. . . . The siege lasted from Christmas 1944 until February 13, 1945, resulting in great suffering and destruction. They reduced to ruin all bridges in Budapest. . . . More than one million people fled from the Red Army to the West and more than one hundred thousand never returned." The third-person-plural personal pronoun, "They," is sufficiently vague to leave the interested visitor in the dark, who might think that it was the Soviets who destroyed the city. The bridges, in fact, were blown up by the Germans; Budapest was bombed mostly by Allied airplanes. A large number of the "more than one million people" who fled from the Red Army were Hungarian soldiers, perpetrators, war criminals, and members of the political elite responsible for Hungary's participation in the war who were fleeing from justice. However, once more the sentence is syntactically more or less correct: they fled as long as they could, before the Red Army arrived.

The half room, which is the threshold between the Nazi and Communist versions of terror, is dedicated to "cross-dressing." As the "Changing Clothes" flyer explains:

After 1919 the Communist Party was organized illegally and, until the Soviet occupation, it had only a few hundred members. During the Second World War, only a few dozen Communist activists could usually be counted on. When the Hungarian Communist Party was organized in the wake of the Red Army's arrival, the growth of party membership became of decided importance. After the members of the Hungarian Communist Party succeeded in getting their hands on the internal and military-political investigative organizations, they had access to the Arrow-Cross membership records as well. Following this, the Communist party was joined in great numbers by people who "to a greater or lesser extent were infected by the counterrevolution and fascism epidemic," said Mátyás Rákosi. The newly admitted "small Arrow-Crossers" in the Communist Party had to declare when and how long they had been members of the Arrow-Cross party, and state that this membership had been a mistake which they wanted to remedy. These declarations were sufficient no doubt to intimidate and blackmail those who signed them.

Communists and members of the ÁVH were thus either Jews who came back with the Soviets or former members of the Arrow-Cross, that is, Hungarian Nazis. Neither of the groups could be classified as true-born Hungarian. (Hitler's Germany, in fact, did not really support the Arrow-Cross Party, which was rather suspicious about claims of German superiority. Germany did not provide either political or financial help to the Hungarian Fascists and did not take the Arrow-Cross Party seriously until 1944. Hitler openly stated in 1938 that the right-wing Hungarian government was commendable and should be taken more seriously than a would-be National-Socialist administration.)[80]

The director of the Soviet-style Political Security Department [later on the ÁVH] was a certain Gábor Péter, who had four years of primary school education and was trained, but never worked, as a tailor's assistant. . . . Gábor Péter himself could not avoid fate. The head of the ÁVH and more than a dozen of his uneducated officers ended up behind bars in January 1953, due to Stalin's pathological anti-Semitism. . . . The Soviet dictator had given the order for the construction of a so-called Zionist conspiracy. His most faithful student, Mátyás Rákosi [the secretary general of the Hungarian party], unhesitatingly gave up the mainly Jewish ÁVH officers, who for many years followed his inhuman orders, as prey.[81]

These statements are put forward as if the world did come wrapped up in a chain of isolated facts, which did not have anything to do with other facts with which they are strongly connected. As if representation of the world were unambiguously determined by a few facts taken in their complete isolation; as if facts were not—in part—"the consequences of

80. Cf. Ungváry, "Kik azok a nyilasok?" pp. 58–59

81. From the flyers "Anteroom of the Hungarian Political Police" and "Room of Gábor Peter, head of the Hungarian Political Police," respectively.

ways in which we represent the world."[82] ("Facts are not individuated before any inquiry, though that does not mean that the inquiry creates them
out of nothing.")[83] Some of the brute facts of these sentences, like some of
the isolated data compiled in other flyers, should be accepted. As proper
sentences—notwithstanding the awkward style and the syntactic and grave
spelling mistakes—and as historical statements, however, they do not
pass. History writing is not the morally uninformed art of chronicling isolated events of the past, understood as unrepeatable particulars located in
space and time. A noticeably arbitrary selection and sequence (and omis-
sion) of a few disconnected brute facts in support of an obvious ideological preconception, which aims at constructing a worldwide, racially
grounded conspiracy theory, from the perspective of actual political
needs, in order to stigmatize an all-too-well defined group of humans, is
offered by the House as history. A script, and a rather familiar one, is put
forward as a normal (normalized), that is, obvious, neutral presentation
of history.

Taxpayers' money was used to construct the House of Terror as a
"memorial dedicated to the victims of both the Nazi and the Communist
terror." On the perforated roof of the House there are both the arrow-cross
and the five-pointed star. The inspirers, ideologues, and politicians who
built this House, and devoted only two rooms to the close to six hundred
thousand Roma, Jewish, and left-wing victims of the Holocaust, needed the
"Hungarian Nazis" in order to put the Communist terror in context. The
latter was longer lasting, thus deeper, more devastating, and more infectious
than the former. The Communist terror was near to, in the vicinity of, and
related to the Nazi terror, especially since the victims of the Nazi horrors,
later on, seized the very first opportunity and became the perpetrators of the
devastating Communist dictatorship. The Jews were not only the victims of
the Nazis, not only the perpetrators of the Communist terror, but also their
own executioners: they, themselves, would not have been able to defend
themselves from themselves. Only the Hungarians, the true victims and the

82. Cf. Ian Hacking, *The Social Construction of What?* (Cambridge, MA: Harvard
University Press, 1999), p. 33. See also Hacking, *Historical Ontology*, esp. pp. 1–26. As my
argument shows, I do not fully subscribe to Latour's or even Hacking's somewhat milder
constructivist position.
83. Williams, *Truth and Truthfulness*, p. 257.

enemies of both kinds of terror, who found themselves in the midst of the crossfire of the life-and-death fight between these terrorists, could finally put an end to the slaughter.

*

The last room of the House is dedicated to "Farewell." On one side of the door the visitor can watch a video of the live coverage of Imre Nagy's 1989 reburial, where Viktor Orbán (prime minister of Hungary in the year 2002) as a young radical, anti-Communist, liberal, new-age politician demanded the withdrawal of Soviet troops from Hungary. On the opposite wall, several television monitors follow the farewell, the last move of the last division of the Soviet army, as it left the country on June 19, 1991. And on the other side of the door, the very last image of the memorial is the opening ceremony of the House of Terror on February 24, 2002, on the eve of the "Memorial Day Dedicated to the Victims of Communism," less than six weeks before the next Hungarian general election, which was due in April 2002. Thus the story comes full circle: the pilgrim who comes to visit the House reads on the marble stone at the entrance that it was the prime minister who had the House built. And on the last image, the prime minister, in front of a crowd hundreds of thousands strong announces the opening of the House. His word became flesh: the Russians cut and run and the terror is over; it is turned and locked into the House that he, the leader of the new right, has built.

The young leader, the youngest prime minister ever in Hungarian history, on the pedestal in front of the dreaded building, which he alone had the courage to tame, surrounded on this festive occasion by hundreds of thousands of his ecstatic adherents, under forests of the national tricolor, was rejuvenation incarnate. From the perspective of the opening, which on the inside was turned into the very last image in the last room of the House of Terror, the story of end and beginning became unambiguously comprehensible: after the long decades of decay—starting with the German occupation on March 19, 1944, and terminating with the disgraceful retreat of the Soviet troops on June 19, 1991—the new era had begun. Leader and his native people under the flag finally found each other and were ready to embark on the clear-cut road leading to future, which cannot be but the extension of the present.

Critics of the House of Terror repeatedly pointed out that the Arrow-Cross was evoked only in order to implicate the Communists by association.

They argued that the House was nothing but an ideological and political construct; it was neither a memorial to the victims of Communism, who were exploited and cynically used for mean political propaganda, nor a monument to the hundreds of thousands who perished during the Fascist times, since they were barely visible. Both the chronological and the narrative frames of the House were carefully devised: the demonstration started with the "double occupation"—as if the German and the Soviet occupations had been coinstantaneous, and the Arrow-Cross rule had started immediately after the occupation, as if there had not been seven long months in between the coming-in of the Germans and Arrow-Cross takeover, as if the five hundred thousand Jews had not been deported during those months (in fact, in less than two months)—and in this way Horthy's rule, which lasted until October 15, 1944, together with the deportation, had been pushed back (or forward) in this phantasmagorical chronology, and thus excluded from the decades of decline and degeneration. Horthy's interwar Hungary could thus be incorporated into the mythic prehistory of the present.

The criticism was partly mistaken, however: the House of Terror in fact—in part as a consequence of the very invisibility of the victims of Fascism and the grave asymmetry of the arrangement—is a proper memorial of Fascism. The House in its context (the "blade-walls," the prison-gray color of the building, the televised and recorded opening ceremony, the film of the mass rally shown in the last room, the blocked entry at the gate, which meant to artificially produce a permanent queue visible from everywhere on the busy Andrássy Boulevard) is almost a literal embodiment—and definitively, not just an illustration—of the emerging post–cold war, a temporary consensus on the definition of "generic" Fascism. In the words of Roger Griffin, probably the most prolific, and certainly the most dedicated and self-promoting exponent of this new consensus: "Fascism is a genus of modern, revolutionary, 'mass' politics, which, while extremely heterogeneous in its social support and in the specific ideology promoted by its many permutations, draws its internal cohesion and driving force from *a core myth that a period of perceived national decline and decadence is giving way to one of rebirth and renewal in a postliberal new order.*"[84] (This insis-

---

84. Roger Griffin, "Introduction," in *International Fascism. Theories, Causes and the New Consensus,* ed. Griffin (London: Arnold, 1998), p. 14; emphasis added. In his *The Nature of Fascism* ([London: Routledge, 1993], p. 23), Griffin provided a more concise core definition,

tence on the past of national decline and decadence versus the imminent rejuvenation that springs from the popular will of the people sharply distinguishes Fascist and neo-Fascist ideology from its suspected double, Communism; radical, bloody transcendence from the brutal project of transformation. Freedom for the Fascist is the triumph of the will as opposed to recognized necessity in Communist ideology. Instead of decadence and degeneration, the past, in the Communist imagination, is the succession of necessary stages, which eventually, following the iron laws of history, should lead to the ultimate end of history. This explains the lack of vitalism as an essential defining feature of Communism, the lack of eroticism of official Communist art, the inherent clumsiness of Communist propaganda, and so on.)

The House of Terror indulges in horror, in pain, in the suffering of the victims, primarily that of the victims of the Communist terror. The barely hidden perverted visual program, the deep and aggressive, mostly black and red colors, the surfeit of images, and the sensual, melodramatic music that surrounds the visitor cannot conceal the aesthetic pleasure of the curators and the designers: it aims at arousing weird fascination.[85] From the layout, the design, from the whole show, from the captions, from the text of the flyers, and on the Web, the visitor can memorialize the history, the words, and the world that Fascism made. The House is a monument of Fascism.

---

which he repeated in his Fascism's new faces (and new facelessness) in the "post-Fascist" epoch. "Fascism is a political ideology whose mythic core in its various permutations is a palingenetic [renewalist] form of populist ultra-nationalism" (Mimeo article for *Erwaegen, Wissen, Ethik* to be published with twenty responses in 2004, p. 10).

The beginning of the emergence of a "Fascist minimum" (Ernst Nolte's phrase), most probably started with the publication of Nolte's famous *Der Faschismus in seiner Epoche* [The Three Faces of Fascism], published in 1963. See also Eugene Weber, *Varieties of Fascism* (New York: Van Nostrand, 1964); George L. Mosse, "Towards a General Theory of Fascism," in *Interpretations of Fascism*, ed. G. L. Mosse (London: Sage, 1979). See also the entry "Fascism" in the *Blackwell Dictionary of Social Thought*, by Roger Griffin ([Oxford: Basil Blackwell, 1993], pp. 223–24).

85. "Between sadomasochism and fascism there is a natural link. 'Fascism is theater,' as Genet said. . . . Sadomasochism is to sex what war is to civil life," stated Susan Sontag in a somewhat seductive manner (Susan Sontag, "Fascinating Fascism," *The New York Review of Books* 22, no. 1 [February 6, 1975]; reprinted in Susan Sontag, *Under the Sign of Saturn* [London: Vintage, 1980], pp. 73–105; quote is from p. 103). On fascination with Fascism, see also Jeffrey T. Schnapp, "Fascinating Fascism," an introduction to vol. 31 of *Journal of Contemporary History* (1966): 235–44.

The prefiguration of the House of Terror, most probably, cannot be found either in Daniel Libeskind's Jewish Museum in Berlin, or in the Holocaust Memorial Museum in Washington, or in the Yad Vashem in Jerusalem. It is advisable to look further, if not spatially, at least, temporarily. Almost seventy years before the right-wing Hungarian prime minister opened the door of the House of Terror, on October 28, 1932, on the tenth anniversary of the March on Rome, the Duce opened the gate of the "Mostra della rivoluzione fascista," the Exhibition of the Fascist Revolution. The Marca su Roma, Mussolini's entry to Rome in 1922, itself had symbolic meaning: it recalled both Caesar's crossing of the Rubicon and the march of Garibaldi's Mille. According to Margherita Sarfatti, one of the most important cultural ideologues of Italian Fascism, the exhibition "for the first time in the modern world brings an event in recent history into the fervent atmosphere of affirmation and of a religious ceremonial. . . . [It is] conceived as a cathedral whose very walls speak."[86]

The exhibition bombarded the lost and disoriented visitors with documents, objects, signs, symbols, images, facts, and artifacts. The distance between fact and fiction, construction and reconstruction, genuine historical documents and artistic recreation disappeared. The ephemeral ritual space swallowed up the viewers, who were denied the detachment needed for contemplation or just for understanding the sight. The ambition of the organizers, the architects, the historians, the curators, and the politicians, who conceived the show, was to build a total, self-contained environment, the *apotheosis* of the movement and the Duce, that aimed at, not the rational, but the emotional reactions of the visitors, immersed in the flow of unexpected visual and rhetorical impulses.[87] (See Figures 6.6 and 6.7.)

The exhibition made use of techniques refined by the futurists, the expressionist theater, and rationalist and constructivist architecture; the curators recruited *novecento* artists and supporters of traditionalist order in art. The use of the so-called *plastica murale*, which turned flat surfaces into moving images, turned the *mostra* into a real modern-day three-dimensional multimedia show. According to contemporary reports, descriptions, and

86. Margherita Sarfatti, "Architettura, arte e simbolo alla mostra del fascismo," *Archittetura* (January 1933): 10; quoted by Emilio Gentile, *The Sacralization of Politics in Fascist Italy* (Cambridge, MA: Harvard University Press, 1996), p. 117.

87. Cf. Carla Susan Stone, *The Patron State: Culture and Politics in Fascist Italy* (Princeton, NJ: Princeton University Press, 1998), pp. 128–76.

FIGURE 6.6. Mario Sironi's Gallery of Fasci. Exhibition of the Fascist Revolution, Rome, 1932. Mostra della Rivoluzione Fascista.

FIGURE 6.7. Entrance to the House of Terror. Photo: János Szentiváni.

photographs, documents were sometimes presented in anthropomorphic forms; other times documents were used as frames, framing other documents or fictitious objects; immensely large-scale images alternated unexpectedly with surprisingly small-scale presentation.

The visitors had to follow the set pilgrimage route, which led through nineteen chronological and thematic halls, covering the period from the outbreak of World War I until the victory and achievements (in five additional rooms) of the Fascist revolution: from chaos through revolution to order. At the end of the pilgrimage the shaken visitor found herself in "Room U," the seven-meter-high Sacrarium of the Martyrs, designed—similarly to the House of Terror—by a theater designer. The "Hall of Tears" in the House of Terror is a clear reference to the shadowy, mysterious "Hall of the Martyrs" at the Exhibition of the Fascist Revolution: at both sites the mixture of modernist and antique, Christian and profane elements, super-imposed by sound and music, aim at overwhelming the upset pilgrims. The cross is the central object in both cases (although the House of Terror was supposedly built—in part—to commemorate the victims of both the Fascist and Communist terrors, among them the deported Jews). (See Figure 6.8.)

The dead at both sites are used as props for the show. In Budapest, a sign assures the dead are mostly the anti-Communist martyrs (among them persecuted members of the higher clergy), but includes also the victims of the Holocaust: "The sacrifice for freedom was not in vain." In Rome, the victory of Fascism was meant to provide retroactive meaning for death in the trenches of World War I. The senseless death of hundreds of thousands of mute victims was exploited for obvious and explicit political aims at both places. Whereas in Washington and Berlin, despite the didactic and over-simplified presentations, there are solid bridges between the museum and the outside world, and the museums were built with the well-documented and sincere intention of respecting the available evidence so that the inno-cent dead could be remembered in a justified way, in Rome and Budapest the victims are cynically used for obvious political purposes. The House of Terror, similar to the Exhibition of the Fascist Revolution, was not meant to be a space of memory; the Budapest building, influenced by its prede-cessor in Rome, is a total propaganda space, where death and victims are used as rhetorical devices.

The mostra turned out to be a fantastic success: in two years close to four million visitors paid homage to Fascism at the Palazzo della Espozioni, the facade of which had been rebuilt in rationalist style. Besides Göbbels and Göring, Simone de Beavoir, Jean-Paul Sartre, Le Corbusier, and the pupils of a Hebrew school visited the exhibition. Pilgrims, two Hungari-ans and two blind men from the Dolomites among them, went to see the mostra by foot.

The Fascist exhibition was not without antecedents either. Mario Sironi, one of the most noted *novecentista* painters, had designed the 1928 Italian press pavilion at the Cologne International Press Exhibition, where he became acquainted with the work of the Soviet constructivist artist, El Lissitzky, who influenced his four rooms at the Fascist exhibition, among them "The March on Rome" and "The Hall of Honor, Dedicated to the Person, Ideal and Works of the Duce." The Soviet material at the 1928 Venice Biennale and the 1929 Russische Ausstellung in Zurich also exerted direct influence on the anti-Bolshevik Rome exhibition. Giuseppe Terragni, the greatest ratio-

FIGURE 6.8. "The Hall of Tears," the "Sacrarium" in the House of Terror.
Photo: János Szintiváni.

nalist architect, the designer of "Room O" and "The Year 1922 up until the Events of October," the architect of the famous Casa del Fascio in Como, borrowed from both El Lissitzky and Konstantin Melnikov.[88]

It is no wonder that there were visitors who found the Fascist exhibition so Bolshevik in spirit that "with a change in emblems the pieces would bring applause in Moscow."[89] The connection between Rome and

88. See Thomas Schumacher, *Surface and Symbol: Giuseppe Terragni and the Architecture of Italian Rationalism* (New York: Princeton Architectural Press, 1991). On the *mostra*, besides the works cited, see also Giovanna Fioravanti, *Archivo centrale dello stato: Partito nazionale fascista—Mostra della rivoluzione fascista* (Rome: Archivo di Stato, Ministero per I Beni Culturali e Ambientali, 1990); Emilio Gentile, *The Sacralization of Politics in Fascist Italy*, trans. Keith Botsford (Cambridge, MA: Harvard University Press, 1996), esp. pp. 109–21; Jeffrey Schnapp, *Anno X. La Mostra della Rivoluzione fascista del 1932* (Rome-Pisa: Istituti Editoriali e Poligrafici Internazionali, 2003).

89. Quoted by Jeffrey T. Schnapp, "Epic Demonstrations: Fascist Modernity and the 1932 Exhibition of the Fascist Revolution," in *Fascism, Aesthetics, and Culture*, ed. Richard J. Golsan (Hanover, NH: University Press of New England, 1992), p. 26.

Budapest is not accidental: the architect of the House of Terror, a well-known set designer, who in past years designed the set of some Italian opera productions, had in the 1970s and 1980s worked together with László Rajk on several neoconstructivist architectural and design projects. Rajk was one of the architects of the neoconstructivist catafalque for Imre Nagy's reburial in 1989.

*

The exhibition starts on the second floor and after a labyrinth-like descent, the visitor arrives at a glass elevator on the first floor. It takes three and a half long minutes to lower the cabin two floors down, while a slobbery, unpleasant-looking elderly man, the former cleaning attendant at the executions, recalls at an extremely slow pace how the prisoners in the cellars were hanged. One has no choice but to stare at the distasteful face on the huge plasma monitor, which fully covers one side of the elevator. At the end of the unbelievably slow descent the visitor arrives in the cellars, the symbolic center of the House of Terror. The long flyer, which describes the "reconstructed prison cells," devotes four lines to the short Arrow-Cross horror; the rest deals with the extreme brutality of the Communist terror, which was similar to methods from "the Middle Ages." "Based on recollections," assumes the text, "the building's cellar system had several floors. When the house was rebuilt, no signs of additional floors were found under the cellars. Nevertheless, it cannot be excluded that additional cellars of the labyrinth were dug into the earth."

Under the ground the organizers reconstructed a "water cell, where prisoners had to continually sit in the water," a "fox-hole, where there were no lights and the prisoner could not stand up," "the guards' room" where "the ventilation system" from the reconstructed prison cell in the cellars of the Historical Office was reinstalled (this was the tube, through which, presumably, poisonous gas or a substance that could modify the consciousness of the prisoners was blown in). The gallows were also re-created in the cellars. Whereas most of the objects on show do not carry the name of the donor or the lending institution, in the case of the gibbet, a small plaque authenticates the object. It was donated by the National Penal Authority, and according to the flyer, it was used until 1985. At the end of the long tour, for the first time since October 30, 1956, the underground became really identifiable and visible: a real prison, with water in it, with real spy holes and the real gallows. Instead of the site where imagination resides, the underground found a concrete physical location where direct and personal encounter is offered to the visitors. Water in the cells, the tube, and the gibbet are—in the context of the prison—objects of ritualized display: they work as relics. The secret, the ultimate proof (although, in the end, it was another cellar, not the one under the Budapest Party Committee building on Republic Square) has come into sight and become physically perceptible for the pilgrims.

The House of Terror is not a marginal institution on the fringes of the city. It was built with about twenty million U.S. dollars, a large amount of taxpayers' money in Hungary (the sum is almost twice the cost of the reconstruction of the Budapest Opera, which incidentally is also on Andrássy Boulevard). The opening of the House was an integral part— probably the most important event—of the 2002 election campaign. The principal aim of the governing radical right-wing party—the former young liberal party, turned radical right—was to win over the electorate of the Hungarian Truth and Life Party in order to avoid the need for a formal postelection coalition with the Hungarian Fascists. The opening was scheduled on the eve of the "Memorial Day of the Victims of Communism," a new remembrance initiated by the right-wing government to compensate for and balance the "Holocaust Memorial Day," introduced by the previous government.

Tens of thousands of the activists and sympathizers of an extreme right-wing radical party assembled on that day on Republic (Köztársaság) Square in front of the Socialist party headquarters, at the site of the siege in 1956. The leader of the Hungarian Truth and Life Party pointed at the former Budapest party headquarters and baptized it the "First House of Terror." At the end of the rally the mass was ordered to bend down, and the demonstrators pressed their ears to the pavement to listen to the sound coming from below, from the prison under the ground over the distance of forty-six years. Then the participants stood up and the crowd marched over to Andrássy Boulevard to unite with the other tens of thousands of supporters of the political right in power, who were waiting for the prime minister in front of the House of Terror, which was bathing in sharp red light. As the leader of the Truth and Life Party remarked, in front of the House of Terror, the forces of the Hungarian anti-Communist right finally joined forces and became at last visibly and firmly united.

"We have locked the two terrors in the same building, and they are good company for each other as neither of them would have been able to survive long without the support of foreign military force. . . . In the very last minute, before it could return, we slammed the door on the sick twentieth century," said the young prime minister, referring to the upcoming election. (Six weeks later, the Socialists, together with the Liberals, won a narrow victory and came back to power. It became known only after the elections that the new Socialist prime minister had been a top-secret counterintelligence officer in the 1980s, during the Communist times.) "The evil promised to redeem the world but instead, it tortured the people under the ground in the cellars."[90]

In July 1295 Pope Boniface VIII sent a mandate to the Bishop of Paris, Simon Mattifart de Bucy, allowing him to build a chapel in the parish of St-Jean-en-Gréve, on the site of what was probably the most famous case of host desacration accusation. The *capella miraculorum* emerged, which housed the *canif*, the knife, which became holy, as the miraculous consequence of the devious effort by a local Jew, who not believing in the dogma of transubstantiation, tried to test the holy host by piercing it with the knife. The miraculous host was locked in the parish church of St-Jean-en-Gréve. According to the *De Miraculo Hostiae* (Of the miracle of the host), the Jew took out a knife and struck the host, which remained intact and began to bleed. He pierced it through with nails but the host continued bleeding. The Jew then threw the host into a fire, then finally threw it into boiling water. The water turned red, and the host was transformed into a crucifix. A poor Christian woman gave up the Jew; he was tried, found guilty, and burned. The Jew asked to hold his book when in the fire and thus be saved. The book and Jew were burned to ashes, while his wife and children converted.[91]

The story was thus converted, transformed into a concrete miraculous site: into a chapel, on the site of the demolished house of the Jew, with elaborate rituals; into an order, the Brethren of the Charity of the Blessed

90. Orbán: rács mögé zártuk a múltat. Tizezrek a Terror Háza megnyitóján [Orbán: We Have Locked the Past Behind Bars. Tens of Thousands at the Opening of the House of Terror], Index, February 24, 2002.

91. "De miraculo hostiae a Judaeo Parisiis anno Domini MCCXC," in *Recueil des historiens des Gaules et de la France*, vol. 22, ed. M. Bouquet and L. Delisle (Paris, 1840–1904), p. 32. Reprinted in Miri Rubin, *Gentile Tales: The Narrative Assault on Late Medieval Jews* (New Haven, CT: Yale University Press, 1999), esp. pp. 40–45.

Virgin, charged with the guardianship of the chapel. It was not just hearsay anymore that fueled the accusations; it was now possible and indeed sufficient, merely to point without hesitation at the chapel, and the solid structure provided concrete and massive evidence. "The news from Paris very soon existed in Latin and in French, and traveled to the adjacent regions . . . to the Low Countries, to southwestern Germany and to northern Italy by the very late thirteenth and early fourteenth centuries."[92] Visible facts, as Maurice Halbwachs reminded us in his *La topographie légendaire des évangiles en terre sainte*, "are the symbols of invisible truth."[93] "No full-blown . . . accusation which resulted in vindication and violence was complete without the creation of an enduring sign to mark the event. . . . Ruins were not allowed to stand as traces of a still open past, but were assumed into new, polished structures," concluded the historian from the lessons of the postaccusatory practices of the Middle Ages.[94]

The cellars under the House of Terror were neither invented nor recreated but finally found. Although the Communists had tried to cover all the traces of their heinous acts, the cellars could not be completely buried. The archaeologists of the Communist terror found them and laid them bare to the gaze of the victorious posterity. The visitor turned witness who was finally confronted with unmediated truth became now entitled to provide authentic account. The House is full of identifiable images (on the wall the photographs of the perpetrators are lined up as if they had been assembled in a photo spread for an eyewitness test: a few Fascists are mixed with a large number of ÁVH officers and Communist officials), recognizable names, abundant dates, and concrete objects. What the visitor is confronted with is clear evidence, which seems to be visibly objective, not invented, not made by the hands of the curators, but that unveils the so-far-invisible truths well hidden in the depths.[95] The cellars, turned into *sacramentum*, sing of (until now) hidden things.

Invisible truth, in turn, argued Halbwachs, needs to find firm roots in concrete facts; only claims based on concrete facts might leave long-lasting,

92. Ibid., p. 45.

93. Translated by Lewis A. Coser, *The Legendary Topography of the Gospels in the Holy Land* (Chicago: University of Chicago Press, 1992), p. 224.

94. Rubin, *Gentile Tales*, p. 90.

95. On historic notions of objectivity, cf. Daston and Galison, "Image of Objectivity"; and the essays in Lorraine Daston, ed., *Biographies of Scientific Objects* (Chicago: University of Chicago Press, 2000).

persuasive impressions.[96] Ideas should take on perceptible, concrete, tangible, localizable forms in order to find a firm place in memory: "If a truth is to be settled in the memory of a group it needs to be presented in the concrete form of an event, of a personality or of a *locality.*"[97]

In an earlier version of her analysis of the host desacration accusation, Miri Rubin concluded:

In those areas where the narrative had become most endemic . . . it was a real presence, of atrocities remembered, commemorated in local shrines. . . . The tale . . . grew in complexity and ambition, in size and ramification. No longer a single Jew, curious or malevolent, attacking a host with his kitchen-knife, but conspiracies of Jews. . . . The narrative evolved and converged with the growing desires for separation and excision of Jews from central European urban communities.[98]

The architect and the interior designer of the House of Terror, Attila Ferenczfy Kovács, was the set designer of the Academy Award–winning film, *Mephisto*, directed by István Szabó—his first film was on the Holy Grail. (At that time the set designer was known simply as Attila Kovács; he started using Ferenczfy, referring to his title of nobility, only after 1989.) In an interview after the opening of the House of Terror, he traced the influences that led to his design of the terror: "My first serious film-set design was *Dániel Szerencsés*, directed by Pál Sándor. . . . Quite a few elements from that film show up in the House of Terror too. How were you able to study the atmosphere of the most brutal terror in the years of 'soft dictatorship'?" inquired the journalist. "There was an extremely depressing hotel interior in that film, and when I was designing the set, the environment that had been so familiar from the Moscow metro helped me in my work. That overdecorated, desolate, and unbearably gloomy underground space found then its way to the House of Terror."[99]

96. For an excellent theoretical reworking of Halbwachs's important insights, cf. Jan Assmann, *Das kulturelle Gedächtnis* [A Kulturális Emlékezet], trans. from the original German into Hungarian by Zoltán Hidas (Budapest: Atlantisz, 1999), esp. pp. 35–49.

97. Halbwachs, *On Collective Memory*, p. 200; emphasis added.

98. Miri Rubin, "The Making of the Host Desacration Accusation: Persuasive Narratives, Persistent Doubts" (paper given at the Davis Center Seminar, Princeton University, October 15, 1993), pp. 31–32.

99. "A Mennyei Seregektől a Terror Házáig" [From the Heavenly Army to the House of Terror], *Magyar Nemzet*, April 2, 2002.

Owing to its mysterious origins and the need people have to give history a meaning in our godless world, *The Conspiracy* soon became a kind of bible, teaching that there is a "mysterious dark, and dangerous force" lurking behind all history's defeats, a force that holds the fate of the world in its hands, draws on arcane sources of power, triggers wars and riots, revolutions and dictatorships—the "sources of all evil." The French Revolution, the Panama Canal, the League of Nations, the Treaty of Versailles, the Weimar Republic, the Paris métro—they are all its doing. (By the way, métros are nothing but mineshafts under city walls, a means for blasting European capitals to the skies.) (Danilo Kis, *The Encyclopedia of the Dead*, trans. Michael Henry Heim [Evanston, IL: Northwestern University Press, 1997], p. 169)

7

Transition

At around 3:20 PM on August 19, 1989, historical justice was done. Some 118 years earlier, the Habsburgs had been denied the chance to play a decisive, constructive role in the process of German unification when Germany became unified in the *kleindeutsch*, Prussio-centric way, by leaving Austria and the Habsburgs out of the process. This time, German reunification started with the active participation of a Habsburg—Otto, the son of the last emperor of Austria and king of Hungary. On August 19, 1989, the Pan-European Union, under the presidency of Otto von Habsburg, organized a picnic near the border city of Sopron in western Hungary, to propagate the notion of a common Europe without borders. On the basis of a previous agreement between the Austrian and Hungarian authorities, the participants of the Pan-European picnic symbolically opened the border.

After July 15, 1989, large groups of East German citizens took refuge in the buildings of the embassies of the Federal Republic of Germany in Prague, Budapest, Sofia, and a few other East European capitals. On August 13, 1989, the overcrowded Budapest embassy building had to be closed with a few hundred East German refugees remaining behind the closed gates.

An early version of Chapter 7 was published as "Self-non-fulfilling Prophesy," in *The Paradoxes of Unintended Consequences*, ed. Lord Dahrendorf et al. (Budapest: CEU Press, 2000).

According to the testimony provided by the photographs of Tamás Löbenwein, on July 19, exactly at 3:20 PM, several hundred East Germans— who had most probably been tipped off by refugee workers from the Maltese Charity in Budapest—broke through the gate: some 661 of them crossed the Hungarian-Austrian border. Not since the building of the Berlin Wall had such a large number of people escaped across the iron curtain at once. "The pulling down of the Berlin Wall began in Sopron," later stated Lothar de Maiziere, East Germany's last prime minister. And at the celebration of the unification of Germany, Chancellor Helmut Kohl declared, "The soil under the Brandenburg Gate is Hungarian soil."[1]

Between February 17 and March 15, 1990, the Institut für Demoskopie Allensbach, the large German polling organization, conducted a large, representative poll among the citizens of East Germany. The institute tried to find out what percentage of East German citizens had foreseen what was coming, or, to be more precise, what percentage remembered later that they had foreseen the future. Although in such polls people tend to remember that their past expectations were more in line with the outcome of events than was probably the case, this time only 5 percent of respondents claimed that they had been able to foresee what was coming. Sixty-eight percent answered that they had absolutely not predicted the Fall of the Wall and of the GDR. The results of the poll are usually cited as proof

---

1. Whereas before the construction of the Berlin Wall in 1961, on average, more than two hundred thousand citizens left the GDR for West Germany every year; after the Fall the number fell to well below twenty thousand. In 1987 rather fewer than nineteen thousand East Germans emigrated to the German Federal Republic. In 1988—as a sign of the weakening of the hard-line regime of the GDR—39, 832 refugees left for the West. In 1989 the number reached the all-time high of 343,854. Before the Pan-European picnic, in July 1989, 11,707 East German citizens managed to flee their country. In August, however, the number almost doubled to 20,955. On September 10 the Hungarian government officially gave permission for East Germans on Hungarian territory to pass into Austria. As a result the number of East German emigrants totaled 33,255 in September (Hartmut Wendt, "Die deutsch-deutschen Wanderungen" [The German-German migration], *Deutschland Archiv*, 24, 1991, pp. 390, 393; quoted by Albert O. Hirschman, "Exit, Voice and the Fate of the German Democratic Republic," in his *A Propensity to Self-Subversion* [Cambridge, MA: Harvard University Press, 1995], pp. 17, 27). (As a child I happened to be on a summer holiday in East Berlin at the moment when the Wall was built. The family I stayed with had promised that we would visit the western part of the city but, without warning, I was told one morning, that it was no longer possible to cross to the other side, as during the night a wall had appeared to protect the eastern part of Berlin.)

of the pre-eventum inability to foresee on the part of the people, who were then to be directly affected by the changes in which they had played no active part as a consequence of their blindness. The results might suggest that the end of Communism just happened to the people without their having been able to participate in the historic changes.

Had the East Germans been able to foresee what was coming, there would have been no need for them to flee to the West German embassies, to cross the "green border" into Hungary during the night, to make use of the Pan-European picnic, to resort to the helping hand of the successor to the Austro-Hungarian throne in waiting, to go into the streets, to demonstrate in Leipzig and Dresden, or even, before all that, to be mortally wounded at the Wall while, for decades, trying desperately to flee from the so-called German Democratic Republic. It would have been enough just to wait at home for the end of the Communist regime. But had they waited for the inevitable to come, sitting peacefully at home, looking forward to the Fall, would it have come when it did, and would it have happened in the same way? Are we in a position to say that the Fall would in fact have come at all without the voice and exit of the East German citizens, without their participation in the form of flight to the West German embassies, which as we know—if only from the results of the poll—was the direct consequence of their inability to foresee?[2] If, as a consequence of their accurate foresight (that is, that the regime would collapse anyway), they had decided to stay home, and, as a result of this decision, the regime had not collapsed, well, in that case, accurate foresight would have prevented the desired event.

---

2. Hirschman, in his paper, which is a modified version of his original and highly influential theoretical construct (*Exit, Voice and Loyalty: Response to Decline in Firms, Organizations, and States* [Cambridge, MA: Harvard University Press, 1970]) writes, "The very fact that they [the collapse of the Communist regimes, especially the events in the GDR] came as a total surprise to both spectators and actors suggests that our capacity to comprehend large-scale political and social change remains utterly underdeveloped." Commenting retrospectively on the role of the flight of the East German citizens in influencing the total collapse of the regime, he points at the possibility "that when previously unavailable opportunities to exit are forced open, people may experience new feelings of empowerment. They might then consider or reconsider other options, including that of reacting to an odious state of affairs by a direct attempt at change—through voice—instead of flight. This sort of *conjunction* of exit and voice turned out to be exceptionally powerful in the German case. . . . On the whole it was the confluence of the two forces that characterized their interaction in 1989" (*Exit, Voice and Loyalty*, pp. 10, 26, and 34; emphasis in original). Hirschman's paper was originally published in *Leviathan* 20 (September 1992): 330–58, under the title "Abwanderung, Wiederspruch und das Schicksal der Deutschen Demokratischen Republik."

The foresight would not have been accurate at all: this amounts to saying that they would have been unable to foresee the future, which amounts to saying that the future would have been different from the foreseen outcome. We are back to square one, or at least, so it seems.

However, we might entertain the hypothesis that—at least in certain cases—it is precisely the benign lack of foresight that makes it possible to bring about the desired future. Predictions by social scientists that become public knowledge might prevent the predicted outcome. In certain cases, far from the lack of it, it is foresight that can prevent certain events from happening. Sometimes, when something is foreseen and that foresight is made public, it acts as a prohibitive force that undermines the chances of the occurrence of the foreseen event. Had the Politburo of the Soviet Communist Party foreseen the consequences of Gorbachev's election to the post of secretary general of the party, he most probably would not have been elected (he would probably have been immediately shot instead), and this in turn might have given a completely different twist to the history of the Soviet Union.

Unfulfillment is usually considered the unproblematic, one might almost say natural, outcome of prophecies in the sphere of social life. If prophecies are not fulfilled, modern scholarship does not feel that anything would warrant a scientific explanation: it seems obvious that usually there is no connection between prophecy, foreknowledge, foresight, and the later events at which the prophecy was originally directed. If there is a correspondence between a publicly known prophecy and the outcome in the social sphere, then scholarly analysis is usually interested not so much in how the prophet (the social scientist, the politician, the speculator on the stock exchange, and so on) was able to foresee the future, but much more in what the impact of public knowledge was on the behavior of the participants and in what way public knowledge could influence later events, irrespective of the ability of the prophet to foresee. The foreseen outcome is not considered one that might justify the foreseer. In the case of the so-called nomological sciences, we expect scientists to foreknow what is going to happen: we expect them to know in advance when a meteorite is going to strike the earth. But we also know that a car runs over another dog every day, so we do not expect the ideographical disciplines (like history) to give accurate projections. The incidents of yesterday (at least in the social sciences) are not coded information about the events of tomorrow.

Sober, careful social scientists take care not to make predictions in public. Rather, they remain silent, in order to divert possible future scholarly or political blame. But posteventum social scientists rarely take credit for the outcome, arguing that it was exactly their conscious silence that significantly contributed to the end result. However, if publicly circulating foresight might prevent the predicted outcome, that is, might amount to a self-non-fulfilling prophecy, then we might expect there to be a direct correspondence between silence and the occurrence of a specific event.

In what follows, with the help of archival documents, I would like to argue that lack of foresight could be the decisive factor in bringing about certain outcomes. After the Fall of Communism, the blindness of the kremlinologists was blamed for the surprise: they proved unable to foresee. In my view, the accusation was shortsighted: the blindness of the kremlinologists turned out to be one of the crucial contributing factors to the changes. I intend to show that groups of central actors in the course of the transition have not been able to foresee what was coming, and that their inability to foresee (and see the not–so-apparent connections among seemingly disparate events) turned out to be the crucial factor in the end. I would like to argue specifically that members of the Communist nomenclature and officers of the army and the secret police, especially for their inability to foresee the unfolding events, in fact played an important role in bringing down the regime and in facilitating the transition. In a paradoxical way, this would confirm the wildest suspicions of certain political groups on the extreme right of the political spectrum.

*

After the unexpected and surprisingly peaceful historical changes in 1989, in almost all of the affected countries where Communism failed so spectacularly but without major bloodshed, suspicion has taken root about the role of the old Communist nomenclature in the changes. The best-known case is Romania, where various groups have tried to prove that what happened was not a genuine revolution, but rather a coup, a well-orchestrated show, in order to save certain groups of the old elite. According to a recent survey, only 41 percent of the Romanian population continue to believe that what happened in 1989 was a revolution; 36 percent hold the alternative view that it was a coup d'état.[3] After 1989 a predilection for conspiracy theories among all sectors of Romanian society, combined with distrust and suspicion directed toward the former Communists who ruled

3. Cf. Victor Neuman, "A fost Revolutie in decembrie 1989?" *Orizont* no. 1416 (January 20, 2000).

the country from December 1989 until 1996, contributed to the creation of the myth of the "stolen revolution."[4] According to the American political scientist Kenneth Jowitt, the vulnerability of Romanian society to rumor is a legacy of the secretive character of the Romanian Communist elite that managed to survive and maintain its information monopoly.[5] Reports, and even best-selling fictional accounts, by former Securitate officers or individuals who before 1989 were closely linked to the Romanian security service succeeded in substantiating the belief in a well-organized secret plot by implicating either Soviet or Hungarian secret agents or Arab terrorists in the overthrow of the Ceauşescu regime.[6] Even Western analysts contributed to the "stolen revolution" thesis by emphasizing the alleged participation of foreign terrorists in the events, or by accusing the National Salvation Front of having invented a terrorist plot to cover up the coup or to legitimize its power.[7]

In Czechoslovakia, the new parliament was compelled to set up a committee to investigate alleged provocation and the role of the secret services during the Velvet Revolution. On November 17, 1989, student groups in Prague organized a rally to commemorate the fiftieth anniversary of the 1939 demonstrations, the brutal retaliation of the Gestapo, and the closing down of the Czech universities by the Nazis. The police forces of the Communist regime attacked the demonstrators, and the next day Radio Free Europe announced that the police had killed one student. The suppression

---

4. On the tapes recorded at the meetings of the National Salvation Front soon after the changes, one of the army generals who had played an important role during the events of December 1989 told how the National Salvation Front had come into existence well before the December 1989 changes. His words fueled the suspicion that what had seemed to be a revolution had in fact been a well-orchestrated coup (Florin Iaru, "Poporul erǎ sa fure revolutia Securitǎtii" *22* [May 11, 1990]: 8–9; quoted by Mihaela Sitariu, "Revolution or Coup d'état in Romania?" [unpublished paper, 2000], p. 6).

5. Kenneth Jowitt, "The Leninist Legacy," in *Europe in Revolution*, ed. Ivo Banac (Ithaca, NY: Cornell University Press, 1992), p. 209.

6. The novels by Pavel Corut, a former high-ranking Securitate officer, combine Thracian-Dacian mythology, Orthodox symbolism, science fiction, and the exaltation of the Securitate as the stronghold of Romanian patriotic virtue. In spite of, or exactly as a consequence of, their ludicrous fabrications, hundreds of thousands of copies of his novels, such as *Floarea de Argint* and *Cintecul Nemuririi*, were sold. See Sitariu, "Revolution or Coup d'état in Romania?" pp. 9–10.

7. Cf. Richard Andrew Hall, "The Uses of Absurdity: The Stage War Theory and the Romanian Revolution of December 1989," *East European Politics and Societies* 13, no. 3: 501–42.

of the demonstration, and especially the news of the killing, acted as a catalyst that led to the mass protests that eventually brought down the Communist regime. It turned out later that nobody had been killed during the police raid, that probably the news of the death of Martin Smid was a provocation spread by the secret services, and that it was most likely a police agent who lay on the ground pretending to be dead, and so on. (Timothy Garton Ash later met the man who had purportedly played the role of the dead student.)

In his study of the "second life" of November 17, 1989, Oldrich Tuma claimed that, with the exception of the Fall of Communism in Romania, nowhere else could such a broad scale of interpretations of events be found as in Czechoslovakia.[8] According to one of the members of the Commission of the Federal Assembly for the Supervision of the Inquiry into the Events of November 17, there is a long list of possible conspiracies behind the events and the false news of the death of one of the student demonstrators: a conspiracy by the secret police (the StB) to strengthen the position of hard-line Communists in the student movement; a demonstration of power to show the strength of the City Committee of the Communist Party and to intimidate the opposition; a demonstration of power by the Central Committee of the Communist Party; a conflict between liberals and hard-liners in the Central Committee; provocation by the hard-liners in order to strengthen their position before the party congress scheduled for December, and so on.[9] Although the parliamentary investigation finally concluded that the speculation according to which the demonstration was a well-organized provocation and a fraud could not be substantiated, still the conspiracy theory and the questioning of the genuineness of the Velvet Revolution helped to undermine the authority of the post-Communist regime and led to a widespread belief in the theory of the "stolen revolution."

The peaceful nature of the changes, which differed so much from the familiar notions of revolution (that is, radical, sudden, often violent, led by a group of well-organized, usually conspiring cadres), made it difficult to believe that what had taken place before the eyes of contemporaries was real and not staged. Hungary was no exception: after the changes, accusations arose about the "stolen" or "unfinished" revolution. In particular,

8. Quoted by Petr Roubal, "November 17. Renaissance of a Forgotten Revolution" (unpublished manuscript, 2000), p. 3.
9. Ibid., p. 4.

groups from the extreme right of the political spectrum accused the post-Communist elite of alleged collaboration with the Communist secret police and the nomenclature. According to these accusations, the Communists gave their consent to the peaceful transition in order to preserve their economic positions, to exploit the process of privatization, and to become "robber barons," the captains of the economy, in exchange for their lost political leadership. Even today, right-wing politicians and newspapers occasionally refer to the so-called Rose Hill Pact (Rose Hill is the part of Budapest where the nomenclature and the nouveau rich customarily live) between the financially greedy Communist elite and members of the democratic opposition, whereby the latter, in exchange for political gains, promised to forego retroactive justice.

As late as 2002, when following its defeat at the elections, the right-wing media disclosed the fact that the Socialist prime minister had been a counterintelligence agent between the late 1970s and the mid-1980s, a parliamentary commission unveiled the surprisingly large number of former Communist secret agents in the post-Communist governments, especially in the conservative and right-wing governments. The reaction of the political right to these revelations was that the agents must have been planted in the right-wing parties by the Communist secret services as "moles," to be used in the future when the right moment arrived; otherwise it would have been impossible to explain such a large number of former Communist secret agents in right-wing organizations. "These were their agents, it was their plan, so it is their [the Communists'] fault," reacted a right-wing politician, who feared that the revelations would make it difficult for the political right to keep dividing society into former Communists and "good-true-born Hungarians."[10]

In what follows I argue that members of the secret police and the nomenclature of the Communist Party did in fact play a decisive role in the peaceful transition in Hungary, and that there was tacit collaboration between members of the democratic opposition and the secret services. Today, almost without exception, the formerly ruling successor parties in the former Communist world claim that they actually played a decisive role in

10. Tibor Pongrácz, former state secretary in the first post-Communist government, in "Beépítette-e az MSZ(m)P embereit a jobboldali pártokba?" [Did the HS(w)P (Hungarian Socialist {formerly Workers'} Party) Plant its Agents in the Right-wing Parties?], *Magyar Hírlap*, September 23, 2002.

bringing about the demise of the old regime. The failure to use force in defense of the Communist rule is presented as crucial evidence in support of the argument. In Hungary, specifically, former theoreticians of the old regime maintain that the whole post–1956 history of the regime was in fact nothing but the long, incremental preparation for the changes. I will show, however, that it was a lack of foresight on both sides, and not a well-ordered conspiracy, that lay at the root of the cooperation. The outcome, the transition, turned out to be in large part the result of the interplay of concurrent, unplanned events. The recording of meaningful coincidences does not only offer hope for promising explanation, but as the German historian Thomas Nipperdey once suggested, it could also "give back to past generations what they once possessed, what every present possesses: the fullness of the possible future, the uncertainty, the freedom, . . . the contradictoriness."[11]

*

"Even funerals—in some instances especially funerals—can be considered not so much as due concern for the dead as a pretext for the seditious enterprises of the living. It can be the case that the most dangerous person at a funeral is the one in the coffin." Thus has Richard Cobb reconstructed the logic of the secret agent in his book on the French Revolution, written from the perspective of the informer.[12] The index of names at the end of the published minutes of the 1989 Central Committee meetings of the Hungarian Communist Party indicates that the name of Imre Nagy, the executed prime minister of the 1956 Revolution, appears on 150 pages. It is clear even from the minutes that his ghost haunted the party leadership throughout the year of transition. It was he who took the regime with him to the grave. We know from the history of the transition in other former Socialist countries that even without the reburial, something else would have brought the Communists down. But in Hungary, the history of post-Communism starts with Imre Nagy's reburial, and its consequences still play an important role.

From the moment in July 1988 when, at a press conference in San Francisco, the last Hungarian Communist secretary general, Károly Grósz,

11. Thomas Nipperday, *Nachdenken über die Deutsche Geschichte* (Munich: Beck, 1986); quoted by Gordon Craig, "The War of the German Historians," *The New York Review of Books*, January 15, 1987, p. 19.

12. Richard Cobb, *The Police and the People: French Popular Protest 1789–1820* (New York: Oxford University Press, 1970), p. 8.

casually answered a well-thought-out question by saying that the party would allow the relatives to rebury the remains of Imre Nagy, there was no longer any chance for the Communist Party to find a firm foothold anywhere. From that moment there remained nothing else for the Communists but continual withdrawal. "I would simply say," said the last Hungarian Communist minister of the interior,

that I consider this unmanageable. Unmanageable, I repeat. But on the other hand, I agree that we do not have a choice; we have no alternative but to go down the road. Until, perhaps, the end. . . . Once we have started on this road, well, then. And we no longer have the strength to stop anywhere, and we should be aware of this. It would be better if we were able to get into the way of the events, instead of the constant withdrawal that, most probably, awaits us.[13]

Communism did not function according to the logic of civilized common sense, which takes for granted that families have the right to bury their dead. Under Communism, the dead, especially the dead who lost their lives as a consequence of Communist "justice," were taken care of by the party according to its political considerations. The dependence of the living on the party gradually loosened after 1963, while its history, its past, its identity, and thus the fate of its dead continued to be a major preoccupation of the party. The rigid composition of the "Pantheon of the Working-Class Movement" has been strictly upheld. The dead, and especially victims of the party, touched the deepest layers of the identity of the regime, thus no public discourse about them could be tolerated. The dead remained completely dependent on the actual political interest of the party leadership. When, without due reflection, the political authorities gave up the right of disposal over Imre Nagy's body, the party lost its way and, from its own logical system, accidentally fell into a completely alien dimension.

In the course of the continual withdrawal, leaders of the party were preoccupied by one constant fear:

If we decide to give our consent even to this . . . then there remains no hope of stopping anywhere. In that case the next stop will inevitably be October 23. This whole debate about giving or not giving permission for the reburial resembles, hauntingly, the debate on October 23, 1956, when, throughout the day the question was whether or not to permit the demonstration that, in the end, led to the outbreak of the

13. MOL 288. Fond. 1989. 62/4 ő.e. Published in Kenedi, *Kis Állambiztonsági Olvasókönyv*, vol. 2, pp. 240–41.

counterrevolution. . . . Emotions here too might get out of control, and the consequences once more could become frightful and unimaginable. . . . I have already heard rumors that we are, after all, not as stupid as we pretend to be: that the party is deliberately trying to provoke this whole thing; the reburial, after all, is not quite against our wishes, for we need a pretext to be able to strike hard.

This is part of Jenő Fock's monologue at the meeting of the International Legal and Public Administration Committee of the Hungarian Socialist Workers' Party on April 28, 1989.[14] Fock knew very well what he was talking about: in 1956 he was a member of the Central Committee, and in 1958 he was one of the signatories of the minutes of the Politburo's closed session that proved that the highest leadership of the party made a political decision about Imre Nagy's legal case, which ended with his death sentence.

It is clear from the documents of the Central Committee of the party and from the secret-police files that, following the 1956 Revolution, the party leadership was haunted by the memory of October 23, 1956, when, after hours of bloody street fights, the demonstrators had seized the building of the Hungarian Radio. The Communist leaders, the opposition to the regime, and the whole country learned that uprisings start with fighting in the streets, with attempts to occupy the radio station and the vital centers of information control, and with the occupation of the headquarters of power. As the day of the reburial approached there remained nothing else for party leaders and the secret services to do than to try to avoid another October 23.

"I wanted to raise just one more issue, here, which I have already mentioned at the meeting of the secretariat": thus the last secretary general of the ruling Communist Party shared his thoughts with the members of the Politburo. "Should there be a flag on the building [on the 'White House,' the headquarters of the party] on the day of the funeral?" "A black one?" interposed one of the secretaries. "Well, a black one, a red one, and the Hungarian tricolor, for example. But the problem is that we do not have three holes There are only two holes in the wall." "We should build [*sic*] a holder," proposed a practically inclined secretary. "Or what if we had just a red flag with a black ribbon?" "This would also do," conceded the secretary general.

But we can have the tricolor and the red flag with a black ribbon on top of it. The tradition here, in this house, however, as far as I can remember, is to have just a

14. MOL. Fond. 288, 1958. 5/65 ő.e.

black flag. . . . The party has not declared Imre Nagy its dead. He is not our dead. So it would not be a problem not to have a flag at all. But why not? Why not have a flag? Who on earth can prevent us from putting out a flag on our building? Who could argue against it? Only the black one. A few days ago we discussed all the possible alternatives: three flags or two or just the black? Yes, the black; this would be the simplest thing to do.[15]

Just three days before the reburial, the highest and most confused organ of the still-ruling party spent its time discussing the number of holes in the wall and the color of the flag, in honor of an executed and not-yet-rehabilitated enemy, who definitely was not one of the dead of the party.

According to the available documents, in the end all the efforts of the party and its secret services were concentrated on preventing the reburial, the resurrection, and the demonstration from turning into uncontrollable and tragic turmoil, an armed uprising, a violent attempt to overthrow the regime. The leaders of the state security services believed—and under the given circumstances, they could not have been expected to think other-wise—that so long as the secret services were capable of manipulating the leaders of the opposition, of misinforming and misleading the foreign diplomats and the foreign intelligence services; so long as the events re-mained in the desired peaceful channel; so long as there was no sign of the return of 1956; so long as the radio was in the hands of the regime, there was still a good chance for them and for the regime to survive.

Our volunteer agents, under the cover names "Bamboo" in *Magyar Világ* [Hun-garian World] and "Willow" in *Magyar Hirlap* [Hungarian Herald], are publish-ing articles in which the funeral is described as an important political step in the direction of social peace and concord, as proof of the sincere wish of the present leadership to leave behind the mistakes of the past and work for the development of true democracy. . . . With the help of our agents we are initiating the publica-tion of articles in *Magyar Nemzet* [Hungarian Nation, the most important news-paper in 1989] that will call for national reconciliation and the preservation of public order.[16]

The files of the former secret police archives are a rich repository of such orders and suggestions. Reading the newspapers of the spring and

15. Minutes of the meeting of the Politburo on June 13, 1989. In Kenedi, *Kis Állam-biztonsági Olvasókönyv*, vol. 2, p. 350.

16. BM (Ministry of the Interior) III/III Department (the department in charge of the surveillance of the political opposition inside the country). Operational Plan, May 1989;

early summer of 1989, one cannot help feeling that the secret services really did do a successful job: the papers are full of articles and reports calling for reconciliation and caution among all parties involved. But the reader might easily become the victim of an optical illusion. At its May 29, 1989, closed meeting the "State Security Operative Committee in Charge of Preparations for the Funeral of Imre Nagy and His Companions" stated, "The national press, partly on our inspiration but partly independently of us, calls for the avoidance of confrontation and for the paying of tribute to the dead in a dignified way."[17] The journalists and the organizers of the funeral did—and would have done anyway, independently of the maneuvering of the secret services—what the agencies, not having any other options open to them, had planned to do. The secret services presented the situation as if they had been able to manipulate all the actors, who, however, had no connection whatsoever with those secret agencies but were acting out of their best convictions. The files of the secret police archive do not contain any known document from the period between May 5 and July 1989 (that is, the period before and right after the June 16 reburial) that would suggest that the opposition was preparing for anything other than a peaceful and dignified act of homage to the victims of the postrevolutionary terror. Naturally, all the documents are not yet available, but it would have been in the interests of the former Communists and the secret services to make such documents publicly available and to blame the former opposition for conspiring toward a violent overthrow of the regime.

"Now we have the chance here to influence events; partly indirectly, but in part in the most direct way," said one Politburo secretary in charge of national security and the secret services at the meeting of the Politburo on June 14, 1988, almost a year before the reburial.[18] According to the available documents—and fortunately a large quantity of vital documents are publicly available concerning the role of the secret services in the last year of the Communist period—in the months preceding the reburial the services collected information from, infiltrated, informed, and misinformed all the organizations that had anything to do with the upcoming reburial.

---

and BM III/III. Press Plan, May 19, 1989. In Kenedi, *Kis Állambiztonsági Olvasókönyv,* vol. 2, pp. 268–69, 280–81.

17. Ibid., p. 309.

18. Minutes of the meeting of the Politburo of the Hungarian Socialist Workers' Party on June 14, 1988; quoted in Kenedi, *Kis Állambiztonsági Olvasókönyv,* vol. 2, p. 202.

The services felt that they were able to manipulate not only the most important actors in the events but even those foreign governments, including the Vatican, and foreign agencies that played a decisive role in shaping international politics. It is evident from the sources cited by the services, and from the analyses of the secret services themselves, that all the actors involved in the organizational work wanted to use the funeral to pay tribute to the dead and not to incite a violent overthrow of the regime. Since the secret services—in the last months of Communism—had no other option but to accept the fact of the reburial and allow the peaceful event to go ahead, they could proudly claim to the leadership of the party that it was due to their successful intervention and irreplaceable role that no attempt was made at a violent and armed overthrow of the regime; everything went according to the plan of the agencies.

Via our officer in charge in the Ministry of Foreign Affairs, Mark Palmer, the American Ambassador in Hungary, should be briefed and, under the guise of a "friendly chat," he should be asked to make use of his connections in the alternative organizations and to dissuade these groups from turning the funeral into a political demonstration.[19]

Through legal and illegal channels, messages should be sent to the governmental agencies of the NATO member states, especially to the American and German Federal agencies, to warn them that certain extremist forces are trying to prevent the peaceful, dignified funeral and to use the occasion for political adventures, endangering the ever strengthening process of democratization,

proposed the III/III Department of the Ministry of the Interior in one of its internal documents in May 1989. The report reads as if it had been the Ministry of the Interior that had proposed the reburial in the first place to strengthen "the process of democratization."[20]

In the framework of our operation code-named "Canasta," our connection under the cover name "Hedgehog-cactus" will send the following information to CIA headquarters: "Certain extremist groups want to use Imre Nagy's funeral to incite antigovernment disturbances. If they succeed, the government will retaliate with force. The Ministry of the Interior has mobilized its special forces." . . . In the framework of the operation code-named "Ulti," our agent, code-named

19. Memo after the May 9, 1989, meeting of the State Security Operative Committee in Charge of the Preparation for the Funeral of Imre Nagy and his Companions. Kenedi, *Kis Állambiztonsági Olvasókönyv*, vol. 2, pp. 260–61.

20. Kenedi, *Kis Állambiztonsági Olvasókönyv*, vol. 2, p. 265.

"Ragweed," will verbally inform the officers at BND [the West-German Federal Intelligence Agency] about the preparations for the upcoming funeral. He will mention the plans of those extremist groups conspiring to disturb the peaceful event. He will also brief the West German officers about the expected reaction of our party's leadership. He should emphasize that any disturbance and conflict would have a negative impact on the developing democratization process.[21]

Our men have already delivered all the necessary tasks [*sic!*] to the Vatican, which urge the leadership of the Catholic Church to accept the views of the Hungarian church leadership as the only official view in these matters.[22]

All these documents show that the state security agencies—even though they were not able to verify it and obviously did not believe in it at all themselves—insisted on misinforming themselves and claiming that certain groups wanted to use the funeral as a signal to provoke violence. It was obviously in the interests of the services to insist on this: otherwise they would not have been able to cling to the fiction of their own irreplaceable status. They needed the myth of possible provocation; what else could have justified their existence in the summer of 1989?

According to our operational plan, we have accomplished our mission in providing security for the funeral service, aimed at contributing to national reconciliation. . . . According to the planned schedule, at 7 AM the crowd started to assemble on Heroes' Square. . . . No extraordinary event worth mentioning took place in the course of our daily activities. There was no need for any police action

concluded the head of the III/III Department in his report at the close of the day of the reburial, on June 16, 1989.[23] (See Figure 7.1.)

"According to our operational plan" and "according to the planned schedule" were the phrases used by the head of the department in charge of the surveillance of the "internal enemy"—as if the reburial had been planned by the security services; as if it had been their idea in the first place; as if this is what they had always been fighting for: "national reconciliation" and the "strengthening of the process of democratization." "No extraordinary event worth mentioning," wrote the chief security officer, as if reburying the executed prime minister of the 1956 Revolution, who had

21. Ibid.

22. Memo after the May 15, 1989, meeting of the State Security Operative Committee in Charge of the Preparation for the Funeral of Imre Nagy and his Companions. Kenedi, *Kis Állambiztonsági Olvasókönyv*, vol. 2, p. 278.

23. Kenedi, *Kis Állambiztonsági Olvasókönyv*, vol. 2, pp. 385–87.

FIGURE 7.1. The Catafalque. Heroes' Square, Budapest, June 16, 1989. Photo: MTI Photo Archives.

been sentenced to death on Kádár's orders, had been the ordinary, routine activity of the Communist regime. The conclusion of these reports is that so long as it was possible for the regime to withdraw, so long as there was a place to withdraw to, there was still space available for the regime and for its services. This is why it was possible for these services to feel that there was still a sufficiently large ground for them to play on, that they could still play an important role, that eventually it was they who planned, organized, manipulated, secured, and succeeded. Until the regime and Communism fell, they operated and therefore existed. And their existence and their capacity to operate were sure proof of the existence of the regime. It was not pure fiction.

By June 16, 1989, only one real and operative goal remained for the government and its secret services: to avoid the violent overthrow of the regime.

And in my opinion we should try to come to an agreement in advance with them: we should agree that this day of the reburial should not be the day of transition, it should not be the day of regime change. They should not do this, should not transform this day into a day of clashes, because we cannot afford another clash.

We should avoid this. We could, we should, agree that the speeches should not aim at saying, "Let's go and let's start from here, let's get rid of the system," the minister of the interior had muttered at a meeting of the Special Committee of the Central Committee of the party, back on April 28, 1989.[24]

So long as there is no shooting at the radio building the trouble is not terminal.

At the close of the day, the head of the III/III Department wrote a summary, based on "operational reports" and information collected by "technical means" (that is, bugging the reception venue) in which he described the atmosphere at the reception that the organizers gave in the evening following the reburial. The organizers of the reception and of the reburial—despite appearances to the contrary as presented in the reports of the agencies—were not the secret services but the opposition groups, led by the Committee for Historical Justice headed by Miklós Vásárhelyi, Imre Nagy's former press secretary, one of the defendants at the Imre Nagy trial and the chair of the Board of the Hungarian Soros Foundation. "The foreigners, political émigrés among them, had a very positive view of the organization of the funeral," wrote the department head in self-congratulatory mode. "Some former political émigrés expressed their wish to move back permanently to Hungary. Some former political prisoners went as far as to say that this wave of rehabilitation [the reburial of the former enemies of the regime] would make their past role appear as if it had been a fight not against, but for the communist regime, and in the end they may have to feel ashamed of that."[25] The services accomplished the task they had set for themselves: they prevented another October 23 from happening—although nobody had wanted it to happen. And by having prevented something that nobody wanted to happen, they assisted in accomplishing something that nobody noticed when it happened: a peaceful and dignified transition.

After 1956 the opposition was as much afraid of another October 23 as the rulers were: the opposition had also learned that after the first shootings, events become uncontrollable, nobody is fully in charge anymore, acts have unforeseen consequences, the Communists lose their heads, the Soviets come back in, and this can lead to unwanted and unavoidable tragedy. Another 1956 was what the opposition wanted least. The secret

24. Ibid., pp. 241–42.
25. Ibid., pp. 387–88.

services—and this is due to the logic of the workings of such services—always sense conspiracy, secret organization, clandestine plans; these are the things that keep them alive. The lack of such activities, according to the reasoning of the services, cannot be due to anything but the successful working and countermeasures of the services themselves. In this logic, the peaceful nature of the reburial was proof of the splendid performance of those services. They had saved the Communist regime once more. And their logic made them blind to the fact that what they had tried so hard to prevent had already happened with their assistance: the day of the reburial was in fact the day of the transition. They simply missed the moment.

When, after the funeral, the deputy minister of the interior in charge of the secret services, among them the III/III Department, evaluated the lessons of the work of the services at the funeral and started preparing the security measures for the possible October 23 demonstration (the first democratic election took place only in March 1990; in October 1989 the Communists were still in power), he drew the following conclusions:

The activities of the state security forces should be organized according to the same principles that were followed before the June 16 funeral. Our guiding principles should once more be securing the growth of new nationwide reconciliation and peaceful political development. [There is a note in the margin of this document: "development into democratic socialism!, Pallagi F."] We should aim to find a common denominator for all those individuals who fought on different sides of the barricades [in 1956]. This common denominator could be a dynamically developing Socialist Hungary. We should suggest [note in the margin: "If necessary, then very powerfully!!, Pallagi F."] that the society demonstrated its maturity on June 16, but on October 23 what will be needed is a qualitatively higher stage of maturity.[26]

*

Now that the body of "the dead man"—as Kádár used to refer to the taboo—was in his (final?) grave, and June 16 had passed without the siege at the building of the radio, the apparatuses returned to their constant preoccupation, to October 23. As June 16 did not turn out to be the prelude of another 1956, the suspicion then focused on the upcoming October 23. But in 1989 October 23 had already happened on June 16: the corpse of the regime had been buried along with the body of the dead man.

26. Ibid., pp. 398–99. (Ferenc Pallagi was the name of the deputy minister of the interior.)

Although everybody, the leaders of the party and its secret services included, had a tacit comprehension of October 23, it was not easy to find the right way to articulate that knowledge. Both for the leaders and for the subjects of the regime, it was difficult to recover the right words about 1956 after the long decades of almost complete stillness that surrounded the dangerous events and the protagonists. Until the very end of the 1980s muteness over 1956 was a collaborative secret.[27]

When the postrevolutionary terror came to an end, and especially after the 1963 general amnesty, the revolution officially metamorphosed from a counterrevolution into a nonevent. Right after the defeat of the revolution, the restored Communist regime clung to the notion of historical continuity, to the idea of the immortal corporality of the party: this was the entity that had resurfaced from illegality, whose leaders had returned with the Soviet troops from Moscow at the end of World War II; this was the party that had incorporated the Social Democrats in 1948, won the elections, and embodied historical necessity by coming into power in the same year. The life of the political body could not be interrupted. It is true that, according to the immediate postrevolutionary interpretation, one of the causes that led to the outbreak of the "counterrevolution" was the *mistakes* committed by, and the so-called personality cult that surrounded, the Stalinist party leadership that ruled the country until 1956. ("The party can never be mistaken," said Rubashov. "You and I can make a mistake. Not the party.")[28] The mistakes, however, were handled as historical accidents.

Representing 1956 as a counterrevolution served the immediate postrevolutionary retribution well (although "normative inversion [labeling the events 'counterrevolution'] keeps a memory of the other alive because this

---

27. "Dumbness, deadly, infinite and unmovable dumbness is the language of dictatorship. I have known only its weakened, softened version, the soft-porn, the language of which was silence. . . . Under Kádár everybody was concretely silent about 56. 8 times 7 was absent from the multiplication table; 7 times 8 was absent too, as this type of multiplication is commutative. . . . Suppose that in the 1970s we had written these four nice, positive integers: 54, 55, a small balking, a deep breath, misswallowing, and then 57, 58 and would have written above them Four-liner, in that case we would have produced a real, courageous, patriotic poem; most probably it would not have been a masterpiece, but the missing magical number would have been seen as the expression of the eternal longing for freedom of the Hungarian folk, and so on" (Péter Esterházy, *A szavak csodálatos életéből* [From the Wonderful Life of Words] [Budapest: Magvető, 2003], pp. 18–19).

28. Koestler, *Darkness at Noon*, pp. 40–41.

image is needed for contradistinctive self-definition").[29] After the consolidation and its sure sign, the 1963 amnesty, when Kádár summarized the scaled-down ambitions of the regime in the slogan "he who is not against us is with us," the counterrevolution, which had divided the society into antagonistic groups, gave way, however, to a hole in the texture of the past. In the official history of post–World War II communist continuity, 1956 could no longer have a meaningful place. The year 1956 merged with other, supposedly undistinguished years; in fact, according to the official historiography, "correcting the mistakes" had already started in July 1956, before the counterrevolution that, in fact, temporarily blocked the positive developments.

The party not only feared even the shadow of 1956, but it also did everything to reassure itself: nothing was allowed to be (as frightening) as it appeared. At the November 1, 1957, meeting of the Central Committee, which discussed the report about the "behavior of the counterrevolutionary elements" on the first anniversary of October 23, Kádár felt it necessary to remark, "As far as the [high number of] abstention from work is concerned, it is important to remind the distinguished Central Committee that this year, October 23 coincided with the culmination of the flu epidemic."[30]

At the root of the countrywide silence was not what Hannah Arendt thought: "Where violence rules absolutely, . . . everything and everybody must fall silent."[31] From the beginning of the 1960s, when "counterrevolution" gave way to muteness, violence no longer ruled absolutely in Hungary. (Note: one of the lexical meanings of "mute" is "to murmur . . . Muting . . . murmuring, discontent . . . 1665 Fuller Ch. *Hist.* XI, XVII 162. That murmuring and muting against Princess differ only in degree, not in kinde."[32] "We would like to provide modest help to the *silently murmuring* crowd of people above whose heads two minorities—the rulers and their opposition—are quarrelling loudly with each other, in order to enable them to acquire a truer picture of themselves," stated the editors of *Beszélő*, in the first issue of the Hungarian samizdat, which would swiftly become the leading voice of the opposition.)[33]

29. Assmann, *Moses the Egyptian*, p. 216.
30. MOL 288. Fond 4/13. ő.e.
31. Hannah Arendt, *On Revolution* (London: Harmondsworth, Eng.: Penguin, 1973), p. 11.
32. *The Compact Edition of the Oxford English Dictionary* (Oxford: Oxford University Press, 1985), p. 799.
33. *Beszélő* no. 1 (October 1981): 12; emphasis added.

It is obvious that the greater part of the citizenry who supported the revolution took the American "liberation theory" or more precisely the "liberation rhetoric" of the Truman and Eisenhower administrations seriously. They believed in earnest that when the appropriate moment arrived, the American army, faithful to its promises, would come to liberate the oppressed nations. When, in 1956 the seemingly appropriate moment arrived, but not the American army, the people had to understand that Yalta, and the agreement that had allegedly been reached there at the end of World War II, should be taken with deadly seriousness. After the launch of the first Sputnik in 1957 it became clear that the times were not transitory: Communism was there to stay.[34] The defeat of the revolution, together with the inaction of the American army and the nonfulfillment of the American promises, contributed not only to the spectacularly quick consolidation of the returned Hungarian Communists (on May 1, 1957, barely six months after the defeat of the revolution, more than two hundred thousand people took part in the May Day demonstration in front of the tribune from where János Kádár waved to the marching crowd), but also to the stabilization of the Communist regimes worldwide. Not only hope in the future but also the meaning of remembering the past were lost for long decades to come. There remained no public place (and no meaningful reason) for remembering, which would have been dangerous anyway.

The majority of the population was aware of the less and less direct, mostly unformulated, implicit rules of life under the Communist regime. Sophisticated generations were socialized into that formless world, where political, social, and cultural rules and norms had to be learned from in between the lines or from deliberate silences, which enclosed the prohibitions. After the terror subsided, predominantly brute force no longer guaranteed the social acceptance of danger zones. Under the entry "Tabu" of the 1937 edition of the *Encyclopaedia of the Social Sciences*, Margaret Mead wrote, "Tabu may be defined as a negative sanction, a prohibition whose

34. According to one "Information Report" sent to the District Committee of the First District in Budapest, concerning the events between October 23–November 7, 1957: "The Sputnik fever was clearly recognizable in our district. This event, involuntarily, provided great help to our work, as it disarmed and prevented quite a few provocative questions about the technological underdevelopment of the Soviet Union. The workers had no choice but to consider it a great achievement of mankind. The less educated working people were dazzled by the news about the Sputnik" (Kenedi, *Kis Állambiztonsági Olvasókönyv*, vol. 1, p. 66).

infringement results in an automatic penalty without human or superhuman mediation. . . . [Its usage must] be restricted to describe prohibition against participation in any situation of such inherent danger that the very act of participation will recoil upon the violator of the tabu."[35] Taboo could be seen as much a means of self-defense in the vicinity of danger, as an inevitable (implicit or explicit social) prohibition against transgression. This is exactly how de Freycinet, at the beginning of the nineteenth century, understood it, when he translated taboo as *prohibité ou défendu.*[36]

Nontalk was not just a manifestation of power; compliance with the prohibition—which had not been stated directly but whose infringement nevertheless resulted in an automatic penalty—solidified, reproduced, perpetuated, and prolonged power. Taboo is one of the pillars of power, which—in the case of a well-functioning system—becomes deeply internalized; this is why there is less need for using external force or even explicit rules for enforcing the prohibition against transgressions.[37] As "the

35. *Encyclopaedia of the Social Sciences* (London: Macmillan, 1937), vol. 7, p. 502.

36. L. de Freycinet, *Voyage autour du monde, enterpris par ordre du roi, exécuté sur les corvettes de S. M. l'Oranie et la Physicienne, pendant les années 1817, 1818, 1819, et 1820,* 2 vols. (Paris: Imprimerie Royale, 1839), p. 597; quoted by Steiner, "Taboo," vol. 1, p. 115.

According to Steiner's almost forgotten, though extremely knowledgeable study, which exerted a major influence on Mary Douglas's "Purity and Danger," the function of taboo is

> the narrowing down and localization of danger. . . . Taboo is an element of all those situations in which attitudes to values are expressed in terms of danger behaviour. . . . Social relations are describable in terms of danger; through contagion there is social participation in danger. And we find expressed in the same term, those of taboo, two quite separate social functions: (1) the classification and identification of transgressions (which is associated with, though it can be studied apart from, processes of social learning), and (2) the institutional localization of danger, both by specification of the dangerous and by the protection of society from endangered, and hence dangerous, persons. (Steiner, "Taboo," p. 214)

Steiner was an adamant critic of most of the theoreticians of the notion of taboo, including Frazer, Radcliff-Brown, and Freud.

37. In an essay, dated March 1944, Franz Baermann Steiner, the displaced, emigrant Jew from Prague, whose parents would perish in the concentration camp, wrote:

> The demonic sphere lies within our own society. Would anyone who has been in a concentration camp believe that wild animals are worse than a human torturer? This form of torment is new: trapping human masses in close-knit nets, building gigantic cages past which "healthy" life floods by. This is more demonic than the torments of slavery, more horrible than the worst that ever happened before: the religious wars of European Christendom. For the captive does not know why he is captured, the guard does not know

classification and identification of transgressions [are] associated with . . . the process of social learning," the perception of public compliance played a central role in socializing generations into the Communist world of mostly unstated rules.[38]

The construct of the counterrevolution was as much the Archimedean point of Communist historiography, as internalized nontalk was that of perpetuating power. The firm rule over Imre Nagy's dead body, the disappearance of his corpse, and the nonexistence of his life and deeds in public discourse both guaranteed and manifested unchallenged rule over the subjects of the regime. The disappeared dead body was firmly isolated from the society of the living, while the implicit but strict rules isolated the subjects from the locality and source of potential threat emanated by the corpse. Although Imre Nagy's grave was unknown, the exact location of his body on the topography of danger zones was common knowledge. Danger was localized with the help of taboo, and this in turn helped the members of society to defend themselves, through self-isolation, from the locality of the dangerous object. Tacit, although gravely asymmetrical, collaboration between rulers and their subjects perpetuated power relations. The invisible dead body, like the body of the wife of one of the masons, walled into the building in Central European folk ballads, held the construct together.

In the very last years of State Socialism, when the indeterminate, vague contours of a world beyond Communism appeared once more on the horizon, more and more signs pointed at the strange hiatus of history. Gradually, especially after the irresponsible and tentative permission to bury the remains of Imre Nagy privately, it became almost visible that something (or somebody?) was obviously missing. The uncertain permission gravely undermined the firm ground of no-man's land: the classification and signs of transgression started the quick process of erosion. The ex-

---

why he should torment him—and the people outside—alas, what do they know? . . . Of course it is possible to control the organizational activities of the demons within a society just as the demons of the outer sphere [nature] have been pacified, and so create a peaceful society. After all, the forces are already at work. What they can achieve is this: the exclusion of the demons from intra-personal relations, and their removal more deeply into the interior. . . . *What was once outside society, what was later inside society will, when this society triumphs, one day be within the individual.* (Franz Baermann Steiner, "On the Process of Civilization," in *Orientpolitik, Value, and Civilization*, vol. 2: *Selected Writings*, ed. J. Adler and R. Fardon [New York: Berghahn Books, 1999]; emphasis added)

38. Steiner, "Taboo," p. 214.

istence of the unpronounceable secret could be inferred from the official efforts to prevent its return. As Freud remarked, "The phenomenon of latency . . . may be explained . . . by the circumstance that the facts and ideas which were intentionally disavowed by what may be called the official historian, were in fact never lost."[39]

It was Kálmán Kulcsár, the last Communist minister of justice, a former military judge in the early 1950s, who officially proposed replacing the Communist coat of arms, surmounted by the five-pointed red star, with the pre–World War II royal coat of arms bearing the Hungarian Holy Crown. It was evident that the suggestion aimed at preventing the return of the republican, the "Kossuth" coat of arms, the arms of the 1848 Revolution that was, at first informally, then formally, used once more during the days of the 1956 Revolution. The resurrection of the traditional political right (with its obsession with the idea of the Holy Crown) was considered to be less threatening in 1988 even by the old-fashioned hard-liners, than the return of the memory of 1956.[40]

*

If muteness was so deep, and the memory of the revolution was shrouded in darkness, what explains the mystery of the unexpected emergence of the story of the defeated revolution, the figure of the slain prime minister? The answer is literally with the dead: the authority to tell the story—as Walter Benjamin showed—was borrowed from death.[41]

The dead, according to Robert Hertz, in normal circumstances, are only temporarily excluded from human society.[42] It is true, the world of postrevolutionary retribution, the world of the Communists, where the dead could not properly be buried for long decades, where the dead could not be named publicly or in private, where even the executioner imposed silence on himself, could not be considered a normal world; these were far

39. Sigmund Freud, "Moses and Monotheism: Three Essays," in *The Standard Edition*, vol. 23 (London: The Hogarth Press, 1964), p. 69.

40. Cf. Miklós Szabó, "Jobbra át?" [Turn to the Right?], in his *Múmiák öröksége. Politikai és történeti esszék* [The Heritage of the Mummies. Political and Historical Essays] (Budapest: Új Mandátum, 1995), p. 99.

41. "Death is the sanction of everything that the storyteller can tell. He has borrowed his authority from death" ("The Storyteller," in Walter Benjamin, *Illuminations*, trans. Harry Zohn [New York: Schocken Books, 1986], p. 94).

42. Robert Hertz, "A Contribution to the Study of the Collective Representation of Death," in his *Death and the Right Hand*, trans. Rodney and Claudia Needham (Aberdeen: Cohen and West, 1960), p. 86.

from normal circumstances. But the dead can only be temporarily excluded from the society of the living. As it is said in the Bible: "O that thou
wouldest hide me in the grave, that thou wouldest keep me secret, until
thy wrath be past, that thou wouldest appoint me a set time, and remember me!" (Job 14:13).

Power in East and Central Europe, just as in Polynesia, where the
concept of "tabu" originates, was measured by the recognized capacity to
restrict.[43] When, as a consequence of the reforms from the mid-1980s, it
became gradually visible in the Soviet Union and, in turn, increasingly so
in the majority of the other State-Socialist countries that the capacity of
the regime to restrict was becoming fatally restricted, the snowball effect
started to undermine the structure perpetuated by the accepted system of
classification and identification of transgressions.[44] With the introduction
of reforms in the Soviet Union and then in her allies, as the consequence of
the loosening of the control over the past that the Communist regimes
tried so hard to impose in Eastern and Central Europe, in the last years of
the 1980s, the existence of still enforced but terminally weakening taboos
suddenly became apparent.

Nondemocratic, authoritarian regimes cannot exist without deeply
buried secrets, protected by silence that marks off the danger zones. In
Eastern and Central Europe after the mid-1980s, it became perceptible that
silence, almost always, shrouded terrible secrets: the Katyn massacre, the
labor camps, the Molotov-Ribbentrop pact, show trials, tortures, murders,
and executions in all the countries where single parties ruled unchallenged.
From silence that could no longer be tightly protected one could infer the

43. Cf. Steiner, "Taboo," pp. 116–31; and Jeremy Adler and Richard Fardon, "Introduction," to Franz Baermann Steiner's *Orientpolitik, Value, and Civilization*, vol. 2: *Selected
Writings*, ed. J. Adler and R. Fardon (New York: Berghahn Books, 1999), p. 58.

44. On the unwillingness and inability of the military forces and the political police to
enforce the rule, see Brian D. Taylor, "The Soviet Military and the Disintegration of the
USSR," *Journal of Cold War Studies* 5, no. 1 (winter 2003): 17–66; and Amy Knight, "The
KGB, Perestroika, and the Collapse of the Soviet Union," *Journal of Cold War Studies* 5, no. 1
(winter 2003): 67–93.

Vladimir Kryuchkov, the last KGB chief of the Soviet Union, whom Gorbachev appointed in September 1988, had served between 1955 and 1959 as a KGB resident in the Soviet embassy in Budapest. Afterward he became a specialist on Hungary in the apparatus of
the Central Committee of the Soviet Party in the 1960s. Yury Andropov, Krychkov's men-
tor, who headed the KGB before he followed Leonid Brezhnev as secretary general of the
Soviet Communist Party, had been the Soviet ambassador in Hungary during the time of
the revolution in 1956.

existence of secrets that silence was meant to hide; and secrets, almost without exception, as in Pushkin's Boris Godunov, point at crimes that haunt the perpetrator, irrespective of his might and the force that protects his inescapable secret: "Boris, Boris, before thee/All tremble; none dares even to remind thee/O what befell the hapless child; meanwhile/In his dark cell a hermit doth set down/A stern indictment of thee. Thou wilt not/Escape the judgment even of this world,/As thou wilt not escape the doom of God."[45]

The uneasy sense of culpability—although it is almost never possible to measure its binding hold—arguably had an impact on the silent retention of events and figures of the recent past. He, who was at once recognized as the returned, was in fact a constructed image, answering to the needs of the present, in the context of the collapsing regime. It is never he who returns.

"[The] soul has learned everything, so that when a man has recalled a single piece of knowledge—learned it, in ordinary language—there is no reason why he should not find out all the rest, if he keeps a stout heart and does not grow weary of the search, for seeking and learning are in fact nothing but recollection," claims Socrates famously in Plato's *Meno* (81 d 1–5).[46] The myth of recollection, as presented in the *Meno*, and which appears— although in a somewhat different form—in Plato's *Phaedrus*, the *Philebus*, and in the *Phaedo* as well, claims that what has ever been known to us is somehow present, although in a hidden, forgotten form within ourselves and could be relearned—thus remembered—with the help of recollection (*anamnesis*). "[T]here is no such thing as teaching, only recollection" (*Meno*, 82 a 1–2).

According to Socrates or Plato, it is we, who by looking into ourselves—mostly with the help of interaction with others, and not by relying on a teacher who tries to pour knowledge into our head—are capable of actively recollecting things we once knew but forgot. As Aristotle formulated it in his *On Memory*, "For recollection is not the recovery or acquisition of memory" (451a 19–20).[47]

45. Alexander Pushkin, *Boris Godunov*, trans. Alfred Hayes (New York: The Viking Press, 1982), p. 33.

46. *The Collected Dialogues of Plato Including the Letters*, ed. Edith Hamilton and Huntington Cairns, trans. W. K. C. Guthrie (Princeton, NJ: Princeton University Press, 1989), p. 364.

47. *The Complete Works of Aristotle*, ed. Jonathan Barnes, vol. 1, trans. J. I. Beare (Princeton, NJ: Princeton University Press, 1984), pp. 717–18.

Humans—so it might seem—have an ever-present capacity to search, to investigate and deliberate, to uncover the connections among isolated, latently existing facts, and by recalling "a single piece of knowledge [to] find out all the rest" (*Meno*, 81 d 2–4). Anamnesis stems from the urge within the self and, supposedly, is closely connected to the awareness that something, which had been experienced before, has since been forgotten:

Whatever may ultimately make our *learning* possible, an additional internal source . . . is required for our being able to recollect. This source seems to be no other than the mysterious awareness of having *forgotten* what we knew in the past. . . . [T]he phenomenon of "recollecting" cannot be considered without taking into account its "opposite," the phenomenon of "forgetting," while the phenomenon of "having something in one's memory" does not have "forgetfulness" as its "opposite": we either have or do not have memories, we either keep them or lose them, but we lose them without being aware of our losing them, without being aware of our forgetting. To become aware of our having forgotten something means to begin recollecting.[48]

Socrates of the *Meno* recalls what he had heard "from men and women who understand the truth of religion" (*Meno*, 81 a 4–5; in Jacob Klein's translation, *A Commentary on Plato's Meno*: "Men as well as women with an expert knowledge of the highest things"):

They say that the soul of man is immortal. At one time it comes to an end—that which is called death—and at another is born again, but is never finally exterminated. . . . Thus the soul, since it is immortal and has been born many times, and has seen all things both here and in the other world, has learned everything that is. So we need not be surprised if it can recall the knowledge of virtue or anything else which, as we see, it once possessed. (*Meno*, 81 b 3–7 and 81 c 3–7)[49]

Plato argues that latent knowledge—what the Hungarian-born Michael Polanyi, who is not too often cited nowadays, in his *The Tacit Dimension* calls "tacit knowledge"—something that one knows but does not quite know at the same time, can be recollected by asking questions, by being questioned, by "a mode of inference," as Aristotle formulated it.[50] "For he

48. Jacob Klein, *A Commentary on Plato's Meno* (Chicago: University of Chicago Press, 1989), pp. 111–12; emphases in original.

49. *Collected Dialogues of Plato*, pp. 363–64.

50. "For the *Meno* shows conclusively that if all knowledge is explicit, i.e., capable of being clearly stated, then we cannot know a problem or look for its solution. And the *Meno* also shows, therefore, that if problems nevertheless exist, and discoveries can be made by

who endeavors to recollect infers that he formerly saw or heard, or had some such experience, and the process is, as it were, a sort of investigation. But to investigate in this way belongs naturally to those animals alone which are also endowed with the faculty of deliberation; for deliberation is a form of inference" (453a 10–14).

Recollection, which is closely tied to introspection, emerges in the course of the process of active and conscious inquiry. We recollect, insist both Plato and Aristotle—after latency, Freud would add—not by searching in the archives, but by reconfiguring the lateral connections between past experiences. By looking inside ourselves, we look back, to the past, to another life, to things we have known once. We experienced something sometime ago, in another life, under different conditions, when certain things, unlike at a later moment, made sense, but then, when we had to live in another environment, in a different world, under the ban of sanctioned stillness, our once-acquired knowledge could not be used, no longer made sense. "Those elements of knowledge about the past that no longer meaningfully correspond to actual concerns are discarded," claimed Jan Assmann in his analysis of Freud's *Moses and Monotheism*.[51] In the words of cognitive scientists, "Our ability to recall is inextricably linked with our assumptions about how the world is."[52]

In 1981, on the occasion of the twenty-fifth anniversary of the revolution, *Beszélő*, the Hungarian underground journal of the democratic opposition, published a collection of essays and reprints. One of the editors, himself a former participant in the event, noted, "Even five years ago, groups of the present democratic opposition—especially the former reform-Marxists—thought with suspicion if at all about October 23, 1956. . . . They assumed that the uprising of the Hungarian people—unlike the Prague Spring [of

solving them, we can know things, and important things, that we cannot tell. The kind of tacit knowledge that solves the paradox of the *Meno* consists in the intimation of something hidden, which we may yet discover" (*The Tacit Dimension* [Gloucester, MA: Peter Smith, 1966], pp. 22–23).

51. Assmann, *Moses the Egyptian*, p. 215.

52. Chris Westbury and Daniel C. Dennett, "Mining the Past to Construct the Future: Memory and Belief as Forms of Knowledge" (Mimeo, Center of Cognitive Studies, Tufts University, 2003), p. 7.

"What we call recollection can never be more than the most plausible story we come up with (or, perhaps, only a story which is plausible enough) with the context of the constraints imposed by biology and history" (ibid., p. 7).

1968]—had not brought closer the dream of 'socialism with a human face.'"[53] Four years later *Beszélő* devoted its nineteenth issue to the thirtieth anniversary of the revolution. The lead editorial of the special issue asserted:

Ever since the "consolidation" of the regime it is not easy to find people in Hungary who have not tried hard to forget the circumstances of how the post–1956 regime came into being. The rulers have asked for forgetfulness in exchange for concessions, but it was necessary for the subjects to forget too, otherwise they would not have been able to love the hand, which, a few years before had beaten them mercilessly. It was only a tiny minority that wanted to remember: out of devotion to the idea, and because they could not, would not forgive—in exchange for whatever concessions—for the bloody suppression of the revolution and the hideous terror that followed it. Still, they were not able to provide a political alternative either: what would they had been able to suggest and to whom? There was nothing else left to them but—by the help of their moral standing—to testify in defense of a lost cause.[54]

Before the late 1980s the vague memories of the revolution could not be used in a politically or practically meaningful way. In the words of Moses Finley, the scholar of Greek antiquity: "[memory] is controlled by relevance."[55]

With Imre Nagy's reemergence and his unexpected resurrection, 1956, and especially the retribution that followed the revolution, found a new historical context. It became not only possible but also made sense to rediscover—in a new frame, under new description—the half-lost memories. What happened at the time of the reburial should be seen as "acting out instead of remembering"—as Freud argued in the case of Moses.[56] Around

---

53. Ferenc Kőszeg, "Egy icipicit igazítottak a világon" [They Have Changed the World a Bit], *Beszélő* no. 2 (January 1982): 97.

When in the middle of the 1980s Imre Mécs—who as a student-participant of the revolution had spent nine months on death row, before his sentence was commuted to life imprisonment—joined the "Danube Circle," a civil environmental/democratic movement, I looked at him with certain reservations. I could not quite understand what that man, at least a generation older than most of us, with a technical degree, who had finished his studies as an adult, with a hard-to-believe life story, had to do with our group.

54. *Beszélő* no. 19 (January 1987): 620.

55. M. I. Finley, "Myth, Memory, and History," *History and Theory* 4, no. 3 (1965): 297.

56. Freud, "Moses and Monotheism," p. 89. Freud, however, uses the verb "acting out," not in a literal but in a special technical sense, meaning "repetition," that is, repeating repressed memories. Cf. Freud, "Remembering, Repeating, Working-Through," in *The Standard Edition*, vol. 12 (London: The Hogarth Press, 1964), pp. 147–56, esp. p. 150.

the time of the reburial, memories of 1956 and 1958, the year of the execution of the revolutionary prime minister, were on everybody's mind. In the fall of 1988, a few months after 1956 had resurfaced in public, the Hungarian Public Opinion Research Institute was permitted for the first time to conduct a poll on 1956. More than 75 percent of those included in the representative survey responded that the revolution and especially the fate of the participants preoccupied them heavily at that time. (Never since has the revolution been so important a public issue.) Forty percent of the respondents still considered 1956 a counterrevolution, while another 40 percent characterized it as a revolution. More than 55 percent agreed that Imre Nagy had been a counterrevolutionary. Just a few months later, in the spring of 1989, the repeated poll revealed a dramatic shift: now only 12 percent thought of 1956 as a counterrevolution, and more than 90 (!) percent disagreed with the statement that Imre Nagy had been a criminal. At the time of Imre Nagy's reburial more than two-thirds of the adult population condemned the Soviet intervention.[57] The collection and translation of the scattered bones, the recollection in public, created connections among the scattered, isolated, repressed brute facts.

The ghost of the tragedy that everybody on both sides tried to avoid served as a warning for all the participants at the funeral. The Central Committee, trying hard to domesticate the memory of the revolution, attempted, in a hasty final effort, to include Imre Nagy in the Pantheon of the Communist movement, by emphasizing his Communist conviction, his efforts to humanize the system, and decided that the representatives of the Central Committee—although the former prime minister "was not the dead of the party" (yet)—should stand in the guard of honor at the catafalque. If anybody among the members of that body had been able to see that there would have been no need to prepare for the anniversary of October 23, as the revolution would, belatedly be victorious on June 16, 1989, then the peaceful transition, the miracle, might have been prevented. In

---

57. "Mária Vásárhelyi, Csalóka emlékezet. 1956, Nagy Imre és Kádár János alakja a közgondolkodásban" [Delusive Remembrance. 1956, The Figures of Imre Nagy and János Kádár in Public Memory] *Élet és Irodalom* (June 13, 2003): 6.

On the role of "interpretative activists" in "translating" cultural objects and in mobilizing resources "so as to demonstrate beyond reasonable doubt the overlap between the meaning of the cultural object and the meaning of a particular political idiom," see Peter Stamatov, "Interpretative Activism and the Political Uses of Verdi's Operas in the 1840s," *American Sociological Review* 67 (June 2000): 345–66.

that case, perhaps once more, blood would have been shed in the streets of Budapest. (Later on, after the transition, the successors of the ruling Communists did in fact assert that Imre Nagy had been their dead. By appropriating his legacy retrospectively, they claimed the central role for themselves in the course of the transition. Withdrawal, defeat, was redressed as responsible, piecemeal, peaceful work for change. They [too] had buried the dead, they [too] had stood at the catafalque in 1989; they had not prevented it from happening; they did it. The transition was their deed—and not the opposition's.)

The memory of the invasion in Prague on August 21, 1968, the introduction of martial law in Poland on December 13, 1981, even the recollection of the workers' uprising on June 17, 1953, in East Berlin had a constraining effect on both the opposition and the party leadership in the countries east of the River Elbe. Just like in Hungary, the hard-learned fears on the part of both the opposition and the party leadership shaped the peaceful nature of the emerging transition. With the Soviet reforms, the capacity of the regime to restrict reached the point of no return. Communism collapsed as a result of heavily constrained acts on both sides. Monumental changes took place with minimal strife.

The miraculously found dead served the overwhelming majority of the country well. The coming collapse of the regime that had been supported by the greater part of the population in the previous decades could not be mistaken. The situation demanded an immediate explanation: How was it possible to support the Communists and Kádár himself, in the face of such a heinous crime? Inversely, how can one explain the sudden anti-Communist sentiments in the light of the decades-long collaboration with the executioners? *Mortus aperit oculos viventis,* "the dead open the eyes of the living," holds an old Latin proverb, which, used in a literal sense, might suggest an answer.[58]

Silence served as the explanation: the muteness that, allegedly, they, the executioners had woven around their crime. The dead had been buried

---

58. In the reading of Baldus de Ubaldis, the noted fourteenth-century Italian legal scholar, a possible figurative legal meaning of the Latin text is that someone born unfree could become a freedman on the death of his master. Kantorowicz argues that the French legal maxim, "Le mort saisit le vif" ("the dead seizes the living"), could—via Baldus—also be connected to the same source. (In the French case the maxim relates to the law of inheritance, which is far from my literal reading of the Latin text.) See Ernst Kantorowicz, *The King's Two Bodies* (Princeton, NJ: Princeton University Press, 1957), pp. 393–94.

in a deep, unknown grave that was so immensely difficult to find even for the authorities in 1989. The dead had been with great care hidden from sight, built into the wall; this is why the people of the country—so the reasoning went—could not be held responsible for their ignorance. In fact, even for their ignorance, for their almost voluntary support, for their deeply uncomfortable situation in the face of all these unexpected and embarrassing questions, the majority found in the person of the suddenly discovered executioner the right one to blame. The country was shocked; without the self-indulgent shock the greater part of the country would have been embarrassingly lost, left without an answer. The dead man took Communism to the grave with himself. The mourners claimed absolution from him. He could not refuse; he had been killed and forgotten thirty-one years before.

A violent, defeated revolution and a victorious, peaceful, negotiated transition is an antinomy. However, in my view, it was in large part due to the memory of the bloody and tragic revolution that the transition in Hungary could take place without bloodshed, in a peaceful, sad, and almost dignified way. And in this process, unexpectedly, without proper knowledge of what they were doing, the secret police collaborated with the opposition to the regime. It was not only Imre Nagy's body that served as a tie between 1956 and 1989: in a strange way, the peaceful transition was the post mortem, late—for too many too late—victory of the revolution. It was not exactly his victory: he died as a reform-Communist.[59]

59. "My only consolation in this situation is," said Imre Nagy on June 15, 1958, in front of his judges, "that sooner or later, the Hungarian people and the international working-class will acquit me." He was careful when choosing his last words: he did not appeal to the international working-class movement, led by the Soviet Union. Instead, he put his trust in the international working class.

Index

Cultural Memory | *in the Present*

Jacques Derrida, *Negotiations: Interventions and Interviews, 1971-1998*, ed. Elizabeth Rottenberg

Brett Levinson, *The Ends of Literature: The Latin American 'Boom" in the Neoliberal Marketplace*

Timothy J. Reiss, *Against Autonomy: Cultural Instruments, Mutualities, and the Fictive Imagination*

Hent de Vries and Samuel Weber, eds., *Religion and Media*

Niklas Luhmann, *Theories of Distinction: Re-Describing the Descriptions of Modernity*, ed. and introd. William Rasch

Johannes Fabian, *Anthropology with an Attitude: Critical Essays*

Michel Henry, *I am the Truth: Toward a Philosophy of Christianity*

Gil Anidjar, *"Our Place in Al-Andalus": Kabbalah, Philosophy, Literature in Arab-Jewish Letters*

Hélène Cixous and Jacques Derrida, *Veils*

F. R. Ankersmit, *Historical Representation*

F. R. Ankersmit, *Political Representation*

Elissa Marder, *Dead Time: Temporal Disorders in the Wake of Modernity (Baudelaire and Flaubert)*

Reinhart Koselleck, *The Practice of Conceptual History: Timing History, Spacing Concepts*

Niklas Luhmann, *The Reality of the Mass Media*

Hubert Damisch, *A Childhood Memory by Piero della Francesca*

Hubert Damisch, *A Theory of /Cloud/: Toward a History of Painting*

Jean-Luc Nancy, *The Speculative Remark: (One of Hegel's bon mots)*

Jean-François Lyotard, *Soundproof Room: Malraux's Anti-Aesthetics*

Jan Patoc<hac>ka, *Plato and Europe*

Hubert Damisch, *Skyline: The Narcissistic City*

Isabel Hoving, *In Praise of New Travelers: Reading Caribbean Migrant Women Writers*

Richard Rand, ed., *Futures: Of Jacques Derrida*

William Rasch, *Niklas Luhmann's Modernity: The Paradoxes of Differentiation*

Jacques Derrida and Anne Dufourmantelle, *Of Hospitality*